The Institutional Imperative

SHORENSTEIN
APARC
STANFORD

THE WALTER H. SHORENSTEIN
ASIA-PACIFIC RESEARCH CENTER

Studies of the Walter H. Shorenstein Asia-Pacific Research Center

Andrew G. Walder, General Editor

The Walter H. Shorenstein Asia-Pacific Research Center in the Freeman Spogli Institute for International Studies at Stanford University sponsors interdisciplinary research on the politics, economies, and societies of contemporary Asia. This monograph series features academic and policy-oriented research by Stanford faculty and other scholars associated with the Center.

The Institutional Imperative

THE POLITICS OF EQUITABLE DEVELOPMENT
IN SOUTHEAST ASIA

Erik Martinez Kuhonta

Stanford University Press
Stanford, California

Stanford University Press
Stanford, California

Printed in the United States of America

Library of Congress Cataloging-in-Publication Data

Kuhonta, Erik Martinez, 1973– author.
　The institutional imperative : the politics of equitable development in Southeast Asia / Erik Martinez Kuhonta.
　　　　pages cm
　Includes bibliographical references and index.
　ISBN 978-0-8047-7083-5 (cloth : alk. paper)
　ISBN 978-0-8047-8688-1 (pbk.　　　　)
　　1. Economic development—Southeast Asia.　2. Southeast Asia—Economic policy.　3. Southeast Asia—Social policy.　4. Southeast Asia—Politics and government.　I. Title.
　HC441.K755 2011
　338.959—dc22
                                                    2011017098

Typeset by Newgen in 11/14 Garamond

To my parents—Precioso and Cleofe Kuhonta
And to Kazue Takamura

Contents

Illustrations

MAPS

Abbreviations

AOP	Assembly of the Poor
Bt	Baht (Thai currency)
BAAC	Bank for Agriculture and Agricultural Cooperatives
BN	Barisan Nasional (National Front, Malaysia)
CPAR	Congress for a People's Agrarian Reform
CPM	Communist Party of India, Marxist
CPP	Communist Party of the Philippines
CPT	Communist Party of Thailand
DA	Democratic Alliance (Philippines)
DAP	Democratic Action Party (Malaysia)
DMP	Debt Moratorium Program
DNU	Department of National Unity
EDCOR	Economic Development Corps
EGAT	Electricity Generating Authority of Thailand
EPF	Employment Provident Fund
EPU	Economic Planning Unit
FELDA	Federal Land Development Authority
FMS	Federated Malay States
FPTP	First Past the Post
GDP	Gross Domestic Product
ICP	Indochinese Communist Party
ICU	Implementation Coordination Unit
IMF	International Monetary Fund
JKKK	Jawatankuasa Kemajuan dan Keselamatan Kampung (Village Development and Security Committee)
KMT	Kuomintang (Nationalist Party, Taiwan)

LP	Liberal Party (Philippines)
MARA	Majlis Amanah Rakyat (People's Trust Council for Indigenous People)
MAS	Malayan Administrative Service
MCA	Malaysian Chinese Association
MIC	Malaysian Indian Congress
MNP	Malayan Nationalist Party
MP	Member of Parliament
NAP	New Aspiration Party (Thailand)
NCC	National Consultative Council
NDP	National Development Policy
NDPC	National Development Planning Committee
NEDB	National Economic Development Board
NEP	New Economic Policy
NESDB	National Economic and Social Development Board
NFP	National Federation Party (Fiji)
NIC	Newly industrializing country
NOC	National Operations Council
NPC	National Planning Council
NSCB	National Statistical Coordination Board
PAP	People's Action Party (Singapore)
PAS	Party Islam (Parti Islam-Se Malaysia)
PF	Popular Front (Philippines)
PMIP	Pan-Malayan Islamic Party
PNC	People's National Congress (Guyana)
PPP	People's Progressive Party (Guyana)
RIDA	Rural Industry and Development Authority
RM	Ringgit (Malaysian currency)
SAP	Social Action Party (Thailand)
SAWARI	Satu Wilayah Satu Industri (One Village, One Product)
SEPC	State Economic Planning Committee
TDRI	Thailand Development Research Institute
TRT	Thai Rak Thai
UMNO	United Malays National Organization
UMS	Unfederated Malay States
UNDP	United Nations Development Programme
VASS	Vietnamese Academy of Social Science
VCP	Vietnamese Communist Party
WDI	World Development Indicators

Note on Terms and Spelling

Malaysia was known as Malaya until 1963, when it became the Federation of Malaysia through the inclusion of Singapore, Sarawak, and Sabah. Singapore was expelled in 1965. I use the term *Malaya* when describing specific events in pre-1963 politics, but I use *Malaysia* both for events after 1963 and for describing the more general historical trends of the country as a whole, even when they involve events before 1963.

Thailand was known as Siam until 1939. I use *Siam* to describe specific events before 1939, but I use *Thailand* to describe general trends and patterns in the country's history, even if they relate to politics before 1939.

Thais and Malays are commonly referred to by their first name. I have spelled out the full name the first time and subsequently used only the first name. In the reference section, Thai and Malay authors are listed by their first name. In most instances, I have not included honorifics (with the occasional exceptions of *Tunku* and *Tun*).

There is no uniformly accepted method of romanization from Thai to English. My method has been to follow pronunciation. However, for Thai names, I have kept the spelling that is generally preferred by the individual. This spelling often does not conform to actual pronunciation. For example, Samak Sundaravej is pronounced "Samak Sundarawek." For names of Thai political parties, I sometimes use the Thai name and sometimes the English name. I do this following the convention in the literature.

Lastly, I should point out that I use the terms *race*, *ethnicity*, and *communalism* interchangeably throughout the book. This is in large part because the literature on Malaysia tends to use *race* and *communalism* to describe ethnic groups.

Note on Currencies and Measurements

In 1975, the Malaysian ringgit (RM) replaced the Malaysian dollar as the official currency of the country. The value of the Malaysian dollar and ringgit has ranged from about 2 to 3.8 to the U.S. dollar.

The Thai currency is the baht. With the exception of the Asian financial crisis in 1997–98, its value has ranged from about 20 to 40 to the U.S. dollar. During the boom years in the 1980s and 1990s, its value was about Bt25 to US$1.

Thailand's unit of measurement is the *rai*. One *rai* is equivalent to .16 hectares, or .395 acres.

Acknowledgments

This book grew out of my concerns with poverty and inequality in developing countries, particularly in Southeast Asia, as well as analytical arguments about the role that institutions can play in addressing the dilemmas of the developing world. I take great pleasure in finally having the chance to thank in writing the many people who have supported me in the numerous years it has taken me to complete this book. Those who helped me at the early stages of this project include Atul Kohli, Lynn White III, Kent Eaton, and Deborah Yashar. Lynn has been unfailingly supportive in my research endeavors, and I want to thank him for his kindness and generosity. Atul has had an immense influence on me, and my debt to him is deep. His imprint on my thought process and on this book is abundantly clear. He has been a superb mentor and role model—challenging, encouraging, and always inspiring.

Many people helped me better understand politics in Thailand and Malaysia, either in my fieldwork research or on more informal occasions. In Thailand, I wish to acknowledge Nethitorn Praditsarn, Worawut Smuthkalin, Sumanee Pongpo, Alex Mutebi, Pannate Rangsinturat, Jirawat Poomsrikaew, Decha Siripat, Saroja Dorairajoo, Pasuk Phongpaichit, Chris Baker, Viengrat Nethipo, Khun Kaew, Patcharin Lapanun and the Khon Kaen University anthropology team, and the late Nikom Chandravitun. In Malaysia, I thank Khoo Boo Teik, Jomo K. S., Khoo Khay Jin, Shamsul A. B., Tan Siok Choo, Ahmad Shabery Cheek, Susan Paik San Teoh, Kikue Hamayotsu, Lorraine Salazar, James Jesudason, Ragayah Mat Zin,

Greg Felker, Bill Case, Meredith Weiss, Diane Mauzy, and the late Noordin Sopiee. My warm thanks to Uncle Raju and Aunt Devi—my gracious hosts in Bangsar Baru—who made my first extended stay in Kuala Lumpur especially pleasant and memorable, and to Mr. Kana of the Institute of Strategic and International Studies, who helped me to find my hosts and who has graced me with many acts of kindness. Sincere thanks also to Neric Acosta and Chito Gascon for sharing their knowledge of the inner workings of Philippine politics, and for their inspiring idealism. Some people listed here may not agree with the central argument of the book, so no one should be implicated in what follows. Nonetheless, I am very thankful for advice and support.

I am extremely grateful to the following people for thoughtful comments on the manuscript in its various stages: Eun Kyong Choi, Kent Eaton, Antonis Ellinas, Don Emmerson, John Gershman, Paul Hutchcroft, James Jesudason, Ben Kerkvliet, Arang Keshavarzian, Ehito Kimura, Atul Kohli, Junko Koizumi, Manuel Litalien, Jim McGuire, Illan Nam, Phil Oxhorn, Hendro Prasetyo, Jim Spencer, Richard Stubbs, Kazue Takamura, Tuong Vu, Meredith Weiss, Lynn White III, and Deborah Yashar. I especially wish to single out Tuong Vu for identifying several overarching problems in the manuscript and for showing me how to rectify them. Many thanks also to the three anonymous reviewers. All were incredibly helpful and supportive. One, in particular, provided penetrating, insightful, and extensive comments that heavily guided my revisions. I want to thank this reviewer for showing me how valuable peer review can be. At Stanford University Press, I thank Andrew Walder and Stacy Wagner for shepherding the manuscript through the review and publication process. A special thanks to Jay Harward at Newgen North America for his outstanding professionalism in the production process.

I also wish to acknowledge some excellent friends who have been a great source of intellectual stimulation: my fellow "young" Southeast Asia political scientists who are all trailblazers in their own right, Tuong Vu, Kikue Hamayotsu, Allen Hicken, Dan Slater, and Viengrat Nethipo; some very generous and supportive "senior" Southeast Asianists, Paul Hutchcroft, Rick Doner, Ben Kerkvliet, Jojo Abinales, and Don Emmerson; two scholars who inspired me to major in political science as an undergraduate at the University of Pennsylvania, Frederick Frey and Akiba Covitz; an incomparable intellectual and treasured friend from Penn, Carlos Lopez-Reyna; an extremely busy UN assistant secretary-general, Jomo K. S., who gave me some invaluable last-minute advice in a hotel room in Philadelphia; my former Princeton colleagues who provided camaraderie and support, Arang Keshavarzian, Eun Kyong Choi, and Illan Nam; and a fellow Princeton graduate, superb friend, and endless conversationalist about political science, Antonis Ellinas.

McGill graduate students Parminder Chopra, Alessandra Radicati, Rory Raudseppe-Hearne, and Suranjan Weeraratne provided excellent research assistance. Special thanks to Alessandra for copyediting and Parminder for all kinds of last-minute tasks. Many thanks to my McGill colleagues, Phil Buckley, Juliet Johnson, Takashi Kunimoto, Matt Lange, Sonia Laszlo, Catherine Lu, Lorenz Lüthi, Hudson Meadwell, Khalid Medani, Phil Oxhorn, and Christina Tarnopolsky, for stimulating conversations and collegial support. I especially wish to acknowledge Rick Schultz, the chair of my department, for his support of junior faculty and for funding a workshop that helped improve the book.

For funding and institutional support that provided me time to write or do research, thanks are due to the Center of International Studies and the Woodrow Wilson Scholars Program at Princeton University, the Walter Shorenstein Asia-Pacific Research Center at Stanford University, Tony Reid and the Asia Research Institute of the National University of Singapore, the East-West Center in Honolulu, the Center for Southeast Asian Studies at Kyoto University, the Fonds de Recherche sur la Société et la Culture (Québec), and the Social Sciences and Humanities Research Council of Canada. I have benefited from the use of libraries at Princeton University, Thammasat University, Chulalongkorn University, the Institute of Strategic and International Studies in Malaysia, University Kebangsaan Malaysia, University of Malaya, Stanford University, the National University of Singapore, the University of Hawai'i, Kyoto University, McGill University, and the National Library of Thailand.

This book is dedicated to three people who have always believed in me— my parents and my wife. My parents, Precioso and Cleofe Kuhonta, taught me from early on the importance of education and scholarship. They constantly nurtured my knowledge, and they impressed on me a concern for the world of politics. They have supported me in every turn in my life, and I cannot thank them enough for such unconditional love. My wife, Kazue Takamura, has dissected my arguments, helped me clarify and articulate my ideas more carefully, served as my sounding board, and edited every page of the manuscript. Her vast knowledge of Malaysia has been indispensable for some of my fieldwork and for the overall argument. Just as indispensable to me has been her moral character—selfless, generous, and always interested and concerned with the world we live in. I thank her especially for understanding what motivates my work and for believing in it. It is no exaggeration to say that without her support this book would not have been completed. Finally, I thank my son, Javier ("Habi-chan") Takamura Kuhonta, whose boundless energy, insatiable curiosity, and irrepressible mischievousness have at times distracted me from my goal of completing this book but have also made my life so much more fulfilling.

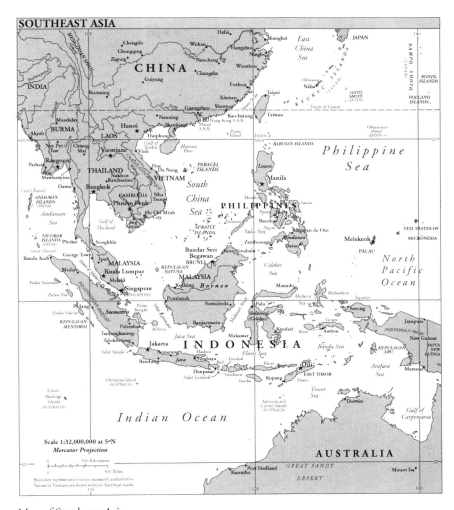

Map of Southeast Asia

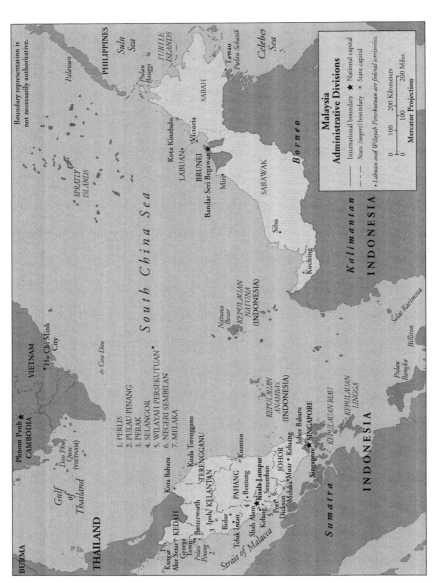

Map of Malaysia

Map of Thailand

PART ONE

Introduction and Theory

ONE

Introduction

> Perhaps the most significant aspect of Malaya's success is that it was achieved not by separation of political power from development, but by an infusion of that power into the development effort.
>
> —*Gayl Ness*[1]

> The main challenge for Thai policy-makers is to work out a development strategy which will try to redress the social and regional imbalances existing in the society following a period of rapid economic growth. At the same time, however, a development plan to harmonize the objectives of growth with social justice also requires some kind of political and institutional structure which has a clear sense of purpose and which will be innovative enough to bring about the necessary reforms.
>
> —*Saneh Chamarik*[2]

> Without strong political institutions, society lacks the means to define and realize its common interests.
>
> —*Samuel Huntington*[3]

Introduction

The pursuit and achievement of equitable development—economic growth rooted in a strong pro-poor orientation—is a rare feat. Most countries in the developing world have difficulty achieving economic growth, let alone growth with equity. Only a few countries across the world have achieved growth with equity. The most prominent have been in Northeast Asia—Japan, South Korea, and Taiwan—but a few others are sprinkled around different regions of the world, including Costa Rica, Mauritius, Kerala (India), and Malaysia.

In 1955, the economist Simon Kuznets hypothesized that economic growth would affect the level of inequality through a parabolic process.[4] As the economy took off, inequality would rise but would then stabilize as the economy developed and finally decline at the more advanced levels of economic development. This was known as the inverted-U hypothesis. The Kuznets curve was compelling because it had a clear deductive logic at its core: intersectoral shifts between agriculture and industry would lead to rising inequality in the early stages of modernization. It also cemented analytically what seemed intuitive at the ground level: that there were significant costs to industrialization. Yet a review of the vast body of literature on the Kuznets curve concluded that there is in fact no necessary, logical relationship between economic growth and inequality.[5] In some developing countries, economic growth has not inexorably led to rising inequality. What, then, distinguishes the rare cases of growth with equity from those with growth and inequity?

This is a general theoretical question that can be addressed from different angles, including through large-N statistical studies focused on economic variables; case studies emphasizing particular economic, political, or sociological characteristics of a country; and comparative studies seeking to highlight specific factors that account for different developmental trajectories. In this book, I employ the latter strategy. I propose to answer the general theoretical question of variation in patterns of inequality through a comparative historical analysis in which political institutions, especially institutionalized political parties and cohesive interventionist states, play a central role in shaping outcomes of development.[6]

The central thesis of this study is that institutional power and capacity, along with pragmatic ideology, are crucial to the pursuit of equitable development. Institutionalized, pragmatic parties and cohesive, interventionist states create organizational power that is necessary to drive through social reforms, provide the capacity and continuity that sustain and protect a reform agenda, and maintain the ideological moderation that is crucial for balancing pro-poor measures with growth and stability. Strong institutions are the political foundations for equitable development because they ensure that public interests supersede private interests. Central to the politics of social reform must be the creation of institutions that are centered on representing collective goals rather than personalistic ones.

This book advances this thesis through a structured comparison of two relatively similar countries in Southeast Asia: Malaysia and Thailand. The study explains why Malaysia has done significantly better than Thailand in achieving equitable development. It takes a comparative historical approach to the problem, emphasizing the roots of inequality in both countries and the institutional structures that have emerged to address the dilemma of inequality. The book then places the comparative analysis of these two countries within a broader framework of two other Southeast Asian cases, the Philippines and Vietnam, two countries that also represent different points on the spectrum of equitable development, with the Philippines demonstrating lower levels of success like Thailand, and Vietnam being more similar to Malaysia.

The Puzzle and the Argument

In Southeast Asia, Malaysia stands out as the most successful case of equitable development. In terms of growth in gross domestic product (GDP), Malaysia has outpaced its Southeast Asian neighbors (Singapore excepted), with a 2009 per capita GDP of US$7,030.[7] Poverty fell from a high of 49.3 percent in 1970 to as low as 3.8 percent in 2009.[8] Most critically, Malaysia's Gini coefficient declined from a peak of .529 in 1976 to .441 in 2009.[9] By 2005, less than a quarter of the population was working in the traditional agrarian sector.[10] Within the context of the Southeast Asian newly industrialized countries (NICs), Malaysia has led the group in GDP per capita, poverty reduction, and income distribution.

What especially distinguishes Malaysia is its sharp reduction of income inequality. No other country in the region has been able to significantly reduce the uneven distribution of income in the context of high growth rates. Although Malaysia's distribution of income rose in the 1990s, when viewed in the long term, the trend has been a significant decline in income inequality largely through the evening out of interethnic disparities. In the context of the debate regarding the relationship between growth and equity, Jacob Meerman writes: "[H]ere is a case [Malaysia] where social policy may have been the instrument that made growth at all possible."[11]

Thailand's development has been impressive in terms of growth rates. In the late 1980s and early 1990s, Thailand's galloping growth rates set records in the developing world. With an average growth rate of 9 percent during the boom years from 1985 to 1995, it succeeded in lowering poverty to 11.6 percent before the eruption of the Asian financial crisis in 1997.[12] In 2009, its GDP per capita stood at US$3,893.[13] Yet what stands out in Thailand's developmental trajectory beneath the impressive growth statistics is the stark rise in inequality. In 1975, the Gini coefficient was .426; by 1992, it had peaked at .536. From 1992 to 1998, the Gini coefficient dropped to .509, but in 1999, it had risen back to .531. In 2004, it declined slightly to .499, but in 2006, it was .515.[14] In essence, from the mid-1980s until 2006, the Gini coefficient has moved upward, despite a few years of slight decline, but has generally hovered around or greater than .50. Between 1981 and 1992, the period during which the boom began and a democratic transition occurred, the average income of the top 10 percent of households tripled, whereas the income of the bottom 30 percent of households registered little change. The gap between the top and bottom income groups widened from seventeen to thirty-eight times.[15] And despite high growth rates, Thailand's social structure has not changed as much as Malaysia's, with between 40 percent and 50 percent of the population still employed in the agrarian sector. These trends in inequality stand in stark contrast with those of Malaysia, where the Gini coefficient has decreased since 1976 (see Figure 1-1). "Nowhere in Southeast Asia, or even in Asia, has this twin problem of growth-equity trade-off become more unique and more interesting than in the case of Thailand," observed Medhi Krongkaew, an economist who has studied Thailand's distribution of income throughout his career.[16]

Given these different trends in equitable development writ large, this empirical puzzle therefore arises: why has Malaysia done much better than Thailand? In Malaysia, a highly institutionalized ethnic party, the United Malays National Organization (UMNO), has forcefully sought to implement pragmatic social reforms along ethnic lines. Along with a capable bureaucracy, it has advanced a battery of policies that have gradually reduced the uneven distribution of income between the Malays and the Chinese. By contrast, Thailand has been devoid of institutionalized parties with programmatic agendas. Its bureaucracy has stimulated high growth rates but has remained largely aloof with respect to the concerns of the popular sector. Strong institutions—especially institutionalized parties and effective interventionist states—are thus key to the pursuit of equitable development.

In Malaysia, the problem of inequality has deep roots that go back to the British colonial policy of "divide and rule." Colonial authorities divided the

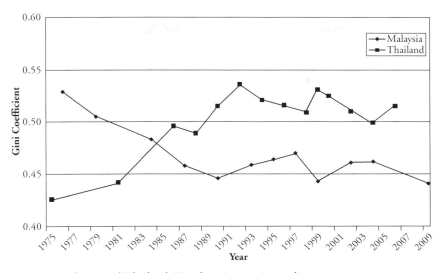

FIGURE I-I Malaysia and Thailand, Trends in Income Inequality, 1975–2009

SOURCES: Malaysia 1986, 1996, 2001, 2006, 2010; Ragayah 2008; Somchai 1987, 2001; National Economic and Social Development Board 2003; Medhi 2008; Warr 2009.

economy across ethnic lines, relegating the Malays to traditional economic sectors while giving the Chinese free rein over the more modernized areas of the economy. This ethnic division of labor became deeply entrenched in the Malaysian soil, aggravating Malays' anxieties that their status in a land that they believed belonged to them was under grave threat. This came to a head in devastating ethnic riots in Kuala Lumpur on 13 May 1969.

Breaking through structural inequalities compounded by ethnic divisions is not an easy task. Countries facing similar problems and with comparable demographics have been consumed by ethnic violence (Guyana), civil war (Sri Lanka), and cyclical coups (Fiji). Malaysia, however, was able to tackle ethnic and class divisions through a combination of party organization, state intervention, and moderate policies of redistribution. Institutional resilience has been crucial to Malaysia's ability to address social reforms without destabilizing the polity. An institutionalized party has been able to channel grievances from the grass roots into the policy arena, to maintain a consistent focus on its programmatic agenda, and to monitor the implementation of policy in the periphery. This institutional depth provided Malaysia with the political foundations for wide-ranging social reform.

Ideological moderation has been a crucial element of Malaysia's reform agenda. Although UMNO was born of anxieties of ethnic survival and has upheld a strong ethnic raison d'être throughout its history, its policies and political behavior have not been characterized by ethnic chauvinism or violence against rival ethnic groups. The Malaysian state has used authoritarian measures within a semidemocratic environment since 1969 to enforce its redistributive agenda, and it has discriminated against the large Chinese minority. The politics of equitable development in Malaysia has not come without costs. But on a comparative level, these authoritarian tactics have not been as severe as in other countries facing the same problems of ethnic inequality, such as Fiji or Guyana; nor have the policies been so draconian as to completely marginalize the ethnic minority and drive it to wage war for a separate state, such as in Sri Lanka. Furthermore, in its redistributive mission, the Malaysian state never seized assets through a nationalization program like that of Venezuela under Hugo Chávez.

In Thailand, inequality can be traced to a pattern of laissez-faire growth, in which incomes from export-oriented industrialization have heavily outpaced incomes from agriculture. Compounding this income differential has been the slow pace of labor absorption in modern industry, where the rural sector's decline as a share of GDP has not been matched by a similar decline in the rural population. Although industrialization has taken off, about 40–50 percent of the population still remains within the rural sector. Compared with countries with a similar GDP share of industrialization to agriculture, Thailand's failure to absorb the rural population in the modern sector is striking. A tendency to concentrate economic resources in the capital, Bangkok, also exacerbates this imbalance. With the recent exception of the Thai Rak Thai (TRT) Party, no political institution has emerged in Thailand to fundamentally tackle uneven growth and rural-urban disparities.

Unlike Malaysia, in Thailand personalism has largely shaped political parties. Parties have not stood for public agendas but rather for private interests. Most parties have had shallow organization, amorphous ideology, and brief life spans. They have therefore lacked the motivation and the capacity to represent the poor or any collective group. Furthermore, a conservative bureaucracy has dominated policy making, and the military has perennially intervened in the affairs of civilian politics, thereby preventing the sustainability of any social reforms. Despite having achieved some of the highest growth rates in the world, Thailand also experienced a severe worsening of its distribution of income. Most notably, the democratic transition dating from 1988 led not to improvement in the distribution of income but to its worsening.

The populist policies of the Thaksin Shinawatra government (2001–06) and the TRT Party were a notable effort to incorporate the interests of the poor and change the trajectory of Thailand's development model. For the first time, a slew of pro-poor policies, ranging from universal health care to a debt moratorium for farmers, was implemented in an organized and sustained manner. But with the exception of the universal health-care program, these policies did not make fundamental changes in the livelihoods of the poor. Although some of the spending programs provided the poor with short-term opportunities to reduce their debt or to engage in small-scale entrepreneurship, the long-term effect does not appear to have been sustainable in terms of significant advancements in capacities and in income. This is, in part, because some of these policies represented the party's more populist orientation.

Analytical Contributions of the Study

This book intends to make several contributions to the study of the comparative politics and political economy of developing nations. First, the book emphasizes the importance of political institutions, especially institutionalized parties, in effecting equitable development. Institutionalized parties are crucial to the reduction of inequality because they provide the "organizational weapon" necessary for a state to implement social reforms.[17] Institutionalized parties back reforms with organizational power, sustain policy continuity, maintain dialogue with the grass roots, monitor the bureaucracy's implementation of policy, and emphasize programmatic policies rather than personalistic and clientelistic exchange. All of these factors are necessary for advancing social reform. Above all, an institutionalized party reinforces the importance of public over private interests. Without institutionalized parties, a state with some rational-legal traits may be able to achieve high rates of economic growth, as Thailand did, but it will lack the political power and the links between state and society that are necessary to drive through more challenging structural change.

Precisely because the poor suffer numerous disadvantages vis-à-vis the upper classes, organization is crucial for addressing their interests. Elites can rely on capital and personal networks to influence policy, but the lower classes lack those resources. Therefore, organization, particularly through a political party, becomes the key mechanism for articulating and advancing the interests of the popular sector. The presence of an institutionalized organization is not sufficient to ensure that reform will make headway, but without organization, we can be certain that the interests of the poor will not have a lasting influence on government. Referring to Brazil, Scott Mainwaring makes this point eloquently:

> Weak parties have been a pillar of a system in which the state usually functions mostly for elites, in which these elites enjoy privileged access and favors, in which codified universalistic rules are frequently undermined in favor of personalistic favors, in which public policy is constantly undermined by personalistic exchanges and favors, and in which, as a consequence of all the above, the poor suffer.[18]

A key avenue for addressing social reform in the developing world thus rests with institutionalized parties.

Second, this study emphasizes state capacity and intervention. To transform society, the state must intervene forcefully, but it must do so with the mind-set of a bureaucratic "iron cage" rather than simply that of an iron fist.[19] In the push to reduce inequality, numerous forces will be arrayed against the state. Even beyond structural opposition, a redistributive agenda necessitates massive coordination and planning if the state is to succeed in restructuring society while still ensuring that the economy continues to grow and that those whom the redistributive program disfavors are not so thoroughly marginalized. To achieve its goals, the state must intervene effectively through the use of proficient civil servants; systematic procedures; close coordination between center and periphery; and above all, an executive that sustains its focus on its policy agenda.

Third, this study underscores the importance of pragmatic ideology and moderate policies. For equitable development to be achieved, without sacrificing either growth or equity, policy reform must not antagonize the upper class, drive out capitalist groups, or foment unrest and instability that will ultimately hurt the poor. Were a state to undertake large-scale redistributive policies through nationalization or the seizure of assets, it would undermine the possibilities for economic growth by marginalizing the entrepreneurs who are necessary to create jobs and investment. Many social revolutions and populist movements have sought to redress inequalities, but their radical ideologies have often spurred widespread violence and lower growth rates, which have been to the long-term detriment of the poor. A party rooted in pragmatic ideology will be able to pursue redistributive reforms that can improve the conditions of the poor while still ensuring that economic growth provides them with opportunities for upward mobility. Reforms that focus on education, health, and agricultural productivity stand a better chance of reducing inequalities because they are less likely to destabilize the polity and the economy. Therefore, the difficult balance between growth and equity depends heavily on a party with a pragmatic ideology.

A comparative historical approach provides the analytical framework for this study. For the purposes of this book, there are four important contributions of this particular analytical approach. First, the historical perspective allows one to conceptualize inequality as a long-term structural problem and to examine different periods in a country's history in which social reforms were essayed. In Malaysia, a historical approach emphasizes inequality's deep roots in that country. One has to understand how deeply embedded those roots are to fully appreciate the extent of the progress the state has made in reducing inequality.[20] A long-term framework also provides a deeper understanding of the numerous efforts made in a country's history to tackle inequalities. Although Thailand represents analytically the "negative" case, its history is littered with a number of attempts to pursue pro-poor reforms. Most of these failed because institutions were unable to aggregate, channel, and shape policy reform.

Second, a comparative historical framework allows one to analyze how institutions have evolved and adjusted in relation to structural problems. The key issue in the politics of equitable development is how institutions respond to social crises when inequality can no longer be tolerated at a "normal" level. In some cases, institutions can respond coherently to social demands, but in other cases, institutions falter. Relative institutional capacity hinges in large part on prior institutional formation. By tracing and comparing the historical development of institutions, we will see how they have been able to adapt in relation to demands for social reform.

Third, if we constricted the framework to the contemporary period, we might end up relying on variables that appear to intuitively explain equitable development. In the case of Malaysia, for example, one may be led to believe that the country's social structure "naturally" explains its success in redistribution. That is to say, the correlation between demographics and an economic outcome provides the analytical explanation: where an ethnic group is the economically disadvantaged majority and also controls the government, we should expect economic outcomes in its favor. A historical perspective shows us that social structure does not provide such a neat answer. Institutional and policy changes that paved the way for equitable development occurred *after* 1969, despite the fact that social structure was constant. Although this does not mean that social structure is unimportant, one should look closely at institutional changes over time to identify the critical causal variables.

Fourth, the comparative approach sharpens the development of theory that would not be possible through a case study alone. It is important to put Malaysia in comparative perspective because of a tendency in the Malaysianist literature to explain Malaysian politics only through the country's most prominent social structural characteristic—that of ethnicity—which thereby makes the study of Malaysia sui generis. A comparative perspective pushes one to examine variables across cases and to move beyond the particular features of one country. Furthermore, a comparative approach makes it abundantly clear that Malaysia has done significantly better than its regional neighbors in equitable development. Studying Malaysia without a comparative lens reinforces a shortsighted view that not much has improved in this long-standing semidemocratic regime. In fact, much has changed in terms of equitable development, even if certain structural patterns (e.g., a dominant party regime, ethnic divisions) still persist.

Studies of political economy in Thailand have also been notable for their lack of a comparative perspective. Although there are numerous studies that focus on social development writ large, such as poverty, environmental degradation, labor rights, and so on, few seek to place the Thai experience in a comparative framework. The pitfall here is that without a comparative yardstick, it is difficult to really know how severe the social problems in Thailand are and to evaluate what kinds of political reform are possible.[21]

Finally, one of the central themes advanced in this book is that politics requires difficult trade-offs. Some readers will recoil at the claim made in this book that a hegemonic, competitive authoritarian (or semidemocratic) state has been able to advance social reforms and that ethnic preference has driven those reforms. Both the authoritarian and the ethnic cast of Malaysia's social reform package are understandably disturbing to many academics, practitioners, and laypersons. I do not intend to deny or gloss over the unpalatable aspects of Malaysia's development. However, the reality of politics is that the public goods we desire, such as development, stability, democracy, and equity, cannot always emerge as a "clean" package.[22] Historically, it is often the case that some public goods have to be sacrificed for the attainment of others. This should not be surprising to students of the East Asian developmental model, where authoritarianism has historically gone hand in hand with economic growth.

Politics should be understood in the context of constraints—that is, political actors operate under difficult conditions in which available choices often fail to offer the most pleasing alternatives. This does not mean that one should accept, from a normative level, these trade-offs or that one should not try to seek changes in the way policies have been implemented and in the way politics gets played out. Nor should one assume that Malaysia's pattern of development based on elements of coercion and ethnic loyalty is an appropriate model for other countries. The goal of this book is not to prescribe but to analyze and document the structural realities involved in the politics of equitable development. Furthermore, it bears emphasizing that the theory of this study pivots on institutions, not on democracy or authoritarianism. If there is a prescriptive claim that emerges from the analytical argument, it is that powerful and capable institutions are critical for addressing structural inequalities.

Research Design

The comparative framework is crucial to the methodology and theoretical thrust of this study. The Malaysian and Thai cases represent variation on the dependent variable: equitable development. Figure 1-1 shows the divergent trajectories of inequality for Malaysia and Thailand. Although Thailand's Gini coefficient has risen steadily since the mid-1970s, Malaysia's has declined overall.

The research design fits within the "most similar" systems approach in that Malaysia and Thailand share a number of similar properties so as to make them comparable. They are geographically proximate; are endowed with extensive natural resources; have a low population density; and most critically, are the countries with the largest percentage of a significant ethnic minority, specifically the Chinese, in Southeast Asia. Recent figures show that Thailand's Chinese population is 14 percent, whereas Malaysia's is 24 percent.[23] Some may argue that comparing Thailand and Malaysia neglects differences in ethnic pluralism, yet such criticisms fail to take into account the fact that Thailand is ethnically more diverse than its current exterior facade portrays. Although in Malaysia ethnicity is the very public face that the nation wears, in Thailand ethnicity hides behind the mask of national integration but remains a salient social force, particularly in the economy.

This book is based on a range of primary and secondary materials. The analytical framework is shaped largely by secondary materials. Fieldwork in Thailand (for a continuous full year of research and numerous shorter trips) and Malaysia (for a period of six months) provided empirical material for this study.[24] Fieldwork research involved the gathering of local and government documents, as well as interviews with bureaucrats, politicians, nongovernmental organization representatives, villagers, farmers, journalists, and academics in Bangkok, Suphan Buri, Ubon Ratchatani, Kuala Lumpur, Kelantan, and Penang. I also spent a few weeks in Manila to attend political meetings and conduct interviews.

The comparative framework is based on explaining variation in the politics of inequality and in the relationship between growth and equity. The analytical and descriptive focus of the case studies, particularly in the contemporary period, has thus been influenced by the different periods in which inequality became an urgent political issue in each case. In Malaysia, inequality stems from the colonial period and was addressed successfully only during the period of the New Economic Policy (NEP, 1971–90), during which the country's trajectory of growth with equity was being shaped. Therefore, the focus in the Malaysian case is on understanding the politics of the NEP rather than more recent policy issues. In Thailand, inequality began to rise in the 1970s and peaked in the early 1990s, when growth rates were also at their apex. Therefore, with respect to Thailand, I focus on the contemporary political scene, particularly issues of rural debt, dam construction, and health policy. In recent decades, these issues have become deeply contested precisely because inequality has risen starkly during Thailand's economic boom. The empirical material and the time frames are therefore not symmetrical in the sense that each case covers exactly the same policy sectors or the same time period. However, the thrust of the argument is in explaining and comparing overall trends in the politics of equitable development.

Some Clarifications

For its goals and analytic scope to be understood, it is important to clarify what this study does not argue or do. First, it is important to emphasize that the book does not claim that Malaysia has conclusively resolved problems of inequality. In the 1990s, Malaysia's distribution of income worsened under liberalization policies and the demands of globalization for differential wages and skills. Under Prime Minister Mahathir Mohamad, the state began a gradual process of retrenchment from several policy sectors, significant privatization, and reduction of its absolute focus on poverty and interethnic inequality. The effects of these policies as well as some deinstitutionalization of UMNO under Mahathir slowed down the equitable thrust of the Malaysian state, although they did not change the overall direction, as can be seen in Figure 1-1.[25]

The rising bump in inequality in the 1990s does not alter the overall claim that, in the long run, Malaysia has made huge strides in reducing inequality and in improving incomes of the poor Malays. The argument of this book should be understood from a long-range, historical perspective. What I seek to analyze is a general categorical trend. The general trend since the NEP was instituted, given a short time lag, has been a clear decline in overall inequality; an evening out of the income gap between the Malays and the Chinese; and the growth of a robust, professional Malay middle class. It is this trend that I wish to highlight and whose relationship to political variables I aim to elucidate. When placed in a comparative historical perspective, Malaysia has thus been relatively successful in reducing an uneven distribution of income, particularly along ethnic lines.

Second, it is crucial to clarify what I aim to explain as an outcome and the measures I employ to define that outcome. The dependent variable of this study, in its broadest sense, is equitable development, that is, the successful pursuit of growth with equity. This is measured in aggregate terms through a combination of growth rates and income distribution, especially the Gini coefficient. The Gini coefficient is important because, as an aggregate number, it provides an immediate, graspable figure for income distribution. But for the purposes of this study, the Gini coefficient is also a tricky measure to use for two reasons. First, as a measure of inequality, it is affected not only by government policy but also by external conditions, such as fluctuations of prices of commodities and currencies in global markets or the demands of multinational firms for higher skills or lower wages.[26] Therefore, if we measured the dependent variable *only* in terms of the Gini coefficient, we would lose focus on our central concern: government pro-poor outcomes. Second, the economic literature gives very different numbers for the Gini coefficient. This is because the Gini coefficient can be calculated differently—despite use of the same surveys—on the basis of how one weighs and adjusts the data, or because it is sometimes calculated in terms of income and sometimes in terms of consumption. The data are not standardized across countries or even within institutions.[27]

My strategy to address these issues is the following. I use the Gini coefficient as a broad aggregate measure of a country's *trends* in income inequality. This is necessary to conceptualize the big picture. However, my interest is, above all, in the *politics* of social reform, especially in the ability of a government to *implement* pro-poor policies. It is, after all, in the implementation stage where party institutionalization, state intervention, and pragmatic policy and ideology—the independent variables—make a difference. Thus, while keeping sight of the numerical trend of the distribution of income, the case studies herein focus on how a government has dealt with social reform and whether it has been able to implement policy in favor of the poor. The key issue under scrutiny here is a state's pro-poor position, as measured by its capacities to follow through on policies that support the poor. On the issue of the data of the Gini coefficient, my strategy has been to use local sources, both from the government and from academia, on the assumption that those sources are in better sync with realities on the ground.[28]

Chapters That Follow

Chapter 2 sets out the theoretical framework for this study. It provides a theoretical discussion of the relationship between party institutionalization, state intervention and state-party dynamics, moderate policy and ideology, and crisis on the one hand and equitable development on the other hand. In particular, the chapter stresses the analytical significance of party institutionalization for equitable development.

Part Two of the book comprises chapters 3 and 4, on Malaysia's politics of equitable development. A brief discussion of Malaysia's economic trends introduces the chapters. Chapter 3 begins the narrative with the origins of ethnic inequality in the shadow of British colonialism. It then narrates the postwar rise of UMNO and the early efforts to address the uneven ethnic social structure. Chapter 4 opens with the antecedents of the May 1969 crisis and then discusses the effect of the crisis on institution building and social reform. The chapter then zeros in on the politics of reform under the NEP and looks particularly at the policies of land settlement, education, and health.

Part Three of the book consists of chapters 5 and 6, on Thailand's politics of equitable development. A brief introduction discusses Thailand's economic trends. Chapter 5 begins by describing the origins of the bureaucratic state under King Chulalongkorn. It then turns to analyze the impact of the 1932 revolution on institutional and social reform. After addressing the lost opportunities for reform during the postwar period, the chapter concludes with the Sarit Thanarat regime's bureaucratic reforms that provided a basis for rationalizing economic policy and propelling Thailand's first economic boom. Chapter 6 begins with the turmoil of the mid-1970s and then turns to the more democratic period of the late 1980s. It analyzes the role of parties in both the 1970s and the recent democratic period, showing how weak institutions limited the prospects for reform. It then looks closely at a few policy areas, including rural debt, dams, and health care, which have affected equitable development and that were engaged by the Thaksin government.

Part Four of the book contains chapters 7 and 8. Chapter 7 extends the argument about states and parties to two other countries in Southeast Asia, the Philippines and Vietnam. The chapter analyzes how the Philippines has historically been plagued by weak institutions that have denied it the potential for growth, let alone equity. The other half of the chapter turns to Vietnam, where a highly institutionalized party has successfully carried through social reforms, thereby creating a relatively equitable society and, in its more recent phase, managing to stimulate economic growth without excessively exacerbating the distribution of income. Chapter 8 summarizes the argument and highlights the similarities and differences across the four cases.

TWO

Institutions and Social Reform

Introduction

This chapter first surveys several alternative arguments that may explain equitable development. It then zeros in on the central argument of this study, focusing on party institutionalization, state structures, the content of policy, and social crisis. The chapter concludes by discussing the importance of balancing the abstraction of variables with relational or contextual fields. Although the chapter seeks to abstract out the broader analytical lessons of the politics of equitable development in Southeast Asia, one should keep in mind that these variables "fit together" in explaining variation in development because they are anchored in contextual cases.

Alternative Explanations: Democracy, Class, Ethnicity

In comparative politics, equitable development can be explained by at least three theoretical approaches different from the one I propose here. These include a focus on democracy, on class, and on ethnicity. All of these explanations hinge on the importance of social forces and on numerical superiority. The argument advanced in this book engages social forces but emphasizes institutions. In going through these rival explanations, it is important to understand their distinct theoretical approach and why they do not fully explain variation in equitable development.

The view that democracy can improve the lot of the poor is premised fundamentally on the idea that a broader distribution of power will lead to improvements in social equity.[1] There are several variants on this theme. The first and simplest one is that numbers matter. This is the pluralist logic, by which the size of different groups is important in explaining economic outcomes. Tracing its lineage to Alexis de Tocqueville and John Stuart Mill, and framed historically by the close relationship between working-class movements and the expansion of the franchise in Europe, proponents of this thesis argue that majoritarian demands work to reduce inequality.[2] A related strand in this literature claims that democracy provides electoral incentives that may favor the poor or the median voter.[3] Political parties, irrespective of their ideologies, address the interests of the poor because they compete for their votes. Competition forces parties to be more accountable to the electorate and therefore to pursue some social policies. Finally, a more open polity means that there is more space for social mobilization, freedom of expression, and freedom of association through civil society. Under democratic regimes, groups in civil society have the opportunity to voice and advance their interests.[4] Particularly in countries where political parties are weak and fail to represent the interests of the poor, civil society groups are the crucial link, in that they bring issues of poverty to the political agenda. Thus, numerical advantage, political competition, and open space for mobilization and expression provide the basis for greater equity-enhancing reforms under a democracy.

The problem with arguments focused on regime type is that they are built on the premise that there are already effective institutions that can incorporate and aggregate the interests of the poor. This assumption is based largely on the European historical experience, particularly at the turn of the twentieth century, which makes its generalizability questionable.[5] In developing countries, competitive elections may be held regularly, and civil society may have room for mobilization, but political institutions may lack organizational structures and ideological bases to channel social interests and effectively represent them in the policy arena. Simply holding elections and having opportunities for political voice does not ensure that reform will be implemented. Often, institutions operating in electoral democracies in developing countries do not represent collective groups but simply advance the interests of elite factions.

A second problem with the regime-type argument is that it assumes that incentives for redistribution can come primarily from electoral competition. Again, we are led in this direction because reform in Europe occurred in the context of an expanding franchise. Yet in developing countries, authoritarian or semidemocratic regimes have also pursued pro-poor policies. Underlying these regimes have been institutions that seek legitimacy through performance as a basis for rule.

Thus, if we compare Malaysia to the Philippines or Thailand, we can illustrate the problem of relying on regime type as a basis for explaining pro-poor outcomes. Malaysia can be categorized as a semidemocratic or competitive authoritarian regime, where electoral competition is real but also heavily skewed in favor of the dominant party. The Philippines and Thailand are more openly democratic in terms of the space the state grants to civil society and political parties. Yet democratic periods in the Philippines and Thailand have not been conducive to pro-poor reform. There is intense competition among candidates to woo voters, but this does not result in policy geared toward the median voter. Instead, elites dispense patronage and spoils before elections to gain votes but do not seek to aggregate and channel interests of collective groups into policy. Despite the depth of social inequalities in Thailand and the Philippines, this equilibrium persists. By contrast, in Malaysia, an institutionalized party has forcefully addressed the interests of the poor through organizational depth and ideological consistency. In Vietnam, an even more closed regime has forged a strong equitable outcome through a committed left-wing party. But this does not mean that authoritarian regimes are *generally* more pro-poor than democratic regimes. One need only point to the Marcos period in the Philippines or the Sarit-Thanom period in Thailand to reject this position. Regime type cannot explain a developmental outcome because a policy outcome must depend on the kind of institutions available in the polity. Ultimately, it is institutions that implement policy. Those institutions that can advance social reforms, I argue in this chapter, must be cohesive, organizationally complex, ideologically consistent, and rooted in society.

Related to the argument of democracy is that of class. Here the claim is that working-class mobilization pressures the state to initiate social reforms. Arguments that emphasize the importance of class are also rooted in the Western historical experience, where democracy, labor unions, and left-wing parties support working-class interests.[6] For example, Friedrich Engels's claim that the working class "shall grow into the decisive power in the land before which all others will have to bow" was premised on the expansion of suffrage throughout Europe. The underlying assumption of this literature, known as "power resources" or "political class struggle" and focused on the European welfare state, is that the working classes have organizational capacities. Through organizations—labor unions and left-wing parties—the working class can build the necessary power to challenge conservative forces. This literature hence begins with class struggle but ends with organization.

When we dissect this class-based argument, we see that its portability is limited because it is heavily based on the European experience, in which leftist parties and unions worked in tandem to represent working-class interests against conservative forces in an electoral democracy. Underlying this position are the following assumptions: parties represent social groups, ideological divisions across classes are salient, unions are strong, and electoral democracies are not just present but furthermore allow for free competition. All of these assumptions are problematic in developing countries. In Southeast Asia, parties often do not represent social groups, party ideologies are often vacuous, ethnicity may trump class consciousness, and the state often represses or co-opts unions. One is hard pressed to find cases where the lower classes, whether rural or urban, have had enough power to shift policy in their favor. In Vietnam, the rural peasantry was able to make gains, but crucially this could occur only because of the mediating presence of an institutionalized, communist party in a nondemocratic regime. In most other countries in the region, left-wing parties have not been major players. Class does matter for social reform, but it can have an impact on a policy outcome only through institutions. Furthermore, those institutions do not necessarily have to be of a socialist character, nor do they need to operate under fully democratic conditions.

The third alternative explanation for patterns of equitable development is more specific to the literature on Malaysian politics. The overwhelming majority of the literature on Malaysia stresses the importance of ethnicity in shaping policy choices, whether in terms of redistribution or in terms of industrial transformation. Studies on political parties in Malaysia have highlighted ethnicity as the major impetus for advocating certain programs of social reform. Hence, in Malaysia, the fact that the political elite and the poor are Malay provides the political basis for social change.[7]

I concur that the correlation between ethnicity and class is important. In Malaysia, it is the correlation between ethnicity and class that has created the incentives to redistribute resources in favor of the economically disadvantaged Malays. But I want to emphasize that, by itself, this correlation is not a satisfactory explanation for Malaysia's pattern of equitable development. Focusing primarily on ethnicity and class tends to reduce political outcomes simply to the content of social structure. This type of explanation has two pitfalls: it is reductionist, and it particularizes Malaysia on the basis of its social structure, thereby limiting possibilities for comparative analysis (other than with plural societies). In such studies, Malaysia becomes sui generis, a case that stands on its own.[8] It is precisely comparative analysis on dimensions other than ethnicity that I seek to promote in this study.

I present a two-pronged argument to challenge the claim that Malaysia's social structure explains redistribution: one based on comparative analysis of countries with a similar social structure and one based on within-case analysis. First, let us look at three countries that have the same social structure as Malaysia (i.e., one ethnic group controls capital, whereas the other ethnic group, generally indigenous, controls the state and is also economically disadvantaged). These three countries with similar social structures—Fiji, Guyana, and Sri Lanka—do not have the same outcome of equitable development as Malaysia.[9] Furthermore, unlike Malaysia, systemic instability—coups, ethnic violence, and civil war—has characterized their politics. Comparative analysis shows us that we should not assume that a similar social structure will uniformly lead to a positive outcome of equitable development simply because the disadvantaged ethnic group is at the helm of the state. The relative capacity of the state or party and the particular ideological leanings and their effect on elites' policy choice ultimately determine how a country addresses structural inequalities. Putting the Malaysian case in comparison with cases with similar social structures indicates that Malaysia's relative success in equitable development, as well as in political stability, is unique. The discussion of the three cases, Fiji, Guyana, and Sri Lanka, is elaborated in further detail in the appendix.

Second, it is important to emphasize when Malaysia began to successfully attack structural inequalities. The evidence shows that it was only after the 1969 riots that the state shifted its course decisively and intervened more forcefully to redistribute income and that the dominant party became more institutionalized and more focused on social reform. Between 1957 (independence) and 1969, the state pursued pro-poor, pro-Malay policies, but those met with minimal success. In both periods, pre-1969 and post-1969, the country's social structure was constant, yet it was only after 1969 that Malaysia began to see significant changes in patterns of inequality.[10] A within-case analysis, therefore, shows that it is not social structure that explains the change in the outcome (equitable development) but specific institutional changes in the polity that affected policy and in turn shifted the direction of the economy. Lest this discussion be misunderstood, I want to be very clear that I am not denying the importance of social structure in shaping Malaysia's inequality. Furthermore, it should be clear that institutions are embedded in social structures and should not be considered autonomous from interests constructed by social forces.[11] Nonetheless, if we are to pinpoint *analytically* what has led to structural change in Malaysia, it is critical to highlight the role of institutions, specifically the party and the state.

Party Institutionalization and Social Reforms

Instead of focusing on regime type, class, or ethnicity, I argue that institutions provide a more compelling theoretical lens for explaining variation in equitable development. This is so because institutions provide the weak with a collective material structure that allows them to unify and articulate their interests. Institutions can overcome the disadvantages of capital, geographical dispersion, informal networks, personal influence, and organizational fragmentation. They enable subaltern groups to organize and mobilize effectively, to articulate their interests in the halls of power, to maintain a coherent channel for advancing those interests, and to ensure constant monitoring and enforcement of those interests so that policy formulation actually is effected at the implementation stage. Above all, institutions provide the poor with the organizational weaponry to subdue and constrain the politics of personalism—a pernicious form of politics that inevitably undermines their long-term interests.

The significance of institutions for mobilizing the interests of the poor has its origins in leftist politics. From the social democratic parties of Europe to the communist parties across the globe, organization has been vital to the political strategies of the left.[12] In Europe and in developing countries, the only way the left has historically been able to challenge the status quo was by organizing and mobilizing at the grass roots. As Chilean President Eduardo Frei put it: "The great masses of Chileans have no organization, and without organization no power, and without power no representation in the life of the country."[13] In India, Atul Kohli made a compelling argument for the significance of disciplined, cohesive organization within a left-of-center party that could tackle social inequities.[14] Rare cases of successful equitable development—such as Kerala, India; Costa Rica; and Mauritius—have been explained in part in terms of cohesive social democratic institutions.[15] Although not concerned with the left, Kurt Weyland has also articulated an institutionalist argument in the case of Brazil, arguing that institutional breadth is crucial for there to be successful redistributive reforms.[16]

This study builds on these insights but seeks to broaden out the argument about institutions, moving it beyond their rootedness in a leftist movement or in a democratic setting. Most studies emphasizing party organization implicitly or explicitly have either the left or democracy as a broader canvas within which they situate organization. What I argue instead is that organizational power for social reform does not have to have an elective affinity with leftist ideology, nor must it be rooted in a democratic regime. Particularly in developing countries, where regime type can often be extremely nebulous, fitting neither fully democratic nor authoritarian categories,[17] or where class structures may be less salient than ethnicity, it is important to move beyond the general parameters within which pro-poor organizations are often theorized. Furthermore, in highlighting this difference with studies framed by leftist politics or democratic regimes, we should also realize that initiatives to attack inequality can also stem from institutions that may not match our normative preferences, whether in terms of the use of coercion or in terms of the advancement of one ethnic group over the other.

In Malaysia, the United Malays National Organization (UMNO) stands out as a powerful organization with a social agenda dictated by ethnicity. Ideologically, the party does not match the leftist inclinations of the social democratic parties in Europe, Latin America, or India. Quite the opposite— the party elite had its roots in the aristocracy and colonial bureaucracy, whereas the elite today includes significant elements from the capitalist class. Yet *organizationally*, UMNO matches the social democratic parties in many respects. The party is internally democratic, has a vast membership with a strong voice in the direction and leadership of the organization, is actively involved at the grassroots level, and at the same time maintains a strong center with the ability to discipline and enforce the party agenda. Like many social democratic parties, UMNO also tends toward pragmatic politics and policy. It is driven above all by concerns over Malay survival and power, but it is not a party with chauvinistic or violent tendencies toward other ethnic groups. Its mode of governance and its policy agenda have always been based on some bargaining and compromise with non-Malays. This moderation becomes especially apparent when we compare UMNO with other ethnic parties in the developing world, such as in Sri Lanka, Fiji, and Guyana, that have employed violence against their ethnic rivals.

What is also notable about the Malaysian case is that it has advanced social reforms in a semidemocratic, illiberal regime. After the 1969 riots, the Malaysian state imposed martial law for twenty-one months, and the regime that emerged after 1971 was significantly more closed than in the pre-1969 period. In contrast to the Communist Party of India, Marxist (CPM) in West Bengal, which Kohli discusses, social reforms did not occur in a democratic setting in Malaysia. Rather, authoritarian practices structured the basis for reform and helped provide more coercive power behind them.

Underlying the thesis of organizational power are the concept and theory of institutionalization, most famously articulated by Samuel Huntington.[18] Huntington defined institutionalization as the process by which organizations and procedures acquire value and stability.[19] This concept was framed within an effort to understand and theorize the possibilities for achieving order and stability in a developing world where tentative democratic experiments had spiraled into social upheaval and military coups. Dominant parties, such as the Soviet Communist Party, India's Congress Party, South Africa's National Party, and Mexico's Institutional Revolutionary Party, served as the exemplars of institutionalization—disciplined and organized parties that could represent *and* control their constituents. Irrespective of regime type, institutionalized parties shaped the basis on which order could be achieved.

Four variables were at the core of the concept of institutionalization: adaptability, coherence, complexity, and autonomy. Adaptability refers to the party's continuity through time, measured by generational change in the leadership and functional change in the party (e.g., from opposition to government). Coherence is defined in terms of discipline and organization in the party, such as through routinized procedures to elect members of the executive board. Complexity means that the party has institutional depth, made up, for example, of differentiated units rather than centered on a single, dominant personality. Autonomy refers to independence from social forces, such as landed elites or labor unions. An autonomous party may have links to social forces, but those forces should not dominate it.

Huntington's work inspired a vast literature,[20] but one in particular, the work of Scott Mainwaring and Timothy Scully, provides an important corrective to the concept of institutionalization.[21] A critical difference is Mainwaring and Scully's emphasis on rootedness in society as a key component of institutionalization, in contrast to Huntington's focus on autonomy. Most concepts of institutionalization tend to focus on the structure and persistence of the organization and on its autonomy, but not on its linkages with society. In Huntington's worldview, institutionalization is less about rootedness and more about autonomy precisely because the threat to order in the developing world comes from social forces. Were social forces to penetrate institutions, institutional coherence would fray.

On some level, autonomy is necessary for institutions to maintain their value separate from social forces.[22] But Huntington's concern for stability leads him to undervalue the significance of social forces for party strength. For a party to have structural continuity and consistency, it cannot remain separate from social groups.[23] Social forces, whether based on class, ethnicity, language, or region, provide value to the party and unite its members in a collective agenda. Parties rooted in society will tend to have an ideological agenda that provides the party with consistency that is crucial for sustaining programmatic policies.[24] Furthermore, rootedness in society allows the party to maintain constant dialogue with its constituents, which enables the organization to respond to needs at the grass roots effectively. In turn, constant feedback from the grass roots strengthens the party's grip on power by ensuring that it is responsive to the members' needs. For a party to sustain its presence in a polity, it thus must be embedded in the social landscape. Without this link to society, a party is likely to be shaped less by ideology than by clientelism. Parties without a social base are often built solely around strong personalities.

A second key difference between Mainwaring and Scully's and Huntington's concepts is that the former were concerned with the relationship between institutionalization and democratic consolidation. In fact, their concept was premised not on party institutionalization but on the party *system*. This allowed them to move away from Huntington's vision of hegemonic parties as the emblematic forms of institutionalization. Much of the recent literature on party or party system institutionalization has been concerned with democratic consolidation, marking a clear shift from the concerns of Huntington. Though understandable, this also has the unfortunate tendency to stretch the concept of institutionalization such that it often has more to do with democracy than with value infusion of an organization.

My concern in this book is not with the relationship between institutionalization and order, nor between institutionalization and democracy, but with institutionalization and social reforms. Institutionalization affects social reforms in at least three ways. First, it provides a cohesive structural apparatus within which pro-poor ideologies and social movements can be channeled, aggregated, and articulated in the policy realm. Second, it provides a long-term, patterned structure within which policy can be implemented effectively. Third, it subdues the narrow-focused and short-term goals of charismatic, populist leaders and traditional patron-client relations in favor of long-term, collectively driven, programmatic policies.

A central aspect of institutionalization is that it provides discipline and cohesiveness for the articulation of interests. Without cohesiveness—one of Huntington's criteria for institutionalization—pro-poor movements and ideologies may not find a way to have their agenda implemented in the halls of power. "No idea has ever made much headway without an organization behind it," writes Samuel Barnes. "Wherever ideologies seem to be important in politics they have a firm organizational basis."[25] To the extent that cohesiveness suggests internal strength, an institutionalized party may also serve as a powerful bulwark against reactionary forces that resist reform agendas. There is no guarantee that cohesive, institutionalized parties—which Philip Selznick describes as "organizational weapons"[26]—can in fact defend their agendas against more repressive forces, but it is worth emphasizing that the building of organizational coherence is one avenue for strengthening or protecting one's policy initiatives.

Social movements mark the history of pro-poor struggles, but the success of those movements does not match their proliferation. This is because they have often not been incorporated and shaped by an organization. In Vietnam, during the colonial period, rebellions sprang up in protest against state authorities' relentless taxation despite poor harvests. In the Philippines, agricultural workers in the late 1940s protested against unfair tenancy conditions, thereby spurring the Huk Rebellion. In Thailand, villagers in the north and northeast rallied in the 1990s to protest against large infrastructural projects that displaced their means of livelihood. These movements failed to improve the livelihoods of the poor because they could not translate mobilization into policy output.

Civil society groups, particularly development nongovernmental organizations (NGOs), have been extremely active in Thailand and the Philippines, mobilizing and organizing the poor, and functioning as their only genuine representative. But this form of politics is inherently limited because it does not contain within it the means to directly shape policy outcomes. Civil society actors bargain with government officials on behalf of the poor, they craft research papers showing the significance of grassroots development, and they oppose policies that are unfair and repressive. These actions are crucial, but they do not have a sustained and direct impact on policy. For pro-poor policies to stick and succeed, they must have forceful political backing and coordinated efforts to channel resources toward their goal. For this, political parties are necessary. Furthermore, without institutionalized parties that can channel and integrate social demands, mobilization by social forces is likely to dissipate once the state represses it. Institutionalized parties thus have a unique role as an organizational weapon that can bind social interests together and then use the power of a cohesive institution to drive through social reforms.

Cohesive parties must also be socially rooted, for cohesiveness implies not just internal unity but also a consistent link with a particular social group.[27] Parties characterized by coherence maintain consistent ideologies and are closely rooted with a relatively bounded social group.[28] Programmatic coherence therefore creates a basis for social rootedness, wherein the party consistently seeks to keep its eyes and ears focused at the ground level to address the interests of its members. A party rooted in society thus listens to the grass roots, responds to it, and channels those interests into the appropriate governmental structures. Without social rootedness, parties would simply function as vehicles for elite interests.

One of the distinct characteristics of UMNO is its consistent efforts to remain rooted at the grassroots level. State assembly members and members of Parliament (MPs) maintain a constant presence at the local level, visiting the branch offices of the party to confer on the needs of their constituents. The executive explicitly instructs UMNO politicians to visit their districts regularly, to be proactive on the ground, and to report back to the center on their activities in the field. This endows the party with a genuinely representative function. At the same time, this representative function allows the party to better control its constituents and to maintain its grip on power. As Harold Crouch has nicely put it, UMNO's equilibrium is a "repressive-responsive" one.[29]

By contrast, few parties in Thailand can be thought of as representatives of particular social groups or as rooted in society. Split constituency returns provide strong evidence that parties lack a social base, as this means that voters do not have allegiance to a particular party.[30] From 1986 to 1996, more than 50 percent of constituencies had split returns.[31] With the exception of the Democrat Party and Thai Rak Thai (TRT), the membership base of parties is extremely shallow.[32] In general, the incentive for membership development lies less in genuine efforts to establish deep organizational structures than in complying with laws on political parties and receiving public subsidies. The shallow nature of membership development is especially apparent in the disjuncture between a party's membership numbers and its actual votes. In the 2001 election, Chat Phattana, New Aspiration, and Chat Thai all received significantly fewer votes than their membership numbers.[33] Parties have even been known to seek out members simply by sending application forms to factories; the workers would then sign and return the forms in exchange for some material reward.[34] Even more problematic is the fact that parties have not linked up with any social groups, such as labor unions, women's groups, or ethnic communities. Only the Democrat Party has established a firm regional base in Bangkok and, most prominently, in the south.[35] Emulating the strategy of the Social Action Party (SAP) in the mid-1970s, TRT was able to gain the loyalties of rural villagers in the north and northeast primarily through its populist programs, but the depth of the linkage between party and individual has occurred less through organizational penetration and active involvement of social groups than through the charisma of its leader and the popularity of the party's social reforms.

The second function that institutionalization plays in terms of social reforms is as a structure to maintain policy continuity. A party that has longer staying power is more likely to advance programmatic policies rather than clientelistic ones, as it will be focused on a long-term vision. An institutionalized party is not just more likely to initiate programmatic policies but also is more likely to make them stick. An institutionalized party tends to have an entrenched presence in the polity and will therefore be able to monitor the trajectory of its policy programs. Parties lacking institutionalization may promise social reform but may fail to deliver as a result of their unstable foundations. Pro-poor policies, in particular, must rely on the continuity of their institutional proponents because, as these policies encounter opposition, the proponents will need organizational backing and resoluteness to bring the policies to their envisioned destination.

In Malaysia, UMNO has been in power since the first elections were held in 1955. In terms of Huntington's criterion of adaptability, this is a party that has lasted and has been able to ensure generational change in leadership as well as function in different roles, first as a conservative nationalist movement and then as a governing party. Most crucially, UMNO's unbroken tenure in power has enabled it to fulfill its reformist agenda. Without a long period during which to plan, initiative, implement, and adjust policies in relation to feedback, it would be difficult to make headway on structural change. A massive agenda for reform, like the post-1969 New Economic Policy (NEP), requires continuity of elites in power.

By contrast, in Thailand, reform efforts have collapsed because of the instability of the party system. In the mid-1970s, when social reform stood some chance of success, a number of reform bills could not be passed into law and therefore be implemented, including one that would have reduced the stranglehold of local elites in the periphery. With numerous parties sharing little in common in the governing coalitions of the 1970s, parliamentary continuity was always on fragile ground, and the military's threats to step into the fray further constrained party development. In the 1990s, repeated efforts by rural villagers, displaced by dams, to gain concessions from the state foundered as a result of the parties' weak institutionalization. Two parties, Chat Thai and New Aspiration, did negotiate a broad compensatory package with the rural poor, but both packages collapsed when the governments of these clientelistic parties fell apart. Both governments fell apart because of factional wrangling within the leading parties and the broader coalition. Lacking any durability in the party system, civil society actors and rural poor who negotiate with the state have no guarantee that their arduous efforts will be implemented. Only one party in Thailand, the Democrat Party, operating since 1946, can lay claim to durability and adaptability. But this is a party that has historically shown little concern for the rural poor. The TRT Party was more effective than other parties in effecting social change in part because it lasted a full four-year parliamentary term. It was able to make a compromise over the Pak Mun Dam hold while also putting into place a number of social policies, including a universal health-care program. Yet TRT also did not last long, as it found itself ousted in a military coup.

The third and final area in which institutionalization contributes to social reform is on the question of organizational complexity and value. This is perhaps the most abstract issue within the concept of institutionalization, but it is also the most fundamental. Institutionalization has powerful implications for social reform because it implies the rationalization and systematization of policy above and beyond charismatic, personalistic, or traditional values. Institutionalized parties, where procedures, organizational structures, and programs are valued in and of themselves reduce the influence of personalism, whether within the party system or within the polity more generally.

Whether one conceives of personalistic power in terms of charismatic populist leaders or more traditional, clientelistic networks, politics based on personalism tends to be narrowly based, short term, and elite driven.[36] Within the party system, the pernicious effects of personalism are evident in politicians' constant party switching. There is virtually no loyalty to parties in Thailand and the Philippines and therefore little interest in strengthening parties as instruments of broader collective agendas.

What drives the party system in Thailand are factions, based largely on personal ties, whether family or friends, and on financial or political benefits (e.g., a shared vote canvasser, known as a *hua khanaen*). These factions are the movers and shakers of power in the party system. Their constant search for greater spoils is largely the cause of the system's high electoral volatility. The goal of factions is not to advance a particular policy agenda but simply to gain a cabinet seat as a means for patronage that will then benefit faction members. Powerful factions can anoint one party as the dominant force in one election and in the next election elevate another party to the apex. From 1979 to 2001, factional conflict led to the downfall of at least five of eleven governments.[37] As a consequence of high electoral volatility, parties do not remain in control of government for long and therefore are unable to sustain a programmatic agenda. This is to the detriment of policy stability in general, but especially for the poor, whose avenues for reform are limited compared with those of the upper class.

By contrast, in Malaysia, the party system is valued in and of itself; electoral volatility is extremely low; parties manifest highly complex structures;

and although factionalism exists, it is generally held under check. All parties in Malaysia have extensive branches and active memberships. For example, UMNO has an elaborate structure with a supreme council at the apex, followed by divisions and branches in the periphery. Elections are regularly held for positions on the supreme council, and rank-and-file members have considerable say on the direction and agenda of the party. Auxiliary organizations bringing in youths and women also broaden the party structure. The party and the auxiliary organizations are proactive at the branch level in areas that range from politics to mundane social activities. Party switching is extremely uncommon, and although sharp factional infighting has transpired at a number of points in UMNO's history, only in 1988 did it go so far as to split the party. But even after that split, a reconfigured UMNO was still able to win subsequent elections. There have also been periods in which strong personalities sought to establish their supremacy over the organization.[38] Yet, despite periods during which factionalism or personalism has risen above the norm, in the long run the party organization has always reasserted itself.[39]

In political systems where populist politics predominates, the interests of the poor are under threat.[40] Populism often tends to sharpen class cleavages, which in turn leads to greater social polarization, heightened violence and instability, and ultimately a counterreaction from entrenched elites—all outcomes that are not favorable for improving the conditions of the poor. Economic policies under classic populist regimes tend to be fiscally reckless and to spur hyperinflation.[41] In many Latin American countries, populism sharpened divisions between the middle class and the working class, precipitated an economic crisis, and opened the door for military coups. Instead of improving the conditions of the poor, populism often worsened their situation in the long run.

Like populism, clientelism centers on personal relations and short-term rewards in exchange for political support.[42] Rewards can come in the form of financial, moral, or material incentives. Although local elites or party officials in weakly institutionalized systems may provide numerous welfare benefits, such as financial loans, medical care during emergencies, or assistance with everyday village problems, the nature of this support is intermittent, short term, and contingent on support for the patron. Unlike institutionalized parties, clientelism generally lacks long-term goals and systematic plans for reform. Only when a favor is needed do material benefits pour down.

The short-term, narrowly focused, exchange-driven nature of personalistic politics suggests that there may be more corruption and less accountability both within parties and within the broader polity under such conditions than in institutionalized parties.[43] However, it would be misleading to suggest that institutionalized parties are not prone to corruption, clientelism, and patronage. Institutionalized parties also reward their supporters with material benefits in an effort to gain votes. Notable examples are Japan's Liberal Democratic Party or Mexico's Institutional Revolutionary Party.[44] Many Malaysia observers have also pointed to the deep clientelistic aspects of UMNO.[45]

I do not want to overdo the dichotomy between institutionalization and personalism, whereby we assume that institutionalized parties are devoid of all the vices inherent in clientelistic exchange. However, we should understand that in making these distinctions, we are trying to establish differences in kind rather than differences in degree. No analytical category is completely bounded, but there is arguably a *qualitative difference* between a social variable that has stronger properties of X than of Y. Two points should be emphasized on the overlap between institutionalization and clientelism. First, traditional clientelism tends to be defined by a chain of transactional relationships, with elites themselves as the recipients of spoils at the local level; however, modern party organizations that practice clientelism are more likely to dispense benefits to collective constituencies, with the intent of gaining their political support rather than that of local notables alone.[46] Second, there is a qualitative difference between institutionalized parties that also have aspects of clientelism and clientelistic parties that have no institutionalized structures at all. The former may play the politics of patronage within a programmatic agenda, whereas the latter simply dole out spoils or seek personalistic power without any programmatic vision. This difference goes to the very heart of the contrast between the party system in Malaysia and that in Thailand, and between parties that seek some social reform and those that are oblivious to reform. In Malaysia, parties may have elements of clientelism, but they are unequivocally institutionalized and programmatic, so that clientelistic exchanges do not overwhelm the institutionalized and programmatic aspects of the organization. In contrast, in Thailand, clientelism overshadows any systematic or rationalized aspects of party organization and behavior.

State-Party Dynamics

The relationship between states and parties can prove extremely valuable for development and particularly for redistributive reforms.[47] There are three ways in which state-party relations matter. First, state capacity and intervention are crucial pillars of a redistributive agenda. They provide the institutional weight and proficiency to sustain a party's ideological vision. While the party steers the political compass, the state bureaucracy provides the institutional capacities to intervene in financial and labor markets, to restructure social institutions, and to execute policy at the grassroots level. Without an effective bureaucracy that possesses some degree of corporate coherence and that operates with an interventionist mind-set, it will be difficult for a reformist party to actualize its goals. Second, the combination of state and party can result in the building of a dominant regime. Such political dominance may be necessary to surmount social crises and concentrate power for redistributive ends. Third, an institutionalized party can monitor, check, and spur the bureaucracy to accomplish its policy agenda. The relationship between state and party can thus be synergistic, but it can also function in terms of a check-and-balance, with the party standing above the bureaucracy to ensure the fulfillment of its pro-poor agenda.

Without forceful state intervention, economic growth alone is unlikely to restructure society. In Thailand, since its first economic boom in the 1960s, the state has generally resisted direct intervention in the market. When it has intervened, however, it has often acted in a repressive manner, concerned more with control of the rural sector than with economic restructuring or redistribution. Several economists have defined state behavior in Thailand as plagued first by the sin of omission and then by the sin of commission.[48] Until 1969, the Malaysian state adhered to a laissez-faire policy that failed to improve the inequitable conditions between the ethnic groups and that then precipitated ethnic riots. Intervention in the markets for labor, education, and finance was crucial in ensuring that redistribution worked effectively. Overall, the Malaysian state demonstrated a forceful interventionist position that went beyond redistribution goals alone but encompassed a broader developmental strategy. Although the Malaysian state intervened in specific markets for the purpose of ethnic redistribution and as part of a broader industrial strategy, it still operated under broad market conditions, creating incentives for foreign investment and export industrialization.[49]

State intervention by itself provides no guarantee that particular policies will achieve their intended purpose. Crucial to the effectiveness of intervention is the capacity of the bureaucracy. The civil service must have systematic control over production resources, rationalized long-term planning, and consistency in policy formulation. It must also be defined by corporate coherence, extensive technical and analytic skills, and relative autonomy in terms of broad macroeconomic policy. This has been one of the primary lessons coming out of the developmental state literature.[50] State intervention without bureaucratic capacity and policy coherence may end up simply fomenting unrest, disorder, and economic collapse. In Zimbabwe, for example, land-reform initiatives led by Robert Mugabe have been driven less by solid institutional foundations than by political zeal. By contrast, the developmental states in Northeast Asia and in Malaysia have intervened judiciously through a competent bureaucratic corps and through purposeful and systematic rationalization of policy.

The second area where the state matters for social reform is in terms of its close relationship with the governing party. This relationship helps infuse the governing regime with power and control, thus creating a dominant party system.[51] This in turn allows the regime to push through its policy agenda unconstrained by an opposition and to ensure a smoother transmission of policy.[52] This is problematic from the point of view of democracy, but in a situation where redistribution becomes an imperative issue, state-party dominance may be essential to achieving this end. Two elements of this relationship are especially important: coercion and resource advantages.

A close state-party dynamic allows the dominant party to take full advantage of all coercive levers in the state's arsenal. These may include not just the employment of the executive as a bully pulpit and a source of moral suasion but also the deployment of the police or army in the case of resistance by vested interests; the employment of bureaucrats to execute challenging policy; and the use of laws that severely restrict political participation, such as internal security acts that allow detention without trial.

Resource advantages, particularly through control of public financing, are critical for dominance because they allow parties "to outspend challengers at every turn, saturate the media, pay armies of canvassers, blanket the national territory with their logo, and generally speak to voters through a megaphone while opposition parties speak with a whisper."[53] Through such acts, parties can dictate their policy interests and overwhelm the opposition. Dominant parties can use resources in both legal and illicit ways. Legally, they can target legislation and pork-barrel projects to their particular regional, ethnic, or class constituencies. At the same time, dominant parties can employ illicit means to control resources. They can shift funds from state-owned enterprises toward their party's goals; they can channel public funds to their party chest; they can use their control of public sector employment to build electoral support; and they can use public, administrative resources for partisan ends.[54]

In Malaysia, the close relationship between state and party, rooted in a party that civil servants founded during the colonial regime, has created a formidable political machinery. By controlling Parliament, most state assemblies, the bureaucracy, judicial courts, the police, the media, and other state institutions, the party has the power to define the policy agenda, restrict the voice of the opposition, and execute its goals. Strong opposition persists against the UMNO regime, as evident in tight elections in 1959, 1969, 1999, and 2008. But this opposition has never reached the point of breaking through the institutional weaponry of the state and party. By maintaining control of the institutional pillars of the state, the UMNO regime has had the means to implement, sustain, and legitimize its pro-Malay redistributive agenda.

Dominant party regimes in Taiwan, China, Vietnam, Malaysia, and Singapore—and, to a lesser extent, Thailand under TRT—have all been successful in pushing through pro-poor policies, whether through land reform, housing policy, mass education, or health-care reform. Their use of coercion and resource advantages has given them ample space to execute their goals. In all of these cases, institutionalized parties pursued pro-poor policies in a context of authoritarian or semiauthoritarian coercion. Dominant party regimes may not always be driven by a redistributive agenda, or succeed in that pursuit, so we should be careful not to assume that they fulfill a sufficient condition for pro-poor reforms.[55] But to the extent that a pro-poor agenda is already on the table, a dominant party regime may serve as a powerful organizational apparatus to implement policy.

The third aspect of a state-party dynamic that matters for social reform is the ability of the party to monitor and check the bureaucracy. Having a party that looks over the shoulders of the bureaucracy can be especially useful to ensure that policy follows the political agenda of the government. In contrast to a developmental state like Japan, where, in Chalmers Johnson's words, "the politicians reign while the bureaucrats rule," for redistribution to be the central impetus of the state, it is the party that must rule. The developmental state literature has focused on bureaucratic capacity as crucial for economic change, and although I have noted here this importance, a state's emphasis on equity-enhancing reforms also requires much more than capacity. It is imperative that the party sit above, motivate, and steer the bureaucracy. This ensures that, unlike the Northeast Asian developmental states, the popular sector is not shut out from policy formulation. To the extent that a party is institutionalized and, above all, rooted in society, its strong presence over the bureaucracy keeps the direction of policy in line with the party's social base.

In their discussion of mechanisms to strengthen state intervention for redistributive purposes, Dietrich Rueschemeyer and Peter Evans observe that a valuable "integration mechanism is the creation of dual bureaucratic structures in which a strand of offices more responsive to intentions of the center parallels the operative main-line organizations, serving to inform the center as well as acting to control and guide the main body of the bureaucracy through sanctions and normative appeals. Such dual lines of control can take many forms, among them ideologically informed parties."[56]

In Malaysia, UMNO has often operated as a "dual bureaucratic structure" in monitoring the work of the bureaucracy. In the 1960s, Deputy Prime Minister Abdul Razak traveled throughout the country making surprise visits to district offices to make sure that rural development programs were being executed as planned. In this way, the party maintained its oversight of the bureaucracy. Even more intrusive in the periphery has been the dominance of UMNO officials on local development committees.[57] Rather than bureaucrats shaping policy at the local level, it is UMNO officials who control the agenda. In rural development in Malaysia, where oversight is perhaps more necessary than in the urban sector, which can be more easily monitored, UMNO has kept its nose burrowed closely in the affairs of local bureaucracy.

Studies in India have also noted the need for political parties to monitor the bureaucracy. For example, left-wing parties have effectively checked the lack of professionalism at a primary health center or bureaucratic fraud and sluggishness in land reform.[58] In Kerala, "if a PHC [primary health center] was unmanned for a few days, there would be a massive demonstration at the nearest collectorate [regional government office] led by local leftists, who would demand to be given what they knew they were entitled to."[59] In Taiwan, the Kuomintang (KMT) has also watched over state institutions, maintaining "a hierarchy of political officers running parallel to the ordinary military hierarchy."[60]

In Thailand, the relationship between party and state has been largely antagonistic. Since 1932, the Thai state has been a powerful bastion of military power. Parties have been forced to operate in the shadows of the "bureaucratic polity." The state's constant interventions in the democratic party system have led to parties living an intermittent existence, thereby preventing parties from becoming institutionalized. The 1970s were a crucial moment when parties could have made inroads in redistribution but were felled by bureaucratic intransigence, especially at the periphery. In the 1990s, in the instances when parties and bureaucrats worked on the same side, their goals were hardly redistributive. Only under the ill-fated TRT government was there some close collaboration between technocrats, especially in the health sector, and a party agenda in favor of the poor. But this has been the exception that proves the rule.

The Content of Policy and Ideology

Beyond structural factors—states and parties—the content of policy has an important effect on patterns of equitable development. Some types of policies may be easier to implement, whereas others may be more challenging. The degree of difficulty in terms of implementation is crucial, because successful implementation—rather than policy articulation alone—often defines the difference between countries that have mitigated structural inequalities and those that have not.

We can assess the likelihood of policy implementation using Merilee Grindle's framework. Development policies can be categorized in terms of those which (1) are zero sum or positive sum, (2) have collective or divisible benefits, (3) require behavioral adaptation, and (4) have short-range or long-range goals.[61] Policies that tend to be zero sum, such as asset redistribution, are more difficult to implement, whereas those that are positive sum, such as health and education, are more likely to be implemented effectively because they do not incite as much opposition. Programs that provide collective goods, such as light and water in urban slums, may be easier to implement because these types of programs are more likely to invite compliance rather than conflict. Programs that require significant learning and adaptation may be more difficult to implement than programs that do not require a change in behavioral patterns. For example, programs that require training for agricultural development or entrepreneurial skills may take longer to see some dividends than, for example, housing schemes for the poor. Finally, policies that have long-range goals may be more difficult to implement than those whose goals are short term and therefore more immediately tangible. Preventive health policies or affirmative action policies for education, which tend to have longer-term goals, may not be as easy to implement as urban housing. Thus, successful implementation is more likely where there are positive-sum gains, collective benefits, a low degree of behavioral adaptation, and short-term targets.

How do these propositions map onto the cases in this study? The Malaysian experience complexifies these general propositions. At first glance, from the perspective of the policy's ethnic bias, the NEP might be categorized as zero sum with divisible benefits. The NEP was meant to rebalance economic resources away from the Chinese and toward the Malays. But this assessment needs to be carefully scrutinized. The NEP was not zero sum if we look at the policy in its broader context. The NEP was never meant to deny Chinese rights to private property, to employment and education, or to competition in the market. The NEP intended to provide structural leverage for the Malays to improve their economic conditions and therefore to be granted significant advantages over non-Malays, but the government was emphatic in stating that all ethnic groups would continue to grow through an expanding pie. Stripping Chinese of their assets was never part of the NEP process. Furthermore, the state later also rebalanced the initial disadvantages for the Chinese by allowing for Chinese public primary and private secondary schools, granting space for private universities that mitigate the quotas that favor Malays in public universities, and allowing Chinese firms to operate state contracts with Malays as front men. "What resentment existed was mitigated, in the economy growth years of the 1970s and early 1980s, by the spinoff benefits for non-Malays that the NEP generated, joint ventures and preferential access for restructured firms to government-controlled opportunities," writes Donald Horowitz. "Piecemeal expansions with side benefits are least likely to generate collective opposition."[62]

In terms of the specific redistributive policies pursued under the NEP, the Malaysian state focused not on land reform as a means of evening the income distribution but instead on education programs, skills training, affirmative action in employment, and health care. Asset redistribution was sought through the stipulation that 30 percent of corporate equity should end up in Malay hands, but this was done through market transactions. Benefits were skewed toward the Malays, but they were largely collective benefits, and even certain social sectors, such as health, were not explicitly tilted toward Malays.[63]

The types of policies required in this redistributive scheme did require significant behavioral adaptation. Training programs, such as Majlis Amanah Rakyat (People's Trust Council for Indigenous People, or MARA), were set up to improve the skills of the Malay working class. Affirmative action programs in universities were meant to push Malays into more technical subjects, such as engineering and the natural sciences. Agricultural schemes, such as the Federal Land Development Authority (FELDA), provided land, technical assets, and training to effectively cultivate private property. The Malaysian state was unyielding in its belief that the Malays had to adapt to modernity if they were to compete with the Chinese. In contrast to the expectation that higher behavioral adaptation makes success less likely, the Malaysian experience shows that it is possible to push through reforms that require behavioral change. For that to occur, the Malaysian state made every effort to pour resources into institutions that would train the Malays to gain more skills, become more entrepreneurial, and increase their productivity.

The Malaysian case also challenges the view that a policy that has long-term gains will be less successful than one with short-term gains. The Malaysian redistributive program was heavily geared toward long-term structural changes. It was only in the mid-1980s that the positive redistributive effects of the NEP became evident in the aggregate data. Education policies often take a generation for the benefits to ensue. Few of the policies that the Malaysian state implemented had immediate tangible benefits: FELDA may have provided land immediately for farmers, but it would take several years for the new landowners to see benefits from their new plots of land. Overall, the thrust of Malaysia's NEP was long term, as the goal focused on structural change in society.

In Thailand, Grindle's framework appears to have more predictive power. Radical reforms that were perceived as zero sum, such as Pridi Bhanomyong's socialist Economic Plan and programs for land-tenure adjustment and land reform in the 1970s, quickly fell by the wayside. But other programs have had moderate success, including the Tambon Fund of the mid-1970s and, more significantly, the recent universal health-care program. Here we see that at least three of Grindle's factors are found in the successful policies in Thailand: positive-sum gains, collective benefits, and low behavioral adaptation. Although the characteristics of policy content do not define the overall equitable trajectory of a country, it is clear that they have some influence on policy outcomes, such that in Thailand the few successes in policy execution have come from programs that have not incited a conservative reaction, destabilized social structures, or required significant learning. But this also indicates the limits of social reform in a country like Thailand.

What we may infer from this analysis is that what matters most for social reform in terms of policy content is that it not be too radical or destabilizing. Some degree of redistribution is possible as long as it is not in the form of expropriation and there are collective benefits. This is a lesson that a Marxist party like the CPM of West Bengal learned in recalibrating its agenda in the 1970s from its earlier, more radical position.[64] In Malaysia, the NEP was a gradual, moderate program of income and wealth redistribution that reflected the party's pragmatic ideology. Despite its pro-Malay agenda and its rhetorical flourishes, UMNO has always operated with an interest in compromise and bargaining with the non-Malays. This stems in part from the close demographic balance of the ethnic groups but, more critically, from the origins of party building, wherein the British called for a multicommunal democracy, and the Malay and Chinese elites found that they could cooperate given their similar class backgrounds and the radical challenges that surrounded them. Despite the 1969 crisis and the decision by UMNO to assert itself more forcefully over the multiethnic coalition that had governed since independence, it still insisted on upholding a grand coalition with non-Malays. Ideological pragmatism has thus characterized UMNO, which in turn can help explain the character of the pro-Malay redistributive program. Policy moderation is thus crucial for redistribution, but this can only come from a party that believes in flexibility, compromise, and bargaining.[65]

Crisis as Catalyst

What spurs a major initiative for social reform? A broad explanation would point to a major social crisis as a catalyst for reform. What constitutes a crisis is difficult to define, but we can start by using Sidney Verba's definition:

> [A] crisis [is] a situation where a "problem" arises in one of the problem areas [penetration, participation, legitimacy, distribution, identity] . . . and some new institutionalized means of handling problems of that sort is required to satisfy the discontent. . . . A crisis is a change that requires some governmental innovation and institutionalization if elites are not seriously to risk a loss of their position or if the society is to survive.[66]

A crisis is a turning point during which elites have to respond if they are to maintain power and order in society. A crisis goes much beyond routine problems because it calls into question the very coherence and survival of the polity. During moments of crisis, opportunities open up to advance innovative policies: "under conditions of perceived crisis, the likelihood of change occurring may be greater than when the policy reform is considered a matter of routine."[67] A "crisis may stimulate action and hence learning on a problem on which insight has been low and which for that very reason has not been tackled as long as it was in a quiescent state."[68]

A number of crises in Asia that precipitated social reforms include Japan's defeat after World War II; the KMT's defeat on mainland China; the 1969 ethnic riots in Malaysia; and more recently, the Asian financial crisis and its effects throughout the continent, particularly in Korea, Indonesia, and Thailand. In Latin America, the period of structural adjustment in the 1980s and the social crisis that it spurred led in the long run to the populist movements and social democratic victories across the region. In the United States, many changes in social policy occurred during the Great Depression and after the assassination of President John F. Kennedy.

In his analysis of the developmental state, Johnson emphasized the quasi-revolutionary characteristic of the state—a characteristic generated by a pressing social crisis. As Johnson puts it:

> This one overriding objective—economic development—was present among the Japanese people after the war, among the Korean people after Syngman Rhee, among the Chinese exiles and the Taiwanese after Chiang Kai-Shek acknowledged that he was not going home again, among the Singaporeans after

the Malayan Emergency and their expulsion from Malaysia, among the residents of Hong Kong after they fled communism, and among Chinese city dwellers after the Cultural Revolution.[69]

In all these states, a sense of urgency spurred transformative change.

To Johnson's list of Asian non-Leninist revolutionaries, one can add Malaysia. Malaysia's impetus for development in terms of growth with equity was one of survival—not from external threats but from internal implosion. The May 1969 riots had rattled the governing regime to its very base and had made the elites realize that massive structural reforms would be necessary to ensure stability and order. This quasi-revolutionary mentality pervaded the state as party elites and bureaucrats moved to implement structural reforms. On some level, a war mentality was already present in some bureaucracies, such as the Ministry of Rural Development, which had been influenced by the internal war against the communists, known as the Emergency. But the May riots suddenly infused the state with a whole new purpose. Indeed, Malay politicians and civil servants often referred to them as a "blessing in disguise."[70] Without the 1969 social crisis as a backdrop, it would be impossible to understand the drive with which the Malaysian state pursued its developmental projects.

A social crisis, however, does not guarantee that reform will be sought or effected. A crisis creates "a point of choice"[71] for reform initiatives, but "it does not necessarily result in either predictable or recommended policy changes."[72] Just like arguments about the pro-poor potential of democratic regimes, incentives (electoral or crisis driven) are helpful, but they cannot explain why some actors respond positively to incentives and others do not. A social crisis—no matter how systemic—should be thought of more as a crossroads, in which a number of options become available to elites, rather than as an automatic stimulus for reform or institutional change.[73] A stimulus is crucial for elites to be moved to action, but even more crucial are the choices elites take. The immediate options available are repression or reform. Elites may find repression less costly, so the choice of reform is by no means given. What leads to a positive response that addresses the social aspects of the crisis?

What this book argues is that institutionalized parties are best positioned to respond effectively to a social crisis.[74] Institutionalized parties with pragmatic tendencies are more likely to respond to a social crisis through policy change rather than to employ repression against the forces of unrest, because their behavior is generally driven by programmatic policies that are rooted in a social base. Institutionalized parties are more likely to gravitate toward programmatic rather than extreme responses, because such organizations can constrain demagogic reactions through their experience with routinized procedures and systematized structures. Institutional constraints can check immediate tendencies to lash out and can therefore center a response toward a more balanced approach. Furthermore, ethnic parties that seek to help their brethren in the wake of a crisis do not necessarily choose the reform option. The historical record shows that ethnic elites may often opt for repression.[75] It is institutionalization—not ethnic bonds—that explains an elite's choice.

Conclusion

To summarize the argument of this chapter, I have emphasized three variables in explaining variation in equitable development—party institutionalization, state intervention and close state-party ties, and moderate policies—and have also stressed the importance of a crisis that can serve as a catalyst to potentially spur reform.[76] Party institutionalization is fundamental because it provides the organizational structure within which policy reforms can be implemented in a sustained and disciplined manner. An institutionalized party, with attributes of adaptability, coherence, complexity, and rootedness in society, has the basis for implementing pro-poor reform. It upholds discipline within the organization; is responsive to its social base; is consistent in its ideology; and above all, is able to maintain the value of the organization over that of individual politicians. Institutionalized parties by themselves are not necessarily pro-poor. But without institutionalized parties, pro-poor reforms are on much shakier ground. On the whole, institutionalized parties move the polity toward greater concern for public programs rather than private interests, and this can only benefit the poor in the long run.

The state is also a crucial player in driving through pro-poor policies. These policies need direct state intervention to channel economic resources toward the disadvantaged sectors in society. But this intervention must be based on competency rather than naked politics. Therefore, intervention that helps the poor must be based on rational goals, technical proficiency,

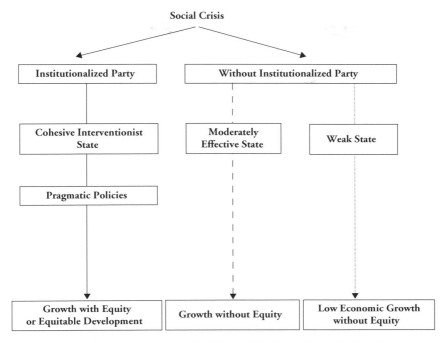

FIGURE 2-1 Theoretical Framework for Explaining Variation in Equitable Development

and systematic procedures. The combination of state and party directed toward a common goal can be of great use in pursuing an equitable program. This combination creates a dominant regime in which organizational resources and coercive power limit resistance and challenges to the reform agenda. At the same time, a party can serve as a forceful check over the bureaucracy and ensure that policy is being executed in line with the party's ideology.

The type of policies implemented is crucial to the success of the whole enterprise. Policies that are positive sum and that produce collective gains are more likely to succeed. Redistribution is one of the most difficult things to achieve in politics, but it can be done as long as it is not carried out in a zero-sum manner. If redistribution occurs in the context of a growing economy and of market-conforming practices, rather than outright asset seizure or nationalization, then it is less likely to trigger bitter opposition or to incite mass exodus. Underlying this choice there must be a party that is anchored in pragmatism.

Finally, a social crisis has to appear on the horizon for the immediacy of action to register in elites' minds. But crisis does not automatically generate reform. It can just as well incite state violence. The likelihood of reform being chosen over repression hinges on the presence of an institutionalized party that can moderate extreme tendencies. The argument is illustrated in Figure 2-1.

In concluding this chapter, it is worth briefly discussing the issue of generalizability. The goal of this chapter has been to develop a theoretical framework within which the cases that will be discussed in the next chapters can be situated and to provide a basis for generalizability beyond the cases. But it bears emphasizing that the key variables in this study— party institutionalization, states, and policy content—should be understood as operating in a contextual or relational field.[77] That is to say that their positive effect on equitable development works to the extent that there is a conjunctural relationship among the variables.[78] The framework I have just set forth is, in the end, a result of both deductive and inductive research. One cannot simply take these variables out of their context and assume that they will have the same effect if they were separated from their conjunctural relationship. The Malaysian case thus comes together as having a positive impact on equitable development because of the conjuncture of several interacting variables. If one of the necessary variables discussed here had not had the same value, it is possible that the outcome could have been different because a conjunctural relationship would have been lacking.

Institutional variables therefore operate within a configurational and historical field and must always be kept in that context. Like the literature on the developmental state, we should care about the generalizable implications not just for the sake of knowledge accumulation but also because, as students of development, we are concerned with improving the human condition *in general*. But the benefits to policy, if any, can come only from a balance between some abstraction and close contextual analysis.

PART TWO

The Politics of Equitable Development in Malaysia

We must do what we can to help the depressed sections of all communities because we believe that unless these imbalances are corrected and quickly too, we will not be able to achieve the national unity which we cherish so much and which is essential to our continued existence as a people and nation.

—*Tun Abdul Razak, prime minister of Malaysia and architect of the New Economic Policy*

Introduction

Malaysia's developmental trajectory is distinct in Southeast Asia for its successful pursuit of growth with equity. Although Vietnam's communist regime has made important strides in redistribution and Thailand has achieved some of the highest growth rates in the developing world, Malaysia since 1970 has maintained a developmental course of steady growth with declining inequality. In the 1970s, Malaysia achieved a solid growth rate of 7.6 percent and in the 1980s grew even faster at 8.9 percent.[1] In 2009, its gross domestic product per capita was US$7,030.[2] The incidence of poverty declined from 49.3 percent in 1970 to 3.8 percent in 2009.[3] The Gini coefficient fell from a peak of .529 in 1976 to a low of .441 in 2009.[4]

The achievement of growth with equity has come against significant odds. In 1969, Malaysia faced ethnic riots, deep inequalities across race and region, and dangerously high levels of youth unemployment. The country's success in implementing a program of equitable development can be traced to its cohesive institutions. A pivotal element underlying the success in equitable development was the government's emphasis on moderation: redistribution across ethnic lines within a framework of overall growth. While the Malays were favored in income redistribution, no ethnic group was to lose in absolute terms, although foreign capital's share of assets would decline sharply.

The centerpiece of Malaysia's strategy of growth with equity was the New Economic Policy (NEP), implemented from 1971 to 1990. The NEP sought to eradicate poverty irrespective of race and to end the association between race and economic function.[5] To reduce poverty and income inequality, the Malaysian government focused heavily on investments in rural development, expansion of human development, and high rates of growth. Rural development programs were crucial to uplift the poorest Malays and enable them to increase their productive assets. This would allow them to benefit from economic growth. Human development was the key strategy, for this allowed Malays to exit the traditional agricultural sector and gain more productive employment in the modern economy. Education in particular was prioritized to provide the means for Malay upward mobility. Finally, high levels of growth had to be sustained for the economy to generate the necessary amount of employment.

It bears emphasizing that it is the state's pursuit of economic growth *and* its direct targeting of the poor through specific, interventionist policies that allowed Malaysia to reduce inequality. Had redistribution been sought without growth, it is unlikely that the government would have succeeded in its aim to restructure society. By ensuring that the economy grew at high rates, it was able to provide the necessary employment for a rising Malay middle class and extract the necessary revenue to fund its social programs. At the same time, had the government not clearly targeted the poor by providing them with the capacities and assets to participate in the expanding economy, it is unlikely that the benefits of growth would have been broadly distributed.

In the World Bank's 1993 report on the East Asian Miracle, Malaysia was singled out as one of the High-Performing Asian Economies.[6] The Malaysian economy registered high growth rates from the 1970s until 1997 (although not as high as Thailand), averaging 7.6 percent in the 1970s and 5.8 percent between 1981 and 1985.[7] During the period of the NEP (1971–90), the economy grew at a rate of 6.7 percent.[8] From 1986 to 1995, the economy grew at an average rate of 7.7 percent, and from 1991 to 1995, it grew at a breakneck speed of 8.7 percent (see Table II-1). Increasing liberalization of the economy, heavy foreign investment, and sustained competitiveness in export markets—especially of electronics, processed agricultural products, and textiles—spurred this heightened growth. Except for a recession in 1985 and the 1997–98 financial crisis, Malaysia's economy has consistently grown

TABLE II-I
Malaysia, GDP Growth Rates, 1955–2009 (percentage)

Period	Growth rates
1955–60	4.0
1961–65	6.4
1966–70	6.0
1971–75	7.1
1976–80	8.6
1981–85	5.8
1986–90	6.7
1991–95	8.7
1996–2000	4.7
2001–05	4.8
2006–09	3.8

SOURCES: Malaysia 1965, 1971a, 1976, 1981, 1986, 1991a, 1996, 2001, 2006, 2010.

NOTE: Where there are discrepancies between government figures, I have listed the most recent figure given adjustments made in subsequent years.

at high rates. During the Asian financial crisis, the economy went from a growth rate of 8.7 percent in 1996–97 to −7.4 percent in 1998 and back to an impressive 7.2 percent in 1999–2000.[9] Overall, growth averaged 6.4 percent over three and a half decades since 1970.[10]

As measured by the Gini coefficient, the distribution of income has gone down since the implementation of the NEP. In the first two decades since independence in 1957 until the mid-1970s, the Gini rose, peaking in 1976 at .529. From the mid-1970s until the mid-1980s, with the NEP beginning to take effect, inequality declined starkly, going down to .446 in 1990, the year in which the NEP was officially meant to end. In the mid-1980s, the Gini coefficient plateaued, and between 1990 and 1995, with greater liberalization in the economy, it rose to some degree.[11] Nonetheless, by 2009, the Gini coefficient had declined to .441. The overall downward trend in income inequality between 1976 and 2009 is thus abundantly clear (see Table II-2).

Furthermore, the income disparity between Malays and non-Malays

TABLE II-2

Malaysia, Distribution of Income, 1970–2009: Gini Coefficient and Income Shares

Year	Gini coefficient	Percentage income of the bottom 40%	Percentage income of the middle 40%	Percentage income of the top 20%
1970	.513	11.5	32.9	55.7
1976	.529	11.1	31.2	57.7
1979	.505	11.9	32.4	55.8
1984	.483	12.8	34.0	53.2
1987	.458	13.8	35.0	51.2
1990	.446	14.3	35.3	50.4
1993	.459	N/A	N/A	N/A
1995	.464	13.7	35.0	51.3
1997	.470	13.2	34.4	52.4
1999	.443	14.0	35.5	50.5
2002	.461	13.5	35.2	51.3
2004	.462	13.5	35.3	51.2
2009	.441	N/A	N/A	N/A

SOURCES: Malaysia 1986, 1996, 2001, 2006, 2010; Ragayah 2008.

narrowed considerably since the NEP. In 1970, the disparity between the Malays and the Chinese was 1:2.29. By 2009, it was 1:1.38. The disparity between the Malays and the Indians also improved. In 1970, it was 1:1.77. By 2009, it was 1:1.10.[12] This evening of disparities between Malays and non-Malays, but especially with the Chinese, has been the most significant political aspect of Malaysia's developmental trajectory and has largely dampened the chance for resentment and violence against the Chinese.

The incidence of poverty has also registered strong declines since the mid-1970s. The trend has been unequivocally down with two exceptions: the 1985 and 1998 recessions. In 1970, the incidence of poverty stood at 49.3 percent. By 1976, it had gone down to 39.6 percent, and by 1995, it had reached 8.7 percent. The financial crisis generated some fluctuations in the statistics, as the incidence of poverty in 1997 stood at 6.1 percent, rose to

8.5 percent in 1998, and then subsequently went back down to 7.5 percent in 1999. In 2009, the poverty incidence was 3.8 percent (see Table II-3).[13]

There is some debate over the government's measurement of the data. In particular, there are doubts as to whether the different surveys are comparable and whether adjustments made to the poverty threshold are appropriate. Jomo notes that part of the registered poverty reduction between 1976 and 1984 may have been due to the lowering of the per capita poverty-line income from RM33.00 in 1970 to RM30.30 in 1987 in 1970 prices, or from RM74.15 in 1970 to RM68.09 in 1987 in 1987 prices. Furthermore, methods of measurement appear to have changed, as evidenced by the Fifth Malaysia Plan's emphasis on a more comprehensive concept of income.[14] Although these criticisms are valid, they most likely do not alter the overall trend of decreasing poverty incidence.[15]

The most powerful evidence that reductions in inequality and poverty have had an effect in society is in the rise of the Malay middle class. Among

TABLE II-3
Malaysia, Incidence of Poverty, 1970–2009 (percentage)

Year	Total
1970	49.3
1976	39.6
1984	18.4
1985	20.7
1990	16.5[a]
1995	8.7[a]
1999	7.5
2004	5.7[b]
2009	3.8

SOURCES: Malaysia 1986, 1991a, 1996, 2001, 2006, 2010.

[a]The percentage for 1990 is given as 17.1 in Malaysia 1991a and 16.5 in Malaysia 1996. The percentage for 1995 is given as 8.9 in Malaysia 1996 and as 8.7 in Malaysia 2001. In both cases, I went with the most recent Malaysia Plan, assuming that corrections were made in the interim.

[b]In 2005, the government changed its methodology for determining the poverty-line income, raising the threshold on the basis of social and economic changes (see Malaysia 2006: 327–29).

the Malays, the proportion of managers, professionals, and administrators increased from 4.0 percent in 1970 to 16.7 percent in 2000. The increase among the Chinese was from 7.1 percent to 17.1 percent. If we break down the categories into managers and administrators, and professionals and technical workers, in each category the increase in the Malays was larger than that of the Chinese. In the managerial and administrative category, Malays increased in absolute terms by eighteen times, whereas Chinese increased by ten times. In the professional and technical category, Malays registered an increase of 9.6 times compared to 4.7 times for the Chinese.[16] By 2008, Malays made up 51 percent of professional and management jobs.[17] These data point to the positive effects of growth on the whole population, but especially to the faster impact on the Malay population, in line with the goal of income redistribution along ethnic lines.

The two chapters that follow are divided on the basis of the events of 1969. Chapter 3 discusses politics before the 1969 riots. It begins by tracing the roots of racial inequality to the early colonial period. It then discusses the formation of Malaysia's political parties in the late 1940s. The chapter then addresses the social reforms that were attempted during UMNO's early period of governance (1955–69). The chapter looks at two policy areas in some detail: rural development and education. Although UMNO made a stab at alleviating poverty and inequality, its efforts generated limited progress, in large part because the elites remained wedded to a laissez-faire mentality.

Chapter 4 continues the story in the post-1969 period. It is after the 1969 riots that the Malaysian state went on a full-frontal attack against poverty and racial inequality. This chapter details the institutional changes that ensued within UMNO to deal with the social crisis. Changes within the party and state provided the basis for a more interventionist orientation toward development and a more hegemonic and institutionalized pattern of governance. The chapter then shows how UMNO successfully addressed social reform in the areas of rural development, education, and health.

THREE

From Colonialism to Independence
A Festering Crisis

Introduction

The roots of Malaysia's ethnic inequality developed under the British colonial policy of dividing ethnic groups according to economic function. Malays were trapped in the traditional, agrarian sector, whereas non-Malays were involved in the modern rural and urban economies. At the same time, the British granted Malays posts in the lower rungs of the bureaucracy. Ethnic divisions in the economy and polity persisted despite independence in 1957. By this point, the United Malays National Organization (UMNO) had been born as a party committed to protecting Malay rights; it had emerged in response to a British postwar proposal to grant non-Malays equal citizenship rights. Despite UMNO's origins as an advocate of Malay rights, the party held to a relatively moderate position both in terms of ethnic relations and in terms of economic policy. Its development plans sought to reduce Malay poverty while sustaining a free market economy, which was a central concern of UMNO's Chinese partners. The government channeled vast resources toward rural development, but these did not reduce the wide gap between the Malays and the Chinese. For this to occur, a crisis of systemic proportions would be necessary to break the laissez-faire mold within which UMNO elites operated.

The Roots of Ethnic Inequality: The Early Colonial State

> What is our policy? It is that indicated by Mr. Sweetenham—
> that we should govern the Protected Native State for the benefit

of the natives. This is the first and primary duty of the English Administrator.

—*Cecil Clementi Smith*[1]

In the political sphere it has been felt necessary to maintain a façade of Malay rule, or at least, of Malay participation in government, but there was no such necessity in the economic sphere. The result has been . . . that the Malay has been economically dispossessed in his own country.

—*Rupert Emerson*[2]

If they had so desired, the British could have used the tremendous leverage provided by their command of the modern state apparatus to effect different types of changes. That this is not fanciful is shown by the ability of the post-colonial government to alter significantly the occupational and social structure of the Malays, especially since embarking on the New Economic Policy.

—*Lim Teck Ghee*[3]

The early colonial period was the crucible within which the dilemmas that would confound contemporary Malaysia were formed. In this early stage of colonialism, dating from the late eighteenth century, the British politicized every aspect of ethnicity. By shaping the economic structure of the peninsula according to ethnic categories and entrenching the Malays in the bureaucracy, the British molded Malaya into a classic case of *divide et impera*. As the polity and the economy were riven in a manner that held little logic except that of British colonial interests, the roots of future conflict were planted deep into the soils of the Malayan Peninsula. The colonial state was the most decisive force in shaping Malayan society, and in constructing the central dilemma of the contemporary Malaysian polity: that of ethnic inequality.

Two crucial legacies of the early British colonial era should be highlighted. First, the British forged sharp ethnic cleavages in Malaya, thereby shaping the contours of what would become a classic case of a plural society.[4] They did this by actively opening the country to migration from India and China, and then channeling the migrants to particular niches of labor.

Non-Malays were largely involved in modern enterprise, especially trade, rubber, and tin, and they were geographically concentrated in western Malaya. In eastern Malaya, the Malay peasantry predominated in the traditional sector, comprising smallholder agriculture, primarily rice, rubber, and coconut. This dual economic structure set the foundations for the uneven development of ethnic groups and regions.

Second, the British maintained the facade of traditional Malay governance by instituting a form of indirect rule through which the Malay sultans were nominally the heads of the state. The displaced Malay aristocrats were made civil servants in the lower rungs of the administration. By maintaining some element of authority in the colonial period, it became easier for the Malays to take over the reins of state in the postcolonial period. The British had thus sown the seeds for divisions between the economy, dominated by the non-Malays, and the polity, held by the Malays.

THE ADVENT OF THE EARLY COLONIAL STATE

Before the arrival of the British, the Malay Peninsula was territorially divided among various states ruled by sultans and an aristocratic class. The British first made inroads onto the peninsula on 15 July 1786, when Francis Light led his troops into Penang on the pretext of assisting the sultan of Kedah against Thai influence. Rivalry between the Dutch and the British for control over commerce in Southeast Asia eventually led to the establishment of the Straits Settlements, which included Malacca, Penang, and Singapore.

In the 1840s, global demand for tin increased, driving Chinese merchants in the Straits Settlements to recruit more labor from China to open tin mines in the Malay states on the peninsula. To gain access to the tin mines, merchants had to establish relations with the Malay rulers, who received royalties and tribute from the mines. This eventually led to tensions between the Malay rulers and the expanding Chinese merchants, as well as within the Chinese community. From 1862 to 1873, warfare erupted among various Chinese factions. Such tensions opened the way for British intervention, and on 20 January 1874, the Treaty of Pangkor was signed, ostensibly ensuring stability for the state of Perak, where most of the mines were located.

This treaty established British dominance over the peninsula, beginning with the lands that were richest in tin. The treaty stipulated that a British Resident should be appointed in the state of Perak and that his advice should be sought for everything except Malay religion and custom. In the 1880s, this system was expanded to central Malaya. The artificiality of this advisory system imposed on the Malay sultans was best noted by Hugh Low, the Resident of Perak, who commented that "we must first create the government to be advised."[5]

Pressured by commercial interests for greater coordination among state governments, the British created the Federated Malay States (FMS) in 1896, which comprised the states of Selangor, Perak, Negri Sembilan, and Pahang.[6] The British then marched further north toward the states under the influence of Siam: Kedah, Perlis, Kelantan, and Trengganu. In 1909, Siam agreed to install British Advisers in those states, which became known as the Unfederated Malay States (UMS). In 1914, the last remaining independent state, Johor, on the southern edge of the peninsula, became part of the UMS.[7] The main distinction between the FMS and the UMS was that the former were governed more directly, whereas the latter had maintained traditional governing structures.

Colonial policy of indirect rule was from its inception a transparent charade to legitimize occupation by force. However, in the 1890s, the Colonial Office in London began pushing the authorities in Malaya to incorporate the Malays into the bureaucracy. This was a result of both ethical considerations and a shortage of colonial officers. Under pressure from London and with some amount of support from more reformist local officials, the British decided in 1910 to admit Malays from the aristocratic class to the lower rungs of the Civil Service in the FMS.[8] This was known as the Higher Subordinate Class Scheme, later changed to the Malayan Administrative Service (MAS).

Through the MAS, the traditional Malay aristocratic class was strengthened even as the British remained in control of the state. By the 1930s, Malays were being promoted to the more prestigious Malayan Civil Service under a system where slightly more than half the posts would be reserved for the British.[9] The British stipulated that only Malays of aristocratic background could join the MAS, and they were adamant that non-Malays not be allowed access to the bureaucracy, as such an allowance would lead to serious opposition from the Malay rulers.[10] By creating such restrictions, the British ensured that the postcolonial elite would be largely drawn from the landed and aristocratic classes and dominated by the Malay ethnic group.

THE PLURAL SOCIETY AND THE ETHNIC DIVISION OF LABOR

The emergence of the plural society in Malaya was both a direct and indirect consequence of British colonial policy. Although the British had a systematic means of importing Indian labor into Malaya, the attractions of commerce, as well as internal pressures in China, triggered large-scale Chinese migration. In the early nineteenth century, the Chinese population in Malaya started to grow rapidly, prompted by British expansion of trade in the Straits Settlements and the western Malay states, as well as by difficult economic and political conditions in mainland China, especially the Taiping Rebellion of 1851. Most migrants came from Guandong and Fujian in southern China.

The emergence of a large Indian migrant population began in the mid-nineteenth century and then picked up speed in the late nineteenth century. This was because of the British need to find cheap labor for the rubber plantations; rubber had become the key cash crop along with tin in the late nineteenth century. The British generally viewed the Indians as hardworking and, for that reason, made a sustained effort to bring them to Malaya with the inducement of a better standard of living.[11]

The mass migration of Chinese and Indians into Malaya transformed the landscape of the peninsula. On the western side, large swaths of land were converted into rubber plantations, and tin mines cropped up in many areas in Perak and Selangor. The eastern side of the peninsula, however, was relatively untouched by the modern economy, as the Malays continued to plod on in small-scale agriculture. Here lay the beginnings of the uneven economic structure. In terms of ethnic balance, by 1935, all the FMS members on the west, except Pahang, were dominated by the Chinese and Indians, whereas the UMS members were still overwhelmingly Malay.

The British made explicit efforts to divide the economy into ethnic groupings so as to facilitate their commercial interests. What the British needed were hardworking laborers to extract resources for export as well as local intermediaries to connect the local producers and consumers with the manufacturers and financiers in England. A policy of open migration provided the initial impetus for the recruitment of labor for the mines and plantations. More directly, however, the British cemented the ethnic division of labor by ensuring that the Malays would remain in rice-paddy agriculture while the non-Malays would work the modern export economy. This was necessary to maintain a constant food supply, to limit the loss of

TABLE 3-1
Malaysia, Number of Rubber Estates by Ethnicity, circa Early 1930s

Number of estates	Europeans	Malays	Chinese	Indians
100–1,000 acres	357	23	287	118
1,000+ acres	296	0	12	0

SOURCE: Emerson 1937: 184.

foreign exchange for rice imports, and to prevent Malay smallholders from competing with the owners of rubber plantations. Even more, such a policy guaranteed a modicum of political stability by preventing the disparate ethnic groups from joining together against the imperial authorities.

The British authorities implemented numerous policies that purposefully sharpened the ethnic division of labor. In the rubber sector, they raised the cost of its cultivation for Malay smallholder peasants largely by restricting usage of land for rubber cultivation. The government also provided better land and infrastructure to the plantation estates, thereby weakening the ability of smallholders to compete. In 1912, the British prohibited rubber from being cultivated in new lands alienated to Malays. Following the passage of the Malay Reservation Enactment in 1913, they discouraged rubber planting in Malay reservations. In 1917, they implemented the Rice Lands Enactment in the FMS, which made it easier for the state to preserve paddy cultivation. After 1917, the colonial authorities made it more difficult for peasants to apply for land for rubber cultivation and then imposed higher rates of premium for new land. The scale of land rents also tipped in favor of paddy, coconut, and subsistence agriculture, and against smallholder rubber cultivation.[12]

Statistics of the rubber estates in the 1930s show clearly how deep the impact of colonial policy was and how far behind the Malays trailed in the modern export economy. Although the Malays dominated landholdings smaller than a hundred acres cultivated for rubber, in the huge estates the Malays were a tiny minority (see Table 3-1). Furthermore, in terms of the share of labor in the rubber estates, the 1931 census shows that there were 203,036 Indians, 37,863 Chinese, and 7,373 Malays.[13] In tin mining, Malays were completely absent. Where the Malays did dominate was smallholder agriculture, such as rice paddy and coconut, as well as in fisheries.

The Birth of UMNO

The social, economic, and political conditions that the British had established in the early colonial period persisted in the postwar era despite the Japanese interregnum from 1941 to 1945. However, the ease with which Malaya and Singapore had capitulated to the Japanese made the British realize that major changes were necessary, especially in terms of building a more cohesive state and a more unified multicommunal nation. They viewed the fragmentation of administration and ethnic divisions as contributing to the weak defense of the peninsula. London's Colonial Office therefore embarked on a plan to rationalize administration and to create a more secure foundation for Malaya.[14] This crystallized in a plan to create a Malayan Union that would transfer sovereignty form the sultans to the crown, unite the nine Malay states and the Straits Settlements (excepting Singapore), pave the way toward self-government, build Malayan national consciousness, and grant equal citizenship rights to the various ethnic groups in Malaya.[15]

For the Colonial Office, the question of citizenship was the most difficult issue to adjudicate. Traditionally an advocate of the Malays, toward the end of the war, the Colonial Office shifted its stance regarding Malay dominance on the peninsula. China's tenacious resistance against the Japanese and active support for the British, coupled with Malay collaboration with the Japanese, moved the British to consider the interests of the Chinese more favorably in regards to citizenship rights.[16] Thus, the emerging distrust of the Malays and the sympathetic view toward the Chinese led the Colonial Office to view the Chinese community as the likely bastion of support for the postwar colonial regime and to therefore break from the traditional colonial vision of indigenous political preeminence.

The Malayan Union was officially announced in October 1945 and then promulgated in April 1946.[17] Initially, the Malayan Union elicited minimal reaction from the Malays, even gaining the consent of the sultans.[18] But as details surfaced in the white paper in January 1946, visceral reaction ensued. Malay elites objected to the reduced powers of the states and sultans but, above all, to the weakening of the Malay people's political primacy. With the granting of citizenship rights to the Chinese, the Malay elites feared they would lose the only advantage they held in a land they considered theirs. The extent of their anxieties is best understood in terms of the demographic makeup of Malaya at that time. From 1921 to 1947, the three major censuses taken showed that the Chinese were rapidly increasing as a share of the total population of Malaya.[19] By 1941, the Chinese had replaced the Malays as the largest ethnic group, making up 43 percent of the population to the Malays' 41 percent.[20]

Onn Jaafar, an aristocrat from the state of Johor, led the charge against the proposal. He quickly realized that it was crucial to pull together the Malays to effectively challenge the union, despite simmering anger against the sultans' meek acquiescence to the British plan. In the Malay newspaper *Majlis*, Onn Jaafar called for a Pan-Malayan Malay Congress, which was then held from 1 March to 4 March 1946 at the Sultan Sulaiman's Club in Kuala Lumpur, and attended by two hundred representatives from forty-one Malay regional and local associations.[21] Here they discussed the possibility of establishing an organization that might prevent what Onn called "the ignominy of racial extinction."[22] This was to become the United Malays National Organization, or UMNO. At the next Pan-Malayan Malay Congress in May 1946 in Johore Bahru, UMNO's charter was approved and the organization was inaugurated as a political party. To coordinate activities against the union, UMNO created the Malayan Union Opposition Department and the Propaganda Department.[23]

With its core mission firmly set, UMNO rapidly moved forward to block the Malayan Union. It mobilized peasants and townsfolk by tapping into Malay bureaucratic strongholds and traditional social structures, and it called for demonstrations and widespread protests. Crucially important was that UMNO found itself in the advantageous position of having the skeleton of Malay authority largely intact under colonial rule and simply needed to bring it together in a modern political machine. In effect, UMNO exploited the colonial ruling framework to undermine the British initiative by tapping the core elements of imperial rule—the bureaucracy and the traditional elite. Furthermore, by virtue of their traditional elite status and rank, UMNO elites could exert significant influence over village heads and district chiefs.[24]

Thus, UMNO mobilized civil servants at the center to lean on district officials and then on the administrative village official (*penghulu*) and the village elder (*ketua kampong*), who then activated the grass roots.[25] One assistant district officer reported how he "travelled by motorcycle from *mukim* to *mukim* informing the *penghulu* of the forthcoming meeting. As a result, groups of Malays from kampongs all over West Johore set off to walk perhaps a journey of two to three days in order to attend the rally."[26]

In this manner, an incipient party penetrated deep into the countryside, awakening the Malays to a sense of ethno-nationalism and in the process transforming the traditional structure into the gridiron of a modern political machine. Above all, the mobilization spurred by the Malayan Union established a mass base for UMNO. Tied to both bureaucrats and local elites, the party had quickly extended its reach and occupied the political center of gravity.

For several months, UMNO organized various forms of active resistance to the union, including boycotting advisory councils and official ceremonies installing the governor of the union and governor-general for Southeast Asia, coordinating the wearing of white on one's cap as an act of protest, and leading rallies throughout the peninsula. Two British parliamentarians touring Malaya noted: "In every hamlet, village and town that we visited we were met by what appeared to be the whole of the population. . . . [T]here have been demonstrations running to thousands of people. Malaya has undoubtedly become acutely politically conscious overnight."[27] Faced with intense opposition, the Malayan Union was withdrawn in July 1946.[28] In its place emerged the Malayan Federation in 1948, whose provisions included special rights for the Malays and restricted citizenship for non-Malays.[29]

Within a few months, UMNO had established a mass base, achieved its immediate goal of defeating the Malayan Union, and become the central political force that would negotiate the path to independence. This stunning success owed a lot to organization. In defeating the Malayan Union, "the leaders of UMNO were able to add the ingredient of organization," wrote Gordon Means. "Within a short period, UMNO was transformed from a loose association of Malay societies into a unified political party having its own separate membership, leadership and an effective system of political communication."[30] By 1946, the party had 110,000 members.[31]

This revolt against the Malayan Union and its British overlords was a relatively rare occurrence, for the colonial regime had largely accommodated Malay elites. Compared to Indonesia and Vietnam, the form of nationalism that became dominant in Malaya was not radical in nature—in fact, it had been largely conservative and gradualist in its orientation.[32] Indeed, "it was not the continuation of colonial rule which caused . . . disillusionment with the British, but rather the postwar policy which promised to end colonialism in such a manner that the Malays would not inherit the mantle of governing authority."[33]

Nonetheless, when the revolt against the Malayan Union erupted, it set in motion a series of events that shaped the incipient party in three distinctive ways. First, the party became the institutional articulation of Malay interests. Second, the need to mobilize across urban and rural sectors against the British led to the foundations of a strong organization. Third, although the party represented Malay interests, it expressed a pragmatic ideology that became cemented with the advent of democratic elections.

The union itself was the catalyst for the birth of the party, but other structural factors helped further party building. The relative support of the colonial authorities in the postwar period for a more participatory public sphere and encouragement of party politics provided the space for UMNO to develop. The fact that UMNO elites were relatively conservative and the perception of the British that the party was "safe"[34] granted it a virtual laissez-passer. Although the British sought to foster political liberalization and self-government, they were not willing to cede that ground to the left, let alone to any communist parties or movements. Therefore, UMNO was the perfect vehicle through which to cultivate democratic politics for a soon-to-be independent Malaya.[35] Similarly for UMNO, accommodation with the British after confrontation was an optimal strategy in light of leftist threats to their embryonic national authority.[36] Thus, UMNO benefited from British support, British efforts to repress Malay radicals in 1948, and the predominantly Chinese Malayan Communist Party's somewhat surprising decision not to attack UMNO out of fear of antagonizing the Malays.[37]

The left, both Chinese and Malay, emerged as a strong challenge to UMNO's conservative nationalism. The Malay radicals, in particular, exemplified by the Malayan Nationalist Party (MNP), were dismayed by negotiations between UMNO and the British in reworking the constitutional arrangements for Malaya in the wake of the defeat of the union. In their view, this collaboration with the colonial authorities was an abandonment of the interests of the Malays and a clear example of the "feudal" tendencies of the rising Malay leaders.[38] The MNP and the Chinese organizations both shared a distaste for the exclusivist pro-Malay nationalism that was being carved out through UMNO-British negotiations.[39]

Although under attack from both Malay and non-Malay critics, it was the challenge emanating from Malay nationalist groups, particularly the social and economic initiatives of the MNP, that was crucial in stimulating UMNO to articulate more precisely its agenda for its Malay constituents.[40]

In particular, UMNO was intent on maintaining its dominant position as the institutional articulation of Malay interests and in response to the MNP it strengthened its organization and programmatic agenda. First, UMNO created new rules for direct membership of individuals rather than membership in the party through affiliate Malay regional and local associations.[41] These associations were then dissolved into state branches so as to reduce the looseness of the party, institutionalize its structure, and tighten membership fees. The party also moved to strengthen its secretariat, establishing departments of finance, religion, economics, politics, education, women, information, labor, youth, general welfare, and trade and industry. The secretariat was vital for coordination and implementation of the party's agenda. The youth section, Pemuda, was led by Hussein Onn, a future prime minister and son of UMNO's founder, and it was meant to recruit youths away from the more militant leftist organizations. The youth section was to become a key auxiliary organization within UMNO that would enable the party to maintain deep roots in society. A women's section, Kaum Ibu (later called Wanita), was also established and in 1947 consisted of twenty thousand members.[42] Finally, to show its commitment to the welfare of the Malay villager, the party developed numerous economic and educational schemes, including the *Five-Year Economic Plan, 1947–51*.[43] By 1949, the party had become significantly more institutionalized.

The party's social base has historically come from two streams. One stream, defined by the national elite, has been characterized by bureaucrats and aristocrats,[44] and by a good number of nonbureaucratic professionals, including doctors and lawyers. Most received their education in English.[45] A second stream, representing the branch levels and grass roots of the party, came from peasant upper-class and lower-level government backgrounds. These included teachers, clerks, small shopkeepers, village headmen, and landowners. Teachers were particularly important, because they were some of the most ardent champions of nationalism in the early years of UMNO's growth.

The 1949 UMNO constitution delineated the party's four core principles: (1) organizing and maintaining an efficient organization, (2) making progress toward an independent nation-state, (3) advancing the interests of the Malays, and (4) upholding Islamic religion. The central plank of the party, the key issue that has always held the party together, is the issue of ethnicity, or Malayness. "The underlying axioms upon which all UMNO policy is based are UMNO political dominance and Malay unity."[46] It is out of the concern with ethnic political dominance that UMNO was born and continues to hold together.

But besides the core principle of Malay hegemony, the party has acted in a remarkably moderate and pragmatic manner.[47] In the words of Abdul Rahman, the second leader of UMNO: "We are ready and willing to accept anything that we earnestly believe is either politically or socially good and productive. . . . There are no water-tight compartments in our policies. . . . In my party we are right and center and left according to what is needed and what we think best."[48] The leadership of Abdul Rahman and Abdul Razak, UMNO's defining figures, was characterized by a moderate form of politics: "indeed flexibility—better expressed as pragmatism—became so highly valued that at times it constituted an ideology of its own right."[49]

The leadership's moderate position is notable for several reasons. First, given the perennial demands from the grass roots for more repressive action against non-Malays, it is often difficult for an ethnic party obsessed with survival of its group to maintain a moderate stance vis-à-vis its ethnic rivals. Comparative evidence reinforces this point. For example, in Fiji, Guyana, and Sri Lanka, parties of the numerically dominant ethnic group have often acted in an ironhanded and autocratic manner against the competing ethnic group.[50] Second, the party has often been buffeted from within and without by calls for more extreme acts against non-Malays. Malay newspapers like *Utusan Melayu* incited UMNO to take a more aggressive pro-Malay stance, whereas rank-and-file party members as well as the UMNO Youth have consistently advocated more antagonistic policies toward the Chinese.[51] Party divisions regularly submitted resolutions that called for banning journalists, magazines, and newspapers that insulted Malays, proscribing parties advocating multilingualism, tightening requirements for citizenship, and warning Muslims abroad not to marry foreigners.[52] Third, the leaders themselves often began their careers as virulent pro-Malay advocates. Although Onn Jaafar ultimately left the party he founded because it refused to open its doors to non-Malays, he had at one point said:

> We shall always firmly maintain that this land belongs to us. I speak so because I notice that the other races in the peninsula affirm that they have the right to demand equality of treatment. Whatever comes we will never consent to this. We wish to make them understand that they are only tenants of the house but not the owners.[53]

Even Abdul Rahman, so lambasted by Malay ultras for having conceded too much to the Chinese, had also made numerous statements questioning non-Malay rights.[54] Thus, despite an inherent potential to see their numerical superiority as an opportunity for repression, despite recurrent rhetoric tinged with chauvinist language from the grass roots, and despite leaders who have played to the street, UMNO—as a party—has behaved in relatively restrained ways.

Why has this been the case? A combination of factors explains this pragmatic stance. Demographics may have played a part, as Malay numerical superiority combined with significant non-Malay populations has not translated into absolute preponderance by any one ethnic group. In the words of a recent UMNO executive secretary, "We cannot [just] throw people in the sea."[55] But though relevant as a background factor, this is too simple an explanation that gives excessive weight to a priori social structural factors. More important are historical junctures, class relations, and structural constraints inherent in electoral contestation.

The initial impetus for some accommodation among the ethnic groups came from the British. Despite their own history of ethnic manipulation for self-serving reasons, they made clear that a central condition for granting independence was communal collaboration in a democratic framework.[56] In January 1949, the commissioner-general for Southeast Asia, Malcolm MacDonald, coaxed Onn Jaafar and UMNO elites to meet with Chinese and other non-Malay counterparts in closed-door, consultative meetings. These meetings, known as the Communities Liaison Committee, were held throughout 1949 and 1950 and formed the basis for discussion, bargaining, and negotiation over the terms of a future multicommunal democratic Malaya. It was in these meetings that the Malays and Chinese began to move to what eventually became known as "the bargain"—an agreement that the Malays would maintain political and cultural primacy, but in exchange, the Chinese would be eventually granted citizenship and be allowed to pursue their private enterprise unhindered by the state.[57] This eventually became institutionalized in the Alliance memorandum to the 1957 constitutional commission, and thus written into the constitution. Once the public became aware of these meetings, they were heartily denounced, particularly by the Malay press. *Utusan Melayu* described it as "a meeting of high-class Malays with rich Chinese under the guidance of a British official."[58]

Utusan Melayu was not off the mark. Indeed, one reason the UMNO elites and the Chinese were able to collaborate in the postwar period was because they shared class backgrounds.[59] As befitted their bureaucratic and aristocratic origins, the UMNO elites were English educated like their Chinese business counterparts. This was also why the British wanted specifically UMNO elites and Chinese business leaders to meet together, for both groups shared a belief in the free market and in liberalism, broadly construed. On economic policy, UMNO was a supporter of capitalism and, until 1969, fully embraced laissez-faire policies.[60] The British were particularly concerned with not allowing the Chinese communists, who were already well organized, or the more radical Malay groups, like the MNP, to seize momentum in the quest for legitimacy and authority in an independent Malaya. They were extremely comfortable ceding power to Malay aristocrats and bureaucrats trained by themselves and to Chinese businessmen who were staunch believers in the British laissez-faire model. The UMNO elites and Chinese leaders—all from the upper ranks of society—were also comfortable with each other's company.

The shared class background of the UMNO and Chinese elites made it easier to bring them together, but it also helped *cement* their incipient alliance. This is because this upper-class alliance stimulated a response from more radical elements on both the Malay and Chinese sides.[61] These forces eventually coalesced into two major opposition parties, the Chinese-dominated Democratic Action Party (DAP) and the Pan-Malayan Islamic Party (PMIP, later Party Islam, or PAS).[62] Both parties rejected the cohabitation of the Chinese and Malay elites and saw such behavior as a betrayal of the interests of their respective ethnic communities. Particularly in elections, as the opposition took over the flanks in the party system and lambasted the centrist parties with rabid ethnic rhetoric, the upper-class Malays and Chinese drew even more tightly together and became more convinced of the importance of interethnic compromise and moderation. They thus held on to the center and anchored that center in pragmatic values.[63]

Yet while the elites were economically conservative, they also saw themselves as a vanguard force for uplifting the masses and ushering them into modernity. As Onn, UMNO's founder, stated: "The UMNO has been formed not only for the purpose of opposing the Malayan Union, but also to fight against the Malays themselves. We have to find ways and means of how we shall change the habits and way of life of the Malays in order to enable them to realize their duties and responsibilities."[64] Although Malay and Chinese elites could cohabit together, the Malay elites had rallied in the first place to defend their ethnicity and after that first success, the party's goal was to strengthen the political and economic position of the Malays. But the distinct aspect of UMNO was that the agenda was to be pursued in a gradualist, pragmatic, and nonrevolutionary way.

Throughout UMNO's history there have been attempts to push the party in a more radical direction, but the party has often rejected such efforts. Some ideas advocated by radicals, particularly after 1969, penetrated the party and helped shape its platform, but they were reformulated or articulated in moderate and unantagonistic terms. Other early radical proposals were resolutely rejected. In the early 1960s, Minister of Agriculture Abdul Aziz bin Ishak, the most prominent UMNO member representing the left-wing faction and a rare leader with a peasant background, sought to make cooperatives the central economic unit of the country. This was a direct attack on the Chinese because it would enable the Malay farmers to bypass the credit and marketing middlemen, who were largely Chinese.[65] This proposal generated heated debate within the party but was rejected, as was a similar proposal put forth at the UMNO General Assembly in August 1966 that a welfare state be created. Although UMNO from its beginnings was determined to stand as the main institutional advocate of the interests of the Malays, it did not espouse a socialist vision that might radically transform the country. Rather, until 1969, it consistently propounded growth through laissez-faire and respect for property rights.[66]

The pragmatic position of UMNO was reinforced by an event that had surprisingly huge repercussions in Malaysia's political system. This was the first democratic election, in February 1952, for seats on the municipal council in Kuala Lumpur—a city dominated by the Chinese. With the backdrop of the Emergency[67] and of British efforts to find a reassuring liberal multicommunal governing structure, numerous parties were engaged in negotiations to create an electable, moderate coalition.[68] The UMNO founder Onn, who had left the party after it rejected his proposal to open full membership to non-Malays, had by then formed the multicommunal Independence of Malaya Party.[69] He attempted to ally with the Chinese, but his efforts backfired, leading to an alliance between the conservative party representing the Chinese, the Malayan Chinese Association (MCA), and UMNO.[70]

The UMNO-MCA partnership swept the elections, winning nine of the twelve seats. The success of the Kuala Lumpur municipal elections led to the formalization of the Alliance at the national level. Because the elections were held in Kuala Lumpur, the MCA was indispensable politically as well as economically. The MCA had in fact won six of the nine seats. Had national elections preceded municipal elections, it is much less likely that UMNO would have been compelled to forge an alliance with the MCA.[71] Thus, a combination of Chinese political strength at the municipal level, vast economic resources that the Chinese could use to finance national campaigns, the national political strength that a centrist Malay party could generate, and the fortuitous fact that local elections preceded national elections created the basis for a formidable alliance. At the helm of these two parties, furthermore, were two leaders, Abdul Rahman and Tan Cheng Lock, who respected each other and shared a "common stake in the preservation of the capitalist order."[72]

The national leadership of the two parties realized that, to win elections in a plural society, it was necessary to court one's own ethnic group within a broader partnership with a like-minded ethnic party. In October 1954, the Alliance was completed with the entry of the Malayan Indian Congress (MIC). In the first national elections held in August 1955, the Alliance asserted its electoral dominance again by winning fifty-one of fifty-two parliamentary seats.[73] In 1957, the Alliance Organization switched its name to the Alliance Party and was duly registered as a political party.

Through the Alliance, a consociational arrangement was formed that would serve as the bulwark for multicommunal stability. Two councils—national and executive—ran the Alliance Party, with the National Council vested with the authority to choose candidates for federal office and the Executive Council vested with the power to discipline and expel renegade members. This, in effect, gave the Alliance some control over membership within its three constituent parties.[74] In government, the MCA had limited cabinet seats but was given control over major portfolios: finance, commerce, and trade and industry.

The Impending Crisis: Laissez-Faire Growth, 1955–1969

Having surveyed the political conditions in the pre-1969 period, we now turn to the economic conditions that governed Malaysia during this period.

We will look first at the overall direction of Malaysian development, followed by a closer view of two important areas where reform was being attempted to improve the living conditions of the Malays: rural development and education. In these two sectors, the state made some progress in its reforms, but it was not until after 1969 that both sectors contributed to an easing of the income divide between the ethnic groups.

In its early years, Malaysia's development planning was largely based on laissez-faire growth. This was due to the colonial legacy as well as to an influential 1954 report of a mission of the International Bank for Reconstruction and Development. The report advised the Malayan government to focus in its first five-year plan (1955–60) on strengthening the private sector as a means for generating economic growth.[75] The first five-year plan of the Malayan government concentrated on three areas: (1) agriculture, particularly rubber replanting and irrigation schemes; (2) infrastructure, utilities, and communications; and (3) education, health, and social services. Throughout the plan period, the government stayed on the safe side by restraining spending even when there were budget surpluses in 1959 and 1960. The Ministry of Finance, headed by the MCA, was intent on protecting the government's liquidity shortage and reserve position rather than investing for development purposes. By 1960, the government's actual expenditures fell below the plan target by 15 percent.

The second five-year plan (1961–65) continued the emphasis on laissez-faire growth, but under pressure from the 1959 elections in which opposition parties scored important victories, particularly in the northeastern Malay states, the government sharply increased its allocations for development. The second plan stated clearly that the rural areas would be given more attention, especially to diversify the base of agricultural commodities and to increase rural employment.[76] About half of the budget was geared toward rural development. Social services were also given a higher priority than in the first plan. In the first two years of the plan, education received 40 percent more spending than did the whole first plan. In 1962, education was the only sector allowed to exceed the expenditure ceiling set by the Treasury. The health sector also saw major increases in spending. In 1960 alone, expenditures for health equaled the total of the previous plan.[77]

The First Malaysia Plan (1966–70) maintained the same trajectory of laissez-faire growth with an increased emphasis on rural development.[78] For the first time, however, the plan noted explicitly that growth was not trickling down and that the uneven distribution of income was a key concern of the state. Notably, however, it did not make any mention of ethnicity (except for the aborigines) when addressing inequality. Rather, it painted the problem of distribution in terms of urban-rural and regional differences:

> The fruits of economic growth so far have been unevenly distributed. Several groups in Malaysian society receive much lower private incomes and fewer public services than the rest of the population. These groups include the unemployed and other obviously weak segments of the population such as aborigines in Malaya and shifting cultivators in the Borneo states. But the problem is not limited to these groups. Most smallholders do not have easy access to markets.[79]

By mentioning the difficulties of smallholders, the government made oblique reference to the fact that Malay farmers were often constrained by largely Chinese middlemen in selling their goods.[80] But one can only infer this from the plan. This is a clear contrast with the post-1969 plans, where ethnicity and national unity stand out starkly as the dominant themes of development planning.

Anticipating a crucial factor that contributed to the 1969 riots, the first plan noted that youth unemployment was on the rise. Of men between fifteen and nineteen years old, 16 percent were now unemployed. In major towns, the unemployment rate of this group was 27 percent, whereas in rural areas it was 6 percent. Among men between twenty and twenty-four years old, unemployment was 10 percent in large towns and 6 percent in the countryside. A significant problem underlying high unemployment levels was the lack of skills among youths. In 1964, public service recruitment filled only 70 percent of the available positions, whereas in schools about five thousand teaching positions were unfilled or filled by unqualified teachers.[81] Throughout the fateful year of 1969, the *Straits Times* continued to highlight the deepening problem of unemployment.[82] In his 9 January 1969 budget address, Finance Minister Tan Siew Sin warned the government of the impending dangers of unemployment:

> The real basic problem . . . which we face in the coming years is the problem of growing unemployment. It is not only an economic problem, it could well become an explosive social and political problem unless we tackle it in time and overcome it, and the only realistic way of dealing with this problem is to achieve an adequate rate of economic growth.[83]

In the mid-1960s, the government also noted with alarm that private investment was not in line with its second-five-year-plan estimates. Although Deputy Prime Minister Razak admonished capitalists to forget "individual interests," the government refused to move beyond persuasion and fiscal incentives. It could have—but did not—intervene more forcefully to tilt private investment toward development concerns, particularly in terms of distorting labor or capital markets in favor of the Malays.[84] Lacking a forceful strategy to attack inequality, the government came under fire from numerous critics. Most vehement were those from the rural northeastern states that continued to feel deprived of the benefits of growth. Underneath the growth model chosen by the Alliance government, the Malay masses were fuming with frustration. This was well captured by Abdul Aziz bin Ishak, the former minister of agriculture, who was ousted because of his espousal of populist policies:

> Beyond the façade of apparent prosperity lies the quiet anger of a people who feel that they have been defrauded by the fruits of Merdeka [independence], and the price of freedom has turned to sand in their mouths. Our people are watching and they see that the entire colonial structure is intact excepting that a few brown faces have replaced the white faces in the air-conditioned offices and the big American cars.[85]

Rural Development

From the independence period until the 1970s, rural development was the focal axis of the state's redistributive policies. With the Malay population overwhelmingly based in the rural sector, the government actively sought to develop the agricultural sector. From 1957 until 1969, the state pumped huge sums of money into the rural sector.[86] This went to a vast range of programs, including drainage and irrigation works, such as the Muda and Kemubu programs in Kedah; physical infrastructure, such as roads, bridges, and piped water; land development; subsidies and credit to farmers; health clinics; and general institutional support. Donald Snodgrass argues that this period should be understood as a holding period in which the incomes of the countryside neither increased nor declined.[87]

In August 1950, the British established the Rural Industry and Development Authority (RIDA). Although RIDA turned out to be an ineffective institution, its creation signaled the beginning of state or quasi-state organizations that were geared toward the developmental interests of the Malay populace. In 1956, the government established an agency for land resettlement, known as the Federal Land Development Authority (FELDA). This agency became the centerpiece of the government's rural development programs, with its ambitious effort to create pioneer landowners in jungle areas. In its early attempts to alienate land and reduce poverty, it had mixed results. However, in the long run, FELDA succeeded in its goal of resettling Malay subsistence farmers and providing them a means for higher incomes. This is discussed in greater detail in chapter 4.

In need of a focal point for coordinating rural development, the government created the Ministry of Rural Development in 1959. The ministry, headed by Razak, who held concurrently the position of deputy prime minister, functioned as a "super-ministry," with influence over technical ministries, such as those of public works and agriculture; direct access to state party governments; and considerable leverage over financial and administrative resources. Fashioned on the model of the war council that had been operational during the Emergency, the ministry operated with a militarylike regimen that reflected the importance the government placed on rural development. "[I]t is the intention of the government to marshal all available resources and to deploy them with such determination and energy," declared Razak, "as were used to free the country from the menace of Communist terrorism."[88]

In terms of policy implementation, the ministry operated through federal-, state-, and district-level rural development committees. The goal of these committees was to expand infrastructural investment in areas such as schools, health centers, roads, wells, and utilities. These committees were composed of civil servants, heads of technical departments, and elected party officials. At the state level, the chief minister was in charge; at the district level, the district officer headed the committee. At each level of government, operations rooms were established to assess, coordinate, and target development policy as if it were a military strategy. Wall maps, graphs, and charts evaluating the progress of projects filled the room. The operations rooms explicitly mimicked the army's "operation briefing" techniques employed during the Emergency.[89]

The Rural Economic Development program (Red Book) was the framework through which development policy was planned and implemented. The Red Book began as a means of recording project proposals at the district level. Through village meetings, or through internal committee discussions, priorities for development spending were established. To organize the amount of information being collected, the Red Book contained an inventory of all basic data at the district level with a map showing land use, projects, physical layout, and transportation networks. Once all the proposals had been collected, a copy of the Red Book was sent to the state operations room, one copy to the national operations room, and one copy kept at the district operations room.[90] The structure on which the Red Book was based was particularly efficient because it provided a fluid channel for disbursal of funds from federal to state to district levels, and it granted districts decision-making authority over the projects.[91] In the second five-year plan, 20 percent of total public investment was allocated to Red Book projects.[92]

Meetings that brought together civil servants and elected officials were regularly held, thus enabling effective communication and coordination between bureaucracy and party. Meetings with the minister were often held in conjunction with briefings at the district and state level that provided a forum to immediately assess bottlenecks in program implementation. These briefings were then followed by field inspections of projects that allowed Razak to impress on the local population the seriousness of the state's rural development agenda and to emphasize the close relationship between party programs and state action.[93] Particularly indicative of the government's commitment and drive for developmental success are the instructions in the Red Book directed to the district rural development committee. Directives such as "Decisions must be translated into action," "Reasons in support of each project will be given in brief, clear, and forceful language," and "Necessary correspondence will be kept to a minimum and written briefly and to the point. Unnecessary correspondence will not be written at all" showed without a shadow of a doubt the seriousness with which Razak and the ministry took their mission.[94] But what was also significant, Gayl Ness concluded from his many interviews with district officers and other bureaucrats in the field, was that civil servants understood that there were clear procedures and standards that were expected—and adhered to—by the ministry. Reward and punishment for performance was rational, and this in itself helped motivate bureaucratic efficiency.[95]

The significance of the Ministry of Rural Development lay especially in its administrative structure through which it generated extensive capacities for policy monitoring and implementation. Crucial to the success of the structure was the importance given to it by the party leaders. As Ness observed, "The structure of the party and the cabinet provided paramount power to the new Ministry."[96] Razak regularly visited operations rooms and other agencies involved in development, checking project sites and progress, exhorting civil servants to achieve their targets, and promoting those who succeeded and punishing those who misrepresented their work.[97] In 1962, he attended 118 district rural development committee briefings, traveling forty-three thousand miles throughout the country.[98] Razak noted: "I therefore set up development planning at the three main levels of Federal, State, and District, and I continue from time to time to give directives to these teams as to how to set about their business of development plan implementation."[99] The fact that the deputy prime minister who would later become prime minister and chief architect of the New Economic Policy (NEP) was the founder of this super-ministry indicates the salience that rural development held in the minds of the political elite.[100]

Other important institutions established during the early 1960s were the Village Development Committee, which served as a feedback organization for the state; the Adult Education Division, which was in charge of village-based literacy classes and functioned as a membership and voter-recruiting machine for UMNO; and the Farmers' Association, which built branches at the village level to support farmers' production. The proliferation of these institutions at the village level was instrumental in enabling the state to penetrate society and achieve its symbiotic goals: the effective implementation of its rural development projects and the consolidation of its electoral base.

More development institutions were established at the local level in the late 1960s. The Federal Agricultural Marketing Authority was geared toward assistance for marketing and to eliminate the role of middlemen. In 1966, Majlis Amanah Rakyat (MARA) was created to support Malay entrepreneurs. In 1966, the Federal Land Consolidation and Rehabilitation Authority (FELCRA) was instituted to assist the landless and unemployed in the cultivation of unused land. Perbadanan Nasional Berhad (PERNAS) was formed in 1969 to provide capital and managerial and marketing services for Malay entrepreneurs.

Thus, from 1955 to 1969, the Malaysian government churned out one institution after another to promote rural development programs. These programs reflected the intensity of effort given to uplifting the Malay rural masses. They were also intended to enable the government to penetrate the countryside to win over votes, particularly after the 1959 elections in which the Islamic party, PMIP, made inroads into government territory. This vast institutional infrastructure implanted the state into the countryside and was important in cementing a framework through which development programs could operate and be monitored effectively by the governing party. But at this point, the efforts were not sufficient to bridge the burgeoning gap between the Malays and the Chinese. The Red Book program, though extremely innovative, focused largely on "output goals . . . items that could be constructed. There was no place for the analysis of human productivity, or of the organization of either production or distribution."[101] A formidable institutional infrastructure was in place that could disburse funds efficiently, but it did not effect deep structural change in terms of economic relations or improved capacities and skills of the rural Malays.[102] For this to occur, greater emphasis would have to be given to employment generation in the modern economy through active efforts to mold and manipulate economic growth. More critically, UMNO and its partners would have to break away from a primarily market-oriented framework where "planning . . . remained tied to a socially conservative political doctrine."[103]

Education

Throughout Malaysia's history, the educational system has been heavily unequal, with the roots of such inequality going back to a policy of benign neglect under British rule. The British allowed the private sector to dictate the pace of education, whereby the Chinese in the urban sector made advances by building their own language schools while the Malays were left to traditional schooling in the countryside that befitted their place in the economic hierarchy.

A number of English-language primary and secondary schools were established at the turn of the century. The Chinese dominated enrollment in these schools. By 1938, they occupied 80 percent of the seats. The fact that the Malays were often suspicious of the Christian orientation of these English-language schools, whereas the Chinese were not, helped widen the educational gap.[104] But more significant is the fact that the Chinese were closer geographically to the schools, which were located in urban areas and more concentrated in the Straits Settlements. Furthermore, the Chinese early advantage in higher income allowed them to bear the costs of these schools. Once in school, the Chinese did better and stayed longer than the outnumbered Malays. Thus, Malays were at a heavy disadvantage geographically, economically, and in this case even religiously. This yawning gap in the educational system could only help compound the economic disparities between the ethnic groups.

In the years leading to independence, there was much debate over how to unify the educational system. The governing elite conceived of the educational system as a means to bring together the disparate ethnic groups with the prominence of the Malay language in schools as the very pinnacle of national consciousness. The proliferation of English and of vernacular schools (Malay, Chinese, and Tamil) under colonial rule was criticized for creating different standards of education and for weakening national unity. Furthermore, the English language stood as an immense obstacle for the Malays. Although there was instruction in the Malay language in primary schools, its absence at the secondary level ensured a dead end in the opportunity structure for the Malays. Thus, the central issue in the politics of education during the period of independence was as much one of national unity as one of expanding access and opportunity for the disadvantaged Malays.

A series of committees attempted to address the tension over the major language of instruction. In 1951, the Barnes Report proposed a bilingual (Malay-English) primary school system. The government initially accepted the report's recommendations (although the Chinese community strenuously rejected them), but they were never implemented because of financial constraints. In 1956, the Razak Report staked out long-term goals of establishing a universal primary system and of promoting national unity and consciousness through education. In the short term, it pressed for the establishment of two types of schools on the primary and secondary level—standard schools (for primary) and national schools (for secondary)—that would use Malay as the language of instruction, and standard-type schools and national-type schools that would use English or Mandarin as the medium. All schools would also require the teaching of English and Malay languages as required courses.[105] In 1960, the Rahman Talib Committee recommended that public support for secondary education be limited to Malay- and English-language schools, thus dealing a heavy blow to the Chinese community and its aspirations for a multilingual educational system.

Another important change in the educational system that was meant to assist the Malays was the abolishing in 1965 of the Malaysian Secondary

School Entrance Examination. This exam, inherited from the British educational system, sought to weed out the academically minded from the vocationally inclined, resulting in a 65 percent failure rate. The Ministry of Education finally reasoned that the exam was premature in cutting off students from academic education. Therefore, it eliminated the exam to guarantee at least three more years of education at the lower secondary level for all students, but it kept in place the entrance examination to the upper secondary level.[106] The results were immediate: students in the Malay-language schools increased from 10,841 in 1964 to 36,171 in 1965.[107]

By the late 1960s, it was increasingly clear that Malay would become the dominant language in public schools. However, it was not until 1969 that the English-language schools fully converted to using the Malay language.

Conclusion

In the postwar period, Malaysia was able to overcome a number of challenges shared by many countries in the developing world, including achieving independence, establishing parliamentary democracy, and maintaining multicommunal stability. In all of this, the formation of an institutionalized party, UMNO, was a crucial piece of the puzzle. As the emerging dominant political institution, UMNO became the anchor for a relatively stable postcolonial transition. Unlike Thailand, where the absence of an alien imperial force weakened the impulse necessary for the emergence of a nationalist party, in Malaysia, a number of events—a misguided postwar colonial plan, ethnic anxieties, threats from more radical Chinese and Malay parties— stimulated the formation of an ethnic, pragmatic, and programmatic institutionalized party. This development, in the long run, would be of great importance for the country's political trajectory. But in the short run, UMNO had not yet found a way to break loose of the structural burdens that the British colonial regime had implanted on the peninsula.

From the early 1950s until 1969, the Malaysian government made strenuous efforts to address the predicament of the Malays, who remained overwhelmingly poor and disproportionately in the traditional, rural sector. But the pre-1969 economic policies did not make enough of a dent in the key problems hindering Malay advancement in the modern sector: lack of adequate skills whether in farming or in industry; insufficient capacities to move into urban, industrial jobs; and an unfavorable educational system.

Although some progress was being made toward making schools more Malay based, and in the area of rural development, government had sharply increased its spending, overall, the state did not pursue structural reform to its fullest extent. Despite the government's commitment to improving the conditions of rural Malays—amply evident in Razak's relentless efforts and exhortations to deepen the development machinery in the countryside—it did not succeed in increasing their incomes. Agricultural incomes grew at an annual average rate of 2.6 percent, which was less than the rate of rural population growth. The government relied heavily on strengthening export commodities, especially rubber and tin, to improve the incomes of the rural sector, but those commodities were too vulnerable to fluctuations in the market. Furthermore, although building a solid infrastructure in the urban and rural areas was important to stimulate the private sector, this sector did not meet the government's hopes of generating adequate employment. Unemployment rates among youths remained dangerously high. An editorial in the *Straits Times* underlined the inadequacies of rural development: "Basically, the rural scene has not changed. True there has been material progress—more roads, schools, mosques, improved social and recreational amenities—to attest to the success of rural development. But rural poverty has yet to be reduced in any significant degree."[108]

The central problem was that UMNO and the government bureaucrats remained stuck in a laissez-faire model—a result of its colonial heritage, the party leaders' class background, and its close cohabitation with the business-oriented MCA. The possibility of using all the levers of the state machinery to redirect capital, resources, and labor; to forcefully mold the pattern of growth; and to ultimately restructure society at its very core was still not at the forefront of the UMNO agenda. Active public investment in the pre-1969 period was thus insufficient to break away from the structures of social inequality because the government's "planned development was conceived within the existing framework of ownership and control in the Malayan economy. This static conception of planning could not cope with inherent immobilities in private investment patterns in the inherited colonial-type economy, nor did it resolve class and ethnic inequalities in the division of the benefits of economic growth. . . . The ruling Alliance ideology prescribed a development strategy geared to the existing social and institutional order, such that economic change was predicated upon and circumscribed by the unchanging pattern of stratification of society."[109]

Although the model the government followed was understandable, given the immediate need of postcolonial states to create a suitable environment for growth in the early stages of development, it was severely inadequate for alleviating poverty and inequality, particularly where ethnicity overlay patterns of stratification.

Thus, with UMNO still mentally trapped in a model of laissez-faire growth, the elites did not attack inequality head-on, nor did they realize the extent to which the Malay masses felt increasingly betrayed by their own ethnic kin. Only once ethnic riots shattered the capital city on 13 May 1969 was the UMNO mind-set pushed to think outside the box—a reality forced on it by the fears of a veritable national implosion.

FOUR

Reforming State, Party, and Economy

Introduction

The year 1969 was a critical juncture in Malaysian history. Devastating ethnic riots in the capital made abundantly clear that ethnic disparities could no longer be left to long-term, trickle-down effects of the free market. The state had to intervene decisively to rectify structural imbalances. From independence until 1969, the United Malays National Organization (UMNO) committed significant efforts to improve the conditions of the rural Malays, but its efforts did not yield major changes because the party did not seek a sharp transformation in economic relations. After 1969, UMNO attacked the problems of social and economic inequality much more forcefully through a sweeping program called the New Economic Policy (NEP). Crucial to this effort was a revamping of the party and efforts to penetrate more deeply into the periphery. Although UMNO was still rooted in its moderate multiethnic coalition, it imposed itself over its partners and opponents in a much more hegemonic manner.

Post-1969 Reforms

> From our past experience, we fully realize that it is not sufficient to provide only the economic infrastructure. This is obvious from the events of May 13, 1969[,] which nearly tore this nation asunder.
>
> —*Prime Minister Tun Abdul Razak*[1]

Since independence in 1957, the Malays had high expectations that the state would rectify the imbalances generated by British rule. Although the state made genuine efforts in this direction, primarily by increasing its spending in the rural sector, the dilemmas of Malay poverty and income inequality were difficult to overcome, especially because the state maintained its inclinations toward laissez-faire policies. The fate of Abdul Aziz bin Ishak, who was rebuffed by the party in his attempts to disband the Chinese middlemen and replace them with cooperatives, exemplified UMNO's position regarding social reform. Abdul Rahman maintained a close working relationship with Tan Cheng Lock and later his son, Tan Siew Sin, and was reluctant to advance any policy detrimental to Chinese capitalist interests. The fact that the Malaysian Chinese Association (MCA) held the Ministry of Finance throughout the prime ministership of Abdul Rahman was indicative of the government's support of unencumbered free enterprise.

In the 1960s, three socioeconomic issues gained particular salience: the weakness of the Malay business sector vis-à-vis Chinese business, the poverty of the Malay farmer, and rising unemployment. Although the economy had been growing, with per capita income increasing by 25 percent between 1957 and 1970, inequality had increased significantly. In the rural sector, the ratio of Malays to non-Malays was 3:1, whereas in the modern sector, the ratio was largely reversed—non-Malays outnumbered Malays by a ratio of 5:2. In 1970, the mean household income for Malays was M$179 per month, for Indians it was M$310, and for Chinese it was M$387. Among those below the poverty threshold, 74 percent were Malay. Within the ethnic groups, 65 percent of Malays were classified as poor, while for Chinese this was 26 percent and for Indians 39 percent.[2] The rates of unemployment among youths increased drastically in the 1960s. For men between fifteen and nineteen years old, 16 percent were unemployed. In major towns, the unemployment rate for this group was 27 percent. Among men between twenty and twenty-four years old, unemployment was 10 percent in towns.

The Malay business community was especially incensed that the state had not done more to support its interests. A government report indicating that Malays controlled 1 percent of corporate equity galvanized the Malays to lobby for structural reform. In June 1965, the state convened the Bumiputera Economic Congress. This congress passed sixty-nine resolutions supportive of Malay economic advancement. It also led to the establishment of two institutions for redressing economic imbalances: a Bumiputera bank created to grant loans for Malays in commerce and industry, and Majlis Amanah Rakyat, or People's Trust Council for Indigenous People (MARA), an organization that would help support and train Malay entrepreneurs. Ghafar Baba, then chief minister of Malacca and a central figure in UMNO, was made the first chair of MARA. The second Bumiputera Economic Congress was organized in September 1968, when more pledges were made to advance the economic concerns of the Malays. Although the congresses reflected significant efforts to improve the position of the Malay business class, in actual practice, their position saw little improvement before the NEP.

The political structure in Malaysia during the 1960s also deteriorated. First, the UMNO and MCA elite had become increasingly remote from the masses as they continued to make decisions behind closed doors. The close relationship between the leaders of the two parties also made it more likely for UMNO to favor the concerns of the Chinese elite rather than those of its own mass base. Stable relations at the top echelon were secure, but beneath, both the Malay and the Chinese masses were becoming increasingly agitated. Although UMNO maintained a solid mass base and had a strong membership throughout the country, its elite members had lost sense of the deep-rooted frustrations of their ethnic brethren.

Second, between 1964 and 1969, ethnic tensions rose sharply. The decision to bring Singapore into the Malaysian Federation in 1963 suddenly made the Chinese a much more powerful force, even though Sarawak and Sabah, on the island of Borneo, had been incorporated to balance Singapore. Lee Kuan Yew had promised to keep his People's Action Party (PAP) out of electoral politics on the peninsula, but he quickly reneged on this deal and brought the PAP in direct confrontation with the Alliance in the 1964 elections. The PAP's call for a "Malaysian Malaysia," a code for greater Chinese political rights, greatly perturbed the Malays. This eventually compelled the government to expel Singapore from the federation. On the other side of the aisle, Chinese anxieties increased when the National Language Bill was passed on 31 August 1967, making Malay the sole national language.

Third, the Alliance, and UMNO in particular, had begun to decay from their original organizational complexity toward a more personalistic, even sultanistic, authority structure.[3] Abdul Rahman exhibited increasing autocratic proclivities in his personal decisions and unwillingness to abide by organizational procedures.[4] In 1959, angered by the MCA's public ultimatum calling for increased seat nominations in the upcoming election, Abdul Rahman decided to personally select all MCA candidates. He repeated this personal selection for all Alliance seats in the 1969 elections. Abdul Rahman furthermore excessively personalized the leadership of the party by convening the meetings of the Supreme Council at his home and by holding only two meetings of the council in 1967–68. He was also the main figure responsible for Singapore's expulsion from the Malaysian Federation in 1965. At one point, a Maoist-like cult even began to surround the Tunku.[5]

Mounting economic and political crises climaxed, with disastrous results for the Alliance in the national elections of May 1969. In these elections, the opposition were able to come to an agreement in which the parties would not compete with each other in the parliamentary districts. This agreement, coupled with rising dissatisfaction among the electorate, increasing assertiveness of the Chinese population, and an extended period of campaigning, led to surprising results. The Alliance still won an outright majority at the national level, but for the first time, it did not gain two-thirds of the seats.[6] The MCA emerged as the biggest loser, having been successfully challenged for the Chinese vote by two opposition parties, Gerakan Rakyat Malaysia and the Democratic Action Party (DAP).

The more serious problem for the Alliance was its failure to retain several state assemblies. The Alliance had lost the states of Kelantan, Penang, Perak, and it was in a virtual tie for Selangor. Never before had the government confronted such a dramatic electoral turnaround. With the government paralyzed by the results, Chinese supporters of the Gerakan and the DAP marched through the streets of Kuala Lumpur to celebrate their victories, taunting Malays with shouts of "*balik kampong*" (go back to the countryside) and other racial epithets. In response, the embattled *mentri besar* (chief minister) of Selangor, Harun Idris, whose position hung by a thread because of the electoral stalemate in the Selangor Assembly, rallied Malays to his residence the following day. The rally quickly turned violent, as many had come armed with weapons. Within two days, rioting, burning, and ethnic massacres had devastated Kuala Lumpur. The final government report stated that 178 people, mainly Chinese, had been killed.[7] Independent estimates were much higher.[8]

INSTITUTIONAL REFORMS

In the wake of the May 1969 riots, UMNO made drastic organizational changes within the party and the Alliance. The party came to the realization that it had to assert greater control over the economy and the polity to appease the Malay masses without completely alienating the Chinese. Thus, UMNO was compelled to navigate a treacherous course between Malay dominance and multicommunal flexibility. Once the riots had been quelled and order restored, UMNO's first move was to centralize power within the newly formed National Operations Council (NOC). Parliamentary democracy was temporarily suspended while all critical decisions were made through the NOC, headed by Razak. The composition of the NOC was made up of the same multiethnic corps that formed the directorate of the Alliance. But now Razak would make all final calls.

The NOC quickly made three important decisions. First, all sensitive issues, which had caused the riots, would from then on be completely off the political agenda. This meant that it was illegal to question the special rights of the Malays as enshrined in article 153 of the Constitution. Second, the NOC decided that the state had to drastically redirect economic policy toward the needs of the Malays, in terms of both their poverty levels and their inability to access capital. Failure to do so could incite further ethnic riots and threaten national integrity. Third, a new national ideology, the Rukunegara,[9] was devised as a means of strengthening national unity.

Amid all the recriminations and soul-searching for the causes of the riots, UMNO realized that its own institutional failures had allowed the situation to spiral out of control. Although the immediate reaction was to blame communists and Chinese opposition parties, UMNO also committed to internal reforms in response to the crisis. Razak, in particular, was adamant that the government and UMNO perform more effectively and genuinely represent the interests of the country. After the riots, Razak met with a few close UMNO colleagues in the Cameron Highlands and agreed that the pre-1969 system was no longer viable. They decided that the state needed a more decisive and long-term policy agenda, that democratic politics had to be constrained, and that UMNO must maintain its predominant position.[10] Overall, the party had to become more decisive and forceful in establishing its political authority and its policy agenda. As R. S. Milne puts it: "The general mood of the government, from May 1969 onwards, was no longer to 'sweep things under the carpet' . . . but to lay them on the line, spell them out."[11] In January 1971, at the first party general meeting since the riots, Razak stated that "UMNO members and leaders must be responsible in determining the guidelines to coordinate the policies of the government and those of the party so that the aspirations for change among the people can be fulfilled."[12] Razak therefore began a series of organizational and ideological reforms within the party that were central to its institutionalized structure. The thrust of these reforms was to centralize and institutionalize power within the party, to strengthen its bureaucratic and procedural structures, and to ensure that the party stood forcefully above government and above its partners.[13] "In contrast to the previous era," writes Gordon Means, "Razak's administration was based on the assumption that UMNO was to provide the mass base of political support for the government. UMNO was to be, much more than before, the foundation for the political system."[14]

First, UMNO passed constitutional changes to tighten party discipline. In May 1971, a special UMNO general assembly made important changes in the party constitution. The Supreme Council was vested with greater power and institutional longevity. Instead of being elected every year, it would be elected every three years. It also was given the authority to select electoral candidates and discipline party members. Other reforms at this assembly included making party members more aware of their rights and responsibilities by making those explicit and fostering a more egalitarian environment within the party by employing terms such as *presiden* instead of *yang dipertuan agong* (officially translated as "president," but with feudalistic connotations) and *wanita* (women) instead of *kaum ibu* (mother).[15]

Second, UMNO solidified the party secretariat to improve organizational effectiveness. This was done primarily by enlarging the research section. Three new members were added to the then staff of one person. One new important task of the research section was to examine monthly political reports sent by divisions and elected representatives. The secretariat also expanded its territorial reach by appointing salaried, full-time organizing secretaries to all party divisions. It furthermore initiated a campaign to spread a "mental revolution" throughout Malay society that was based on an eponymous book written by senior UMNO officials and academics. The campaign sought to advance values among the Malays such as thrift, hard work, rationality, and achievement orientation.

Third, UMNO sought to increase party vigor and dynamism by encouraging frequent meetings at all levels. To ensure greater institutionalization, the meetings of the Supreme Council were moved from the president's home to the party headquarters and were held once a month. Bureaus connected to the council became more active, churning out papers that had an impact on council decisions. On the local level, party divisions and branches of the party were called on to "transform UMNO into an 'action-oriented' party that would monitor economic and social activities at the local level."[16] Throughout 1973, state organizations held a number of conventions that brought together national leaders and local party members. After the 1974 elections, the party also sought to separate elected officials' offices from their residences. Members of Parliament (MPs) and state assemblymen were required to establish their constituency offices in the divisional headquarters, which would "act as the nerve center for meeting and serving the people."[17]

Razak also called on MPs and assemblymen to be more directly involved in their district. Carrots and sticks were employed to ensure that MPs were more involved in the field. Allowances for MPs were raised as incentives for more extensive fieldwork, but the specter of losing their jobs was also raised if the party felt the MP was not working in line with the new directives.[18] Furthermore, as members of district action committees and the state liaison committees, MPs were strongly encouraged to listen to their constituents' needs and channel them to the center.[19]

Finally, Razak sought to clean out bad elements from party and state. He directed UMNO to actively weed out corrupt members and bring in fresh faces, especially intellectuals and younger members. The bureaus of the Supreme Council, for example, were increasingly staffed by senior civil servants and academics.[20] Beyond the party, Razak forcefully pushed for cleaning up the bureaucracy and for building a more responsive government. In his first speech as prime minister–designate, Razak addressed the civil service, stating that officers at the lowest rung were "the eyes and ears of the government. . . . So, if any officer treats them [the people] badly, they immediately conclude that the government is not good and not serving their needs. . . . We must bring in fresh air into all government departments, a new image—an image of a dedicated, efficient, and incorruptible civil service."[21] He further warned the bureaucracy not to become "integrity risks." The government decided to increase salaries of the civil service and to provide loans for purchasing homes to ensure greater integrity and public purpose among officials.

To execute his goals, Razak sought to get rid of venal politicians and officials who would sully the image of the government. He therefore provided the director of the Anti-Corruption Agency, Harun bin Hashim, with broad authority to attack malfeasance within the government. Two corrupt chief ministers from Perak and Terengganu were removed from office under his tenure, and three more were ousted in subsequent years. Hashim concluded his anticorruption drive in 1970, having arrested 67 government employees and 115 private individuals, with disciplinary action taken against 87 public officials.[22]

HEGEMONIC PRAGMATISM

Although the government's immediate concern following the riots was the centralization of power to stabilize the polity and ensure that the interests of the Malays would no longer be forsaken, it gradually returned to its consociationalist tradition. In January 1970, it created the National Consultative Council (NCC) and invited almost all key representatives of sectoral, regional, and ethnic interests, including opposition parties, to join. The NCC included representatives from the National Operations Council, state governments, political parties, the states of Sabah and Sarawak, religious groups, professional associations, public services, trade unions, employers' associations, the media, and teachers. Only the opposition Chinese party, DAP, opted not to join the NCC. Like the postwar British-initiated Communities Liaison Committee, the NCC was meant to provide a closed-door forum for discussions that could strengthen national unity. Like the consociational format of the pre-1969 Alliance coalition, the discussions of the NCC were closed to the public in order for the representatives to discuss issues away from the more partisan and heated sentiments of the masses.

Between 1970 and 1974, UMNO slowly began reestablishing its multicommunal coalition, this time renamed the Barisan Nasional (BN, or National Front). On 1 June 1974, the BN was officially registered as an organization with nine constituent parties.[23] The cabinet formed in 1974 was the broadest to date in terms of ethnicity, party, and regional representation. Of the nine parties in the BN, the inclusion of Party Islam (Parti Islam-Se Malaysia, or PAS) was especially significant because it uprooted a forceful competitor for Malay votes.[24] The creation of the BN eliminated a significant amount of political competition, reduced radical elements in the party system by pushing parties to the center and obliging them to take part in governance,[25] and thereby helped provided a bulwark of stability. Razak stated as much: "The National Front concept is a positive effort towards reducing political tension so as to allow the government to concentrate on intensifying development."[26] The combination of internal reorganization of the party, increased discipline within party ranks, and the co-opting of many opposition parties as well as greater use of authoritarian measures in society led to significant institutionalization and stability in the party system. Electoral volatility, a key measure of party system institutionalization, declined from 38.8 between 1955 and 1969 to 8.6 from 1969 to 2004.[27]

Although UMNO was fully convinced that it alone must determine the direction of the country, it did not jettison its earlier pragmatic belief in multicommunal governance. Rather, it saw the incorporation of opposition parties with its traditional partners of the MCA and Malaysian Indian Congress (MIC) as necessary bulwarks of stability. By bringing in the opposition parties, particularly the non-Malay ones that UMNO had accused of provoking the riots, UMNO believed it could find the optimal equilibrium necessary for stable governance. As Ghazali Shafie notes: "If political parties did not hang together now during this period of development, history would hang them individually."[28]

With the opposition parties under the BN umbrella, conflict between them and the government could be smoothed over behind closed doors rather than in public view. Furthermore, by incorporating the opposition, UMNO had made clear who was in control. The parties were given the option of entering the BN on UMNO's conditions. They could hope for some influence in government or be decisively shut out. Only the DAP chose to stay out. The co-optive strategy of UMNO also worked to weaken the position of its erstwhile ally, the MCA, by playing divide and rule with the Chinese parties. By taking in several Chinese parties in the peninsula and in Borneo, including the Penang-based Gerakan, it ensured competition between the Chinese parties for favors with UMNO, on the one hand, and for legitimacy as the genuine, governing representative of the Chinese, on the other hand.

Like the Alliance, the BN should be understood as more than an ad hoc electoral coalition formed after the results of elections. Unlike most parliamentary coalitions, the multicommunal coalitions of the Alliance and the BN are highly institutionalized. They have their own constitution and their own directorate (executive council made up of representatives from each party), and they act as a unified party during elections, putting up one candidate from the coalition per constituency. But in contrast with the Alliance, the Barisan Nasional is not just a broader tent with a new name.

The BN became unambiguously UMNO dominated in the way the Alliance was not.[29] Although cabinet seats are apportioned among the parties in the BN and their interests are taken into consideration,[30] it is UMNO that decisively dictates. In contrast to the pre-1969 Alliance, UMNO now chose to take control of all the key ministries, with the MCA's control of the Ministries of Finance and Trade and Industry over. After 1969, there could be no other alternative than UMNO dominance. This was a significant change from the government of Abdul Rahman, for it meant that the party would unequivocally seek to advance social and economic reforms for the Malays.

Despite its increased hegemonic status, UMNO still made an effort to steer toward the center rather than the extreme. Given the repercussions of May 1969 and the defensive position in which the non-Malays and the opposition parties found themselves, UMNO could have behaved very differently by running roughshod over the Chinese. Although it was pressured to take a more hard-line stance by Malay "ultras"[31]—university students[32] as well as young party elites, such as Musa Hitam[33] and Mahathir Mohamad—ultimately it did not cave in to chauvinist politics.[34] Responding to student radicalism, Abdul Rahman had said: "These people only want Malay rule. I asked them: 'Can you really do this? Can you really do without the other races?'"[35] He was then able to have the Supreme Council oust Musa and Mahathir, but his days were numbered and he soon ceded the party leadership to Razak. Yet although Razak was identified with the more radical group then emerging in the post-1969 period, he was careful to filter the radical aspirations of people like Mahathir into more moderate institutional channels. Razak agreed that forceful state intervention was necessary, but he would do so in a pragmatic way: "[T]he first basis for economic development," he emphasized, "is the type of political leadership which will not waste national emotion on non-essential rabble-rousing."[36] The calls for a pro-Malay agenda were in the end heeded, for it would have been almost impossible not to move in such a direction. But the push for radical action was molded and implemented shorn of the rabid rhetoric and extreme exhortations of the ultras. Despite the greater Malay emphasis, the post-1969 coalition government thus retained, in Donald Horowitz's view, a "consensus to exclude extreme positions and arrive at a compromise."[37]

For more than a decade after independence, UMNO did not overturn the basic structure of the economy and polity, even if it was clear that the Malays were consistently lagging behind the Chinese and Indians. As long as the country maintained a stable course, no major structural reforms were necessary. Therefore, it is worth stressing that as much as UMNO is a Malay party, for a significant period, it did not attempt to advance the interests of its own ethnic group to the degree that it would displace the interests of the Chinese partners in the Alliance. Only when it became apparent that such arrangements could no longer be sustained did UMNO change its course toward state interventionism and hegemonic politics—but never outright ethnic chauvinism. Had UMNO responded to the 1969 crisis with retribution against the Chinese, it would have been virtually impossible to maintain economic growth.

In the post-1969 period, a political structure thus emerged that was ideologically inclined and organizationally capable of executing a policy regime directed toward social reform. Ideologically, UMNO made it emphatically clear that national stability as articulated in the Rukunegara would form the guiding vision of the nation. Unlike any other event in Malaysian history, the crisis of May 1969 made it starkly evident to the elite that the most urgent issue the country faced was the socioeconomic gulf between the Malays and the Chinese. Interethnic equity was crucial for national stability to be achieved. The UMNO elites were able to address this dilemma in a coherent, pragmatic, and decisive way. Organizationally, UMNO had made significant reforms to strengthen party goals and to build a more coherent bureaucracy. Politically, it had made a firm decision to assert its hegemony over the coalition to fulfill its pro-Malay policies. However, this hegemony was still nested within a multicommunal setting.

Growth with Equity: The New Economic Policy, 1971–1990

The laissez-faire growth model came to a brutal end with the 13 May 1969 riots in Kuala Lumpur. In its place, the Razak government put forth the New Economic Policy. The NEP was a comprehensive endeavor to transform the relationship among the state, society, and the economy.[38] Its fundamental political assumption was that the state had to intervene more forcefully to redirect the trajectory of economic development and move away from the earlier free-market predisposition. The free market could no longer be left to its own workings, for it had clearly shown itself incapable of addressing the concerns of the restive masses.[39] In Khoo Boo Teik's view, 1969 occurred "fundamentally . . . because the Alliance's laissez-faire capitalism could not resolve the destabilizing contradictions of an ethnic division of labor."[40] Now "instead of a relaxed laissez-faire approach all economic categories were urged to be motivated, action-oriented, dynamic, disciplined, dedicated, efficient and in the terminology of *rukunegara*, progressive and oriented to science and technology."[41] The state was thus called on not just to create market incentives but also to actively shape economic outcomes.

Key aspects of the NEP were its economic and political moderation and its effort to pursue equitable development with national unity in mind.[42] The NEP was to be achieved through a "strategy of economic balance . . . founded on the philosophy of active participation, not on disruptive redistribution."[43] The NEP would foster growth with equity through an "expanding pie" in which all groups would see their incomes rising.[44] No group would be left behind for the NEP to achieve its goal of national unity. Razak made this clear: "I would like to underline the watchword 'participate' because it is our belief that this [NEP] will be achieved without taking away, or least of all, depriving the legitimate rights and interests of other communities."[45] If the government's goal of an expanding pie was to be attained, growth had to remain at the heart of the NEP. The UMNO elite understood very well that they could not solve the problem of unemployment without relying on the private sector, which remained predominantly Chinese. Therefore, the government maintained free-market incentives so as not to stifle capitalist investment, but with new regulations concerning employment quotas and corporate equity imposed on the private sector.

The two key goals of the NEP were (1) to eradicate poverty irrespective of race and (2) to end the association of race with economic function.[46] These twin problems are so interrelated that the actual division of the NEP into two separate goals is somewhat artificial. The correlation of race with economic function stems from the concentration of Malays in low-paying economic sectors and of non-Malays in the modern sectors of the economy. Malays dominated the traditional, rural sector, whereas the non-Malays were in control of the modern urban sector and the modern rural sector (plantation estates and tin mines). Malays worked largely in the paddy fields, in fishing, and in rubber tapping. Within industry, most Malays were in the lower-skilled and unskilled niches. Non-Malays worked as shopkeepers, restaurant workers, factory workers, construction workers, hawkers and stallkeepers, petty traders, and farmers of modern cash agriculture. They also predominated in the managerial, professional, technical, and clerical fields.[47] Compared with non-Malays, Malays were clearly concentrated in low-productivity sectors. This factor alone led to a difference of 20 percent between average Malay and non-Malay incomes per worker.[48]

Malays were therefore more likely to be poor than the non-Malays because they were heavily employed in low-paying sectors. In 1970, the mean monthly income of Malay households was M$179, whereas that of the Chinese and Indian households was M$387 and M$310, respectively. Malays made up 85 percent of the households earning less than M$100. In the middle-range income of M$400 to M$699, Chinese households made up 56 percent, Malays 31 percent, and Indians 12 percent.[49]

The NEP's first goal of reducing poverty irrespective of race must clearly be seen in light of the fact that most of the poor were Malays. The second goal of redistribution sought to create greater balance between the social groups and the economy. The key issue here is that, if economic function is to be more broadly spread out in terms of ethnicity, then poverty among the Malays had to be reduced, especially through upward mobility. However, redistribution in the NEP was also directly targeted toward the creation of a Malay bourgeoisie that might balance the Chinese capitalist class. In this sense, the NEP was not just about poverty and income redistribution but also about capital or wealth redistribution. This is important from the point of view of political leverage, for it created greater cohesion and support for the NEP from all Malay classes.

To reduce poverty, the NEP advanced three broad measures: (1) increasing the productivity of those in traditional sectors of the economy, largely through advances in agricultural development; (2) increasing opportunities for intersectoral mobility from low- to higher-productivity activities in rural and modern, urban sectors; and (3) providing subsidized social services, such as housing projects, health services, and educational opportunities, to raise the standards of living for the low-income groups.[50]

The NEP sought to avoid an excessive dependence on agricultural development as a means to reduce poverty. This had been a serious shortcoming of the Abdul Rahman government. The government continued to invest heavily in agricultural development, particularly through the Federal Land Development Authority's land resettlement schemes, but it realized that raising incomes in the agrarian sector would not be enough to ameliorate the distribution of income.[51] To avoid the agricultural trap, the government sought to increase opportunities for Malays by broadening out its scope to industrial restructuring and human development, especially education. The aim of the NEP, then, was to ensure that Malays would possess greater skills and capacities to improve their employment prospects and that industry would give preferential treatment to incipient Malay entrepreneurs. Overall, industrialization was meant to supersede agriculture in big strides and to be driven predominantly by Malay mobility.

One of the crucial factors underlying the riots was the lack of employment of young, restive Malays.[52] By the mid-1960s, labor supply had far exceeded the pace of new job generation. Furthermore, many of the unemployed were severely deficient in technical skills and education. In 1970, unemployment had risen to almost 8 percent from 6.5 percent in 1965.[53] More than three-fourths of the total unemployed in 1967 were between the ages of fifteen and twenty-five, and almost two-thirds were first-time job seekers.[54]

To prevent such a situation from recurring, the NEP made abundantly clear that economic growth was a crucial component of equitable development.[55] The expansion of the public sector and policies that would stimulate the private sector would underpin growth. The private sector was pushed to maintain a hiring policy that would eventually lead to an employment structure that would reflect the ethnic makeup of the nation. This meant that firms had to hire more Malays than non-Malays in the early years of the NEP, so that Malays would eventually constitute about 60 percent of the modern labor force. Private firms were encouraged to establish training schemes by themselves or by pooling resources.[56] The government also undertook more actively productive enterprise through wholly owned firms and joint ventures with the private sector. In these enterprises, the government made a conscious effort to focus on labor-intensive production.[57] Foreign firms were also encouraged to set up factories in Malaysia. Although they were subject to employment quotas, they were willing to accede to this, in part because government policies on unionization were also in favor of capital.

The bulk of the financing for the NEP would come from institutional sources and from revenue generated from extremely effective tax collection.

The well-managed Employment Provident Fund (EPF), a legacy of British colonialism, was tapped to provide more than half of total funds.[58] Other sources included provident and trust funds, social security funds, and the Post Office Savings Bank. Insurance companies and finance companies were also encouraged to increase their purchases of government securities.[59]

We get an overall picture of the immense efforts the state poured into the redistributive agenda by looking at its public investment during the NEP period. In 1960, federal expenditure and lending was equal to 16.6 percent of gross national product. By 1972, this had doubled to 32.6 percent.[60] A major study conducted for the World Bank measuring benefit incidence by focusing on federal outlays per capita for education, medical care, agriculture, and public utilities concluded that public investment was highest in the rural areas; in terms of ethnicity, the benefits per capita to the Malays exceeded the mean by 22 percent, whereas the benefits to the Chinese were 30 percent short of the mean.[61] In terms of public investment, the study concluded that Malaysia could be compared with the welfare states of Western Europe.

Within Asia, Malaysia's level of public spending in the 1980s was one of the highest, and in the late 1970s, its tax effort indicator was the highest in Southeast Asia—more than three times that of Indonesia, when oil revenues are excluded, and almost twice that of Thailand.[62] While Malaysia's public spending was about 40 percent of GDP in the mid-1980s, in other countries it was one-third or half that level.[63] In the 1986–88 period Malaysia's ratio of tax to gross domestic product (GDP) was 18.27 percent—the highest among developing Asian countries.

Although the government gradually reduced its high level of spending in line with privatization under Mahathir, Malaysia still stands out in comparative historical terms through its high ratio of tax revenue to GDP and its concomitant high ratio of public spending to GDP. Relative to other countries, Malaysia's tax revenue and expenditures still remained quite high in the late 1980s, as the NEP began to wind down. Surveying different tax policies in Asia, two economists asked, "Why did Malaysia feel the necessity [in the 1980s] to bring its public spending to such a high level, while Taiwan and Thailand did not?"[64]

The answer should be clear by now, but more crucially what we have been seeking to show is not just why but how. The UMNO had to surmount not just the conventional problems of underdevelopment, such as capital formation, poverty, and institution building, but also the compounded nature of ethnicity and class. Navigating the treacherous waters between Malay and Chinese interests was the most challenging aspect in the crafting of the NEP. Tilting too much to one side could lead to further riots, and tilting too much to the other side could lead to mass migration and capital flight. Yet for the most part, the NEP achieved its goals of reducing poverty and ethnic inequality.

In 1990, the government formally announced the end of the NEP and its replacement by the National Development Policy (NDP). Although the NDP continued the same goals of growth with equity and balanced development, it placed greater emphasis on the importance of the private sector and tertiary concerns, such as science, technology, and the environment.[65] By 1990, the period in which the NDP began, the Gini coefficient had declined from a high of .513 in 1970 to .446, and poverty had fallen from a high in 1970 of 49.3 percent to 16.5 percent. Disparities between the Malays and non-Malays had also narrowed sharply. The income disparity ratio between Bumiputera and Chinese households declined from 1:2.29 in 1970 to 1:1.74 in 1990. The ratio between the Bumiputera and Indian households also fell from 1:1.77 in 1970 to 1:1.29 in 1990.[66] In her survey of trends in Malaysia's distribution of income, the economist Ragayah concludes that "government policies played a crucial role during the NEP period in attaining growth with equity."[67] Despite some increase in inequality in the 1990s, recent data show that in 2009 the Gini coefficient was .441 and poverty had gone down to as low as 3.8 percent.[68]

The government indicated its satisfaction with the pro-poor goals of the NEP in the *Sixth Malaysia Plan 1991–95*, as the focus on poverty and distribution turned toward hard-core poverty in the remote areas of Borneo and of the *orang asli* (aborigines) in Pahang: "The distributional objectives in the Sixth Plan will pay particular attention to the qualitative aspects in dealing with the remaining problems of poverty and economic imbalances among ethnic groups. These problems are no longer as serious as they were twenty years ago. Therefore, the focus will now shift towards selective implementation of programs and projects. Thus, while poverty eradication programs will remain an important aspect of the development strategy, the emphasis will be on targeting the programs for the hard-core poor."[69]

Implementing Social Reforms

Under the NEP, the state sharpened its policy implementation process. Although it already had machinery in place to implement rural development programs, it redoubled its efforts in this area to produce better results. As we will see in the case of FELDA, improvements in coordination and implementation rose sharply after 1971. Under the NEP, the state also finally enshrined Malay as the dominant language in the secondary and tertiary schools and improved access for the Malays. Training schools, such as the MARA Institute of Technology, were rolled out to improve technical skills and raise the rates of Malay employment in the modern, professional sector. Access to health care for the poor also rose. In all of this, organization was crucial to successful implementation.[70]

Before examining in depth several sectors that have been critical to attaining the goals of the NEP, it is useful to have a grasp of the implementing machinery at the state's disposal. At the federal level, development planning is based in the National Planning Council (NPC).[71] The council, consisting of key ministers, is the highest policy-making body for planning and is in charge of the five-year plans. Underneath the National Planning Council sits the National Development Planning Committee (NDPC). This committee is made up of senior government officials and heads of ministries related to economic development, including the governor of the central bank. The NDPC formulates and reviews all plans for development and makes recommendations on the allocation of resources. At the core of planning is the Economic Planning Unit (EPU), which also serves as the secretariat of the NDPC and the NPC, and provides the linkages between ministries and line agencies. The EPU is the nerve center of development planning, where key decisions for the five-year plans are made and enforced. Most important, the EPU sits in the prime minister's unit, which ensures that it is cognizant of the party agenda. Overarching economic policy will thus closely reflect UMNO's interests and strengthen the synergy between party and bureaucracy.

At the local level, similar planning structures are present. At the state level, the State Economic Planning Committee (SEPC) is in charge of approving funding, planning, and implementing projects. The State Economic Planning Unit, like the EPU, serves as the secretariat for the SEPC. The State Development Council has the task of setting priorities among development projects and coordinating line agencies for project implementation through the State Development Committee. At the district and village level, the respective bodies in charge of the implementation of projects are the District Development Committee and the Village Development and Security Committee (Jawatankuasa Kemajuan dan Keselamatan Kampung,

JKKK). The district officer chairs the District Development Committee, in which the various JKKK heads participate. Since 1971, development planning in Malaysia has been reinforced by another body, the Implementation Coordination Unit (ICU). The goal of the ICU is to coordinate development projects at the federal level and to monitor projects at the local level. The ICU also carries out postimplementation evaluation or impact studies to assess the overall trajectory of development policies.

The government continues to employ the systematic strategy of the Red Book in monitoring and implementing policy.[72] Participation in all government levels is encouraged as a means for the central bureaucracy in Kuala Lumpur to gain feedback about rural development and other related programs, such as health and education. The formulation of the five-year plans goes through an elaborate process in which the district officer in consultation with village headmen lists all the important projects in order of priority. The state then examines it and presents it to the federal level. There is thus considerable participation and feedback on policy formulation within the state structure.[73] Efficiency in implementation furthermore benefits from UMNO's historical control of most state governments. The federal government can often lean on its state officials to speed up particular projects based on political considerations, such as elections.[74]

Legislators are also crucial links in the process of policy implementation. Although their role in the formulation of policy is limited, they function effectively as linkages between center and periphery. One study conducted in the 1970s showed that MPs were particularly active in relaying the needs of their constituents to the center, explaining policy emanating from the government, and resolving local conflicts.[75] For example, a Green Book program to improve agricultural productivity in the mid-1970s elicited active involvement by MPs, who communicated with their constituents about the program, listened to their concerns, and relayed them back to the government.[76] Following the 1969 crisis, Razak exhorted MPs to be more proactive at the grassroots level. He provided carrots and sticks to ensure that MPs spent more time in their districts. In the 1974 elections, this proactive grassroots initiative gained greater sway in the party. Furthermore, as ex officio members of district action committees, the MPs have a strong impact on the implementation of policy.

The effectiveness of policy implementation also reflects the interpenetration of state and party, as the party can monitor the bureaucracy and ensure that its political agenda is being executed. The close relations between the bureaucracy and party date back to the founding of UMNO. Much of the bureaucracy worked in tandem with UMNO and could therefore be used to advance the political goals of the party. In the 1955 elections, 80 percent of the UMNO candidates were former officials of the civil service. Of the seven Malays in Abdul Rahman's cabinet, six were former civil servants.[77] The importance given to close ties between party and bureaucracy was made clear by one of UMNO's leaders, Razaleigh Hamzah, in an address to civil servants: "[O]fficers and other government employees are not permitted to be neutral in politics but should support and defend government policies."[78]

A good illustration of the state-party symbiosis in the periphery comes from Shamsul's research in a district in Selangor.[79] Shamsul shows how the NEP's success in the rural areas derives from its deep politicization of the state, district, and village levels. With the advent of the NEP, important administrative changes tipped the balance of state and district organs toward local politicians rather than civil servants. In Selangor, the administrative change led to the Executive Council (Exco), the central political council in charge of development projects, to be composed of nine state legislators and only three bureaucrats. Within the Exco is a steering committee made up of four state legislators, including the chief minister and one bureaucrat.

Administrative officers in charge of the four most important committees focused on development have become political agents of UMNO. Members of these committees are politicians, civil servants of the federal and state governments, and officials of statutory government bodies (e.g., FELDA), but in practice, almost all are in some form or another representatives of UMNO. Although government rules prohibit officials from political activity, such rules have been flagrantly flouted. Almost 80 percent of the government officials in this district are members of UMNO. What this means is that it is the UMNO district office that dictates the decisions of the development committees. Considering the large amount of public funds that these committees can disburse, it is not hard to see how UMNO has succeeded in actualizing its political and developmental goals. Developmental goals are achieved, then, in part because politicians in the periphery overshadow bureaucrats in the planning and implementation of development policy.[80]

REPRESENTATION AT THE LOCAL LEVEL

At the village level, residents also have many channels through which they can directly petition for particular needs. State assemblymen and MPs are in constant contact with their constituents. At the federal and state level, there are service centers with the picture of the relevant MP, complete with his home and cell phone number.[81] The MP regularly visits the numerous *kampong* (villages) in his constituency, attending to grievances and concerns spanning local conflicts to personal problems.[82] The state assemblyman also serves as a central figure in addressing constituents' needs, often acting as a community leader.[83] He is an important link between the grass roots and the party at the local level, responsible for a wide array of issues. For example, in addressing educational needs, he communicates regularly with branch leaders to determine who is eligible for university scholarships.[84] The assemblyman's house is also extremely accessible to villagers.[85]

At the local level, the branch is the most critical link in the party machinery, functioning as a bottom-up and a top-down mechanism.[86] The branch is the smallest unit of the party, made up of between fifty and three hundred people; UMNO maintains branches in virtually every village, where the village head (*ketua kampong*) often serves as the leader of the branch. The branch enables the party to take the pulse of the concerns of the electorate while also operating as the channel through which the national party can communicate its programs and goals.[87] The village head and MP for that constituency meet often, because the village head is closest to local problems and, as UMNO branch leader, functions as the "eyes and ears" of the government.[88] Each branch has a bureau with a specific function such as education, youth, drug use prevention, agriculture, and so on. The agenda of the branch is decided by the party constitution at a higher level. After each branch meeting, the branch leader sends its report to the Registrar of Societies. Delegates from the branches meet periodically at the divisional level, where they channel the concerns from the villages. The meetings at the divisional level provide another forum through which the party can monitor local interests.

In the 1950s, the branch was largely a tool for party loyalty and electoral mobilization. But in line with the changes in the NEP, in the 1980s the branch became a central avenue for promoting social welfare, primarily through the funding of programs promoting agricultural assistance in the form of fertilizer and seeds and piped water; the construction of schools, health clinics, and mosques; and infrastructural projects, including electricity, bridges, canals, and community halls.[89] State assemblymen and MPs are obliged to meet regularly with the branches.[90] Party members are required to return to their constituency on the weekend to meet with the branches and stay abreast of concerns within the constituency. An important innovation to monitor MPs' work at the grassroots level has been the Key Performance Index (KPI).[91] This is a report card that representatives must submit every month to headquarters. In the KPI, they must indicate how many times they go back to their district, what kinds of problems their constituents have, and the programs they are developing in the district. At branch meetings, villagers express their demands or grievances with their representative. For example, if a branch asks for more sports equipment, its MP will look for funding to accommodate such a request. The *wakil rakyat* (people's representative) must therefore be always on the alert to a branch's needs.[92]

The branch thus plays a crucial role in channeling the concerns of the grass roots to the party, ensuring that villagers' needs are not ignored. It is here at the branch level where the party and the *rakyat* (people) meet face to face. Branches have exerted significant pull on the center, expressing disagreements not just over selection of candidates but also over general policies.[93] "Branches perform the important function of keeping the average rural voter informed of changes in the political scene," write K. J. Ratnam and R. S. Milne. "There is thus always some awareness of what the government is doing, and of the arguments for and against its policies."[94] The extensive grassroots and developmental work that UMNO undertakes has in effect "institutionalized the local UMNO branch as the community's chief channel for securing further governmental assistance."[95] This is a party that has penetrated deeply into the villages, established roots with its base, and maintained institutional mechanisms to channel feedback from periphery to center.

The rest of this chapter examines three policy sectors that have played an important role in the NEP's success: land resettlement under FELDA, education reforms, and health policy. The first program helped alleviate poverty in the rural sector by raising the incomes of cultivators of palm oil and rubber. The other two sectors were necessary to build human capital as a means to push the Malays into the modern sector.

Land Resettlement

In 1956, the Federal Land Development Authority (FELDA) was created with a mandate to resettle landless villagers on public lands. Initially, FELDA was tasked simply with the goal of channeling federal funds to local implementing bodies, but a few years later, it was entrusted with the development of land schemes for settlers. The goal of FELDA was to create landowning, small-scale farmers whose income would surpass the current subsistence levels. To achieve this, FELDA developed smallholding schemes that were clustered around villages provided with infrastructural support. Each villager was given approximately ten acres of land to cultivate rubber or palm oil. An average scheme was made up of four hundred smallholdings totaling 3,954 acres. The villagers were provided with loans for the start-up costs, which were to be repaid within fifteen years. Once repaid, the villagers received titles to their land.[96]

In general, FELDA focused its land settlement schemes in the virgin forests of the eastern states. Its early settlements in the jungles of Pahang were intended to populate areas that communist insurgents controlled, thereby providing a basis for infiltrating and domesticating an ungoverned area. Rubber was initially the main crop planted in FELDA settlements because of the available technical knowledge and, more important, the high demand generated by the Korean War rubber boom. After 1970, palm oil displaced rubber because of its higher rates of return and the declining price of rubber in the world market.

In its initial years, FELDA encountered a number of problems.[97] The assumption that settlers would be able to clear land and build their houses fell by the wayside. Therefore, FELDA hired private contractors to clear the jungle, develop the fields for plantation, and build houses. The broad layout of the schemes was also not well integrated. Many projects were scattered and lacked infrastructural support. Other organizational problems included the lack of cooperation between FELDA and state governments, poor coordination within FELDA, a shortage of staff personnel, and a lack of adequate land surveys. As a result, one of the weaknesses in the FELDA operation was its inability to keep up with the demand for settlements. Between 1961 and 1965, the period of the Second Malaya Plan, FELDA was able to provide settlements for only 6,083 of 24,000 chosen settlers. This was 25 percent of its target number. Between 1971 and 1975, FELDA fulfilled 69 percent of its target number. But finally in 1976, FELDA surpassed its target number. Since then, FELDA has generally been able to settle its intended number.[98]

The system FELDA uses to manage the land to derive the highest returns has gone through numerous changes. First, FELDA employed the collective work concept allowing settlers to work anywhere in the field. The idea that this would lead to mutual cooperation quickly proved wrong. Second, FELDA allocated specific plots of land for each settler. This resulted in varied standards of maintenance. Later, FELDA adopted a block system, in which fifteen to twenty settlers joined together to cultivate plots of land of about 148 to 198 acres and received equal income. This system was faulted because it did not create enough incentives for hard work. In 1985, FELDA attempted to institute a land-share ownership system, in which settlers would be given an equal number of shares rather than individual lots. Settlers would receive wages and then be given an equal share of the profits. This too proved unsuitable. Thus, FELDA returned to the individual lot-ownership system, which remains in effect today.

Until the mid-1970s, FELDA's achievements were of a mixed quality. Trial and error marked its early years. The proliferation of other land resettlement programs, such as the Federal Land Consolidation and Rehabilitation Authority, also added to a lack of effective coordination. Eventually, the Ministry of Rural Development streamlined the land resettlement process by putting FELDA in charge. It was only after the mid-1970s that FELDA began to find its rhythm, settling many more peasants at a faster rate. Later, FELDA picked up the pace of resettlement as part of the NEP's agenda of poverty eradication and social restructuring.

In the big picture of development and inequality, FELDA stands out as the linchpin of the state's efforts to alleviate rural poverty. Although other programs in the 1970s were also significant, such as the Rubber Industry Smallholders Development Authority, formed in 1974 to aid farmers in the replanting of rubber, and the Farmers' Organization Authority, established in 1973 to coordinate rural cooperatives and to provide financial, technical, and managerial support to rural smallholders growing crops other than rubber and palm oil, FELDA was the most extensive and highly coordinated state program.[99] Moreover, FELDA made every effort to ensure that settlers received ample support to succeed. After the early trial-and-error period in which FELDA realized that concentrating programs would be more cost effective, villages were configured as growth centers that agencies such as MARA, Bank Pertanian, and other state development authorities could then support. A field insurance program was initiated in 1987 to compensate settlers for crop losses stemming from pests and diseases. In addition, FELDA has supported research and development in biotechnology, production technology, and agricultural and marketing research. It has also made efforts to improve education for families in FELDA through building schools in the settlements, and since 1969, it has provided loans and scholarships.[100] By the 1980s, FELDA had begun to shift its orientation toward nonfarm activities as well as greater diversification downstream through integrated commercial activities, including vegetable gardening, livestock, homestays, retail business, and handicrafts under the Satu Wilayah Satu Industri (SAWARI, or One Village, One Product).[101]

CRITICISMS OF FELDA

Despite FELDA's success in providing a vast array of social services and raising incomes through both farm and nonfarm activities, there are numerous criticisms of the program. For example, FELDA has been faulted for providing land to only a small percentage of the landless, for failing to raise the incomes of more people, for making peasants dependent on the state, and for selecting peasants on the basis of party allegiance rather than degree of poverty.

If one were to measure the number of families or individuals that FELDA has absorbed given the growth of the rural population, one might be able to claim that FELDA has not been particularly successful. By the mid-1980s, less than 15 percent of the rural Malay population had gained from this program.[102] Yet the fact that this program was providing an increasing amount of villagers with cultivable land should not be overlooked simply because it did not meet the full absorptive capacities that were then needed.

One study based partly on fieldwork in Pahang asserted that FELDA settlers were unhappy with a number of conditions on the settlement.[103] These included low prices for produce, excessive deductions from one's income, and the implementation of a collective farming system. Settlers expressed their anger toward FELDA by selling their produce in private markets rather than to the FELDA mills, by striking, or by engaging in everyday forms of resistance. In these disputes, settlers protested to the local UMNO branch, which then intervened with FELDA management officials. In a number of these complaints, UMNO's intervention led to changes in FELDA policy. Collective farming and the shares system, for example, were scrapped after settlers expressed their intense dislike of both systems.

The ubiquity of UMNO in every FELDA scheme is an important element that allows settlers to let off steam against FELDA management policies. The

UMNO branches are linked to local and state party chiefs, which in turn are connected to the central party offices in the capital. Given the importance of keeping the rural population closely allied to the government's developmental goals and political agenda, settlers know that their grievances will find a sympathetic ear. For example, in the district of Jerantut, Pahang, 60 percent of settlers are registered members of UMNO. Thus, in 1983, the UMNO Division of Jerantut, Pahang, acting on settlers' grievances, wrote a memorandum to the minister of land and regional development calling for the resolution of a number of demands, including an increase in the price of produce that would be commensurate with the price that private mills paid.[104] In another case, FELDA's Lasah 2 land scheme drew complaints that the FELDA mill's price for produce was too low, and the UMNO branch led the protests against FELDA.[105] Many strikes on FELDA schemes have been the work of the local UMNO branch openly supporting the settlers' demands.

Even if the UMNO regime is one in which the party and state work hand in hand, the party still operates as a counterweight to state agencies. The party serves an important representative function and can challenge a state agency when its constituents demand such action. When settlers were unhappy with FELDA, they were able to use the channels of the party to have their grievances addressed. Like Shamsul's discussion of rural development policy in Selangor, this example shows that UMNO plays an important role overseeing government work in the periphery.

The criticism that settlers are often chosen on the basis of their party affiliation is perhaps the most damning charge against FELDA. Syed Hussein Wafa observes that "there is a consensus among settlers (and those that failed to receive land) that places in FELDA schemes are awarded to those who support the ruling Alliance Party and therefore they are expected to continue their support."[106] It is also estimated that 20 percent of places in the land development schemes are systematically held for former members of the armed forces.[107] The fact that politics rather than outright need plays a role in the selection of settlers partly taints FELDA's mandate to alleviate poverty. However, the relationship between selection and party affiliation reinforces the point that pro-poor policies have a basis in a party agenda. The mission of FELDA is to alleviate poverty, but this must also provide dividends for the government. Currently, there are sixty seats at the parliamentary and state levels in FELDA schemes, which indicates the political importance of maintaining the support of settlers.[108] Razak's scion, Prime

Minister Najib Razak, expressed no hesitation in linking government policy to electoral support: "[S]ettlers and their families have benefited [from FELDA]. In light of this, we also hope the settlers become the backbone supporters of the government."[109]

Despite these criticisms, FELDA's success is unequivocal. A 1982 study reports the following improvements through the work of FELDA: (1) households in FELDA schemes tended to own more durable consumer goods than those in other rural areas; (2) the infant mortality rate in the FELDA schemes (2.6 percent) was lower than the average in rural Malaysia (4 percent); (3) enrollment in secondary education in FELDA (69 percent) was higher than the national average (62 percent), although the enrollment in primary education in FELDA (87 percent) was lower than the national average (96 percent); (4) more than 55.2 percent of women practiced family planning, compared to the national average of 35.5 percent; and (5) 78.9 percent of women took advantage of postnatal health-care facilities.[110]

By 1976, the year in which FELDA was finally able to place its targeted number of settlers, FELDA had opened 186 schemes, settled 37,435 families, and planted 812,684 acres.[111] The 812,684 acres was a 50 percent increase compared to what rubber smallholders cultivated in 1952.[112] Furthermore, by the 1980s FELDA had been able to redistribute population from the population surplus states to those with surplus land. Pahang and Negeri Sembilan, for example, recorded net gains in population.[113]

In 2005, FELDA had 275 schemes with a total of 103,156 settlers and their families, of which 60 percent had received their land titles.[114] This means that since 1956, more than half a million people, formerly paddy farmers or rubber tappers, have been able to attain a secure livelihood and, more important, place their children in management, professional, and technical jobs. Before entering a FELDA scheme, the average income of a settler was RM70 per month. In 1994, the average FELDA settler received a monthly income of RM1,119 for oil palm schemes and RM977 for rubber schemes. This represented an increase of sixteen to nineteen times one's income level.[115] The income for a FELDA settler has consistently stayed above the poverty threshold.

A World Bank survey of land resettlement programs found that Malaysia's has been one of the more successful. Whether in terms of improving rural incomes, providing extension services, or making correct choices about which crops to grow, Malaysia tends to do better than most other land resettlements.[116] Comparisons with other programs in similar developing countries thus support the position that FELDA is a relatively successful program. This success has come through the state's relentless efforts to improve the livelihood of the rural peasant, and through UMNO's efforts to address the needs of its rural constituents, even going so far as to challenge FELDA authorities when necessary.

Education

On 11 July 1969, two months after the ethnic riots in Kuala Lumpur, the Ministry of Education decreed that English-language schools would convert to Malay-language instruction one grade at a time. This was the final step that significantly strengthened the Malay position in the educational system. Although primary schooling in Chinese and Tamil would still be allowed, along with private secondary Chinese schools, the move away from English and toward Malay radically shifted the balance from the Chinese community to the Malays. No longer was Malay education a dead end in the opportunity structure. Now Chinese vernacular schools were relegated to the disadvantaged position in the educational system.

The struggle over language is important in the overall context of growth and equity because of the correlation between language, ethnicity, and poverty. By gradually changing the system toward Malay language, the government expanded opportunities for the Malay community in schooling and in the economy more generally. Whether the quality of education has improved has been intensely questioned, yet the goal of providing universal education to both urban and rural communities became easier with Malay as the dominant language of instruction.

The Malaysian educational system reflects not just a pro-Malay and pro-poor bias but also a pro-rural slant. This was especially so from 1970 to about 1990.[117] This pro-rural bias is tied to ethnicity, but it is not solely about ethnicity. Many of the programs that are pro-poor do not discriminate on the basis of ethnicity. The Ministry of Education generally seeks to ensure that rural areas are not marginalized. In policy-planning meetings, the first question that is often discussed is "how [to] deal with the remote areas."[118] Funding for schools is based on the number of students in schools, but allocations are weighted differently for remote, rural areas. If there are fewer than 150 students, funding is increased relative to the normal scale.

Numerous programs have also been instituted to alleviate hard-core poverty among students. These include a textbook-loan scheme, a nutrition program, a milk program, and scholarships based on need and merit for students at the upper secondary level.

Strengthening education in the rural areas depends heavily on recruiting and maintaining well-trained teachers. Teachers are required to stay for five years in the countryside, but they are often eager to reduce their length of stay. The ministry induces its teachers to stay by providing highly subsidized housing (even in the urban areas) and by increasing the salary by 5 percent for those teaching in Sabah, Sarawak, and Pahang (among the *orang asli*).

Statistics bear out significant improvements in access and equity. By 1960, the educational system registered 90 percent net enrollment. By the early 1970s, the enrollment ratios between the ethnic groups had equalized, and the gender gap had diminished significantly, although large disparities still remained in the enrollment and retention rates of different economic classes. In 2007, the gross enrollment ratio at the primary level was 97 percent; at the secondary level, 68 percent; and at the tertiary level, 32 percent. The primary completion rate was 96 percent.[119]

If we compare Malaysia's record within Southeast Asia, Malaysia stands out on a number of fronts. First, it does not charge any tuition at all levels of public education.[120] Second, in terms of spending for education as a percentage of GDP, Malaysia ranked highest in Southeast Asia in the 1980s, although the recent trend in spending has been downward. Third, Malaysia's distribution of spending on education contrasts with most of its neighbors. Most countries in Southeast Asia spend more than 50 percent of public spending on education at the primary level. Only Malaysia and Singapore spread out spending in roughly one-third proportions for the three levels of education. This difference is important because increased spending at the secondary level than at the primary level is considered particularly critical for addressing inequality.[121] An earlier cost-benefit study of educational investment concluded that incremental returns to secondary schooling in Malaysia are two to three times higher than other levels of education and much greater than the estimated opportunity cost of capital.[122] By contrast, the returns to primary and tertiary education are less than capital's marginal productivity. Both studies reinforced the Malaysian government's policy choices: its decision to abolish the entrance examination to the secondary level in 1965 and the high levels of funding it has disbursed to the secondary level.

DEVELOPING MALAY PROFESSIONALS

Since the implementation of the NEP, the focus of education policy has been on expanding Malay enrollment at the tertiary level, particularly in engineering, medicine, and the sciences—areas in which Malays are disproportionately lacking. This is in line with the government's intent to restructure the economy, as tertiary education plays a central role in increasing opportunities for upward mobility. Affirmative action policies therefore have been utilized to skew enrollment at universities in favor of the Malays. Officially, 55 percent of seats at public universities have been reserved for Malays, but unofficially, the estimates during the NEP reached as high as 75 percent. Furthermore, of the several thousands of government scholarships available, 80 percent have been given out to Malays. Malays have also been favored in administrative and faculty positions.[123]

One of the key instruments for building up the professional and entrepreneurial class in Malaysia has been the MARA Institute of Technology, which succeeded the Rural Industry and Development Authority after the first 1965 Bumiputera Economic Congress. Its goal was to create entrepreneurs at the professional and subprofessional levels. In practice, this meant increasing the employment rates of the Malays in areas such as management, engineering, accounting, banking, insurance, and architecture. This entailed transforming rural Malays into urban professionals by strengthening their analytical and technical skills.

One of the central concerns of MARA was to inculcate a professional mind-set into its students.[124] More than 80 percent of the student body hailed from the countryside; therefore, MARA faculty provided considerable guidance and advising to channel students into the area of study that suited them best. In every course of study, MARA students were required to learn business and entrepreneurship. To drill into the students' minds the importance of efficiency, MARA's first principal attended to every detail of the curriculum, even dictating that the lunch cafeteria serve only sandwiches so "students wouldn't waste time eating."[125]

In 1965, the MARA Institute of Technology had three hundred students. By 1975, eight thousand students were enrolled. Known today as Universiti Teknologi Mara (UITM), the institute has more than one hundred thousand students in various branches spread across the country.[126] One gauge of success, according to its first principal, was that it was able to graduate five engineers within one year.[127] Today, many MARA graduates are in strategic posts.[128] Its significance for addressing inequality can be best understood by comparison with Thailand. Unlike Malaysia, Thailand has not created a major institution to strengthen the skills of the rural sector. As a consequence, urban industry has failed to effectively absorb the rural population. Despite the industrial sector outpacing agriculture, the population balance still leans heavily toward the rural sector in Thailand. The comparative strength of MARA has precisely been the ability to provide the rural sector with skills to compete in the modern sector.

Health

The Malaysian state has been heavily involved in the provision of health care since independence, especially in the rural sector. As with education and rural development, the provision of health care has been a central prong of the government's developmental strategy. Malaysia's health-care record has been quite successful in both absolute and relative terms. Mortality rates have decreased, life expectancy has increased, and communicable diseases have been controlled. When one compares the critical health indicators for survival (life expectancy at birth and infant mortality rate), it is evident that Malaysia's record is closer to South Korea's than to those of its Southeast Asian counterparts (see Table 4-1).

In looking at the health statistics, it is important to emphasize that much of the achievements in Malaysia are not just due to economic growth but also to an active public sector. An Asian Development Bank report notes that the decline in infant mortality rates in the region occurred before the takeoff of most East Asian economies and that significant improvement in health in Asia is due to increased access to health services.[129] Thus, although growth may be important in sustaining better rates of health, what appears to be more important is the government's role in providing access to health services.

In general, public expenditures for health care as a share of the budget have been relatively low. Since 1961, spending on health has declined, although from 1986, it began to increase. In the mid-1990s, the expenditure of the Ministry of Health was between 5 percent and 6 percent of the budget. In 1999, health expenditure was 6.93 percent of the budget.[130] When one compares total health expenditures (private and public) as a percentage

TABLE 4-I

East Asia, Health Indicators, 1975–1999

	Life expectancy at birth (years)		Infant mortality rate (per 1,000 live births)		Under-five mortality rate (per 1,000 live births)	
	1970–1975	1995–2000	1970	1999	1970	1999
Indonesia	49.2	65.1	104	38	172	52
Malaysia	63.0	71.9	46	8	63	9
Philippines	58.1	68.6	60	31	90	42
South Korea	62.6	74.3	43	5	54	5
Thailand	59.5	69.6	74	26	102	30

SOURCE: UN Development Programme 2001.

TABLE 4-2

East Asia, Ratio of Health Expenditure to GDP, 1998

	Ratio of total expenditure to GDP	Ratio of public expenditure to GDP	Ratio of private expenditure to GDP
China	3.8	0.7	1.9
Hong Kong	5.0	2.2	2.7
Indonesia	1.7	0.7	0.9
Korea	5.4	0.5	3.7
Malaysia	2.7	1.4	1.5
Philippines	2.4	1.0	1.0
Singapore	3.3	1.2	1.9
Taiwan	5.0	0.6	1.7
Thailand	3.9	1.6	1.9

SOURCE: Malaysia, Ministry of Health 2001: 270–73.

of GDP, Malaysia is behind many of its Asian counterparts (see Table 4-2). Although Malaysia is the third-highest country in Asia in terms of public expenditures as a percentage of GDP, it is notably behind Thailand. In terms of private expenditure to GDP ratio, Malaysia ranks above only the Philippines and Indonesia. Despite lower public spending, Malaysia's health indicators surpass those of its Southeast Asian neighbors, which suggests that Malaysia's health system is more efficient. Malaysia's strategy has been to improve health with minimal costs, precisely because it has been focused on rural primary care.

In the mid-1970s, the poorer sectors received much of the government subsidies for health.[131] Specifically, the poorest 20 percent received more than 20 percent of subsidies for rural clinics and midwives. Spending on hospital outpatient services has also been relatively favorable toward the poor. This contrasts with a country like Indonesia (in the 1990s), where the wealthiest sector received 28 percent of public subsidies for health and the poorest received only 10 percent.[132] Data from 1984 show the poor's share of subsidies at 25 percent.[133] Table 4-3 shows how the poor's share has increased in both inpatient and outpatient care. If one compares the inpatient days of the lowest quintile with the highest quintile, it is clear that the poor have made large strides. In 1974, their share was 19 percent, whereas that of the richest was 20 percent. By 1984, the share of the poorest had increased to 25 percent, and that of the richest had decreased to 16 percent. A 1992 World Bank study further confirmed that the government's health expenditures continue to benefit the poor disproportionately. The study found that there was even better targeting than in the past, largely because of the upper strata's lower use of public health facilities.[134] This contrasts with Thailand, where government expenditures on health have generally been channeled toward hospitals in Bangkok and the central region.

TABLE 4-3

Malaysia, Share of Total Inpatient Days and Outpatient Visits, by Quintile of Household per Capita Income, 1974–1984

Quintile	1974		1984	
	Inpatient	Outpatient	Inpatient	Outpatient
1 (poorest 20%)	19	22	25	24
2	27	20	21	23
3	10	23	19	21
4	24	18	20	18
5 (richest 20%)	20	16	16	15

SOURCE: Hanafiah 1996: 762.

The Malaysian government has stood out in Asia through its focus on the free provision of rural health services. The government's efforts in preventive programs began in the late 1950s through malaria education and a national campaign to control tuberculosis in 1961. Its network of rural health services has concentrated on primary curative care, largely through paramedical personnel, and personal preventive care, such as immunization, maternal and child health care, and environmental sanitation work (e.g., the construction of latrines and wells).[135]

The government's policy on public health care has been driven by concerns over equity, spatial, and cost access to services.[136] The organization of rural health care was initially centered on a rural health unit that covered fifty thousand people and comprised three tiers: a main health center and four health subcenters, each of which was linked to four midwife clinics. In the early 1970s, this transformed into a two-tier system, wherein each rural health unit was meant to serve a population of fifteen thousand to twenty thousand people. The rural health unit comprises a health center linked to about four rural health (or community) clinics. Each community clinic covers between two thousand and four thousand people. This structure remains in effect today.

The reliance on rural clinics and on paramedics within the community is a form of noninstitutional care that keeps costs down while ensuring access to most of the rural population.[137] The World Health Organization has endorsed Malaysia's emphasis on noninstitutional care through rural clinics as a model for developing countries. Compared with Thailand, improved health outcomes are attained with low costs.[138] Until now, the rural health infrastructure has formed the backbone of primary health care.[139]

Surveys confirm that access to health-care services and facilities has been especially strong. A 1977 Ministry of Health survey found that coverage was 88 percent in peninsular Malaysia, 58.8 percent in Sabah, and 32.9 percent in Sarawak. In 1993, access to static facilities was 95 percent in peninsular Malaysia and 70 percent in Sabah and Sarawak.[140] These estimates do not include outreach services, such as traveling dispensaries and riverine services, mobile health teams, and dental clinics. Including all forms of health care, static and nonstatic, the Ministry of Health estimated access at close to 100 percent.[141] Comparative estimates of access in Asia range from lows of 50 percent to 60 percent for Cambodia to highs of 80 percent to 90 percent for China and Vietnam. The latter two countries have pursued similar policies as Malaysia in their emphasis on primary health care.[142]

TABLE 4-4
Malaysia, Doctor-to-Population Ratio, 1975–2005

Year	Ratio
1975	1:4,650
1980	1:3,000
1990	1:2,533
1993	1:2,301
2003	1:1,377
2005	1:1,237

SOURCES: Hanafiah 1996: 764; Malaysia, Ministry of Health 2006: 41.

In terms of manpower, the doctor-to-population ratio has been quite high, although it has been improving steadily since 1975 (see Table 4-4). However, Malaysia has emphasized its reliance on paramedics for staffing clinics in the rural sector. In 1975, the World Bank ranked Malaysia thirtieth (of eighty developing countries) in the physician-to-population ratio, but sixth in terms of nonphysician primary health workers.[143] The distribution of doctors in the public sector has also been relatively favorable, although the lure of the private sector has increasingly challenged this. In 1972, the ratio of public to private doctors was 59:41, in 1986, it was 42:58; and in 2000, it had improved to 54:46.[144]

POLITICS OF PRIVATIZATION

Since the mid-1980s, the state has sought to restructure the health sector toward its national policy of privatization.[145] Faced with spiraling costs for health care, in 1993 Mahathir announced that the government would no longer guarantee universal or heavily subsidized medical coverage. This move was intensely debated within the state and challenged from opposition parties and civil society groups. Particularly revealing in this battle over privatization is the presence of a solid tradition of state support for the poor that proponents of the free market cannot easily dismiss. Furthermore, the challenge from social groups for the protection of free public health has crossed ethnic lines, wherein various parties and NGOs have rallied together irrespective of ethnicity.

Although the government has been in favor of reducing the role of the state in health care from that of provider to that of regulator, there is evident tension in such a policy direction. One major planning document, the *Second Outline Perspective Plan 1991–2000*, noted that the government would "concentrate in areas where the market cannot function effectively or in the provision of public goods such as health."[146] The *Seventh Malaysia Plan 1996–2000*, which most clearly leans toward privatization of public health, still stated that "for the low-income group, access to health services will be assured through assistance from the government." Furthermore, given private hospitals' lack of enthusiasm for the government's call to cross-subsidize poor patients, the government passed the Private Healthcare Facilities and Services Bill in 1998, which required a proportion of private hospital beds to be reserved for patients from the poorer strata.

A coalition of opposition parties and citizen advocacy NGOs have so thoroughly opposed privatization of health services that on the eve of the 1999 general elections, Health Minister Chua Jui Meng announced that the cabinet had just decreed that public hospitals and clinics would not be corporatized and would remain under government control and ownership. Furthermore, Chua stated that thirty new public hospitals would be built in the near future and that the state would cover rising costs of medical treatment.

Within the state, there are clear contradictions over the role of privatization in public health. On the one hand, there are those who believe, like Mahathir, that the state must slowly retreat to a role of "steering without rowing" to contain costs and to improve efficiency and quality of services. This was expressed in the government's *Vision (Wawasan) 2020*, its planning document for Malaysia's future as a developed nation.[147] In *Vision 2020*, there is a push to make social welfare reliant on the family rather than on the state. Yet it has not been easy for the government to privatize the health sector, in large part because government officials themselves remain imbued with a tradition of active public support for the poor. The battle over the privatization of health care is still underway, although the trend appears to be an inexorable move toward more private hospitals and the draining of medical personnel from the public to the private sector.[148]

Conclusion

The catalyst for the redistributive policies in Malaysia was the May 1969 riots. Without this crisis, the government would not have undertaken a complete reform of the state, party, and economy. As Merilee Grindle and John Thomas note: "Crisis-ridden reforms tend to emphasize major changes from preexisting policies. That is, prior policies are often considered to be fully implicated in the causes of the crisis and must be rejected if the crisis is to be overcome."[149] But once the government realized that it had to change course, it wasted no time in shifting gears. The party was revamped into a more institutionalized apparatus, the state became more heavily interventionist, and the policy framework and overall climate of political change adhered to a general sense of pragmatism in which economic growth was central to equitable development. Institutional changes were fundamental to reform, but the policy choices the elites made—particularly the emphasis on redistribution within the context of growth—sustained the viability of the reform agenda.

An overhauled, institutionalized party was central to the reform drive. After 1969, UMNO became much more active at the grassroots level, monitoring both bureaucrats and constituents' concerns. The UMNO state assemblymen and MPs intensified their contact with the *rakyat* in the villages and poured a greater amount of funds for all types of development work into the local level. Furthermore, UMNO politicians often checked government agencies in the periphery when such agencies went against villagers' concerns or when they did not fully advance the party's agenda. Although the state already had a heavy hand in the countryside, the added layer of the governing party has provided a mechanism for policy oversight and therefore a means for reinforcing policy implementation. Without an institutionalized party perennially in touch with the grass roots, development policy would be unlikely to be sustained, monitored, and adjusted when necessary.

A second critical factor in explaining the effectiveness of the NEP was judicious state intervention. Unrelenting support for rural development, particularly through land resettlement programs; greater access to education and skills training through changes in the language of instruction and by building institutes and training centers across the country; and policies to attract investment have all exemplified the reach of the state. The fact that Malaysia was one of the highest-spending governments and had the highest tax-to-GDP ratio in Asia in the mid-1980s is a good indication of the state's dirigiste propensities. Without active intervention by the state, both in the rural and in the modern sector, Malays would not have been able to benefit from higher rates of economic growth. Before 1969, Malaysia already had respectable growth rates, but the state's failure to forcefully intervene in the educational system or in the industrial sector meant that Malays could not benefit from any trickle-down effect.

The third critical factor for the NEP's success was its relatively moderate approach. The NEP worked precisely because its goal of balancing the market with the state also reflected the need to balance the interests of the Chinese vis-à-vis those of the Malays. Unlike some redistributive programs in the developing world, the NEP was not based on seizing assets but on redistribution in favor of the Malays within the context of overall growth for all ethnic groups. Had the government squeezed the Chinese too far, capital flight and political instability would have stunted economic growth. Equally important, the NEP needed expanding markets for Malays to gain employment in the modern sector. Thus, by maintaining a free market, economic growth rates were sustained, which in turn raised incomes that began to equilibrate the disparities between the ethnic groups. "While publicly facilitating Malay access to Chinese-owned enterprises, loose implementation of the NEP has enabled even small and medium-sized Chinese firms to seek out state contract work through Bumiputra front men," writes William Case. "The NEP can even be read as having insulated the Chinese role in the exchanges."[150]

Finally, it is necessary to stress that there are many aspects of the NEP that have not been discussed here that have been subject to withering criticism. I indicated in the discussion of land settlement that FELDA has been criticized on numerous fronts. The NEP more generally has been criticized for veering away from its emphasis on poverty and inequality by focusing on building a capitalist class and in that sense has been driven more by the interests of the bourgeoisie and of state officials who would gain from entrepreneurship rather than by the interests of the Malay lower class. It has also ignored the destitution that persists within the Chinese and Indian communities, precisely because it has been driven by ethnicity rather than by class.[151] A further criticism is that, to the extent that the NEP has been focused on building a capitalist class, it has simply created rentier capitalists dependent on state patronage and with no substantive merits.

We should be clear that the NEP had two goals. It sought to reduce poverty and income inequality *and* to create a Malay capitalist class that could compete with the Chinese. One criticism is that the NEP leaned too heavily in the direction of capital formation, thus negating the interests of the lower class. The evidence we have sifted through indicates that the state has poured in massive resources to improve the conditions of the common Malay and that it has *not* neglected the goal of poverty reduction for the Malays in the pursuit of the other goal of a Malay capitalist class. It is true, however, that the NEP has not been concerned with the plight of the lower-class Chinese and Indians. The Indian lower class, in particular, has been almost completely ignored. This is one of the unfortunate aspects of a program that has been ethnically based. But it is also important to note that some policies, such as in health, have had effects that have gone well beyond ethnicity. On the separate question of whether this new capitalist class is simply a rentier class, there is a strong argument here.[152] But for the purposes of this study, my concern is not with the formation of a capitalist class. The emphasis on capital is relevant here only to the extent that it has detracted from reducing poverty and income inequality.

Although the NEP, particularly under Mahathir, did lean heavily toward a concern with the bourgeoisie, on the whole it would be simply misleading to conclude from that criticism that the NEP has not at the same time made major inroads in attacking poverty and income inequality. We must be careful in disaggregating the related, but distinct, goals of the NEP and in evaluating each on its own merits. Statistics on health, education, and rural development attest to significant improvements across the board for the Malays. Overall, the rise of a Malay middle class through heavy public spending on human capital is the strongest indication of the NEP's success in terms of equitable development. This transformation is unequivocal: "Unlike the pre-1970 period, when the new middle class in Malaysia tended to be dominated by those of Chinese origin, the new Malaysian middle class today is multi-ethnic in composition, with the new Malay middle class constituting a major component."[153] By contrast, in Thailand, development has failed to absorb a huge swath of the rural sector, thereby largely limiting middle-class growth to the Bangkok area and, in the process, creating the seeds for conflict between the restive rural sector and the contented urban middle class.

PART THREE

The Politics of Equitable Development in Thailand

Introduction

Following the trajectory blazed by the East Asian Tigers—Korea, Taiwan, Singapore, and Hong Kong—Thailand emerged as the rising star of the second-generation Asian newly industrializing countries. Its phenomenal growth rates in the late 1980s and early 1990s set records in the developing world. From 1988 to 1990, Thailand registered double-digit growth rates: 13.3 percent, 12.4 percent, and 10 percent. Even before the boom of the late 1980s, Thailand had already made huge leaps in economic growth. Beginning with Sarit Thanarat's stewardship in the early 1960s, the economy grew at an average rate of 7.8 percent per annum over a span of thirty years, from the mid-1960s until 1997.[1] In 2009, its gross domestic product (GDP) per capita was US\$3,893.[2] Except for the financial crises of the early 1980s and of 1997–98, Thailand was one of the most dynamic economies in the developing world (see Table III-1).

However, beneath these mammoth strides lay many contradictions and challenges. Among all countries in Southeast Asia, Thailand's economic growth has been most marked by a sharp rise in income inequality. Since the 1970s, income distribution has consistently worsened. In 1975, the Gini coefficient was .426, but by 1992 it had peaked at .536. By contrast, in Malaysia during about the same period, the Gini moved in a completely opposite direction: falling from .529 to .446. In the mid-1990s, the Gini in Thailand registered some decline but then rose again, reaching a high of .531 in 1999. During the Thaksin Shinawatra period, the Gini declined to .510

TABLE III-I
Thailand, GDP Growth Rates, 1961–2009
(percentage)

Period	Growth rates
1961–66	7.2
1967–71	7.2
1972–76	6.2
1977–81	7.1
1982–86	4.4
1987–91	10.5
1992–96	8.1
1997–2001	−0.1
2002–06	5.7
2007–09	1.7

SOURCES: Thailand 1967, 1972, 1977, 1987, 1992; World Bank WDI for 1992–2009.

in 2002 and .499 in 2004, but it then rose to .515 in 2006 (see Table III-2). Overall, from the mid-1980s onward, it has stayed above .500.

The incidence of poverty, by contrast, has declined in line with sustained rates of growth. The poverty incidence fell from more than 60 percent of the total population in the early 1960s to 11.4 percent, or 6.8 million people, in 1996 and 12 percent in 2004 (see Table III-3).[3] However, Medhi and Pranee caution that the income gain from growth has not been as strong as it should have been. Poverty rates have not declined as quickly as one would have expected given the high rates of growth.[4] From 1981 to 1988, poverty declined by only 2.9 percentage points. Medhi and Pranee also show that, if one adjusted the poverty threshold to take into account changes in population structure, pattern and composition of household's food-nonfood consumption, and minimal nutritional requirements, poverty incidence would rise sharply.[5]

Furthermore, although the trend in the decline of poverty has been downward, it has not been consistent. Poverty rose twice, once during a growing economy (1981–86) and once with a contracting economy (after the

TABLE III-2
Thailand, Distribution of Income, 1962–2006: Gini Coefficient and Income Shares

Period	Gini coefficient	Percentage income of the 1st quintile (poorest 20%)	Percentage income of the 2nd quintile	Percentage income of the 3rd quintile	Percentage income of the 4th quintile	Percentage income of the 5th quintile (richest 20%)	Ratio of 5th to 1st quintile
1962–63	.414	N/A	N/A	N/A	N/A	N/A	N/A
1968–69	.429	N/A	N/A	N/A	N/A	N/A	N/A
1975–76	.426 (.439)[a]	6.0	9.7	14.0	21.0	49.2	8.1
1981	.442	5.5	9.3	13.7	21.1	50.4	9.2
1986	.496	4.5	7.9	12.3	20.3	55.0	12.2
1988	.489	4.6	8.0	12.4	20.6	54.5	11.9
1990	.515	4.3	7.5	11.7	19.5	57.0	13.2
1992	.536	4.0	7.1	11.1	18.8	59.1	14.9
1994	.521	4.0	7.3	11.7	19.7	57.2	14.2
1996	.516	4.1	7.5	11.8	19.9	56.7	13.8
1998	.509	4.2	7.7	11.9	19.8	56.3	13.3
1999	.531	3.8	7.1	11.4	19.4	58.2	15.2
2000	.525	3.9	7.2	11.4	19.9	57.6	14.9
2002	.510	4.2	7.6	12.0	20.1	56.2	13.4
2004	.499	N/A	N/A	N/A	N/A	N/A	N/A
2006	.515	N/A	N/A	N/A	N/A	N/A	N/A

SOURCES: Somchai 1987, 2001; National Economic and Social Development Board 2003; Medhi 2008; Warr 2009.
[a]Somchai 1987.

TABLE III-3
Thailand, Incidence of Poverty, 1962–2004 (percentage)

Year	Aggregate	Rural	Urban
1962	88.3	96.4	78.5
1969	63.1	69.6	53.7
1975	48.6	57.2	25.8
1981	35.5	43.1	15.5
1986	44.9	56.3	12.1
1988	32.6 (48.8)[a]	40.3	12.6
1990	27.2	33.8	11.6
1992	23.2	29.7	6.6
1994	16.3	21.2	4.8
1996	11.4	14.9	3.0
1998	12.9	17.2	3.4
1999	15.9	21.5	3.1
2000	14.2	N/A	N/A
2002	9.8	N/A	N/A
2004	12.0[b]	N/A	N/A

SOURCES: Warr 2002: 20; World Bank 2005b: 9, based on National Economic and Social Development Board data.

[a]The figure in parentheses is the incidence based on an adjusted poverty line calculated by Medhi et al. 1991.

[b]In 2004, the National Economic and Social Development Board changed the way it calculated its poverty line to more accurately reflect current consumption patterns of the poor. This raised the threshold line and therefore increased the incidence of poverty. This makes it difficult to compare rates for 2004 and after with those from before 2004 (World Bank 2005b: 10).

1997 financial crisis).[6] Indeed, the World Bank points out that the incidence of poverty in Thailand in the early 1990s was similar to Indonesia, even though Thailand's gross national product per capita was 2.5 times higher.[7] Noting the importance of distribution, Somchai Jitsuchon, an economist with the Thailand Development Research Institute, writes, "Any future poverty reduction policies, or any policies for that matter, cannot ignore the distributional aspects."[8]

These aggregate economic data make clear that inequality is especially acute in Thailand. If we look more closely at some policy sectors, such as land reform, rural debt, dam building, and health care, we will see more clearly that the politics necessary to restructure many policy programs so that they are more effectively pro-poor is particularly challenging. None of the foregoing policy programs, with the exception of Thaksin's universal health-care program, have benefited the poor. The general laissez-faire orientation of the technocracy has also not been conducive to attacking inequalities. What we find in Thailand is that public policy has often been characterized more by the interests of a bureaucratic elite or of emerging capitalists, but not by a concern for the lower classes. Behind this lies the problem of institutional organization.

Absent in Thailand have been political institutions that might break through a conservative veneer that has reinforced inequitable patterns. Thailand's history is not devoid of attempts to form institutions that might tackle inequality. But beginning with Pridi Bhanomyong's People's Party, the initiatives have all foundered. To understand why parties have not emerged as capable interlocutors for the poor, we must analyze the Thai polity on a broader canvas, taking into account the historical origins of institutional development. The two chapters on Thailand here therefore track historical changes in organizational patterns as well as in social reforms. A refrain evident in the chapters on Thailand is that the numerous failures to build organizational power have had a significant and deleterious impact on the trajectory of equitable development.

Chapter 5 begins with the politics of Thailand in the late nineteenth century, for it is there that we find the origins of a modern state. Under King Chulalongkorn (Rama V), the Siamese state embarked on a process of modernization and rationalization of state functions and structures that created the foundations for a centralized state apparatus. Threatened by nobles who dominated the court, and by British and French imperial designs, Chulalongkorn embarked on a sweeping reform program that extended the lease of life of the Chakri dynasty through the creation of rationalized state power.

The modernizing reforms of Chulalongkorn had fundamental repercussions for political development. Chulalongkorn's actions strengthened a conservative nationalist ideology that upheld Thailand's nominal independence as an unmitigated blessing. This in turn hindered the emergence of a nationalist party, which in many other colonized nations had served as the vehicle for political and social reform. Precisely because Thailand remained uncolonized, it did not open up room—in a structural sense—for a strong, mass-driven nationalist movement to arise. Although a coup in 1932 brought the absolute monarchy to its end, it did not succeed, despite some genuine efforts, in forging a movement, an ideology, or an institution that might advance the concept of political representation. Thus, the significance of Chulalongkorn's actions in enabling the monarchy to ride out the colonialist wave was that they prevented a mass-based nationalist movement from taking center stage. When all the dust from the 1932 revolution finally cleared, what emerged at the apex of the state was military rule. In the postwar period, another effort was made to usher in democracy and institutions of a left-leaning nature, but this again was aborted. Thailand's military-bureaucratic state then reached its climax with the authoritarian regime of Sarit Thanarat.

Chapter 6 begins with the period of democracy in the mid-1970s when another major effort in modern history was made to craft institutions with a reformist drive. Although the governments in the mid-1970s responded to calls for reforms, they were unable to make a dent in inequality because they lacked the institutional basis with which to implement policy reform. Furthermore, these weak governments were squeezed between a mobilized and expectant popular sector and a reactionary surge spurred by royalist angst and a revived military. Democracy was restored in 1988, but a more open polity did not lead to changes in the country's inequitable trajectory. Problems ranging from land reform to dam building were neglected and at times worsened by democratic governments. Inequality reached its peak during the early 1990s. The Thaksin Shinawatra government elected in 2001 took the first real stab since the mid-1970s at addressing inequality. Although Thaksin's policies were criticized for their populist basis, they forced other political parties to take issues of poverty and inequality seriously for the first time in more than two decades.

FIVE

The Bureaucratic Polity Ascendant and the Failure of Reform

> The problem still remains a matter of bringing the state machinery under some disciplining power to give it again a firm and directed purpose.
>
> —*David Wilson*[1]

Introduction

In the mid-nineteenth century, Siam was in the throes of major social, economic, and political change. The doors of the economy had been flung wide open through the force of British laissez-faire doctrine; the polity looked increasingly fragile, with a monarchy having to fend off Western imperialist designs and intrigues at the court; and everyday forms of resistance were undermining the feudalistic social structure, known as *sakdina*, whose purpose was to maintain social order and secure labor for the monarchy. The Chakri dynasty—rulers of Siam since the Burmese sacking of Ayutthaya in 1767—was in a precarious state. Yet by the early twentieth century, the Siamese kingdom had regained its footing. A series of modernizing reforms led by King Chulalongkorn (Rama V, r. 1868–1910) gave the state a new lease on life. Centralized, rationalized, and cohesive, the Siamese state not only survived external and internal threats; more important, it had become a veritable bulwark of political power and legitimate authority during a period of intense crisis.

As a consequence of Chulalongkorn's reforms, two closely related institutions gained deeper roots in Siam's soil: a rejuvenated monarchy and an empowered bureaucratic state apparatus. By building a relatively cohesive state apparatus through functional differentiation of the administration, rationalization of taxation and revenue, and centralized control of the periphery, the monarchy had found its basis for survival and growth. With the monarchy and the state closely linked, Siam's political center of gravity at the turn of the century was fundamentally defined. Through his modernizing reforms, Chulalongkorn had ensured that the absolutist state would have a basis for legitimacy that its opponents would later find difficult to overcome.

The solid entrenchment of a modernized monarchy imbued with a strong current of legitimacy had powerful implications for patterns of political development. In 1932, a revolution by disgruntled bureaucrats constituted Thailand's first attempt at a real break with the ancien régime and an effort to graft onto the nation a reformist vision that was grounded, albeit in a very tenuous way, in democracy. But precisely because the revolutionary leaders were challenging a monarchy that had deep roots in society, and whose legitimacy had been solidified by Chulalongkorn, a real break with the past never occurred. Society did not widely perceive the ancien régime as illegitimate, alien, or a threat to national interests. Quite the contrary, Chulalongkorn's modernizing vision had been articulated precisely in national terms, and by doing so, he had occupied the "national space" that anticolonial movements had appropriated in other countries. Thus, without the structural conditions that could arouse popular discontent and a mass movement, the potential for party building, and therefore for some programmatic reformist agenda, could not develop. The 1932 revolution ended up further entrenching Chulalongkorn's bureaucratic pillars. The center of this bureaucratic power moved decisively to the military camp, embodied by autocratic figures like Phibun Songkram and later Sarit Thanarat. Not until the 1970s, when economic growth had opened up social fissures, was there another challenge to the bureaucratic state first crafted by Chulalongkorn.

Social Structure in Premodern Siam

Although it did not go so far as to operate like a caste system, social structure in premodern Siam was extremely hierarchical, rigid, and repressive. At the apex of society was the king, who ruled with the aid of princes and nobles, known as *nai* (lords). Below the *nai* were *phrai*, who served as indentured labor. At the bottom of the scale were the slaves, or *that*. This system was called *sakdina*—a concept mired in extensive debate.[2]

Sakdi means "power" or, more specifically, "something that one possesses as the source of power,"[3] and *na* means "rice field." Thus, if we think of *sakdina* as "power over land"[4] we can compare the system, in broad outlines, with feudalism.[5] Land seems to have been the basis on which this system initially operated. However, the resemblance of *sakdina* to feudalism is tricky for at least two reasons. First, power in premodern Siam was centripetal rather than centrifugal: centered on the king rather than dispersed among nobles, as was more typical of European feudalism.[6] Second, as Quaritch Wales and others have argued, although *sakdina* originated on the basis of land, it later functioned in terms of control over manpower.[7] Akhin Rabibhadana's classic work thus visualizes *sakdina* as a form of societal rankings based largely on the possession of manpower.[8] The source of power was control over the population, precisely because population, not land, was a scarce commodity in Siam and much of mainland Southeast Asia.

At the heart of the *sakdina* system was corvée labor. The *phrai* were divided into two main categories, *phrai luang* and *phrai som*.[9] The *phrai luang* were the king's men. Their position was the worst in the hierarchy—considered even worse than *that* or debt slaves—because of forced labor. *Phrai luang* had to do corvée for six months of the year.[10] Most of the labor required from the *phrai luang* consisted of constructing palaces, fortifications, and temples; canal digging; menial service for the royalty; and military service. The *phrai som* were considered to have better conditions than the *phrai luang* because they were not required to do corvée labor. Instead, they served as the personal retainers of the nobles and princes.

During the Chakri dynasty, the conditions of the peasantry initially became harsher, in large part because the Chakris felt the need to tighten their control over manpower following the shocking capitulation of the Siamese kingdom at the ancient capital of Ayutthaya. In 1774, King Taksin forced all *phrai* to be tattooed on their wrists for more effective control and requisition of the population when needed.[11] The population's hatred and resistance to corvée was legion:

> [W]hen registrars came, some dressed up as Chinese, Indians, or Europeans [who were not liable for corvée]. Some chained themselves up and pretended to be prisoners. Some quickly entered the monkhood. Others bribed the officials to classify them into exempt categories. Attempts to arrest defaulters sometimes resulted in pitched battles. Many took off into forests and formed robber bands. Many others chose to contract debts and fall into the status of *that* or debt bondsmen who were exempt from corvée.[12]

King Mongkut (Rama IV) was aware of increasing resistance to corvée and was no longer convinced that requisitioning labor was useful to the monarchy.[13] But he left it up to his son, Chulalongkorn, to take the radical step of ending the *sakdina* system. Chulalongkorn's push to end corvée labor and slavery would solidify his claim to visionary progress.

Modernizing the State, Protecting the Dynasty

Chulalongkorn became king at the age of fifteen, after Mongkut succumbed to malaria in a scientific expedition in the south. The monarchy was at its most vulnerable point, with one noble family, the Bunnags, in almost complete control of the state.[14] The *upparat* ("second king"), a potential heir to the throne and a rival to Chulalongkorn, also owed his position to Chuang Bunnag. With Chuang Bunnag as regent, his son as head of the Ministry of the Military (*Kalahom*), his brother in control of the Ministry of Finance (*Phra Khlang*), and more relatives and allies in key positions in other ministries and government offices, the Bunnags were the de facto rulers of the Siamese kingdom. Nobles, not royalty, controlled Siam's bureaucracy.

As problematic as Chulalongkorn's grasp on power was his lack of a financial base. The monarchy was increasingly bereft of financial resources. Because the monarchy did not have direct control over the ministries, it was not able to collect revenue for itself. The lack of finances meant that the monarchy had to cede patronage in the ministries and royal offices to the nobles. Similarly, because the nobles as ministers controlled registration rolls of the *phrai*, they alone knew how much commutation tax should be coming in, and they therefore could pocket the taxes.[15]

A third problem for Chulalongkorn was Western encroachment on Siamese territory. With the British in control of Burma, most of modern Malaya, and the Straits Settlements by the 1870s, Siam found itself encircled from northwest to southeast. In 1855, Mongkut had acquiesced to British demands and had accepted the terms of the Bowring Treaty. The treaty established free trade in Siam, with import duties restricted to 3 percent ad valorem and export taxes to 5 percent; it eliminated the monopolies and privileges of the royalty and nobles; and it provided extraterritoriality rights for the British. Although not formally colonized, Siamese sovereignty looked increasingly fragile, as numerous Western powers followed the British lead and imposed burdensome treaties on the Chakri dynasty.

In the latter half of the nineteenth century, outright colonial subjugation inched closer. In their push toward southern China, the French first seized large chunks of Cambodia, which Siam considered part of its realm, and then set up a showdown with the Siamese monarchy in July 1893, the ultimate intent of which was to lop off the Lao territories from Siamese control. This culminated in a short battle at the mouth of the Chao Phraya River, known as the Pak Nam Incident, in which the Siamese were spectacularly outgunned.[16] Following the Pak Nam Incident, the French claimed all territory east of the Mekong River, which significantly included the province of Luang Prabang. In one swoop, Siam lost about one-third of its territory, which corresponds roughly to modern-day Laos.[17]

The Pak Nam Incident was a turning point in Chulalongkorn's reign, as the young king realized that Siam was impotent against Western firepower. Although initially depressed by the humiliating defeat against the French, Chulalongkorn eventually set about reorganizing the state by rationalizing administration and professionalizing the military. These reforms established the foundations for the modern Thai nation-state through its assertion of control over its modern-day boundaries. Before 1893, Chulalongkorn had initiated a number of reforms that were meant to strengthen his position against his erstwhile opponents, but after the Pak Nam Incident, this was intensified.

The incentive for state building was dynastic survival. The noose that Chulalongkorn felt tightening around him could be loosened only through the building—and control—of a modern state. Kullada Kesobonchoo Mead puts it well:

> In order to legitimize his moves to accumulate power in his hands and to gain support against these vested interests, the king stressed the importance of initiating the same reforms that had made the West strong. He emphasized the need for efficiency and economic development, the importance of social justice and the monarch's role as representative of the nation and the people. . . . *But the king's interest in modernizing change was also limited. He did not want to see power pass to the nation-state.*[18]

The paradox of state building under Chulalongkorn was that its modern impulse also contained within it patrimonial features, as Chulalongkorn began his reforms in the context of dynastic interest and survival.

Chulalongkorn's reforms can be divided in terms of labor, administration, and military. On the issue of labor, the king made a first stab toward ending the *sakdina* system by abolishing prostration. This was a symbolic, but powerful, act. Eventually, the monarchy replaced corvée in 1899 with a capitation tax. In 1905, Chulalongkorn officially abolished the corvée system as well as slavery.

In the popular imagination, these acts are widely considered part of Chulalongkorn's liberal impulses, and they helped consolidate the image of the monarchy as an enterprising, progressive, and visionary institution.[19] Yet the move against slavery and corvée labor also had an economic and political logic whose fundamental goal was the strengthening of the monarchy. If laborers were freed from service to the monarchy and to the *nai*, they could be used more effectively in an economy that British free-market intervention had opened up. The more free labor was available, the more productive the economy was; therefore, higher revenue could be gained, especially from the numerous tax farms. Revenue could also be amassed through a head tax. The freeing of labor was crucial politically, to undermine the support base of the nobility. The nobility's wealth was dependent on the labor of the *phrai*, the fees they could earn from their *phrai*,[20] and the sale of slaves. As Tej Bunnag puts it: "[T]he Act concerning commutation tax of 1902 [formalizing the head tax] was the weapon which could be used finally to ruin the provincial nobility's fortune."[21]

The role of the Chinese in the economy was also a central element in the eventual dismantling of the *sakdina* system. By the mid-nineteenth century, Chinese immigration was heavily encouraged as a means of increasing the labor supply necessary for developing the economy under conditions of open trade that had been stimulated by the Bowring Treaty. The Chinese had to pay a poll tax every three years, but beyond that, their labor was not coerced. Chinese were active in commercial agriculture, as well as in shipping and trading. They "were needed, then[,] for the expansion of trade designed to swell governmental and royal revenues. To serve this purpose, they had to be given freedom unthinkable for the Thai masses of the time."[22] The significant role of the Chinese in the economy was thus a clear indication to the monarchy that there were greater gains to be made financially through an open labor system rather than through a coerced manpower system that heavily benefited the noble class.[23]

In administration, Chulalongkorn identified lack of functional differentiation and decentralization of power as critical weaknesses. In terms of administrative coherence, the bureaucracy did not distinguish clearly between civilian and military affairs. The three main ministries in charge of the administration of the kingdom had responsibilities that were regional and functional, thereby blurring any organizational logic. Such incoherent division of labor impeded the state from responding effectively to economic and political crises.[24]

The first significant effort to systematize the administration came in 1888 with the creation of an experimental cabinet composed of twelve ministers with equal rank whose responsibilities were clearly differentiated. The prime ministerships for the civil and military administration and the Ministry of Foreign Affairs were all divested of their regional responsibilities. In 1892, Chulalongkorn institutionalized this experimental cabinet, granting nine of the twelve ministerships to his brothers.

Centralization of state power was another urgent task.[25] Nobles, local chiefs, and tributary lords all had their own fiefdoms and militias. The critical issue was control over the outer provinces and tributary states to secure the kingdom's borders. The means to do this was the installation of commissioners (*khaluang*) in the provinces and tributary states. These commissioners, often princes, including half brothers of the king, or military officials, carried direct authority from Bangkok, were backed by military force, and stayed in the provinces for extended periods of time. They played a pivotal role in weakening the power of oligarchs by forcing the provincial governors and nobles to submit to the authority of the center. They ensured that the provinces would be internally stable, that Bangkok would be able to collect revenue more efficiently, and that in the process, Siam would have a more effective first line of defense against Western powers.

The problem with the military was that it lacked cohesiveness and a system for maintaining regular forces. Authority over the military was lodged in the two key ministries, the Ministry of Civil Affairs and the Ministry of Military Affairs. This had been done to prevent concentration of military power, which might be turned against the throne.[26] The problem with military recruitment was that it relied on commoners' military service under the corvée system. This allowed the king to levy troops when necessary but did not create a regular unit serving in wartime and peacetime that could provide long-term security. Furthermore, most of the militia were non-Siamese, whose allegiance to the throne was often tendentious.

Chulalongkorn's first step toward reform was the establishment of the Royal Pages Body Guard, a unit made up of young, salaried officers in charge of protecting the palace. The Body Guard adopted high standards of professionalism and administrative rationalization, including functional division, accountability, and personnel inducements.[27] Through the placement of his brothers in top echelons of the Body Guard, Chulalongkorn had a military unit directly accountable to him. These more professionalized officers then began to penetrate other military and naval departments.

In 1905, the crucial move toward a regularized, professionalized, national army was taken through the Conscription Edict. The significance of universal conscription was that it decisively ended the corvée system by eliminating disparities in terms of military service among commoners and between commoners and aristocrats. Universal conscription became acceptable to commoners in the long run because its principles were based on compensation and fairness. When serving in the military and upon fulfillment of all military responsibilities, soldiers were not liable to pay the poll tax (which had replaced the tax in lieu of service under the corvée system). Soldiers were also allowed to fulfill their service in their home province. These positive inducements stood in stark contrast to the corvée system. "The new system distributed obligations to the Crown more equitably than the old and, under law at least, gave commoners a new measure of individual freedom," explains Noel Battye. "By comparison with the discriminatory and harsh old system of military service, conscription was just and civilized."[28]

Universal conscription filled two key goals of Chulalongkorn. It struck a final blow against the corvée system, cutting off the last hold of the nobles over commoners. This act was presented as a move toward egalitarianism as well as a means to systematize and centralize a taxation system that would benefit the treasury in the long run. At the same time, it created the armature Chulalongkorn had long been advocating to deal with aggressors on the border. After the humiliation of the 1893 Pak Nam Incident, and following two serious threats in the outer provinces in 1902—the Laotian Holy Man Rebellion and the Shan Rebellion—Chulalongkorn was determined to create a more modernized army. In his view, "if there were no cudgel handy to give some resistance, the hooligans were always likely to be aggressive and disturbing."[29] By the first decade of the twentieth century, the national budget reflected Chulalongkorn's concern with military strength. The portion for military defense took up the largest share in the budget, and by 1910, expenditure for the army had surpassed that of the navy threefold.[30]

Thus, at the end of Chulalongkorn's reign in 1910, the army had been transformed into a more modernized bureaucratic institution. From a corvée system of largely non-Siamese militia, Chulalongkorn had created a national, professional standing army. The army was joined at the hip with the monarchy because the king had placed many of his sons, educated at military academies in Europe, in the top echelons. One of the critical legacies of the military reforms is that the army had become the centerpiece of the state. The praetorian state that emerged in the late 1930s under Phibun and that was consolidated through Sarit in the 1950s can thus trace its origins to Chulalongkorn's military reforms.

In the long run, Chulalongkorn's modernizing administrative and military reforms had deep ramifications for Thai political development. First, the consolidation of the civil and military administration meant that power had been centralized and rationalized in the state. Until Chulalongkorn's reforms, power was diffuse and fragmented. Now the Thai state emerged as a more cohesive structure that would have the capacities to advance the interests of the state qua state.[31] Just as important, the state would stand above other actors through its coercive capacities. This process of state building formed the roots of the "bureaucratic polity"—a concept Fred Riggs developed to emphasize the dominance of the military and civilian bureaucracy in the Thai political system.[32] Furthermore, the overpowering might of the military and its sustained efforts to intervene in civilian politics complicated later attempts to establish civilian institutions, especially political parties.

Second, Chulalongkorn's pioneering reforms fostered an image of the Thai monarchy as a benevolent force. By abolishing slavery, ending nobles' control over commoners, creating incentives for military service, rationalizing and universalizing the tax system, and above all, defending the shrinking territory of Siam both from internal fissures and external encroachment, Rama V ensured his legacy in the annals of Thai history. Ultimately, by endowing the monarchy with an aura of progressive reformism, Chulalongkorn found the means not only to strengthen and consolidate the Chakri dynasty but also to justify its central place in Thai society.[33]

Third, in contrast to other polities in Asia that were colonized, such as India, Indonesia, and Vietnam, or those with decaying monarchies, such as China under the Qing dynasty, the reinforced and domineering presence of the Thai absolutist state made it more difficult for a mass-based nationalist party to emerge as a countervailing force. The space that nationalist parties filled in other countries was, in the case of Siam, held by the monarchy: that is, the institutional and ideological appropriation of public state interests. Precisely because Chulalongkorn used internal and external threats as a springboard for intensive state building and royalist consolidation, Siam could not generate a nationalist party that would mobilize the masses against the ancien régime. Siam's ancien régime was not a colonial oppressor or a traditional force that had failed to adapt to the pressures of modernization; on the contrary, Chulalongkorn had ensured that his absolutist state would withstand and overcome the turbulence of the imperialist age through an agenda of progressive reform. Bureaucratic elites, frustrated by the patrimonial system, did later agitate for change. However, even when they subdued the monarchy, they did not seek to banish it for good. Furthermore, they remained wedded to the bureaucracy, and particularly to its bastion of militarism, as the regnant force in the state and therefore could not conceive of the mass party as an alternative sphere of power.

The 1932 Revolution and Its Aftermath

In the 1920s and early 1930s, discontent against the absolute monarchy was on the rise. The repercussions of the Great Depression compelled the state to increase taxes and decrease spending to maintain a balanced budget, thereby harming many of the interests of the bureaucracy. But the more fundamental problem predating the Depression was the rising frustration of an increasingly educated civilian and military bureaucratic corps. As an incipient urban middle class became increasingly professionalized and entered the ranks of the bureaucracy, it found itself constrained by a patrimonial system that favored entrenched princes and nobles.[34] These younger bureaucrats, adhering to the idea of *lak wicha*, the principle of administration based on law and rationality, sought to end *lak ratchakan*, the principle of royal service.[35]

The initiative for revolutionary change, however, began far from the shores of Siam. In the 1920s, bureaucratic officials from elite families and bright scholarship students had been sent to European capitals for further education in legal, administrative, and military affairs. A young group of dissident bureaucrats began organizing in Paris to discuss ways of reforming and eventually overthrowing the monarchy. The key figure in this circle was Pridi Bhanomyong, a brilliant Sino-Thai who hailed from a provincial middle-class gentry family in the town of Ayutthaya and had excelled in his studies, winning a scholarship for a doctorate in law at the Sorbonne.[36]

The first meeting of the dissident group was held in Paris on 5 February 1927. The group called itself the Khana Ratsadorn, or People's Party. The party articulated six guiding principles: freedom and equality in politics, law, and business; internal peace and order; economic planning to provide economic well-being and work for all; equality of privileges; liberty and freedom; and education for all.[37] Although these principles were quite general, they were shaped by the stirrings of popular revolutions across the world and motivated, above all, by the desire to overthrow the monarchy.[38]

The People's Party was a small, tight, and secretive clique through which the planners of the coup came together. The members of the People's Party were divided into a younger and older group. The older group was made up of military officials, whereas the younger clique comprised civilian and military bureaucrats. It was the younger clique, led by Pridi, that spearheaded the planning of the revolution. Although the People's Party was conceived of as a political party, in practice it operated like a secret society in its early meetings in Paris. Members were careful not to put anything in writing and to invite into the party only those whom they could trust. Most significant, the People's Party was unified not by a commonly held ideology but by the desire to oust the monarchy and by friendships formed in Paris. This rather shallow base of collective organization would prove the Achilles' heel of the party, for once the task of governance came into play, factional rivalry would hinder its development.[39]

In the early hours of 24 June 1932, the Promoters executed their coup with brilliant success.[40] Avoiding bloodshed and with minimal firepower behind them, the Promoters were able to quickly take over the palace, trap and isolate any princes who might have offered resistance, and control the flow of communication in Bangkok.[41] Following the coup, the Promoters realized that they needed the king and well-established bureaucratic officials to provide legitimacy and administrative capacity for the new regime. Because King Prajadhipok (Rama VII) was not completely averse to some reform, having begun tentative efforts to draft a constitution in the early 1930s, and because the Promoters were not intent on founding a republic, they asked the king to play a prominent role in the unfolding of the revolution.[42] In fact, the Promoters apologized to the king several months after the coup and retracted their initial fiery manifesto (penned by Pridi) that had vehemently blasphemed the monarchy.[43] The party also gave the prime ministership to a conservative bureaucrat outside the party and most cabinet seats to conservatives rather than party members. It did this because it felt the revolution needed cover.[44]

The People's Party reform agenda was focused on establishing institutions of democratic accountability and on improving the economic conditions of the Siamese. The party firmly believed that a state that genuinely represented the interests of the citizenry had to replace the patrimonial ways of the monarchy. With a concern for some aspect of popular representation at its core, the People's Party had brought forth revolutionary change in Siam. According to Toru Yano, "[T]he conception of man as an autonomous individual was something that no one in Thailand could have previously envisioned."[45]

Constitutional reform was fundamental to ensuring accountability of the monarchy and the princes and aristocrats. Article 1 of the provisional constitution stated that the "highest power of the country belongs to the entire people."[46] Two features marked the constitution: first, it decisively reduced the power of the monarchy, and second, it provided a three-stage process for the establishment of democracy.[47] Pridi admired Sun Yat-sen's revolution in China, so the provisional constitution followed Sun's political theory of a three-stage revolution. In particular, it included a focus on indirect voting, examination for political candidates, and political socialization of the masses.[48] Even more significant, Pridi adopted from Sun the idea of party tutelage or party dictatorship.[49] The *London Times* commented, "Outwardly the new regime is democratic, but in practice so far it is a one-party government of a mildly fascist complexion."[50] In Pridi's political vision, the party was to reign above the polity, providing guidance and leadership like the Soviet Communist Party and the Kuomintang (KMT). Mirroring the KMT, the People's Party appointed members to the two most important organs of government—the National Assembly and the People's Committee. But in contrast to the Soviet Communist Party, the People's Party, like the KMT, was to advance the interests of all classes rather than those of the proletariat alone. Although advocating democracy, the People's Party appeared to believe that a top-down structure was necessary before popular representation could proceed further.

PRIDI'S ECONOMIC PLAN

The ideology of the People's Party was relatively vague given its disparate membership, but Pridi's *Economic Plan* articulated in full scale a radical vision for reform. As the leader of the party, this plan could be understood as the party's programmatic statement. But the reality was that it was, above all, a reflection of Pridi's intellect, ideals, and social concerns.[51] The plan was marked above all by a strong socialist consciousness. Pridi's ideological vision and sincere desire to implement that vision are clear:

> When the People's Party announced that the new government would find work for everyone, and would draw up a national economic plan so as not to allow people to go hungry, it was not just fooling the people. . . . [T]he fact that the government has not done anything yet is because it has not yet proceeded according to my thinking. When it does proceed according to my thinking that the government should run the economy itself, all the people will have work to do, through the government accepting everyone as a government servant, including children, the sick, the disabled, and the aged who cannot work but who will receive a monthly salary from the government. The people will not go hungry because the lowest level of government salary will be determined as sufficient to buy or exchange for food, clothing, shelter, and so on in accordance with the needs of the people.[52]

The key themes in the plan included the following: (1) faith in the state as the central force for the management of the economy, for the betterment of human livelihood, and for the protection of all citizens; (2) a view that centralization of power under the state ensured efficiency and effective management of all areas of social, economic, and political life; (3) a strong concern for redistribution and for the social protection of all people; and (4) a clear dislike of private industry as well as of "social parasites."[53] Despite Pridi's repeated attempts in the plan to rebut any charges of communism,[54] his opponents labeled it as such. This charge, although meant as calumny, was not completely off the mark, for it is clear that the emphasis Pridi placed on virtually complete state control over resources, on redistribution, and on an end to private industry was shaped by a socialist spirit and shared many aspects of modern communist regimes—even if Pridi was very careful to clarify that there would be no expropriation of property or extreme acts of social engineering.[55]

Pierre Fistié has argued that many of Pridi's ideas on political economy came from a course on the history of economic ideas given by Professor August Deschamps in 1925 at the law faculty in Paris.[56] In particular, the works of French social theorists like Saint Simon, Fourier, and Proudhon made their imprint on Pridi's plan.[57] Pridi himself explained that the ideas for the plan came from his studies in political economy in the law faculty: "So the consciousness arose in me that Siam should have an economic plan which followed the science of socialist theory and which took into account the local situation and contemporary state of Siam."[58] The influence of events in the Soviet Union was also notable, but Fistié qualifies that this influence "appears to have been more of a pragmatic order than of an ideological order."[59] What was especially significant to Pridi was the similarity between the rural conditions of Siam and the Soviet Union.[60] Pridi's emphasis on the state and on redistribution may have been influenced less by a Soviet model than by French and Western European theories of state-led industrialization and social welfare.[61]

The most prominent theme that runs through the *Economic Plan*, known as the *Samud Pokleuang* (yellow-covered book), is the importance of the state. The plan envisioned the state as the fulcrum of the economy. It would take over land, labor, and capital; organize society through cooperatives; coordinate the efficient use of resources; produce, buy, and sell products; and provide salaries and social protection for all citizens. The state was envisioned as the basis for the betterment of the human condition, because in Pridi's vision, its purpose was to represent the people.

The actual mechanism through which the state would manage the economy and society was through cooperatives, which would structure economic and social life. Their compact nature would enable the efficient use of resources, the effective mobilization of society, and the maintenance of order. In part 8 of the plan, "Dividing Work among Cooperatives," Pridi wrote:

> Once people have joined cooperatives . . . it will be easy to organize administration as a municipality including sanitation and health. For example, the cooperative will arrange to have a doctor issue regulations about health care. Education and training will also be easy, because the members live close together. On a day when work is over, the cooperative may issue instructions to come for study or training. . . . The suppression of thieves and criminals will be facilitated. Apart from this, the military may use the cooperatives as a device for giving military training to people before they are conscripted for military service or the reserves.[62]

The extensive role of the state in all aspects of social life was itself a repudiation of private enterprise. Pridi was willing to exempt from state employment the liberal professions, including writers, lawyers, painters, and teachers; to maintain some degree of private trade and farming; and to issue

bonds for land. He was emphatic that his agenda not include expropriation of assets or property of the upper classes. But the general thrust and
rhetoric of the plan is clear: private industry, oppressive and self-interested,
should bow down to the state. In contrast to private enterprise and existing
"social parasites," government would not seek to make profit but to protect citizens: "The government is the representative of the people. So this is
equivalent to the people being the owners of the whole economy. When the
output of the economy is high, the people as workers and government servants will receive higher salaries in proportion. There is no need for government to set aside a portion of the benefit of anyone, for there is no one to
be benefited in such a way. This is different from the case of private factory
owners. It is normal for them to set aside a high profit and exploit the labor
of the workers for personal benefit."[63]

A concern with improving the conditions of the disadvantaged ultimately drove the state's deep immersion in society and economy. The state
would redistribute land, implement an inheritance tax, provide everyone
the salaries and benefits that only civil servants had until then enjoyed, and
create insurance for the weaker members in society—something that private
industry would not do. Attached to the plan was a draft on social insurance
exempting certain sectors of society, such as invalids, the disabled, and preg-
nant women, from having to work while still receiving a salary. This was the
first attempt to create a social welfare scheme in Thailand.[64]

The exposition of the *Economic Plan* marked the climax of the People's
Party. The firestorm it incited from the monarchy and reactionary forces
eventually weakened the party and Pridi's social agenda. A series of government meetings were held to discuss the plan, of which one held in March
1933 was especially important.[65] This last meeting ended up clearly in Pridi's
favor but the sources of opposition to his plan—conservative officials, including the prime minister and a few older members of the party, and the
king—had increasingly stiffened. With younger members of the Assembly
in support of the plan, but with conservative members in charge of the
cabinet opposed, events became more tense with the prospect of either
side of the aisle using violence. On 1 April 1933, with military force behind
him, Prajadhipok dissolved the Assembly, ended any more discussion of
Pridi's plan, and then published his own rebuttal, concluding: "I do not
know whether Stalin copied Luang Pradit (Pridi) or whether Luang Pradit copied Stalin. . . . The only difference is that one is Russian and the

other is Thai."[66] Accused of being a communist, Pridi was forced to leave the country.[67] Dismayed by the turn of events, Pridi's colleagues in the party launched a second coup against conservative forces and finally took complete charge of government. They brought Pridi back into the government but made clear to him that any discussion of his left-leaning economic agenda was over. The revolutionaries were still too vulnerable to allow the specter of communism to hang over their regime.

PARTY ORGANIZATION

With the *Economic Plan* consigned to history, the party lacked a clear social vision. Equally problematic was the development of its organization. Despite Pridi's efforts, the party had a hard time expanding its organizational structure and activating a grassroots membership. It could not move beyond its operation as a select clique of elites, and many of its activities throughout the countryside were more in the likes of a club than of a party.[68] Within less than a year, Prajadhipok's act banning all parties had terminated mobilization through the People's Party and its auxiliary arm, the People's Association. This act was spurred by conflict between organizers of a new party, the Khana Chat, or Nationalist Party,[69] and members of the People's Party, who sought to obstruct Khana Chat from registering.[70] With this conflict as an excuse, the king sought to weaken the revolutionaries by claiming that Siam could not handle conflict inherent in a multiparty system and that the proliferation of parties would divide the nation.[71]

However, at the initial stages of party development, the People's Party had made serious efforts to expand. The People's Association, the auxiliary unit created for the purpose of fostering unity and patriotism among the masses, initiated a relatively successful mobilization campaign. By midafternoon on the day of the revolution, the association's membership drive surpassed all expectations. In six weeks, the association had grown to ten thousand members, and by 1933, this had increased to one hundred thousand members throughout the country. The People's Association also established branches in every province.[72] Meetings were to be held once a month and would report on activities of the National Assembly as well as promote political knowledge through lectures.[73] Party members toured the countryside and spoke to large audiences about their activities.[74] In Bangkok, the party had support from labor, particularly tramway workers, carpenters, and rail workers.[75]

As part of its dissemination strategy, the left wing of the People's Party published two newspapers, *24 Mithuna* [24 June][76] and *Sajjang*.[77] Sanguan Tularaks, owner of *24 Mithuna*, also translated and published a pamphlet by J. W. Kneeshaw titled *Latthi Sochialism Mai Khwam Wa Arai* (What is the meaning of socialism?). Ten thousand copies of the pamphlet were distributed to raise awareness of socialism ahead of upcoming elections.[78] Sanguan furthermore delivered public lectures on the constitutional system hoping to attract more members into the party.[79]

These initiatives ultimately were not deep enough and did not last long enough. Within a year, the party had ceased to exist as an official organization, although its ninety-nine original members continued to refer to themselves as members of the People's Party. The inability to generate momentum from the coup severely hindered the potential for sweeping reforms and for building a nationalist party like the purported model of the KMT. Pridi sorely wanted to avoid a situation that "would merely replace the system of one king with a system of many kings,"[80] but he was incapable of getting past a swarm of conservative forces, both within the party and within the polity; of convincing the masses that a revolution was necessary to their lives; and of promoting an ideological agenda for reform. In all of this, political organization could have made a decisive difference.

The first error that undermined the possibility of sustained revolutionary change was the failure to conceive of reform in terms of a mass base rather than simply on the basis of elite maneuvers. The party did make efforts to build a grassroots base through the People's Association, but most of the activities of the association were largely fairs about the constitution and sporting or leisure events.[81] When these efforts went deeper than fairs they were not particularly effective. As the *Bangkok Times* reported:

> The leaders of the People's Party have been able to study the reaction of the people as a whole to their movement. They have been helped by several itinerant commissions sent out from Bangkok to preach the revolution even in remote villages. These emissaries have probably been themselves taught and slightly saddened in the process. It is not easy to teach those whose energies are spent in the mud of the rice fields and in the thickness of the jungle that liberty and equality are things to which it is worthwhile to sweep kings from their thrones.[82]

The party was thus fundamentally incapable of establishing roots in society. Its failure lay in its origins as a top-down elite party rather than as a movement driven by a cause that incited widespread discontent. Despite

Pridi's modeling of the People's Party on the KMT, in the end it operated like an elite faction rather than an organized party.[83]

The failure to deepen the party's foundations fed into the next error, which was the decision to seek some form of cohabitation with the king and other conservative bureaucrats.[84] Without institutional armature and popular support, the People's Party was ironically forced to embrace the monarchy as a pillar of support to preempt foreign intervention or even popular unrest in favor of the king. Instead of eliminating the monarchy, the party leaders assumed that they could control the monarchy by emasculating it constitutionally. They also thought that it would be wise to put a conservative, but sympathetic, figurehead in power rather than place themselves as the very face of the new regime. In both cases, they miscalculated. Prajadhipok proved adept at countering many (though not all) of the constitutional clauses that would have diluted his power, and the new government's figurehead, Manopakorn, was less interested in supporting the revolution than in asserting his own interests. Instead of relying on the bureaucracy as a means of power, the revolutionaries would have been better served by fortifying their party as an instrument to control the state. This "oversight" goes to the very heart of Fred Riggs's refrain that a countervailing power is necessary to check the bureaucracy: "If the People's Party had hoped to gain political control over the government from outside the bureaucracy, they would have had to build an organization similar to the Communist Party, the Kuomintang, or let us say, the Congress Party or Muslim League in India."[85]

A third error, largely of Pridi's own making, was the decision to pursue an economic plan that was far too radical for anything Siam could have achieved or accepted. Given the lack of a popular base that might back such radical economic change, Pridi's plan was surely skating on thin ice. "His Economic Policy was obviously sincere," noted a close observer of Thailand, "but it was equally clearly impracticable."[86] The impracticable aspect stemmed less from the economic principles themselves than from the lack of organizational power with which to further such ideals. Without an organizational structure within which to base, defend, and promote social reforms, their likelihood of success was extremely limited. The key question that should have been asked was this: "What machinery could have been devised to carry out these schemes?"[87]

More generally, if we place the People's Party's in comparative perspective, we can see that, despite all its own strategic errors, it also faced a very different structural environment than other modernizing parties. For parties that became dominant, institutionalized forces, such as the Congress Party in India, the Vietnamese Communist Party, or the United Malays National Organization (UMNO) in Malaysia, colonialism was an important oppositional force that had the effect of strengthening them by reinforcing their ideological position and compelling them to develop organizational capacities. Although the degree of opposition to colonialism may have varied across the parties, the fact that they were engaged in a struggle against an alien force enabled them to coalesce and mobilize the population under a party. By contrast, the initial, quick success of the 1932 coup executed without popular support ultimately worked against the imperatives of party building at a critical juncture in Thai modern history. The People's Party was therefore unable to avail itself of a social revolution to restructure society because the presence of the monarchy—restored under Chulalongkorn—had removed the impetus for complete social transformation. The year 1932 may have been a change of regime, but it could not be the basis for organizational development or structural reform.[88] The "revolution" that mattered had come earlier. Chulalongkorn's state building was able to outlast the 1932 coup and weaken any reformist impulse it contained, such that Riggs concluded that "the revolution of 1932 involved merely the substitution of one oligarchic elite for another."[89]

The legacy of 1932 was thus to ultimately strengthen military-bureaucratic rule rather than democracy or social reform. Once the dust had settled, the dominant individual who emerged from the party and who then led the government from 1938 until 1944 was Phibun Songkhram, initially a close friend of Pridi from the conspiratorial days in Paris and an artilleryman who eventually became the consummate military dictator. Phibun emerged triumphant amid factional infighting within the People's Party largely because he was able to dominate the army. With firepower behind him and with an ideology of militant nationalism providing him an aura of fascist glorification, Phibun defined the postrevolutionary period and, in so doing, trampled on the reformist vision of Pridi.

The Postwar Period

In 1944, Phibun resigned from the prime ministership because of his alliance with the Japanese. A vacuum of power provided a rare opportunity for liberal and left-leaning forces to start from scratch in their effort to build institutions that redirected the polity toward social concerns. This period, from 1944 to 1951, described as "one of the most violent and critical in modern Thai history,"[90] pitted three groups with strong ideological differences against one another. On one side was a leftist-democratic movement led by Pridi. Pridi's coalition included two parties, the Constitutional Front, composed of liberal members from the People's Party, and the Cooperative (Sahachip) Party, made up of northeastern radicals who had joined the underground Seri Thai (Free Thai) Movement against the Japanese, as well as labor groups and students.

Arrayed against Pridi were royalist forces and the military. The royalists initially formed the Progressive Party led by Kukrit Pramoj, which then merged into a new party, the Democrat Party (Phak Prachathipat) led by Khuang Apaiwongse and Seni Pramoj (elder brother of Kukrit). Khuang had been one of the Promoters but had long felt sidelined by the leaders of the coup. The Pramoj brothers, in contrast, were of royal stock and deeply opposed to Pridi. The Democrat Party's initial raison d'être was not much more than virulent opposition to Pridi. Although initially castigated by its dealings with the Japanese, the military eventually formed the third wing in the ideological competition of the postwar period, even forming a party known as the Tharmathipat. The military's ideological role, however, would be less a civilian one, as it would reprise its use of force to achieve its ends.

The January 1946 elections were the first in which parties mobilized for direct elections. Although these parties were not mass based, they did reflect sharp ideological differences. In the elections, Pridi's Constitutional Front and the Cooperative Party captured the bulk of seats against the Progressive Party. Pridi became prime minister in March 1946.

Once in power, Pridi drafted a new constitution that was the most democratic yet in Thailand's history. It made Parliament completely elective, created a senate that was elected by members of the Parliament, and made political parties legal for the first time. The new constitution also prohibited bureaucrats and soldiers from sitting in the senate, the lower house, or the cabinet. This was intended to prevent a figure like Phibun from holding the position of commander in chief of the army as well as prime minister.

This period also witnessed a rising leftist tide. To appease the Soviet Union and facilitate Thailand's entry into the United Nations, Pridi repealed the anticommunist law. In the August 1946 elections, the Communist Party of Thailand (CPT) won a seat in Bangkok and joined Pridi's coalition. The CPT actively championed student and labor organizations and published a weekly newspaper.[91]

The chances for consolidating democracy under the Pridi government, however, faced numerous obstacles, of which the most threatening was the state of the economy. A shortage of consumer goods had led to rising inflation, in which retail prices stood at eight times their prewar level.[92] Furthermore, rampant corruption within the government and the bureaucracy and against many of the former Seri Thai undermined the legitimacy of Pridi's rule, even if he himself was not tainted by corruption.

What eventually sank Pridi was the death of King Ananda Mahidol. On 9 June 1946, the young king was found shot in bed. Rumors spread that Pridi as the former regent had conspired to assassinate the king. Although the evidence pointed to an accidental death, Pridi's opponents, including the Democrat Party, continued to fan these charges. Unable to repress these rumors, Pridi resigned the premiership.

In elections held in August 1946, Pridi's two parties maintained their majority, but they lacked Pridi's forceful personality to continue a strong national agenda. Throughout the year, the party system began to unravel. In May 1947, a faction split off from the Democrat Party, calling itself the People's Party (Phak Prachachon) and joining Pridi's coalition. Meanwhile, Phibun had created the Tharmathipat Party to reestablish his position in civilian politics. The Democrat Party stood with the Tharmathipat Party against Pridi's coalition. The volatility in the party system, along with the unsolved death of the king and the frailty of the economy, made the country ripe for its third coup.

On 8 November 1947, the military overthrew the civilian government. Although Khuang and the Democrat Party were initially allowed to run the government, in April 1948, the military finally edged Khuang out and reelevated Phibun to the prime minister's office. Yet another coup on 29 November 1951 firmly stamped the military's dominance over the state. The struggle between civilian and military forces was over. After this coup, Phibun restored the 1932 constitution, which allowed civil servants or active military officers to hold seats in the cabinet or the Parliament.

The collapse of democracy in the postwar period was the result of a number of crises. The death of the king was the nail in the coffin that sealed the fate of Pridi's government. But the inability of the government to deal with dismal economic conditions was equally critical. The inflationary conditions of the economy were particularly burdensome for the military. Already angered by the course of the war and their demobilization, many armed officers found that they had no welfare benefits to tide them through a dire economy. A larger problem lay in the consistent failure of reformist forces to focus on organizational power. "Perhaps most serious was [liberals'] lack of discipline and their inability to develop themselves into a cohesive political force," wrote Frank Darling. "Unlike the military leaders who relied on the highly-disciplined armed forces, the liberals failed to build a national party organization on which they could gain political support."[93] Even had Pridi and his allies concentrated on party building, they may have found themselves outgunned by their opponents. But without some deeper efforts toward organizational development, civilian parties had virtually no basis from which to defend their agenda.

Although parties in Thailand did not have a deep social base, they did have some ideological roots. Pridi's coalition was founded on social democratic ideals and regionalist impulses in the northeast. It was also linked with the Central Labor Union.[94] The Democrat Party stood squarely in the conservative-royalist camp, with many of its members coming from the aristocracy, royalty, and landowning class. Further on the right was Phibun's Tharmathipat Party, which represented the military. Clearly, there was some ideological basis for the aggregation of party organizations.

Yet even if there was some ideological clash, these parties sorely lacked a mass base. With the partial exception of the Sahachip Party representing the northeast, parties did not have roots in society and therefore did not mobilize followers. Parties were largely formed to support a leader angling for power in Parliament. Without a mass base, there was little foundation on which to build a party. By contrast, the military forces arrayed against Pridi were united against the civilian government. The military's discipline naturally provided it with greater organizational strength when competing with newly formed civilian parties. Given these shaky democratic foundations, it is not surprising that the party system failed to become consolidated.

The Legacy of the Sarit Regime, 1957–1973

On 20 October 1958, Field Marshall Sarit Thanarat, the chief of the army and a key player in the 1947 coup against Pridi, staged a coup that consummated the military's rise to power since the era of Chulalongkorn. Ending any pretense of democracy or constitutionalism, Sarit banned Parliament, political parties, and political gatherings.[95] Although his military predecessor, Phibun, had made some effort at retaining a facade of constitutionalism, Sarit showed no restraint in proclaiming martial law. What he put in place of the halfway house of military rule with elements of constitutionalism was a self-styled revolution. Although the revolution was in a sense a misnomer, as it was a reactionary movement that restored the symbolic power of the monarchy and infused society with traditional Thai values, it also involved a massive revamping of the state apparatus and the advent of modern economic development.

Two central goals lay at the heart of Sarit's regime: revolution (*pattiwat*) and development (*phattana*). These two ideas were interrelated, for the revolution was meant to usher in development. Sarit saw himself as transforming the Thai polity and offering a completely new path for the Thai nation.[96] For the revolution to succeed, Sarit focused on strengthening the military bureaucracy and rationalizing the civilian bureaucracy, particularly the economic agencies. This had a deep impact on Thailand's developmental trajectory. First, it reinforced and heightened the dominance of the military, especially the army, over the polity. Sarit had risen through the ranks of the First Division of the army—the key unit in Bangkok that had been involved in the 1947 coup that ousted Pridi. He therefore deepened the role of the military in society by directing its energies toward social and economic tasks, especially development programs that were intricately linked with security interests.

Second, in rationalizing the bureaucracy and in legitimizing his regime, Sarit built the structural foundations of the country's developmental institutions. These institutions were staffed by technocrats steeped in classical macroeconomic precepts and were protected from external interference. They were able to propel Thailand onto a staggering rate of growth, outpacing most of the developing world during this period.

Sarit lessened the government's role in the economy, giving more space to the free market. This was a significant change from Phibun. Economic policy gained a whole new dimension: private and foreign investment were encouraged; state enterprises were stifled, except for infrastructure and utilities; and the Chinese business community was no longer harassed.[97] This push toward a more liberalized economy reflected political rivalries among the military elite. Because Sarit's rival, the police chief, Phao Siriyanond, controlled state enterprises in public utilities and import substitution, the move away from direct state intervention in the economy was an explicit effort to undermine Phao's power base.

In the area of bureaucratic consolidation, Sarit created numerous agencies that remain the pillars of contemporary macroeconomic policy. Following the guidelines of a 1957–58 World Bank report,[98] Sarit established the National Economic Development Board (NEDB, later the National Economic and Social Development Board) and the Budget Bureau within the Office of the Prime Minister.[99] Several other important institutions for economic policy were also created: the Board of Investment and the Office of Fiscal Policy within the Ministry of Finance. Sarit, furthermore, made himself chair of the Civil Service Subcommission, which gave him broad authority over the civil servants. During this period, Thailand achieved an average growth rate of 8.4 percent. This was the beginning of Thailand's economic takeoff.

Sarit allowed technocrats ample latitude in implementing economic policy, protecting them from predatory forces, whether these were military officials or politicians. Influenced by the tenets of Anglo-Saxon economics gained through graduate training in the United States and in England and more residually by the tradition of financial conservatism dating back to the influence of British advisers to the monarchy, Thailand's technocrats paved the way for a market-driven economy.[100] For these technocrats, the advancement of the free market was a way to get around the corrupt and rent-seeking practices of the military state. The free market would dictate the pace and direction of development, and the state would confine itself to supporting the needs of the entrepreneurs. Thailand's most revered technocrat, Puey Ungpakhorn, made no secret of his belief in free enterprise: "What is the one single most important factor for progress? My short answer is private initiative. . . . Kill the initiative, as in so many of our neighboring countries, and you can forget about the targets in your five-year development plan."[101]

The First Plan reinforced the importance of the free market: "It is believed that in Thailand increased output will be most readily secured through the spontaneous efforts of individual citizens, fostered and assisted by government, rather than through government itself entering directly into the field of production. The key note of the public development program is, therefore, the encouragement of economic growth in the private sector, and the resources of government will be mainly directed to projects, both in the agricultural and non-agricultural sectors of the economy, which have this objective in view."[102]

During the 1960s and 1970s, government concentrated on building physical infrastructure—roads, highways, communication networks, and irrigation dams. Significant expenditures on agriculture also sought to push export commodities in order to increase the country's foreign exchange.[103] Much of the stimulus for infrastructure expansion arose out of the need to curb leftist discontent. Major highways cut across the northeast and penetrated into provinces that were populated by communist insurgents and leftist sympathizers.[104] Sarit was intent on extracting as much foreign aid from the United States at this time, and the aid went largely toward infrastructure that could penetrate leftist strongholds.[105] The U.S.-backed Accelerated Rural Development Scheme worked to construct roads and infrastructure in politically sensitive areas, thereby linking rural development with state security. The military bureaucracy was increasingly pushed toward functions and skills that would support developmental tasks in the countryside.[106] At the same time, the government sought to increase foreign and domestic investment by repressing wages and creating financial incentives for private enterprise.

Although the technocratic elements of the bureaucracy were rationalized for the purposes of fostering economic growth, inequality was not a major consideration. This was largely because the technocrats in the NEDB and in the Ministry of Finance were less interested in reducing the increasing income gap between the regions and between the rich and poor than in forging ahead with high rates of growth through private investment. As a native son of Isan (the northeastern region), Sarit had shown some interest in social welfare, emphasizing the importance of infrastructure, the provision of clean water, and health and education programs for the betterment of the countryside.[107] Nonetheless, although the agricultural sector was allocated a high amount of funding, it was still given lower priority than industry and physical infrastructure at the center. This was apparent by the rise in the per capita income of Bangkok compared to that of the rural countryside. In 1968–69, villages in the north, south, and northeast had average family incomes that were only 78 percent, 70 percent, and 69 percent of the national income.[108] Medhi Krongkaew notes that, during this period, "the traditional farm sector was not only relatively neglected, one could even say that it was exploited for the benefits of the modern sectors."[109]

Between 1962–63 and 1968–69, the average household money income of the north and northeast increased, but its poverty levels did not decline.[110] As a share of total poverty, the level of poverty in the northeast increased to 47 percent from 40 percent, whereas in the north it just barely went down from 26 percent to 24 percent. This means that the income gains in the north and particularly in the northeast were disproportionately in favor of the rich. Overall, growth was having some effect on income levels, but its impact was skewed toward the upper classes, thereby widening inequality already by the 1960s.[111] Given the substantial allocations being disbursed toward agricultural projects in the 1960s, it is fair to surmise that there was considerable leakage toward wealthier villagers in the north and northeast. Even more, one might deduce that the bulk of spending directed toward defeating communist insurgency, most of this concentrated in the northeast, had negligible effects on the livelihood of the poor.[112]

Conclusion

Chulalongkorn's legacy in Thailand today is an extremely positive one. He is revered as a farsighted king who saved Siam from imperial aggression and modernized the monarchy. As we have seen, however, his legacy in terms of political development has been one of hindering the possibilities for organizational development and in turn for social reform. This is because his modernizing reforms, by reinvigorating the monarchy, had the structural effect of weakening incentives for social mobilization, party building, and social reform.

The 1932 revolution was part of a wave of social and political revolutions that were sweeping across colonized nations. But in Thailand the revolution faltered. "Pridi belonged to the same political generation as Jawaharlal Nehru, Soekarno, Ho Chi Minh, Aung San, and other anti-colonial nationalists of the inter-war period. They all emerged in the same political and intellectual context," write Chris Baker and Pasuk Phongpaichit. But the difference between Pridi and the other nationalists was that they "were all pitted against colonialism."[113] Chulalongkorn's ability to maneuver between the British and the French kept colonialism at bay, which in turn removed the need for social mobilization and social reform. Pridi could not summon the masses to support the People's Party because there was little basis for an uprising. Thus, "denied effective support from the popular masses who had not yet reached the stage of political consciousness," Fistié concludes, "Pridi and his small troupe of partisans did not comprise more than an isolated vanguard."[114]

By contrast, Malaysia's political development did produce structural incentives for party building. Although UMNO was not born of the same radical nationalist roots as India's Congress Party, Vietnam's Communist Party, or Indonesia's Nationalist Party, it still emerged out of opposition to a colonial project—the Malayan Union—that would have weakened Malay power. At the same time, challenges from radical forces and efforts by the British to eventually work with UMNO moderates helped shape the organizational and ideological basis of the party. Without these initial structural constraints, UMNO would not have been born. Unlike Malaysia, Thailand could not use a colonial project as a springboard for party growth and mobilization.

Thus, in Thailand, instead of organizational development and social reform emerging out of 1932, militarism gained ascendancy within the People's Party and throughout the state. A brief period immediately following the war broke the military's momentum—but not for long. Following Phibun, an even more authoritarian figure, Sarit, asserted control of the country. Parliaments and parties were repressed, but economic development was encouraged. This began Thailand's first boom under a highly competent technocracy. However, economic development was focused on growth and not distribution. As a consequence, social and economic gaps ruptured across classes and regions. This, along with a yearning for freedom, was to be the basis of the struggles of the 1970s.

SIX

Growth Without Equity

> Between the hammer of a military coup . . . and the anvil of bu-
> reaucratic indifference or distaste, politicians and political parties
> have led a chequered, impoverished, and precarious existence.
>
> —*John Girling*[1]

Introduction

In the 1970s, Thailand moved from a closed regime to a fully open, mobilized polity in which social forces—students, workers, farmers—pressured
the state for social reform. Although the government initiated numerous
efforts to address rising inequalities, it was incapable of making them stick
in the periphery. Parties lacked organizational power and had no means
of compelling bureaucrats and local elites to abide by the law. With weak
institutions caught between social pressures and a reactionary resurgence,
the democratic regime imploded. In the late 1980s, Thailand returned to
democracy just as its second economic boom began. But throughout this
period, parties remained institutionally weak and disinterested in social reform. The rise of Thai Rak Thai (TRT) in 2000 shook up the polity and
party system. For the first time since the 1970s, a party sought to articulate
the interests of the poor. However, the degree to which institutionalization could reshape inequality was limited by the personalistic control maintained by its founder, Thaksin Shinawatra, over the party, and ultimately
by a military coup that saw Thailand revert to a seemingly insurmountable
cycle of military interventions and weak civilian institutions.

The Turbulent 1970s

The 1970s were a period of great instability in Thailand. Sarit Thanarat's
economic reforms had initiated the country's first economic boom, resulting

in an annual growth rate of 11.8 percent in the latter half of the 1960s. But by the early 1970s, the economy had begun to falter, with growth declining to 2.8 percent in 1971. More critically, inflation rose to 15 percent in 1973 and to 24 percent in 1974. This inflationary surge was unprecedented in Thailand's modern economic history.[2] In 1972, rice production declined by 12 percent, creating a rice crisis, with rice being hoarded and Thais lining up for supplies.[3] Student enrollment at secondary schools, vocational schools, and universities had also increased sharply in the 1960s, but opportunities in the private sector and in the esteemed bureaucracy had not kept pace.[4]

In the midst of these economic travails, any legitimacy held by the two generals running the country, Prime Minister Thanom Kittikachorn and his deputy, Praphat Charusathien, dissipated. Their cavalier dismissal of Parliament in 1971, the naked acts of corruption surrounding their ruling circle, and their unabashed resort to nepotism (anointing Narong Kittikachorn, son of Thanom and son-in-law of Praphat, as successor) precipitated a growing number of acts of defiance and protest by university students. These protests culminated in several days of massive rallies that reached more than four hundred thousand people and were sparked by the arrest of a group of students, professors, and politicians who had demanded a new constitution. On 14 October 1973, students and armed forces clashed, resulting in more than sixty deaths and nearly one thousand injured. The intervention of the king and, above all, the decision by the army commander in chief not to support the Thanom-Praphat-Narong triumvirate rid Thailand of military rule for the first time in twenty-six years.[5]

The collapse of the military regime through a mass civilian uprising— what was in effect the first "people power" movement in Southeast Asia— broke open a dam of latent discontent related not just to freedom but also to growing inequities throughout the country. Despite rapid growth in the 1960s, the conditions of the farmers had deteriorated by the 1970s, and urban workers' wages and benefits had failed to improve. The larger problem was that government economic policy had focused heavily on raising the national income but not on its distribution.[6] Bangkok Bank's vice president–turned–politician Boonchu Rojanasthien punctuated this fact in a major address to the Ministry of Finance: "We all know what the results of [Thailand's] developmental efforts have been: the wealthy have been developed to greater wealth, while the poor are as poor as ever—and not a few of them are worse off than before."[7]

An interim government headed by a former chief justice of the Supreme Court and rector of Thammasat University, Sanya Thammasak, was initially tasked with the goal of rebuilding democratic institutions and addressing social grievances. Parliamentary elections were then held more than a year later, in January 1975, and a bewildering number of parties and candidates ran for office. Forty-two parties and 2,199 candidates vied for 269 seats in Parliament. Many parties were largely vehicles for ambitious personalities and made no effort to contest as parties, simply putting forth one or two members to contest the elections.[8] The multitude of parties and candidates reflected the new democratic opening but also suggested how fragmented and unstable any governing coalition would be.

The party system was deeply fragmented, with twenty-two parties winning seats, of which nine held only one or two seats. Although most parties espoused vacuous programs supporting liberal democracy and Thailand's tripartite moral vision of nation-religion-king (*chat-satsana-mahakasat*),[9] there was also a perceptible ideological divide in Parliament—a consequence especially of the leftist parties' success in gaining a significant number of seats and an emerging divide between progressives and conservatives *within* the largest party, the Democrat Party.[10] On the right were parties that were remnants of the military-backed party of the 1950s and 1960s.[11] The military-linked contingent in Parliament splintered into the Chat Thai (Thai Nation), Social Nationalist Party, Social Justice Party, and Social Agrarian Party. These parties simply reflected the current factions within the military, in effect splintering from the military "mother ship." On the center-right were the Democrat Party and the Social Action Party (SAP), led respectively by the royalist Pramoj brothers, Seni and Kukrit. The SAP was an offshoot of the Democrat Party, distinguished by a prestigious group of Bangkok Bank executives carrying forward an ambitious reform program. Finally, on the left were the New Force Party (Palang Mai) and two socialist parties, the United Socialist Front and the Socialist Party of Thailand.

Although the Democrat Party gained the most seats in the election, its initial attempt to form a governing coalition collapsed after a month. The SAP, led by Kukrit, then maneuvered to form a coalition with thirteen parties, including three major right-wing ones. Kukrit's only means for keeping his coalition together was to divvy up the ministries among his major partners. Because nothing but an interest in electoral power and access to spoils held the parties together, there was no attempt to create a unified policy program within the coalition. Instead, "it soon became apparent that the country was being run by at least three mini-governments—Social Action, Thai Nation [Chat Thai], and Social Justice—rather than by a single effective coalition."[12] Each party sought to maximize its patronage through its cabinet portfolio, with the SAP concentrating its energies on the *tambon* rural development program (discussed subsequently), the Social Justice Party exploiting the Ministry of Agriculture, and Chat Thai cultivating its links with the military.

Political parties in the 1970s thus operated in a situation rife with fragmentation and clientelism. This situation followed from decades of military dominance in which parties had been consistently harassed, their organizations disbanded, and competitive elections outlawed. Except for the Democrat Party—a party that since the late 1940s had become the institutionalized opposition to military regimes and parties—every other party was a new organization with very shallow links to social groups. The leftist parties had some roots in the Socialist Front of the late 1950s, but these were tenuous, based less in institutional structures than in the abiding interests of the northeastern peasantry.[13] Furthermore, the left did not present one united party in the elections but was represented by three major parties, along with a few smaller ones.

Although parties were institutionally weak, social forces were extremely vibrant and articulate. Invigorated by their success in overthrowing the military, students spearheaded the calls for social change throughout the three years of democracy, placing constant pressure on the democratic governments. The National Student Center of Thailand was the organizational heart of the student movement, but other student groups were also active in clamoring for reform. Student groups led countless demonstrations throughout these years, were instrumental in mobilizing farmers, and played a key role in collaborating with labor.[14] What emerged was a triple alliance (*sam prasarn*) linking students, farmers, and workers.[15] This alliance proved effective at fomenting mobilization, raising social awareness, and driving relentless demands onto Parliament, but it was not as effective in allying with institutions in power, and therefore in following through on policy implementation.

SOCIAL REFORMS

It is thus within this open—but institutionally volatile—environment that social reforms were addressed. The major issues that confronted the democratic governments centered on the rights and conditions of urban workers and rural farmers. Throughout the three years of open politics, factory and service workers flexed their muscle. The number of labor disputes and strikes was unprecedented. Between 1973 and 1976, there were 1,233 strikes, with an average of 25.7 per month. By contrast, between 1966 and 1972, there were only 137 strikes, with an average of 1.6 per month. In 1973, 177,887 workers were involved in strikes, and in 1974, this number was 105,883.[16] In 1974, the Sanya government raised the minimum wage by 33 percent to Bt16 per day. A major strike by textile workers forced the government to further increase the minimum wage in Bangkok to Bt20 (US$1) a day, with the stipulation that it would be increased to Bt25 in 1975. In 1975, the landmark Labor Relations Act was passed, which legalized labor unions and gave them a role in the collective-bargaining process.

The rural sector was also ripe for unrest. Population pressures, tenancy, landlessness, and rural indebtedness had risen significantly throughout the countryside, particularly in the central and northern provinces. Tenancy rates across the country increased by 8.7 percent from 1963 to 1973. The central and northern provinces experienced the sharpest increases, by 21.8 percent and 14.7 percent, respectively.[17] By 1976, 41 percent of households in the central provinces and 27 percent in the north were tenants.[18] In the central region, the key problem was absentee landlordism, whereas in the north tensions between landlords and tenants were high. Land tenure was less of a problem in the northeast, yet development programs had yielded minimal benefits. The *Bangkok Bank Monthly Review* noted that, in the northeast,

> new highways were carved and old ones extended . . . [but] in selling their products the farmers remain just as vulnerable to the middlemen because the marketing system has not been modified. Though many storage dams were constructed, in growing their crops the farmers still live in constant fear of drought because of the lack of feeder canals to the farms. Though electricity generation had multiplied, the farmers still have to make do without electricity because most of the power cables lead to Bangkok and the larger towns. The vast strides made in national development have therefore been practically meaningless to the people who most need help.[19]

The Sanya government, under pressure from peasant and student demonstrations, made strenuous efforts to address the inequitable conditions

in the countryside. It established a committee with the authority to real-
locate land, to investigate grievances of landless farmers, and to arrest and
detain uncooperative landowners. By September 1974, it had received more
than 53,650 petitions, which stretched the committee beyond its capacities. In the end, the committee was able to address only 3 percent of the
claims, whereby it persuaded landowners to sell back their land to farmers.[20]
The Sanya government subsequently issued an executive order that sought
to strengthen the rights of farmers. The order allowed farmers to farm on
land they had lost or on other land appropriated for them by the government, to regain land lost due to exorbitant interest rates or to foreclosure,
and to occupy land without government retribution. Furthermore, the government announced that it would punish landlords or moneylenders who
had cheated farmers, would not allow landlords to transfer their rights over
lands that had been seized, and would grant land to the poorest farmers on
a cooperative basis.[21]

In September 1974, the Sanya government established the Farmers' Aid
Fund, which reserved 80 percent of revenue from the rice premium to support farmers and stabilize prices of farm products. The rice premium was a
tax used to lower the price of rice for export paid to farmers so as to reduce
the cost of food to the urban sector. For the first time, revenue from the
export tax on rice was redistributed to farmers. In December 1974, an overwhelming majority in the National Assembly passed the Land Rent Control
Act. This was a landmark bill that granted tenants security of tenure, limited the rent the owner could claim to one crop per year and to one-third
of the rice crop, and provided protection during poor harvests.[22] In January
1975, the legislature under the Sanya government passed a milestone land-
reform bill that allowed for the expropriation of land bigger than fifty *rai*
(twenty acres) through compensation at market value.

The Kukrit government took over in March 1975 and continued the work
begun under Sanya. Kukrit's SAP was a medium-size party, but it included
some Bangkok Bank executives who had ambitious plans for economic development and party building.[23] Realizing the importance of strong institutions as well as of the draw of a programmatic agenda to forge a social base,
these individuals sought to model the SAP on Singapore's People's Action
Party. The SAP developed an extensive reform program that included increases in the minimum wage; full employment within five years; eradication of inflation; the building of twenty thousand public housing units for

low-income workers; free bus transportation for the poor; and most significantly, the Tambon Fund (*ngoen pan*).[24]

The Tambon Fund was the centerpiece of the SAP's reform agenda. The
goal of the program was to disburse funds to the *tambon* councils in the
countryside for local development projects, such as the construction of
roads, irrigation canals, wells, and wooden bridges; the repair and expansion of schools buildings, meeting halls, and health centers; and the installation of electricity lines. The *tambon* is an administrative unit equivalent to
a commune or subdistrict that aggregates a number of nearby villages. The
program was especially intended to help farmers find employment during
the dry season. Besides supporting the rural sector, a larger goal of the program, according to Kukrit, was to "promote decentralization of political authority from the central government to local units of government, thereby
laying the foundation of democracy at the grassroots."[25] The popularity of
this program was evident from the support it received in Parliament. To
initiate the program, Kukrit had to request a special appropriation from
Parliament. This was passed unanimously.[26] In 1975, the program disbursed
Bt2.5 billion ($125 million) to the five thousand tambon councils, and in
1976 this rose to Bt3.4 billion.[27]

The Tambon Fund was intended to go hand in hand with an initiative to
hold regular elections for local leaders and thereby strengthen democracy at
the grass roots.[28] Although the initiative had strong support in two Parliaments, it did not pass because both Parliaments did not last long enough to
have the bill written into law.[29] The first Parliament under Kukrit dissolved
under military pressure, and the second Parliament succumbed to a coup.

The other major initiative of the Kukrit government was to increase the
flow of credit to farmers through the Bank for Agriculture and Agricultural
Cooperatives (BAAC). The bank was established in 1966 to provide con-
cessional credit to farmers, but in 1975 it was given a much heftier role in
supporting the rural sector. The bank was required to increase its portfolio
to Bt3.5 billion from Bt2.65 billion in 1974. Furthermore, the government
required commercial banks to provide the rural sector with 5 percent of
total loans. If they could not do this, they were to deposit the shortfall
with the BAAC.[30] This program helped reduce the dependence of farmers
on informal lenders and radically increased the flow of funds to the rural
sector. One analysis concluded that "the rural credit system was entirely
transformed by this policy."[31]

The Sanya and Kukrit governments pushed social reform the furthest that Thailand had seen until that point. Yet despite the reform efforts and the passage of laws and programs to address the disparities between city and countryside, the livelihoods of the poor did not improve. The greatest obstacle to reform lay at the stage of implementation. The authority of the Sanya and Kukrit governments did not extend far beyond Bangkok.[32] Although a democratic-reformist wind had swept through the capital, it did not reach the bureaucratic functionaries. In the provinces, local bureaucrats, including district officers, village heads, *kamnan* (*tambon* or subdistrict leaders), police, and land registrars resisted substantive change. They had no interest in coordinating with laws coming out of Bangkok, nor could they be compelled to do so. They were tied to local elites or would themselves lose from the implementation of structural reform. Thus, reforms

> stopped at the national level, never really penetrating into the small towns and villages. . . . When it came to implementation, middle- and lower-level bureaucrats, indifferent or opposed to the reforms, failed to carry them out. The reformers' strength was inadequate to compel implementation in the face of such entrenched resistance, and time was far too short to develop a new base of political power.[33]

Unlike Malaysia, there was no synergy between policy makers and policy implementers and no institutional links between the executive and bureaucrats in the periphery.

A policy that required relatively simple disbursal of capital and did not disturb the social order, such as the Tambon Fund, could be achieved on some level.[34] But where a policy required some form of coercion to ensure its implementation, such as the Land Rent Control Act or the Land Reform Act, this could not make headway, as the state did not have the institutional means, and often not the desire, to follow through on the law.[35] Absent in Thailand was a state machinery or party cadres that could use coercion to monitor and enforce law. In both of these major bills, the outcome was not improved land tenure but local elite recalcitrance, harassment of peasants seeking implementation, and manipulation of the law.[36] The primary organization challenging reactionary resistance in the periphery, the Farmers Federation of Thailand, was attacked ruthlessly, with twenty-one leaders in the federation, including its vice president, assassinated.[37]

Although the Land Rent Control Act made clear how rent should be allocated more fairly, in actuality, the decision on the distribution of rent was to be made by the Land Rent Control Committee, made up of government officials, landowners' representatives, and tenants' representatives.[38] The need to go through committees at both the district and the provincial level decreased the chances of implementation according to the stipulated law, as these committees invariably leaned in favor of landlords. Two journalists reporting from the north noted:

> No one interviewed was abiding by the law, nor was anyone they know. . . . The law has yet to be seriously enforced, partially because few tambon committees have been set up to administer it, while those that have are dominated by the kamnan and village headmen who are often landlords themselves. In many cases village headmen refused to even inform villagers of the change in the law.[39]

The failure of the land-reform program was particularly indicative of the limited political will and capacity of the government. Kukrit showed little interest in implementing the bill that had been passed under Sanya's government. Institutionally, land reform never stood much chance. The bill allowed farmers to retain land up to or larger than one thousand *rai* (395 acres) if they could prove they were cultivating it, or if they received government support, or if they were involved in domestic and export markets.[40] These conditions favored wealthy landowners. At the level of implementation, the bill lacked funds to purchase land, required coordination across a fragmented bureaucracy, established subcommittees at the local level that were devoid of farmer participation and dominated by local elites (*kamnan* and *puu yai baan*) who owned land, and did not correlate with the regions that needed it most.[41] Ultimately, the government bought only 88,868 *rai* (35,136 acres) of land from private landowners (of which more than 40 percent was Crown land), and it distributed 34,425 *rai* (13,611 acres) (involving 1,778 households) from public land. Of private land, this was only 4 percent of what the government had planned for land reform.[42]

A larger political problem was that Kukrit himself was not particularly invested in land reform as a means of redistribution. A royalist and a conservative, Kukrit understood the importance of reform, but these reforms had to be gradual ones that did not threaten the social order.[43] His agenda was one of "increasing economic inputs into the rural sector, rather than land-tenure adjustment."[44] His government disbursed Bt2.5 billion to its core program for redistribution, the Tambon Fund, but allocated only Bt45 million for land reform—a difference of more than fifty times.[45] Kukrit's administration also evinced less sympathy (than that of Sanya) for strident farmer demands, rejected their petitions, and repressed the Farmers Federation of Thailand.[46]

WEAK PARTIES

Weak implementation and coordination was fatal to reform, but so was the fecklessness, fragmentation, and questionable political will of the governing parties. In the first place, parties' ability to govern was constrained by a perpetually unstable coalition and a military that continued to exert influence in the background. Kukrit's government survived only thirteen months. When Kukrit's coalition was floundering, the military warned him not to allow a rival, left-leaning coalition to take power.[47] Realizing that such a move could invite a coup, Kukrit dissolved Parliament. The Democrat-led government that followed was on even shakier ground. It lasted six months before being ousted by a coup. Such an environment made it inherently difficult to implement and sustain policy, and to pass legislation that would have to go through numerous debates and changes.[48]

After new elections in April 1976, the Democrat Party took the reins of government. Although the most institutionalized party in terms of both longevity and organizational structure, it was deeply torn in this period between a conservative and a left-leaning faction.[49] To counterbalance the conservative faction's ties to the military,[50] the progressive group began building branches throughout the country to establish deeper roots in society. From 1975 to 1976, this initiative, led by Secretary-General Damrong Lathiphiphat, established sixty-six branches in the central, northern, and northeastern regions.[51] The formation of the branches would strengthen the party horizontally, and an alliance with a powerful pragmatist general, Krit Sivara, would protect the party vertically against other factions in the military.[52] In an extremely fluid environment, the party's strategy to build organizational complexity and external alliances made great sense. However, events on the ground overtook these organizational initiatives. The untimely death of Krit took away the party's key defense against military intervention, and the increasing mass violence and rallies on the streets of Bangkok, culminating in the student massacre at Thammasat University in the early morning of 6 October 1976, overwhelmed any strength that could have been derived from organizational deepening.[53] These efforts at institution building came too late and were no match for right-wing violence.

A larger structural problem in these years of ferment was that the governing parties that were at the center stage of the polity remained too detached from the social groups that clamored for reform.[54] The two leading parties that sought to advance social change, the Democrat Party and the SAP, adopted reform agendas less out of genuine ideological commitment than out of pressure from social groups and concerns for electoral dividends. Although the Democrat Party had a progressive faction, and the SAP had elaborated a sweeping policy platform, these were status quo institutions supportive of liberal democracy, free markets, and a conservative social order. They were not inspired by a social agenda and were reluctant to take the reform movement to its logical conclusion. Thus, the grassroots activism of the National Student Center of Thailand, of the Farmers Federation of Thailand, and of labor unions, was not—and could not be—linked to governing party institutions. These civil society groups were too radical for the governing parties.[55] "There was a wide gap between parties and people," noted Saneh Chamarik, deputy rector of Thammasat University. "The parliamentary system did not express the problems and feelings of the people, and the parties had no real contact with labor unions or farmers' groups."[56]

Yet had some alliance been sought between social groups and political parties, this would have benefited both sides. It would have created a structure for channeling grievances and demands; it perhaps would have moderated demands and strengthened policy coordination; and to the extent that policies were implemented successfully, it would have created a feedback loop that would benefit the governing party.[57] Such an alliance, however, was always a remote possibility. Kukrit's SAP may have been committed to moderate reform, but it was not willing to countenance challenges to the reigning social order from radical farmers and students. In the big picture, intensive social mobilization without institutional linkage and aggregation not only weakened the prospects for reform but also created the optimal conditions for military intervention.

Unlike the United Malays National Organization (UMNO) in Malaysia, the People's Action Party (PAP) in Singapore, or the Vietnamese Communist Party, parties in Thailand lacked organizational complexity, support at the grass roots, and ideological coherence. In the absence of cooperation with the bureaucracy, control over the military, and a long-term time horizon in which to build capacity, the burden on the parties was too high. On one side, they could not satisfy relentless demands for reform, but on the other side, they could not stem the counterreaction by business, military, and the palace. Caught in the middle of restive demands for change and reactionary forces increasingly anxious over the downfall of monarchies in Laos and Cambodia, parties failed in the basic function of state-society intermediation.

Assessing the efforts of the Sanya and Kukrit governments, David Morell and Chai-Anan Samudavanija conclude: "While it was only a modest beginning, in total they constituted the most genuine governmental reform seen to date in Thailand, an awkward attempt to respond to the meaning of the events of October 1973."[58] These three years of democracy and of attempted social reforms broke a long-standing pattern of conservative policy and politics and were therefore of profound importance in Thailand's history. But ultimately, the subaltern classes did not gain from this period because political institutions were weak, fragmented, and conflicted over their commitment to social change. This stands in sharp contrast to the situation in Malaysia, where the dominant party, UMNO, was able to overcome a major social crisis in the late 1960s, thus redirecting the state toward deep-seated reform.

Democratization and the Boom Years

The turmoil and ideological polarization of the 1970s was followed by a period of stability and pragmatism. A rabidly right-wing Supreme Court justice headed the government right after the 1976 coup, but his reactionary fervor soon lost support from centrist generals, who engineered another putsch. An amnesty program then initiated reconciliation with students who had fled to the maquis after the Thammasat massacre. Elections were held again from 1979 to 1988, but the generals retained the prime ministership, first Kriangsak Chomanan and then Prem Tinsulanonda.

In the late 1970s, deteriorating global conditions—the oil price shock, falling commodity prices, and rising interest rates—severely affected the Thai economy. Terms of trade declined sharply, the current account registered a yawning deficit, external debt grew, inflation rose, and budget deficits became more acute. To address these dire economic conditions, the Prem administration in the early 1980s accepted two structural adjustment loans from the World Bank and drew credit from the International Monetary Fund (IMF).[59] The Prem government was successful in tackling the structural imbalances in the economy, and its creditors lauded it as one of the more successful adjustment programs in the 1980s. The 1980 macroeconomic reforms provided economic stability that paved the way for the boom.

In the late 1980s, Thailand's economy took off, registering some of the highest growth rates in the world. From 1985 to 1995, average growth was 9 percent, with three consecutive years of double-digit growth rates. Compared with the 1960s primary commodities boom under Sarit, export-oriented industrialization largely drove this growth. In 1985 and 1986, manufactured exports exceeded primary commodities as a share of gross domestic product (GDP). From 1970 to 1993, agriculture's share of GDP declined from 27 percent to 12 percent, whereas manufacturing rose from 16 percent to 26 percent.[60] Manufactured exports, such as textiles, electronics, jewelry, footwear, vehicles, and toys, contributed heavily to the boom. Despite the shift toward manufacturing, agriculture, particularly agro-processing exports (e.g., canned fish and fruit, broiled chicken), also sustained growth.[61]

A number of factors spurred Thailand's boom. The crisis in the mid-1980s convinced the government to devalue the baht and to take seriously the demands of businesspeople and bankers, as well as World Bank advice, for favorable export-oriented policies. This coincided with the relocation of Japanese, Taiwanese, and Korean firms into Southeast Asia as a result of rising currencies and labor costs. With a devalued baht, cheap land and labor, and relative political stability, Thailand became a magnet for foreign investment. Domestic capital was also crucial for the boom, as Thai firms sought joint-venture opportunities with foreign firms and took advantage of liberalizing policies to acquire technology and diversify their markets in areas such as finance, property, infrastructure, and telecommunications.[62] A drove of rural migrants, estimated around 2 million to 3 million people, formed the basis for cheap labor to work the export industries.[63]

But although Thailand became the economic darling of the 1990s, the negative social and economic consequences of the boom became drastically apparent. Thailand's developmental trajectory in the 1980s and 1990s was conceived of purely in terms of growth rates, investment opportunities, and macroeconomic stability. The Thai economy had clearly found its groove through market-enhancing policies and export-oriented industrialization,

but it gave little consideration to actually molding the country's growth pattern to address the needs of the hinterland. By the early 1990s, Thailand had
the highest income inequality in Southeast Asia. A 1993 World Bank Report
on six East Asian countries noted that Thailand's poverty rate was similar to
Indonesia's, despite its much higher GDP per capita.

Although economic growth raised Thailand's per capita income and created a robust middle class largely based in Bangkok, it did not benefit all
segments of the population. Small-scale farmers, subsistence peasants, forest
dwellers, and informal workers—groups in society who are generally lacking in skills or assets—were left on the margins of development. By one estimate, these groups constitute two-thirds of Thailand's workforce.[64] These
groups have found it exceedingly difficult to reap gains from the economic
boom, and others have had to push back against economic modernization
in an effort to protect their sources of livelihood.

A critical problem in Thailand's developmental trajectory has been the
failure of industrialization to absorb the rural population. Despite the steady
decline in agriculture's share of the economy, at the height of Thailand's
boom, the sector employed two-thirds of the population. Recent figures
show that this has declined to about 40 percent or 50 percent of the population, but this still "is one of the highest proportions found among countries
at a comparable level of development."[65] The source of this problem is low
productivity in the rural sector and an orientation toward capital-intensive,
rather than labor-intensive, manufacturing.[66] The effect has been to sharpen
the divide between those left in the rural sector and those employed in the
modern sector.

With Thailand's economy heating up, the interests of state and business coincided in their quest for maximizing investment opportunities and
boosting growth. The countryside was crucial for this quest, not just in
terms of cheap labor from rural migrants but also increasingly because of the
need for natural resources to propel and sustain the engines of growth. Control over water, forests, and land was critical to generate electrical power, to
transport gas, to plug into lucrative markets for paper and pulp, to build industrial estates, and to deal with industrial waste. Bangkok-centered growth
had to be fed, and the hinterland fulfilled this need perfectly. At times, the
state was the main protagonist, as it constructed dams for electrification,
but at other times, it acted as sponsor, providing concessions to industries
to take over degraded forest land. In the process, state and capital displaced

and repressed the peasantry to make way for the instruments of industrialization. Or as Pasuk Phongpaichit masterfully put it: *amnat* (power in the guise of the state) and *itthipon* (influence in the guise of social forces or business groups) had joined hands to squeeze out the peasant.[67]

This alliance was something new, as Thailand had long been seen as an entrenched "bureaucratic polity" in which the reigning bureaucrats marginalized business. Anek Laothamatas famously claimed that the rise of business meant that a more liberalized polity had sprouted out of the bureaucratic-authoritarian mold. But for the peasantry, there was less to celebrate in the business sector's liberalizing impulse, for in the end, their economic and political position failed to improve in a more open polity. A more pluralistic political environment had surely emerged, but without any increased representation for the poor. Instead, the peasantry found itself constantly engaged in rearguard action to protect its livelihood. The only weapon available to the peasantry to counter *amnat* and *itthipon's* marriage was mass protest.

Unlike in Malaysia, the poor have had no recourse in political institutions. The technocrats in agencies that can be considered "islands of efficiency"— the Ministry of Finance, the Bank of Thailand, the Bureau of the Budget, and the National Economic and Social Development Board (NESDB)— have generally adhered to a conservative macroeconomic model. Technocrats have prioritized monetary stability, fiscal restraint, private enterprise, property rights, and open trade.[68] Although a few technocrats, such as Puey Ungphakorn and Kosit Panpiemras, were deeply concerned about equity, the conservative and market-oriented thrust of these crucial agencies persists until today. The technocratic core of the Thai bureaucracy has therefore been resistant to state intervention that directly attacks inequality.

However, when the state has intervened, it has done so in a repressive manner or in a clientelistic manner, pursuing interests of the private sector. Several economists have noted that the state initially committed the sin of omission and later the sin of commission.[69] A land resettlement program in the 1990s, known as Kho Jo Kor, was allegedly intended to preserve forests, but it used violence in displacing villagers to plant eucalyptus trees in the degraded forests. These trees would bear high yields in the paper and pulp industry. Development projects, such as dams, have been built with claims to improve the quality of life in the periphery, but they have run roughshod over the livelihood of displaced subsistence peasants.

PARTIES UNDER DEMOCRACY

Institutionalized parties are necessary to challenge a conservative bureau-cracy, but Thailand has largely lacked such a resource. Parties in the demo-cratic period followed the pattern of the 1970s. As in the 1970s, the party system remained extremely volatile. From 1979 to 2005, electoral volatility was 36.7—the second highest in Asia, after the Philippines.[70] The effective number of parliamentary parties is also quite high—the highest in Asia. From 1979 to 2005, the average effective number of parliamentary parties was 5.8, and the effective number of parliamentary factions was 21.17.[71] These figures indicate a high degree of fragmentation in the party system. From 1979 to 2001, factional conflict led to the downfall of at least five of eleven governments.[72] Parties rose and fell in factions' battle for spoils rather than because of any struggles over principle. Programs were devised purely for the purpose of elections in boilerplate fashion by professors and business associates who served as party advisers. Personalism pervaded the party system, with virtually every party but one (the Democrat Party) driven by a leader's charisma and political skills rather than by organiza-tional and ideological imperatives. Parties constantly switched in and out of coalitions, such that cabinets in the 1990s lasted an average of only nine months. Party identity had no meaning. It "was governed not by conviction but prediction—which party would be part of the next ruling coalition and thus worth joining."[73] Unlike in Malaysia, parties lacked continuity, institu-tional complexity, extensive memberships, and roots in society.

In such a fluid institutional environment, political representation of social groups is impossible. The only group effectively represented within parties was business. As Chai-Anan puts it: "[O]nly the interests of the privileged groups are effectively aggregated by political parties."[74] In the 1975 Parlia-ment, 35 percent of members of Parliament (MPs) were businessmen. This trend continued in the 1980s, with the emergence of provincial capitalists, when business held almost 50 percent of cabinet portfolios.[75] Big business from Bangkok and the provinces gained complete control of Chat Thai and SAP, and began to exert greater influence even within the Democrat Party.[76]

The only exception to the feckless party system is the Democrat Party. The Democrat Party is the most institutionalized in Thailand, with inter-nal democratic procedures, branches across the country, a relatively strong membership, and consistent support in parts of the country, especially the

south and Bangkok. It is also the only party in Thailand in which the institution supersedes the individual. Unlike most other parties, the fate of the
Democrat Party does not hinge on any one leader. Although the party has
faced problems in organizational development, in the context of the Thai
party system, it has greater cohesiveness, adaptability, and complexity than
any other party.[77]

Yet the Democrat Party is ideologically conservative, with minimal interest in social reform.[78] Its origins are royalist and aristocratic, and much
of its fighting spirit came from opposing Pridi Bhanomyong and his leftist
agenda. Since the 1970s, the party has moved in a more liberal direction,
recruiting young intellectuals, businesspeople, and lawyers and establishing links with social groups, such as students, traders, and Muslims.[79] But
despite this shift, the party has consistently supported the status quo. It
claims to be a bedrock of democratic values, but its record in opposing the
military is rather tame.[80] The party also has a strong affinity with conservative bureaucratic values. In Sungsidh Piriyarangsan's view, the Democrats
have a "bias towards regularly pleasing bureaucrats."[81] As exemplified by the
longtime leader Chuan Leekpai, the party operates in a traditional bureaucratic mode.

The Democrat Party's policy agenda has generally leaned toward laissez-
faire capitalism, fiscal restraint, and strict adherence to the rule of law. From
1992 to 1995, when the party was in power, it initiated some pro-poor initiatives, including land reform to settle peasants who had been squatting
in state forests. But the end result of these programs simply reinforced the
elitist basis of the party. The Democrat MP for Phuket, who was the secretary to the head of the Agricultural Land Reform Office and had a seat
on the provincial committee in charge of recommending land distribution,
used her position to dole out land rights to her relatives. Her husband,
also a provincial councilor, was given ninety-eight *rai* (thirty-nine acres)
of land, and her father was given thirty-seven *rai* (fifteen acres). This land-
reform scandal brought an end to the Democrat government. The party
came back to power during the financial crisis in 1997 and worked assidu-
ously to prop up the financial sector. It was perceived to be a lackey of the
IMF and gained the ire of the rural sector when it tore apart a deal, negotiated by the previous government, to compensate thousands of villagers who
had been displaced by dams. The party's tendency has been to dismiss any
pro-poor demonstrations, claiming that such acts go against the rule of law.

Disdainful of rampant corruption among rival parties and proud of its institutional heritage, the Democrat Party remains deeply antagonistic toward pro-poor reform.

The right-wing Chat Thai, in comparison to the Democrat Party, exemplifies Thailand's clientelistic parties. If Chat Thai has any discernible agenda, it appears to be the growth of the free market and the pursuit of rents through the control of cabinet seats.[82] Its ideology has been one of reactionary conservatism "opposing socialism, communism, and anything leftist."[83] Initially known as the "generals' party," its founding members, Pramarn Adireksarn and Chatichai Choonhavan, were son-in-law and son, respectively, of Phin Choonhavan, a powerful military general in the 1950s.[84] Parmarn and Chatichai were both former generals, who then made their fortune as textile tycoons. The party evolved from its close links to the military to become the übersymbol of a capitalist party interested in capturing public office for private interests.[85] Chatichai's government was known as the "buffet cabinet,"[86] whereas Banharn Silpa-archa, who became leader in 1992 and took the party in a more provincial orientation, was famous for the statement that "being in opposition is like starving yourself to death."[87]

In the 1990s, two parties sought to break from the party system's clientelist mold, but in the long run, they were swept away by the inexorable tendencies of the Thai party system: one collapsed, and the other was absorbed by the new giant on the block, Thai Rak Thai (TRT). The case of Palang Dharma (Moral Force) is instructive in terms of the challenges of party building and programmatic agendas in Thailand. The party emerged in the late 1980s with great hopes for a "new Thai politics."[88] Unlike most parties, it elaborated an ideological vision of moral principle based on Buddhist values,[89] expressed a serious commitment to fighting both corruption and vote buying,[90] operated internally through democratic procedures,[91] and made serious efforts at building a mass-based organization. Its main Bangkok office had more than thirty staff members, as well as an eight-member policy and planning team that coordinated with its elected members.[92] In half the provinces around the country, it established branches that were active yearlong in relaying to the center issues of importance at the local level, in recruiting candidates, and in publishing its activities in the party's quarterly newsletter. The party even operated a "political engineering school" that sought to engage and mobilize individuals interested in the party's program.[93] By 1995, the party had eighty thousand members.[94] Standing out from the crowd of feckless parties, Palang Dharma dominated politics in Bangkok, sweeping parliamentary and local seats in the early 1990s.

Yet within a decade of its founding, the party had disintegrated. Despite some degree of organizational complexity, Palang Dharma was riven by numerous factions to the point that it lacked any coherent vision except that of its charismatic leader, the general-turned-ascetic Chamlong Srimuang. But Chamlong was ultimately less interested in building a strong party than an ethical movement centered on himself. He incessantly played the religious and pragmatic factions of the party against each other and constantly interfered with democratic procedures in the selection of executive members. Furthermore, while elected party members attempted to fulfill the party agenda, the party itself did not coordinate effectively, for example, ignoring field reports from Bangkok district councilors.[95] When Palang Dharma joined the governing coalition led by the übercapitalist-clientelist Chat Thai, all of its moral sheen faded away. Having erupted onto the political scene with high hopes of party building through strong organization and ideology, Palang Dharma found itself trapped within the same structural constraints under which almost all Thai parties labored: burdened by personalism, bloodied by factionalism, and compromised by coalitional alliances based on short-term interest rather than principle.[96]

The New Aspiration Party (Phak Khwam Wang Mai, or NAP) was another effort to break through the traditional mold of the party system. Although the party was to serve as the vehicle for General Chavalit Yongchaiyudh's quest for the prime ministership, it advanced an agenda of organizational complexity that was lacking in other parties. The party sought to recruit one million members; to build branches across the country; and like Indonesia's Golkar, to "recreate the hierarchies, command structures, and certainties of military life."[97] The initial efforts seemed promising, as the party employed eighty staff members at its Bangkok headquarters in preparation for its first election.[98] Furthermore, the party recruited young, committed leftist reformists, who made sincere efforts to address the plight of poor villagers in the northeast, particularly on the issue of the Pak Mun Dam. Under Chavalit's government, the cabinet approved a major reform package for the rural poor that provided them land rights and livelihood security.

However, in most respects, the NAP was not a stark change from the traditional mold of the party system. Its party-building efforts resulted largely from absorbing patronage-type MPs, including the powerful northeastern faction of Sanoh Thientong, whereas numerous party branches were simply houses or offices of their MPs, therefore lacking institutional identity separate from the individual MPs. Its membership level was in actuality significantly below its 1 million mark, at around three hundred thousand.[99] The NAP eventually became associated more with its provincial, clientelist types, who provided the party its margin of victory in 1996. As it went into decline, it folded into TRT in 2002, thereby replicating the trend of rapid life and death in the Thai party system.

Prospects for Reform

In this period when economic liberalization and gradual democratization shaped Thailand's political economy, the weakness of political parties and the conservative nature of the bureaucracy hindered social reform. However, two exceptions should be noted. One emerged from reformist elements within the bureaucracy, whereas the other emerged from a broad coalition led by Chat Thai. In the National Economic and Social Development Board (NESDB), bureaucrats in the mid-1980s had begun to question the excessive growth orientation of the Thai economy.[100] In the Fifth Plan (1982–86), a pro-poor program based on the basic-needs approach classified poor and non-poor areas and identified the 12,555 poorest villages in thirty-seven provinces as immediate targets of developmental programs. Initiated by the head of the agency, Kosit Panpiemras, it sought to increase infrastructure and employment opportunities in the rural sector. The NESDB began to seek greater popular input in its plans.[101] This was most evident in the Eighth Plan (1997–2001), whose drafting was opened up to nongovernmental organization (NGO) activists, community leaders, monks, academics, and businesspeople. The goal was a "people-centered development" that would "move away from the top-down approach practiced by the public sector in the past."[102] However, some economists have questioned the relevance of the NESDB plans for actual policy implementation.[103]

Another pro-poor initiative came, surprisingly, from the right-wing Chat Thai, led by Chatichai. This was the decision to push for a Social Security Act (SSA). Chatichai's support for the SSA was partly a gesture of gratitude to labor for having supported him in defeating General Prem and becoming in 1988 the first elected prime minister since the 1970s. Though of great significance, the passage of the bill did not reflect any pro-poor agenda within the party or from Chatichai himself. The process that led to the SSA was "ad hoc rather than institutionalized"[104]—a combination of an alliance among labor, parties, business, and reform-minded bureaucrats coming together during a more open democratic setting.[105] The implementation phase was languid. After the passage of the act, only one full-time member was assigned to prepare the social security infrastructure.[106] One analyst of the SSA noted the disparity between the actual vote and the enforcement of the legislation: "[W]hile the *vote* for the SSA, covered by all media was considered useful for political purposes, the *enforcement* demands a lot of financial and personal resources and, above all, a reliable and efficient administration."[107]

The most forceful challenge to Thailand's pattern of development, however, came in 2000 from an unlikely figure, Thaksin Shinawatra, the country's richest tycoon. In a sharp challenge to the governing Democrat Party and to the conservative norms of the Thai party system, a new party called Thai Rak Thai led by Thaksin proposed, in the lead-up to the 2001 elections, a sweeping package of social reforms, including a debt moratorium program for farmers; the One-Million-Baht Village Fund, which echoed the SAP's Tambon Fund of the 1970s; a universal health-care program; and numerous other schemes. The scale of the reforms was unprecedented.

The Asian Financial Crisis in 1997 played a crucial role in Thaksin's reform program. The loss of income of workers and professionals, the forced return of many Bangkok workers to the countryside, and the perceived capitulation of the governing Democrat Party to global financiers and liberal international institutions generated a strong social response.[108] Thaksin saw the opening and masterfully took it. As Chuan's Democrat Party sought to steer the economy out of the crisis, it followed closely the IMF's prescription, including allowing businesses to fail, aggressively raising interest rates, and cutting social spending. Thaksin thus entered the fray by juxtaposing his dynamic, entrepreneurial, and nationalistic vision to the plodding and bureaucratic approach of Chuan. The party's slogan *"khit mai, tham mai"* (think new, act new) said it all.

As Thaksin began to cultivate the rural sector, the Democrat Party continued to dismiss it. It showed minimal interest in the myriad problems of the rural countryside, which ranged from agricultural debt to livelihood displacement due to dams and other development projects. The government tore up a compromise package with many villagers displaced by a major dam that had been negotiated with the previous Chavalit government, arguing that there were no longer any funds for it. In December 2000, farmer groups in the country's northeast vowed to "drive the Democrats to extinction" in the next elections because of what the villagers saw as the Democrats' lack of concern for their interests.[109]

Taking advantage of the increasing anger of rural organizations against the Chuan government, Thaksin conferred with pro-poor NGOs and brought into his party prominent intellectuals, NGO leaders, and leftists from the 1970s. "While the Chuan government had worked closely with the bureaucracy to suppress grassroots protest and dissent," write Duncan McCargo and Ukrist Pathmanand, "Thai Rak Thai sought to enlist support from the popular sector."[110] In August 2000, TRT unveiled its populist platform. The package was populist in three ways: it articulated a radical, albeit indirect, critique of the status quo; it forged a direct, top-down relationship between Thaksin and the populace; and it was undergirded by a multiclass coalition with the rural sector at the core. Unlike classic populism in Latin America, which was mostly urban based, Thaksin's populist platform was notable for its focus on the rural classes.[111] To respond to what was emerging as a TRT electoral onslaught, other parties somewhat desperately decided to be pro-poor, too. The New Aspiration Party devised a slogan, "To help a tree grow we have to water its roots. To revive the country we must help the poor," and Chat Thai came up with "Reform thoroughly to solve the country's problems."[112]

In the January 2001 elections, TRT won 248 seats in Parliament, just 2 shy of an outright majority. Moreover, TRT dominated northern Thailand and won half of the seats in the northeast—the country's two poorest regions. By absorbing the small Seritham Party soon after the election, and then taking in the medium-size New Aspiration and Chat Phattana parties, TRT ballooned into an even more dominant force. By 2002, TRT had established a grand coalition—something unseen in previous Parliaments.[113] Within a few months of taking over government, it began to roll out its policy reforms. In 2005, TRT achieved an even more punishing electoral victory, controlling almost four-fifths of the seats in Parliament.

Thus, TRT had shaken the polity and the party system through its electoral dominance. It held on to one full four-year parliamentary term, was hegemonic in Parliament, began penetrating and restructuring the bureaucracy, and had overwhelming support in the rural sector and a mandate for change from virtually all sectors of society. No party in Thailand's history had achieved any of these feats. On some level, the party was thus a new phenomenon. It was programmatic despite its populist catchall aura, was relatively cohesive and could discipline the numerous factions within the party, had some degree of organizational complexity with branches throughout the country, and had roots in society through an expanding membership and party leaders and policy makers who came from the popular sector.[114]

At the same time, however, TRT relied heavily on absorbing traditional clientelistic factions to quickly win elections; membership and branches were largely superficial with minimal feedback from the grass roots and few functional activities at the branch level; and most of all, the party was heavily dependent on its founder, financier, and charismatic leader, Thaksin. In terms of adaptability, the party lacked a system for institutionalized leadership change, unlike its rival, the Democrat Party. This was evident in the difficulty deputy party leader Chaturong Chaisaeng experienced in holding together what remained of the party following the 2006 coup and subsequent court ruling that eliminated TRT. In summary, it is probably correct to conclude that the party "represented a synthesis of the old and the new."[115]

The remainder of this chapter looks more closely at a few policy arenas—rural debt, dams, and health care—that relate to equitable development and have also seen the active involvement of TRT. We examine these policies in a larger context before TRT intervened and assess the role of TRT in each of them.

Rural Debt

Rural debt has been a perennial problem in Thailand. The problem originates from farmers' engagement with commercial agriculture and the consequent need to use cash for a multitude of inputs that aid productivity.[116] The purchase of inputs requires farmers to borrow at exorbitant rates from informal lenders—on the order of 25 percent to 60 percent—thereby setting themselves on the path to debt.[117] The inability to pay back this debt has been a prime cause of increasing landlessness, particularly in the central region.[118] At the same time, farmers have had a hard time borrowing from institutional lenders because of their inability to provide collateral. This is in part because many farmers do not have land titles, but even more because those farmers who do have land titles issued by the Land Reform Office cannot use them for land sales or mortgages.[119]

Until the mid-1970s, the amount of rural credit was miniscule. In 1974, agricultural credit was only 2 percent, or Bt1.3 billion, of total commercial bank credit. The Bank for Agriculture and Agricultural Cooperatives (BAAC) level of credit was also small, at Bt2.7 billion.[120] In 1975, as part of the SAP platform, commercial banks were required to raise the level of agricultural loans to 5 percent of their total portfolio. The level of loans was gradually increased, stabilizing at 11 percent. Before the Thaksin government came to power, the BAAC accounted for 48 percent of formal credit; commercial banks, 46 percent; and agricultural cooperatives, 6 percent.[121]

Notwithstanding the increased infusion of capital into the rural sector since the mid-1970s, farmers remained deeply mired in debt in the 1990s. Recent estimates put the number of families in debt at 4.7 million (out of about 5.7 million farming families). Debt in the northeast and north is around Bt30,000–40,000 per household, and in the central plains it is highest, at about Bt60,000 per household.[122] The problems are manifold, but one of the most important is that institutional credit has bypassed the poorest farmers and been directed to medium- and large-scale operators. This has ensured that informal lenders, with their higher interest rates, retain a critical position in the rural credit market.[123] A survey in the mid-1980s in Nakhon Ratchasima showed that the richest farmers borrowed from commercial banks, medium-income farmers borrowed from the formal (BAAC especially) and informal sectors, and the poorest farmers borrowed from the informal sector only or did not borrow.[124]

One response to the debt crisis in the central plains has been to employ alternative agriculture methods by planting pesticide-free crops.[125] This enables farmers to exit the debt cycle by reducing the need for purchasing inputs, such as chemicals.[126] Nongovernmental organizations have been at the forefront of this shift and have gained support from the NESDB, as seen in the Eighth and Ninth Plans; they also have received funding from the Chavalit government.[127] In 1997, King Bhumibol Adulyadej's annual speech advocating a "self-sufficient economy" further legitimized this move.[128]

The 2001 elections scrambled the dilemma of rural debt with Thaksin's campaign pledge to establish a three-year moratorium on debt repayment.

The debt moratorium plan (DMP) focused on increasing farmers' disposable income and stimulating rural purchasing power.[129] It concentrated its efforts on small-scale farmers who had nonperforming loans with the BAAC. These farmers would join one of two programs, debt suspension (*phak chamra nii*) or debt relief (*lot phara nii*), and would receive advice on farm production.[130] The three-year moratorium was meant to give farmers space to start crop production cycles, sell their products, and slowly reduce their debt.[131] Although senior officials at the BAAC vociferously opposed the policy,[132] farmers across the country greeted it with euphoria. Before the program could be coordinated and implemented, farmers had already announced their intention to stop repaying their debts to the BAAC.[133] The DMP was launched three months after TRT won the election, in April 2001; 2.3 million farmers signed on to the program within three years of the program's launch, of whom approximately 1.17 million entered for debt suspension and 1.14 million for debt restructuring, for a total of about 2.31 million.[134]

How effective has Thaksin's rural initiative been? The evidence is quite mixed. A number of studies show general improvements in the conditions of farmers, but most studies also show that levels of debt have actually increased. One early analysis of the DMP using panel data collected from 2001 and 2003 concluded that in terms of changes in consumption, asset accumulation, and savings of the participating households, the program had fallen short of its objectives.[135] By contrast, a comprehensive study by a research institute at Thammasat University provided much more positive data on the DMP.[136] Based on surveys and focus groups in eight provinces throughout the country conducted toward the end of the three-year program,[137] the study showed that overall the DMP had led to increased income, increased savings, a positive cash flow, and an improved asset-to-debt ratio (see Table 6-1).[138] One key assessment of the study was that a livelihood training program (*khrongan sattham chiwit khong kasetakon*) under the DMP had been particularly useful in improving the conditions of farmers.[139] Government documents confirmed the positive impact of the DMP on farmers' savings.[140]

However, on the specific issue of debt, the data (with one exception) generally indicate that rural debt has actually increased.[141] This is particularly clear in the Thammasat report, where most indicators trend positive with the exception of debt.[142] The study concluded that the program was

TABLE 6-1
Thailand, Survey Data from Debt Moratorium Program, 2004 (percentage)

Issues	Increased	Same	Declined
Income	47.9	29.6	22.5
Savings	46.4	41.8	11.8
Asset-to-debt ratio	52.2	40.9	7.0
Debt	53.7	28.7	17.7

SOURCE: Thammasat University 2004: 142, 144, 147, 152.

successful, but it raised doubts as to the ability of farmers to effectively save and deal with their debt.[143] Other local sources also confirmed rising debt in the countryside.[144] Furthermore, continued protests a year after the program had been implemented by groups of farmers demanding that the state take over farmers' debt through a rehabilitation fund raised questions about the program's effectiveness.[145] Nonetheless, numerous parties, including the Democrat Party, continued to advocate debt moratorium programs after the Thaksin government was ousted in a coup in September 2006.[146]

Dam Building and Peasant Displacement

The construction of dams in Thailand dates to the first five-year plan in the 1960s, but it was in the 1980s that conflicts became acute. The first major struggle over dams centered on the Nam Choan Dam, a dam that was being planned in the mid-1980s in a large forest reserve in Kanchanaburi Province in western Thailand. The dam was intended to feed electricity into Bangkok, but critics claimed that it would flood the forest reserve, lead to adverse climatic effects, and deplete fish and riverine resources. A broad civil society coalition—local community groups, professors and students, NGOs, scientists at the Forestry Department, and some prominent politicians, including former Prime Minister Kukrit—rallied to defeat the project.[147] Although significant, the campaign's success was based largely on the emergence of an ad hoc coalition concerned with environmental repercussions rather than an institutionalized structure focused on social reform. Instead of parties playing an instrumental role in the campaign, they "played an initially insignificant and later an opportunistic role, most waiting until popular opposition was overwhelming before coming out publicly against the dam."[148]

Another struggle over a controversial dam erupted in the late 1980s and persisted for more than a decade. This battle ended on a less successful note than that of Nam Choan. The Pak Mun Dam, located on the Mun River in the northeastern corner bordering Laos, about three and a half miles upstream from the Mekong River, has been the most controversial dam constructed in Thailand and has been the focus of protests and resistance since its inception. The chief purpose of the Pak Mun Dam was to address the increasing peak demand for electricity in the northeast during the economic boom of the late 1980s, especially during the dry months. The project was initiated under the Chatichai government and completed in 1994 under the Democrat Party–led government.

The dam's impact on villagers' livelihood was severe and extensive. Most villagers around the Mun River are subsistence peasants who rely on fishing and the raising of crops and foraging in forests by the river. The loss of fish and land, such as swamps, wetland forests, cultivation strips, and paddy fields, had a drastic effect on their livelihood.[149] The total number of households directly displaced by the Pak Mun Dam was 1,700. By April 1999, 6,202 households had been awarded some degree of compensation for loss of livelihood from the impact on fisheries.[150] In total, the dam affected more than twenty thousand villagers around the Mun River.

Initially, protests centered on just compensation. But these protests yielded minimal gains at an extremely slow pace. The central problem was that villagers lacked political representation. The state agency in charge of the dam, the Electricity Generating Authority of Thailand (EGAT), was able to co-opt local officials, the subdistrict leaders (*kamnan*), and the village headmen (*phu yai baan*) through material incentives.[151] Furthermore, it employed a divide-and-conquer strategy among villagers by enticing some with money and by supplying blatant disinformation on the effects of the dam.[152] The committees formed to address compensation packages were composed of local elites and EGAT supporters, with villagers opposed to the dam shut out.[153]

Compensation packages were inconsistent and difficult to implement. For example, a group of villagers directly affected by dam construction was promised new housing, land for agriculture, and money. In fact, however, some villagers were not given land; for others, the land was unsuitable for agriculture; and for others, the houses were too small and drinking water was inaccessible.[154] Some villagers, upon receiving money, realized this was not enough to buy land titles, so they moved to the forest reserve, where they were more likely to make a living. Upon moving to the reserve, they were labeled "encroachers" on state land.[155]

After years of lobbying for fair compensation, villagers decided to push for the complete decommissioning of the dam. In March 1996, the Assembly of the Poor (AOP, or Samacha Khon Jon), an umbrella organization of NGOs that had been the primary backer of the villagers, held its first major rally for twenty-six days at Government House. About ten thousand villagers joined the monthlong protest. Prime Minister Banharn Silpa-archa of the Chat Thai Party initially equivocated about meeting the protesters but then agreed to some concessions, including granting land rights documents to all who could prove claims to land, allowing some to lease land at low prices, providing compensation for victims of nearby Sirindhorn Dam, and suspending all future dam construction. These were significant concessions, but they did not last, because Banharn's government collapsed in November 1996 amid factional rivalries and allegations of corruption.

In 1997, a ninety-nine-day protest in Bangkok put more pressure on the new government of Chavalit Yongchaiyudh and the New Aspiration Party.[156] In part because Chavalit was a native of the northeast, he appeared more willing to address the villagers' grievances. Chavalit assigned a group of young reform-minded deputy ministers, including Chaturon Chaisaeng and Adisorn Piangket, to negotiate with the villagers. These young ministers made a genuine effort to give the villagers a fair hearing. At one of the meetings in March, the discussion centered on the need to clearly assess the impact of the dam on peasants' livelihood. The Fisheries Department and EGAT claimed that the quantity of fish and the income from fishing had remained stable or even increased since the dam's construction. The NGO representatives responded that their interviews with fishermen indicated that the opposite had occurred and that fishermen's own testimony should be considered expert information.[157] An official from the Irrigation Department then became irate, complaining that "every time the state builds something people always complain to the government, or EGAT, or us. First, we should consider whether this group of people have a right to petition or not. If you accept that they do, then second, is their petition plausible?"[158]

Deputy Minister for Science Adisorn replied: "Here in Thailand everyone has the right to petition. It's part of our democratic system. You probably shouldn't ask such questions. People have a right to petition directly to the government, because I'm well aware that district officials cover things up, or even EGAT covers things up."[159]

On 11 April 1997, Chavalit's cabinet agreed to a sweeping resolution that included measures to protect villagers' lands, compensation for villagers affected by dams and reforestation programs, and a pledge to listen to local opinion before initiating construction on other projected dams. But with the Asian financial crisis then burning down Thailand's economy, Chuan's Democrat Party took charge in November 1997 and summarily revoked the resolutions of the previous cabinet. In March 2000, the siege of Bangkok's government intensified with more than three thousand villagers setting up permanent camps outside Government House.[160] When the Chuan government ignored the recommendation of a government committee to open the sluice gates, 225 protesters scaled the walls of Government House but were beaten back by police.[161]

Despite the AOP's ability to keep the plight of the villagers in the media spotlight, the Chuan government did not budge. Chuan refused to meet the protesters, accusing them of being manipulated by a "third hand" (meaning foreign NGOs). Instead, he focused his attention on rescuing banks and financial companies drowning in debt in the financial crisis. One AOP leader summarized the different prime ministers thus: "Chuan just did not want to talk to us. He was just too conservative. Banharn was a little better. At least he accepted we have a case in principle. But nothing came of it. In the end, he's just a wealthy businessman. Chavalit has done more. He has gotten down to details."[162]

Thaksin Shinawatra's resounding victory in the January 2001 polls was greeted as a positive harbinger in the struggle against the dam. Thaksin pledged to have the sluice gates opened on a trial basis for four months during the rainy season to see whether there would be a significant increase in the stock of fish. In contrast to the plodding, legalistic style of Chuan, Thaksin made good work of his campaign slogan of *"khit mai, tham mai"* (think new, act new). He appeared extremely responsive to the demands of the AOP, and he personally met with the protesters camped outside Government House on 10 February 2001, one day after officially becoming prime minister.

However, protests resumed when the cabinet voted in October 2001 to maintain the four-month opening of the gates rather than a year-round opening. Although the opening of the gates for four months led to the return of 184 species of fish and to the rise of the average yearly household income from Bt3,045 to Bt10,025, this was still significantly less than what the fishermen earned before the construction of the dam, estimated to be a yearly income of Bt25,742.[163]

On 20 December 2002, Thaksin convened a televised conference at Government House. The critical moment in this conference was the report of the Ubon Ratchatani University research team. This team had been commissioned by the government and for the first time officially recommended that the gates be opened permanently. Until then, the report from this research group had limited itself to the more modest task of assessing the costs and benefits of four possible scenarios. The shift in the opinion of the rector of Ubon Ratchatani University was crucial. Prakob Virojanakuj had earlier agreed with the cabinet decision to keep the gates open for four months, but at the conference, he surprised many by calling for the decommissioning of the dam: "The university is in favor of helping the people to solve their problems once and for all by opening the dam sluice gates year-round. This is because EGAT can solve the technical problems, but the villagers cannot change their way of life. Their only mistake was that they were born poor and lacking opportunities. Every party will win (if the dam gates are opened). EGAT wins by helping the government solve the longstanding Pak Mun problem. What the villagers will get, however, is only what they have lost. Nothing more."[164]

On 15 January 2003, Thaksin decided not to repeal the cabinet decision of 1 October 2002 and thus to allow the gates to be open for only four months of the year. The compromise currently remains in place to keep the sluice gates open for four months of the year.

Health-Care Reform

Compared with rural development, the health-care system in Thailand has achieved relatively positive results in terms of access and delivery for the poor. Although government expenditures and resources are heavily skewed toward the interests of the middle and upper classes, in the area of preventive health care, Thailand has done relatively well. The government has

TABLE 6-2
Thailand, Basic Health Statistics, 2000

Statistics	Rates
Infant mortality rate	33.0 per 1,000 live births
Life expectancy	Female, 74.9; male, 69.9
Bed: population	1:454
Doctor: population	1:3,427
Dentist: population	1:14,917
Nurse: population	1:870

SOURCE: Thailand, Ministry of Public Health 2002: 23–25.

reduced malnutrition, provided vaccines for preventable communicable diseases, improved maternal and child health conditions, and eliminated parasitic diseases resulting from poor sanitation. By the mid-1990s, immunization covered more than 80 percent of the population, leading to substantial declines in morbidity. Fewer than 7 percent of school children exhibit any sign of malnutrition, and attendance for prenatal, partum, and postpartum care is greater than 95 percent (see Table 6-2).[165]

GEOGRAPHICAL DISTRIBUTION

The two central problems of the health system in terms of inequality have centered on geographical distribution and coverage.[166] Medical resources have historically been concentrated in the Bangkok area. Although the Ministry of Public Health has strenuously sought to lure medical personnel to the provinces through a generous package of incentives, most doctors and nurses prefer to remain in the capital. In 2002, the ratio of doctors to population in Bangkok was twenty-four times that of the lowest-ranked province, Si Sa Ket in the northeast.[167]

By every important criterion in the health system, the central region and Bangkok dominate—even in the distribution of health center personnel, which focuses on primary care (see Table 6-3). In the national budget allocation, the central region overwhelms the northeast. The northeast's allocation per capita is the lowest among all regions and is less than half that of the central region (see Table 6-4). In looking at the Health Achievement

TABLE 6-3
Thailand, Geographical Distribution of Medical Personnel and Services, 2000: Personnel and Services-to-Population Ratio

	Bangkok	Central	Northeast	North	South
Doctors	1:793	1:3,576	1:8,311	1:4,501	1:5,194
Nurses	1:309	1:825	1:1,702	1:908	1:884
Health center personnel	N/A	1:1,059	1:1,666	1:1,292	1:1,141
Health centers[a]	N/A	1:3,631	1:4,930	1:4,132	1:3,896
Hospital beds	1:202	1:369	1:766	1:493	1:494

SOURCE: Thailand, Ministry of Public Health 2002: 251, 274, 278, 287, 295.
[a]Data for 2001.

TABLE 6-4
Thailand, Allocation of Health Budget per Capita, by Region, 1999 (in baht)

Region	Health budget per capita
Central	768
East	396
West	454
North	367
Northeast	328
South	409

SOURCE: Thailand, Ministry of Public Health 2002: 340.

Index (HAI) developed by the UN Development Programme (UNDP) and the NESDB, we see that of the twenty-four lowest-performing provinces in terms of health, exactly half are located in the northeast, and of the seven worst-performing provinces, four are in the northeast.[168]

However, recent trends have shown some reduction in disparity between the regions. In 1979 the doctor-to-population ratio in Bangkok was 1:1,210, whereas in the northeast it was a staggering difference of 1:25,713. The proportion of the northeast's to Bangkok's ratio was 21.3. Twenty years later, although the northeast still lags behind, the proportion between the two was 10.5.[169]

The imbalance between the regions is also reflected in the inefficient way in which regional hospitals are designated.[170] Regional hospitals are designated to provide services for a population beyond the province in which the hospital is situated. Therefore, regional hospitals should logically be spread out so as to widen their span over broader areas. Instead, a significant number of hospitals concentrated in the central region and the Eastern Seaboard have been designated regional hospitals. For example, Bangkok, Chonburi, Rayong, and Chantaburi all have regional hospitals, yet the distance between each city is relatively minimal. By contrast, in the northeast there is only one regional hospital for a much larger span of territory. This also means that the workload for a regional hospital in the Eastern Seaboard is less than average given the responsibilities that such a type of hospital should shoulder, whereas that of a regional hospital in the northeast is greater than average.

TARGETING VERSUS UNIVERSAL COVERAGE

Until 2001, health insurance in Thailand was divided into four programs: Social Security (SS), Civil Servants Medical Benefits (CSMB), a five-hundred-baht health card, and a low-income scheme. The latter two programs were meant to cover the poor. The low-income scheme was a free medical card that was established in 1976. The health card was introduced in 1983 to provide an alternative to the low-income scheme, which was relatively unpopular because of the way it stigmatized the poor and because the poor did not receive fair and courteous treatment under that scheme.[171] The health card costs Bt500—a relatively low price, but high enough to distinguish it from the low-income scheme, whose lack of cost has ensured poor medical service.

Although by 2001, a total of 34 million people, or about 52 percent of the population, were covered in the low-income scheme (22 million) and through the health card (12 million), major inconsistencies and gaps riddled the health-insurance system.[172] The CSMB scheme, though it comprised only 12 percent of the population, retained the highest allocation in the budget, along with a wide range of coverage and benefits. The SS scheme under the Ministry of Labor and Social Welfare had the second-highest allocation. In 1999, the health card and the low-income program had a budget of only Bt273 per person per year and had limited benefits.[173] These differences in financial allocation and benefits highlight the disparities in coverage.

Even beyond the inequities in the system, the premise of the low-income scheme is based on the idea of targeting, in other words, of identifying the poor and then supplying them with a card. This, however, feeds into and reinforces the patron-client system because the ministry can target the poor only through the recommendation of the village committee, where the influence of the village head (*phu yai baan*) and subdistrict (*tambon*) head (*kamnan*) is decisive. As a result, there is leakage toward relatives and friends of the village and *tambon* leaders. The ministry has attempted to overcome this problem by asking health personnel, teachers, and monks to join the village committee overseeing the distribution of health cards for the poor, thereby limiting the authority of the village and tambon leaders. Yet the results are clear: only one-third of the poor were able to access this card.[174]

Service for the poor under the low-income scheme has also been mediocre. The poor must first go to the primary health-care unit, known as a health center, before they can visit a hospital. However, the health centers provide low-quality health care, as most of the staff are paramedics. It has therefore been difficult to convince the poor that the state was providing them good medical service.[175]

THAKSIN'S REFORMS: THE THIRTY-BAHT UNIVERSAL HEALTH-CARE POLICY

In April 2001, the insurance system was revamped with a thirty-baht policy (also known as the Gold Card, or Bat Thong). This policy was the centerpiece of Thaksin's social reforms. This insurance program provides universal coverage to all Thai citizens at the cost of only Bt30 (less than US$1) for almost any medical service. It replaced the low-income program and the five-hundred-baht health card with the aim of providing more standardized, high-quality medical service for the poor. The scheme's primary goal was to provide universal health care coverage at a minimal fee. Other goals of the scheme included increasing per capita funding for the medical needs of the poor, emphasizing primary health care while keeping costs low, rebalancing funding toward provincial hospitals, and having a single benefit package and standard of quality for all Thai citizens.[176]

The Thirty-Baht Health-Care Program was a milestone in Thailand's policy reforms for the poor. In terms of expanding coverage, the thirty-baht

TABLE 6-5
Thailand, Medical Coverage, before 2001 to 2008 (million)

	Pre-2001	2002	2005	2008
Low-income scheme (So.Po.Ro)	22	N/A	N/A	N/A
500-baht health card	12	N/A	N/A	N/A
Social security and workmen's compensation fund	7	7.12	8.74	9.84
Civil servants' medical benefit	4	4.05	4.15	5
30-baht universal health-care program (Gold Card)	N/A	45.35	47.34	46.95
Total population	61	61.12	62.81	62.55
Uninsured	17	4.60	2.36	.52
Percentage covered	72	92.5	96.3	99.2

SOURCES: For pre-2001, interview with Pongpisut Jongudomsak, director of Bureau of Policy and Planning, National Health Security Office, June 2003. For 2002–08, National Health Security Office 2009a.

NOTES: The low-income scheme and the five-hundred-baht health card were discontinued with the implementation of the thirty-baht universal health-care program. There are also a few smaller insurance programs not included in this table (see National Health Security Office 2009a).

program made significant headway. Compared with earlier health insurance schemes for the poor, in which approximately 34 million people had been covered, the thirty-baht program expanded coverage to some 45.35 million people in 2002, thus covering 92.5 percent of the population. In 2008, 99.2 percent of the population was covered.[177] After instituting the thirty-baht program, the number of uninsured steadily declined from 17 million before 2001 to 4.60 million in 2002 and 520,000 in 2008 (see Table 6-5).[178]

Under the two previous insurance programs for the poor, the Ministry of Public Health had established a capitation of only Bt273. By contrast, the CSMB scheme had the highest allocation in the budget, even though it comprised only 12 percent of the population. In 2002, this was about Bt2,349 per capita per year. The SS scheme that covered labor in the formal sector had an allocation of about Bt1,450 per capita per year.[179] Under the thirty-baht program, the allocation of funding for the poor received a big boost. In 2002, the budget per capita for the thirty-baht program was set at Bt1,202. In 2009, it rose to Bt2,202 (see Table 6-6). This last allocation was 95 percent of what the National Health Security Office requested.[180] Thus, there were huge strides, from less than Bt300 in funding pre-2001 to the 2009 capitation of Bt2,202.

As part of its redistributive thrust, the thirty-baht program endeavored to shift funding priorities away from the richer hospitals that catered to urban residents. The program initially directed funding toward community hospitals rather than general and regional hospitals located in the urban areas. Before the thirty-baht program, funding was heavily skewed toward state hospitals in Bangkok and the central region. The thirty-baht program sought to change that by targeting population size as the main factor for funding allocation, precisely because the program would increase demand in the poorer areas of the country. Under this criterion, the northeast—the poorest and most populous area of the country—should have gained over other regions.[181]

However, the rebalancing of funding toward community hospitals in the provinces came under fire from the Bangkok-based health-care establishment.[182] The heavy criticism from the health establishment led the ministry to capitulate in 2003 and go against the wishes of the National Health Security Office, which was running the program, by broadening the criteria for funding at the national level.[183] Provincial hospitals therefore lost in this bureaucratic tug-of-war over funding priorities, although this was later reversed in favor of them when a more reformist minister took over the ministry.[184]

TABLE 6-6
Thailand, Thirty-Baht Universal Health-Care
Program Capitation Rates, 2002–2009 (in baht)

Year	Capitation rate
2002	1,202
2003	1,202
2004	1,308
2005	1,396
2006	1,659
2007	1,899
2008	2,100
2009	2,202

SOURCE: National Health Security Office 2009b.

The critical problem following the Ministry of Public Health's about-face became the lack of funding for the provincial community hospitals, because a significant proportion of available resources had to be redirected toward the richer hospitals first. This meant that rural hospitals had to wait longer before their funds come through, and therefore had to contend with the specter of bankruptcy.[185] According to the Rural Doctors Society, of 819 ministry-run hospitals, 265 had accumulated debts of Bt1.3 billion by 2004. Of these, only 19 were general and regional hospitals, and the remaining 246 were community hospitals based in the north and northeast.[186] A research report by the National Economic and Social Advisory Council argued that the revised method of funding allocation was "unfair" because it placed the burden squarely on the shoulders of the rural hospitals, where demand for the program was high. The report noted that the imbalance in funding stemmed from the different rates charged for medical treatment by the three levels of hospitals (community, general, and regional). To rectify the overall problem of budget allocations, the report called for the scrapping of the three-tier system of hospitals and calculating costs for treatments at a general level rather than on the basis of type of hospital and its own calculations of treatment costs.

The funding difficulties of the thirty-baht program have led to concerns about the quality of care and to complaints by doctors that they are being overworked. At Lerdsin Hospital in Bangkok, for example, patient visits increased by about two hundred thousand in 2003 alone.[187] Surveys also indicated large disaffection among Thailand's hospital workers with the program, with many who resigned stating that increased workload was a key factor in their decision to quit.[188]

Despite the problems and criticisms of the thirty-baht program, the post-Thaksin governments have retained it, indeed scrapping the thirty-baht copayment, criticized as an unnecessary transaction cost. Although critics have had a field day lambasting the program as "populist," it has become institutionalized within the health system and has been supported by every government following the TRT.

Conclusion

The democratic period of the mid-1970s provided the first concrete opportunity for social reforms. Unlike the 1932 revolution or the postwar government, this time there was active movement in the grass roots that pushed for more equitable policies. But the parties in power lacked institutional capacity to absorb societal demands and implement them effectively. Since then, the party system has remained largely in the hands of capitalist forces that have lacked any real ideological or organizational foundations. The Democrat Party has been the most institutionalized party in the country, but as the case study on the Pak Mun Dam has shown, it has not had any abiding interest in social reform.

A few social reforms did occur during the more liberalized period, but these resulted largely from ad hoc events. The NESDB's pro-poor initiatives reflected the prominence of a handful of progressive civil servants. The passage of the Social Security Act, a milestone in social reform, occurred through a confluence of democratic forces coming together at an opportune moment. The defeat of the Nam Choan Dam was the result of civil society forces rallying forcefully. Although the mixed outcome of the Pak Mun Dam came through a party, TRT, and a populist leader, Thaksin, reactionary forces later exorcised both from the political system in 2006. Only the universal health-care program appears to have a more institutionalized basis, driven by TRT and supported by every post-TRT government.[189]

These few events of success in social reform are important because they complicate the picture of Thailand as a purely negative instance of equitable development. However, they do not contradict the argument of this study: political institutions are necessary to direct a country's developmental trajectory toward an equitable outcome. Although some pro-poor initiatives were successful, without forceful institutional backing, they will not be systemic or sustainable and will be at the mercy of the personal sympathies of government leaders and the pressure of social forces. The success of the Nam Choan Dam was not replicated with the Pak Mun Dam, and the passage of the Social Security Act was an isolated incident in Chat Thai's tenure in power. Institutionalized parties are thus necessary to anchor reforms solidly and systematically into the synapses of the state.

A clear contrast is thus apparent between Thailand and Malaysia. In Malaysia, the state has exerted massive effort and expended significant resources to advance development. During the New Economic Policy period, public spending reached as high as 40 percent of GDP. Constant efforts to improve rural institutions, to upgrade skills, and to strengthen access to education have reduced poverty in the rural areas, mitigated inequalities, and absorbed the rural population into modern professional jobs. In Thailand, some 40 percent to 50 percent of the population remains in the traditional agrarian sector, despite the economy being heavily based on the secondary and tertiary sector. This has compounded the divide between the rural sector and Bangkok. Thus, compared to Thailand, the Malaysian state has been much more successful at integrating the rural population into the modern economy.

An equally critical problem has been the failure in Thailand of effective political representation of the rural poor. Parties are inconsistent in their efforts to address the predicament of the poor, and those that do seek solutions do not last long, given the volatility in the party system. As we have seen in the case of the Pak Mun Dam, local elites have often sided with government officials rather than the poor. In Malaysia, village heads are often linked with UMNO, and therefore support the rural poor. The presence of UMNO in the countryside in effect provides the necessary backbone for the rural poor. In the absence of a party that penetrates the countryside, the poor are left defenseless against the interests of local elites. From the mid-1970s until the current period, the problem of the rural poor in Thailand has not changed: they have lacked any political party that might advance, protect, and sustain a pro-poor agenda. Only civil society groups have sought to represent the lower classes, but their influence has been limited.

Thaksin's TRT Party and its pro-poor platform served as a shock to the system in suddenly centering the interests of the poor in the polity. Many analysts have been skeptical of Thaksin's motivations, given the fact that he hails from the summit of the capitalist class and that he has blatantly used the state for his own interests, particularly in the 2006 sale of Shin Corporation to Singapore's Temasek. Nonetheless, we should look less at motivations than at policy output. The debt moratorium program, though quite systematic in its goals, has ultimately not made a major dent in reducing farmers' debt in large part because of the moral hazard it creates. In contrast, the universal health-care program has been much more successful in addressing the needs of the poor. Although it encountered strong resistance from conservative elements, the program has been retained in all post-TRT governments.[190]

If we conceptualize TRT as a more institutionalized party, then there is some basis for confirming the argument that institutionalization and state-party dominance are crucial for social reform. Indeed, Thaksin's self-proclaimed desire to emulate UMNO and PAP give us some reason to tack in this direction. The difficulty in sustaining this argument to its fullest is that TRT cannot be considered institutionalized like UMNO or PAP. It clearly differed from the traditional clientelist parties, like Chat Thai, through its emphasis on policy and internal discipline, and its initiatives to link and represent social groups. At the same time, it was also composed of clientelist factions, had limited organizational complexity, and above all, relied heavily on Thaksin for financing and leadership. Ultimately, the impossibility of conceiving of TRT without Thaksin makes one doubt how institutionalized the party was.

On some level, the question of whether TRT would make a long-term difference for the livelihood of the poor was taken out of its hands when the party was ousted in the September 2006 coup. Thailand reverted yet again to a cycle of military coups and weak civilian institutions. Thailand's long-term developmental trajectory, despite TRT's presence, appears to move down the same conservative road. Nonetheless, the importance of Thaksin's policies, even beyond their actual moderate success, is that they have opened up the political agenda for pro-poor reforms. Except for the mid-1970s, no major political party has advanced a serious pro-poor program. After TRT, all parties have tried to replicate its success by parroting its platform. This is still a long way from a more equitable, developmental agenda, but at the very least, the politics of equitable development in Thailand is now fully engaged.

PART FOUR

Extensions and Conclusions

SEVEN

Extending the Theoretical Argument
The Philippines and Vietnam

Introduction

This chapter extends the comparative scope of the book's thesis to two other countries in Southeast Asia that are on opposite ends of the institutions-development spectrum: the Philippines and Vietnam. The Philippines has a dismal record in terms of economic growth rates, poverty alleviation, and distribution of income. This is the case in terms of absolute numbers and, more important, long-term trends. Vietnam still has a lower per capita income than the Philippines, but its growth rates over the past two decades have been extremely impressive. Furthermore, the Vietnamese government has historically shown capacity and ideological commitment to deal with inequality, and its distribution of income has remained relatively even despite liberalizing the economy.

Like Malaysia and Thailand, Vietnam and the Philippines are both newly industrializing countries (NICs). They are also the two most populous countries in the region, following Indonesia.[1] There is some basis, then, to pair them together as contrasting cases that provide further comparative evidence buttressing the theoretical argument of this study: that a combination of state interventionism, party institutionalization, and pragmatic policy and ideology is necessary to pursue equitable development. This chapter begins by looking at the Philippines and then turns to Vietnam. The goal here is to show through broad, comparative historical analysis the external validity of the argument regarding institutional power and capacity.

Philippines

The Philippines is popularly known and lauded as the first democracy in Asia. It is also highly regarded as one of the most literate and English-speaking populations in Southeast Asia. Furthermore, it is often fondly remembered as having had one of the highest gross domestic products (GDP) per capita in Asia in the 1950s.[2] The irony of these accolades, however, is that they highlight how poorly the Philippines has fared in development, despite—or in some cases because of—these "positive" factors.

By the end of the 1960s, the Philippine economy was one of the most sluggish in Asia. In the 1980s, growth rates were negative for two years in a row, with a cumulative decline of 14 percent. Compared to Malaysia, Thailand, and even Indonesia, poverty alleviation has been much slower. A 1993 World Bank report noted that the incidence of poverty in the Philippines is higher than in countries of similar or lower per capita income, which suggests that the limited growth that has been achieved has not been pro-poor.[3] Although poverty rates have declined overall, they have done so at a much slower rate than in fellow NICs. In large part, this is because growth has not taken off the way it has in neighboring countries. However, it is also because the government has not crafted policies that tend to be poverty reducing, whether through redistribution or through structuring the pattern of economic growth. Furthermore, the distribution of income in the Philippines has been highly unequal, although it has remained relatively constant.

The fundamental reason development in the Philippines has not attained the high growth rates experienced in Thailand and has not been able to attack inequality as in Malaysia has to do with weak institutions. Although the state has played a central role in the rise of most of the Asian NICs, either through a systemic developmental machinery or through pockets of bureaucratic capacity, the Philippine state has been stunningly ineffective, trapped in an asphyxiating patrimonial mold.[4] The Philippine state has never been able to establish a clear boundary between public and private interests. From the Spanish colonial regime until the present day, the state has been a site for the accumulation of personal power and wealth and the dispensation of favor and patronage rather than a foundation for the provision of public goods. Whether under a democratic or an authoritarian regime, patrimonialism has structured the nature of public authority and of policy output. Under the dictatorship of Ferdinand Marcos, Philippine institutions degenerated and patrimonialism was centralized and deepened, but as Paul Hutchcroft has shown, this patrimonial structure has deep historical roots that transcend one of the most repressive and corrupt periods in Philippine history.[5]

The weakness of political parties has also been one of the underlying problems of Philippine development. Like the state itself, parties in the Philippines have not been concerned with a public agenda. Rather, parties have largely operated as vehicles for the personal ambition of landed elites and traditional politicians. Since 1901, when the first local elections were held under American rule, the pursuit of public office as a means for private gain has motivated most political parties. Parties have not been concerned with developing programmatic agendas, mobilizing social groups, or representing collective interests. There are a few parties that have bucked this trend, but they face significant challenges in staying afloat in a patrimonial system. Most of these are parties on the left, including the Communist Party of the Philippines (CPP), the Democratic Alliance in the 1950s, and more recently, Akbayan and Bayan Muna. Since the 1990s, the Liberal Party has increasingly become more programmatic. But these are exceptions to a party system that is remarkably devoid of programmatic, let alone ideological, fault lines. The real fault lines in the party system are not between parties but between personalities and family dynasties concerned with amassing spoils. Since the American period, this system of feckless parties has been remarkably constant, unshaken by social, economic, and political crises.

In 1973, Carl Landé wrote that "party membership is not a category but a matter of degree" and that "one finds in the Philippines a much more simple process of favor seeking and favor giving between members of the public and administrative decision makers."[6] Twenty-five years later, a major study on the Philippine political economy employed Max Weber's writings on patrimonialism to hammer a similar point: "Practically everything depends explicitly upon the personal considerations: upon the attitude toward the concrete applicant and his concrete request and upon purely personal connections, favors, promises, and privileges."[7] Philippine political development has thus progressively reinforced a system in which institutions have had minimal value qua institutions and in which oligarchs have been able to dictate the agenda without worrying about constraints on their action or on the need to address public interests.

ECONOMIC RECORD

A recent paper by the Philippines' preeminent expert on poverty and inequality states: "The past-quarter century saw the Philippines lagging behind most of the major East Asian countries in practically all aspects of economic and social development. . . . Further blunting the impact of whatever
growth that occurred on poverty was its persistently high level of economic
inequality."[8] With a GDP per capita in 2009 of US$1,752, the Philippines
ranks significantly below Malaysia and Thailand.[9] Its GDP growth rates in
the 1960s until 1970 averaged 4.9 percent. During the Marcos dictatorship
(1972–86), GDP growth rates averaged 3.4 percent, with two consecutive
years in which growth rates were –7 percent. The latter period of the Marcos regime was marked by a severe economic crisis, driven by government
debt, economic plunder, and mismanagement of the economy. The post-
Marcos period until 2009 saw growth rates average 3.9 percent—a marginal
improvement over the period of the dictatorship (see Table 7-1).[10]

Given these rather dismal figures, it is not surprising that poverty rates
remain still quite high. Although poverty rates have declined from a high of
59 percent to 33 percent, they have not made the same inroads as neighboring Asian NICs, including Indonesia (see Table 7-2).[11] The reason for this,
according to economist Arsenio Balisacan, is the government's failure to sustain high growth rates for a period long enough to make a more decisive
dent in poverty.[12]

TABLE 7-1
Philippines, GDP Growth Rates, 1951–2009 (percentage)

Period	GDP growth rate
1951–60	6.4
1961–70	4.9
1971–80	5.9
1981–90	1.8
1991–2000	3.1
2001–06	4.6
2007–09	3.9

SOURCES: Canlas et al. 2009: 17; World Bank WDI for 2007–09.

TABLE 7-2

Philippines, Incidence of Poverty, 1961–2009 (percentage)

Year	Poverty incidence
1961	59.25
1965	51.47
1971	52.23
1985	49.2 (53.9 in Balisacan 1994)
1988	45.3 (44.2 in Balisacan 1994)
1991	45.2 (44.6 in Balisacan 1994)
1994	40.2
1997	33.0
2000	34.0
2003	30.0 (24.9)[a]
2006	32.9 (26.4)[a]
2009	32.6 (26.5)[a]

SOURCES: Balisacan 1994; Balisacan 1999; National Statistical Coordination Board (NSCB), Poverty Statistics website (http://www.nscb.gov.ph/poverty/2009/default.asp).

NOTES: There is significant discrepancy in the incidence of poverty across sources, including government institutions. For example, the NSCB has the percentage of poverty incidence in 1997 at 33.0 and 2000 at 34.0. However, the National Statistics Office has 1997 at 36.8 and 2000 at 39.4. The trend, however, is similar, in that the poverty rate increased in 2000 relative to 1997. I have stayed with the NSCB data, as this institution provides the official rates of poverty for the Philippines.

[a] In 2011, the NSCB revised its methodology for calculating poverty incidence. The revised numbers are shown in parentheses. Based on this new methodology, the estimates of poverty go down in absolute numbers, but the trend is not significantly different. However, there is a discrepancy in the figures that the NSCB reports when comparing the old and new methodology; compare p. 18 with p. 19 in NSCB 2011.

The distribution of income in the Philippines has been very unequal, although it did not reach the levels seen in Thailand in the mid-1990s, nor did it begin from the same point as Malaysia. In 1961, the Gini coefficient was .486. In 1971, just before martial law, it had barely improved to .478. In 1985, however, it was lower at .447, but by 1994 it had risen to .451, and in 2003 it had reached .461. It then declined to .448 in 2009 (see Table 7-3 and Figure 7-1). Figure 7-1 shows that there have been some shifts in the

TABLE 7-3
Philippines, Distribution of Income, 1961–2009: Gini Coefficient and Income Shares

Year	Gini coefficient	Percentage income of the 1st quintile (poorest 20%)	Percentage income of the 2nd quintile	Percentage income of the 3rd quintile	Percentage income of the 4th quintile	Percentage income of the 5th quintile (richest 20%)	Ratio of 5th to 1st quintile
1961	.486	4.2	7.9	12.1	19.3	56.4	13.4
1965	.491	3.5	8.0	12.8	20.2	55.4	15.8
1971	.478	3.8	8.1	13.2	21.1	53.9	14.2
1985	.447	5.2	9.1	13.3	20.3	52.1	10.0
1988	.447	5.2	9.1	13.3	20.6	51.8	10.0
1991	.468	4.7	8.5	12.7	20.2	53.9	11.5
1994	.451	4.9	8.8	13.4	20.9	51.9	10.6
1997	.487	4.4	7.8	12.2	20.2	55.5	12.6
2000	.482[a]	4.4	7.9	12.4	20.5	54.6	12.4
2003	.461[a]	4.7	8.3	12.8	20.9	53.3	11.3
2006	.458	N/A	N/A	N/A	N/A	N/A	N/A
2009	.448	N/A	N/A	N/A	N/A	N/A	N/A

SOURCES: National Statistics Office (NSO) website (http://www.census.gov.ph/data/sectordata/dataincome.html) for the Gini coefficient; National Economic and Development Agency (NEDA) website (http://222.127.10.196/National/HouseInc.html) for the quintile shares. Both NSO and NEDA base their statistics on the surveys of the Family Income and Expenditure Survey (FIES), administered by NSO. Quintile shares and ratios are calculated by author. Data for 1961–71 is based on Balisacan 1993 and Medhi and Ragayah 2007.

NOTES: Balisacan and Piza 2003 have different Gini coefficients for 1985–2000, but the trend is similar to that of the NSO. Their source is also the FIES.

[a]NEDA's Gini coefficient is .49 for 2000 and .48 for 2003, higher than that of the NSO.

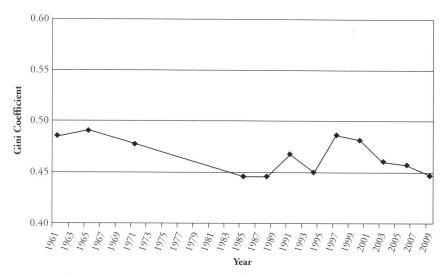

FIGURE 7-1 Philippines, Trend in Income Inequality, 1961–2009
SOURCES: Balisacan 1993; Medhi and Ragayah 2007; National Statistics Office, "Index of Family Income and Expenditure," http://www.census.gov.ph/data/sectordata/dataincome.html.

direction of the Gini coefficient, but the overall trend can be characterized as somewhat static: the Gini has not moved clearly in any direction.

The remarkable aspect of these statistics is not just that they show no improvement in the distribution of income over the long run but that there is little indication that the restoration of democracy has had any positive effect on growth and equity. Between 1971 and 1985, approximately the period of the Marcos dictatorship, the Gini coefficient improved by .031, but during the democratic period from about 1988 to 2009, the Gini coefficient saw no improvement, registering a slight uptick of .001. Although poverty levels have declined, this has come about in very slow increments. In the aggregate, economic growth rates have barely improved from the Marcos regime, and the gap between the rich and the poor has slowly inched up.

POLITICAL DEVELOPMENT

With the economic statistics as a background, we now turn to analyze the political factors that have shaped the Philippine pattern of development. If we are to understand the role that weak institutions have played in the trajectory of Philippine development, we should begin with the colonial period. The roots of a weak state and party system can be traced to the American democratic mission in the Philippines, where elections strengthened provincial power and private interests against the center and public interests. But the American regime itself was grafted onto earlier foundations. It was built "on the residual architecture of the previous Spanish colonial state."[13]

The Spanish colonial state in the Philippines was characterized by a superficial structure of authority. Compared both to its other colonies in Latin America and to other colonial empires, such as the Dutch and the British, the Spaniards made barely an attempt to extend their authority beyond the capital. In the first place, they did not emigrate in large numbers to the Philippines. Until the waning years of the empire, the number of Spaniards in the Philippines never topped five thousand.[14] Second, the colonial authorities evinced no interest in creating state institutions with any rational-bureaucratic capacities that might establish national policy across the archipelago. Although the governor-general in Manila had extensive powers of appointment throughout the colony and the right to overturn directives from the king of Spain, the colonial regime had little ability to shape any systematic agenda or enforce its policies. Spanish official authority was largely limited to governance in the capital. Furthermore, the government officials themselves were often of low repute, prompting Spanish historian Tomas Comyn to report in 1820 that it was "common enough to see a hairdresser or a lackey converted into a governor; a sailor or deserter transformed into a district magistrate, a collector, or military commander of a populous province."[15]

There were two reasons for the failure of the state to deepen its reach and capacities. The most significant had to do with the overbearing presence of the religious friars. The friars acted as a second arm of government, establishing themselves as the virtual rulers of life beyond Manila. The friars were principally concerned with propagating the Catholic faith and amassing power. They ruled the natives with impunity, even going so far as to murder the rare governor-general who sought to reform the administration.[16] Indeed, "in much of the Philippines, the friars were the state."[17] Furthermore, the friars roundly resisted and rebuffed efforts in the nineteenth century to improve governance and accountability.[18]

The other structural weakness of the colonial regime was that it lacked a foundation for institutional continuity. Governor-generals could not hold tenure for more than two years and later for only one year, whereas middle-ranking civil servants could be removed arbitrarily. The short time horizon of the governor-generalship meant "fecklessness of long-range planning" and efforts by the governor-general to "enrich himself in office in the shortest possible time."[19] In the long run, this meant that the colonial regime lacked any clear administrative agenda separate from the particularistic interest of its temporary officeholder. It was expected that officeholders would use their position to make private gains. "No conceptual distinction existed between the public welfare and the officials' private benefit, a confusion that survives today."[20] Overall, the Spanish colonial state lacked any rational-legal foundations.

The Spanish also established no foundations for economic development until the nineteenth century. The Philippines was used primarily as an entrepôt for trade. Unlike the British or the Dutch, the Spanish exerted minimal efforts in developing the economy, such as through mining, agriculture, or shipbuilding. Except for the galleon trade running from Mexico to China via Manila, the Philippines was closed to foreign trade until 1834. However, with the abolition of the galleon trade and the opening of Manila and other ports to international trade, export agriculture began to take hold. By the 1840s, 90 percent of revenue came from cash crops.[21] This shift of the colonial economy toward commercial agriculture and monetization had major consequences. It made land a more valuable commodity, which the upper class (native *principalia* and Chinese mestizos) seized by exploiting the ignorance of the peasants.[22] In this, they built on the earlier practices of the friars in the seventeenth and eighteenth centuries of grabbing land from the peasantry through all kinds of fraudulent means.[23] The dispossessed families became tenant-sharecroppers of the *principalia* and Chinese mestizos, who themselves were renting land from the friar orders. But the elites were able to push the burden of cultivation onto the peasants while taking over their land.[24] Peasants became "virtual slaves of their creditors" because they repaid the loan through labor.[25] Hence, vast agricultural plantations emerged along with small peasant holdings, thus leading to a dual economy.[26] In the peasant's dispossession of land at the hands of friars first and the upper class later, the roots of inequality in the countryside began to take hold.

AMERICAN COLONIALISM

The American presence in the Philippines was both distinct from Spanish rule and derivative. Its distinctiveness arose from the establishment of electoral democracy throughout the country. But it was also derivative because it reinforced the power of the periphery over the center. It did this by auctioning off to the caciques the vast religious estates that the friars had established and by providing these provincial elites a basis for expanding their authority through electoral office. The selling of the religious estates was supposed to lead to land redistribution to tenants to assuage rural discontent, but in fact the American officials sold land at prices that were out of reach of the peasantry, and therefore the land ended up in the hands of the upper class.[27] Meanwhile, elections at the municipal, provincial, and national levels were a central mechanism through which social elites could extract economic resources from their constituencies and from the center. Without any entrenched centralizing structure to guide the direction of national policy, elections at every level of the state allowed for the capture of the state rather than the state's penetration of the periphery. Thus, the combination of land distribution to the caciques and the early birth of an electoral system created the basis for an elitist democracy.

The decision to hold elections first at the municipal (1901), then the provincial (1902), and finally the national level (1907) was due to both political expediency and American liberal ideals.[28] Following a brutal war in which the Americans annihilated fierce Filipino resistance, Governor William Howard Taft realized that, to suppress Filipino nationalist desires, it would be crucial to forge an alliance with the *ilustrado* and cacique class, thereby co-opting the most powerful adversary of the colonial regime. Imbued with both the goal of pacification and the liberal mind-set of Tocquevillian democracy, Taft went about providing space for the elites to share in governance through local elections. The route of pacification through elections was very much part of the liberal worldview that saw local governance, in the likes of New England town halls, as the ideal foundation for an incipient democracy.

The caciques had no difficulties dominating offices at all levels of government because history had already endowed them with overwhelming advantages. During the Spanish period, the commercialization of agriculture toward the middle of the nineteenth century had decisively strengthened their hand. Under the Americans, pacification and economic distribution of vast lands cemented their economic power. The early restrictions on the franchise, in which only 1.4 percent of the population voted, removed any serious electoral competition from the grass roots. Finally, the gradual decentralization of power helped reinforce the strength of local elites as Americans shifted the balance of provincial governments toward elected officials and away from appointed bureaucrats. By the time the National Assembly was elected in 1907, provincial elites were well ensconced in the halls of power. Public office would then serve as an instrument to accumulate more capital and to strengthen one's political position.

In the first decades of colonial democracy, a number of parties were born, including the Federalistas, Nacionalistas, Partido Demócrata Nacional, Nacionalista Collectivista, and Nacionalista Consolidado. But these parties did not have any mass base and largely reflected the jockeying for power in the Assembly between two dominant politicians who had emerged from provincial office, Manuel Quezon and Sergio Osmeña. Party labels rose and fell on the basis of these two leaders' efforts to entrench themselves in power.[29] These early democratic skirmishes set the foundations for an organizationally incoherent and ideologically vacuous party system.

What was notable in these early years was the fact that all the contestants were provincial elites; that what held parties together were personal ties centered on dominant leaders; that there were no major programmatic differences among parties;[30] and that the parties lacked organizational depth, roots in society, and mobilizing capacities. They were largely vehicles for elites to gain power rather than institutions with any representative function toward collective interests. This was especially evident in the concerns of the assemblymen in the first National Assembly in 1907. On the first day at work, the assemblymen voted to increase their per diem allowances. They later passed a bill to exempt uncultivated land from taxation and other measures in favor of their class.[31] "The survival of these early characteristics in Philippine politics of recent times," observes Renato Constantino, "are too obvious to require further comment."[32]

The dilemma that emerged, then, was that American efforts to compromise with the elites and to create avenues for local self-governance ended up entrenching a system of local patrimonialism devoid of any institutional capacity or democratic merits.[33] Taft was well aware of this tension, but he nonetheless pushed ahead in the vain hope that local governance would eventually yield more substantive democratic results.[34] "The most striking inconsistency of the early years, and of the entire American period . . . was the ambivalence displayed toward the Filipino elite," writes Michael Cullinane. "This group was invariably depicted as a major obstruction to the realization of a truly democratic society and the establishment of social justice; yet no significant effort was made to 'uproot' the social and economic conditions that lay at the heart of cacique rule."[35]

What compounded the problem of an elite democratic system was the weakness of the bureaucratic center. Like the Spanish regime, the American authorities never made an effort to develop a more robust bureaucratic core that would be insulated from elected officials and have the capacity to supervise those officials and act as a check on their behavior.[36] The reality was that there was not much incentive for strengthening a central bureaucracy. Compared to European colonialists, the United States did not envision power in terms of concentration at the center through an independent bureaucracy. President William McKinley's instructions to the Taft commission on local government emphasized that "in the distribution of power" under the Americans "the presumption is always to be in favor of the small subdivision."[37]

Furthermore, the tensions and recriminations back home over American colonialism created a disincentive for civil servants to serve for long in the colonies.[38] Major bureaucratic organs were understaffed in the early period of American colonialism. In 1906, the Executive Bureau, the principal agency in charge of overseeing provincial and local government, had only seven employees, who had served since its advent in 1901.[39] Governor-General Francis Harrison's desire to speed up the Filipinization of the bureaucracy, in accordance with Woodrow Wilson's sympathies for national autonomy, also helped undermine the staffing of the bureaucracy with Americans.[40] Unlike other colonial bureaucracies, the conquering power did not seek to forcefully stamp its authority at the core of the state. The consequence of this was that the central government's later attempts to rein in the patrimonial direction of local government turned to naught as they had little institutional means to do so.

The larger problem of Philippine political development can be understood in terms of an unfortunate pattern of historical sequencing, whereby the advent of early democratic elections before state building entrenched a system through which provincial private interests would dominate, define, and distort the idea of the public good.[41] Instead of a strong institutional core capable of pursuing a national agenda, the legacy of American colonial rule was the entrenching of the private accumulation of power. Personal ties, especially centered on the family, were the linchpin of political relations, coalition building, and policy making.[42] A synergistic situation thus developed where the "privatization of public resources strengthens a few fortunate families while weakening the state's resources and its bureaucratic apparatus."[43] The remarkable continuity of a political system characterized by the use of public office for private interests, as a trough for spoils, as a means for entrenching oneself and one's family and friends—or cronies—in power, and as a resource for destroying one's rivals can thus be traced to developments in the American colonial period.

THE POSTWAR PERIOD

Democratic governance from 1946 to 1972 did not lead to any significant changes in terms of development and social reforms. Although the Filipinos were now self-governing, there was no movement toward institution building that could improve economic conditions. During the period, per capita gross national product (GNP) was second only to Malaysia and Singapore in Southeast Asia. Quite significantly, the Philippines was ahead of Thailand in per capita GNP but by the 1980s had been decisively overtaken. Yet other indicators suggest that the government's role in terms of development, as assessed through public spending, was significantly below par. In 1960, the Philippine government's public expenditures fell 7.93 percent below the median for sixteen comparable countries. Expenditures for agriculture, health, social insurance, and housing were notably in the lower end of the budget.[44]

The Philippines could have used this relatively stable democratic period to strengthen its institutions as a basis for economic growth, but instead the patrimonial structure that had been established under the Americans sank more deeply into the crevices of the state. The civil service was particularly vulnerable to the excesses of patronage politics and patrimonial influence. Bureaucrats' decisions were often based on personal favors either for politicians or for friends and family members. Just as problematic was the fact that civil servants had little incentive to stick to a more rational form of decision making. Between 1940 and 1956, the cost of living increased by 350 percent, but the salaries of middle- and upper-level civil servants did not even go up twofold.[45] Indeed, the salaries of Malaysian civil servants were twice those of the Philippines.

The problem of low compensation dates back to the Commonwealth period. A former vice-governor of the Philippines estimated that salaries for the lower rungs of the civil service (about 60 percent of government employees) were severely inadequate and that 25 percent were being paid below a living wage.[46] Under such conditions, it is not surprising that personal favors and other forms of corruption penetrated the bureaucracy. A larger problem in the Philippine bureaucracy was that by entering the civil service, one could bypass a competitive examination. In the postwar period, more and more civil servants gained their position through personal contact rather than merit. In 1964, more than 80 percent of national government employees and 57 percent of high-ranking civil servants had *not* taken an admissions exam.[47]

Continuity in terms of patronage and personalism also characterized the party system in the postwar period. In 1946, the Liberal Party was born from a faction of the Nacionalistas to enable another oligarch, Manuel Roxas, to engineer his way to the presidency. As in the Commonwealth period, there was little substantive difference between parties.[48] Both the Nacionalistas and Liberals were vehicles for occupying the presidential palace, Malacañang, with no ideological or organizational value. Party switching became a perpetual game in Philippine politics that allowed politicians to further their ambitions. Ramon Magsaysay left the Liberal Party in 1953 to run against the Liberal president, Elpidio Quirino. Marcos likewise bolted the Liberals when he realized that incumbent Diosdado Macapagal was going to hold on to the reins of the Liberal Party. Like Roxas, these decisions proved the right ones, as all three of the "defectors" were elected president through their new party. Party switching could even be as dramatic as mass defection when a member from another party won the presidency. In 1961, a month after Macapagal's victory, one senator from the Nacionalistas, a number of representatives, seven provincial governors, more than one hundred mayors, and thousands of municipal and village officials moved over to join the Liberals.[49]

In the 1950s, one significant window of opportunity did emerge in which the institutional lethargy of the Philippine state and the personalistic behavior of its elites might have been shaken. This was the Huk Rebellion in central Luzon that began in 1946 and tapered off in the early 1950s.[50] The peasant rebellion was sparked by increasing discontent among tenants and sharecroppers that landlords were treating them unjustly and reneging on earlier traditions of patron-client relations. As a result of a number of socioeconomic changes, including the commercialization of agriculture, advances in farm machinery, and population growth, landlords were no longer willing to provide income security for tenants. Under very dire economic conditions, landlords no longer gave tenants interest-free loans of rice, rations, fair shares of the harvest, or various forms of financial and social support. Peasants were also being evicted from the land they harvested. Efforts to protest these deteriorating conditions met violent repression from landlords, police, and the Philippine Constabulary. Until the communist insurgency reached its height under the Marcos regime, the Huk Rebellion was the most forceful expression of social discontent. The rebellion did not, however, extend beyond central Luzon. Despite the overwhelming military advantage of the state and the landlords, the Huk Rebellion persisted until the early 1950s.

The Huk Rebellion began to lose its force when the newly appointed defense secretary Ramon Magsaysay took a different approach to rural unrest from that of the oligarchs. Magsaysay understood that the rebellion stemmed from deep-rooted grievances and decided that some institutional and social reforms were necessary for the government to quell the rebellion. While he continued to wage war against the Huks, Magsaysay disciplined the army and improved its morale. In particular, he went out of his way to supervise the troops in the province, praise those who had fought well, and quickly punish those who had abused their position.[51] At the same time, captured Huks were treated with respect and given a fair trial and eventual rehabilitation. As Magsaysay declared, "The army should bleed for the people and not the people bleed for the army."[52]

A central plank in the campaign against the Huks was social reform. Magsaysay built on a prewar program called the Economic Development Corps (EDCOR) by focusing its mission on granting land to landless tenants and small farmers, including former Huks. The corps provided fifteen to twenty acres per family, as well as farm tools, a carabao, a house, and seeds. The plots of land were situated within communities complete with a church and a school. Between 1951 and 1957, 978 families, or 5,000 persons, had settled on EDCOR farms in Luzon and Mindanao.[53] One assessment was extremely positive: "[T]he Philippine government had never offered such attractive terms to ordinary citizens—much less to former dissidents."[54] However, of the families settled, most of them came from outside central

Luzon, and only 250 were from the Huk movement. In many respects, the program, along with a battery of other reforms, including agrarian courts, government-paid lawyers helping tenants, and government-credit facilities, was useful for advancing Magsaysay's reform agenda but not for changing the structures of land inequality.[55]

Magsaysay's reform agenda ended with his death in a plane crash in 1957. His push to make the state's armed forces more accountable and its behavior more just, as well as the moderate social reforms, represented a small opportunity for change. These reforms gave the peasants a reason to have some faith in government again and thereby took the steam out of the rebellion. Magsaysay's death brought back rule by the oligarchs. The concurrent demise of the president and a moderate reform agenda showed that social reform was completely dependent on a leader's sympathy rather than on an institutional structure. Like Thailand, social reform when it has come through has had an uneven quality, dependent above all on the personal interest of the leader rather than on institutionalized structures. Under such conditions, social reform becomes a mixture of benevolent paternalism and patronage rather than institutionalized change. Despite Magsaysay's efforts at reform, ultimately he did not build a strong party that could have sustained a reform agenda beyond his own leadership.

During the late 1940s, peasants in central Luzon had also sought to pursue their interests through the electoral system. Before the first postwar election, two parties representing peasant interests in central Luzon had made some headway: the Popular Front (PF) and the Democratic Alliance (DA). The PF was able to gain several municipalities, but the DA fared much better. The DA's social base consisted of peasants in central Luzon, but also included progressive intellectuals, urban labor unions, and radical Nacionalistas. Its leader subsequently became secretary of justice, and its executive included leftist members of prominent families.[56] Despite massive intimidation and violence, the DA won six seats in Congress in the 1946 elections. This was the Philippines' best chance of having a programmatic party in Congress. The oligarchs, however, did not stand for this. President Roxas was able to expel the DA members from Congress, thereby increasingly forcing disenfranchised peasants to join the maquis.

The postwar era of democratic rule by oligarchs ended with President Ferdinand Marcos's declaration of martial law in 1972. By the early 1970s, unrest had begun to grow throughout the country. In 1971, a bomb at a rally of the Liberal Party that severely injured eight senatorial candidates was symptomatic of the spiraling of political violence. Angered by the blatant corruption in the 1969 elections, university students demonstrated against Marcos. The communist New People's Army as well as the Moro National Liberation Front began to mobilize at this time. Using growing social unrest as an excuse, Marcos declared martial law, claiming that he would restore order in his "New Society."

The first years of Marcos's dictatorship seemed promising. The economy grew by about 7 percent per year from 1972 to 1979. Technocrats were initially given room to implement macroeconomic policies, revenue from agricultural innovations and rice production increased, and manufacturing picked up. Even agrarian reform was given priority. "Land reform is the only gauge for the success or failure of the New Society," Marcos stated. "If land reform fails there is no New Society."[57] However, by the late 1970s, it became increasingly evident that Marcos's New Society was a travesty in every sense. In stark contrast to the Sarit Thanarat dictatorship in Thailand, much of this economic growth was not helping to build a middle class. Under Marcos, no real structural changes were made to the economy, and as the external environment for agricultural commodities deteriorated and the oil crisis hit, the situation began to crumble. Wages for skilled labor in Manila fell 23.8 percent, whereas those of unskilled laborers declined by 30.6 percent during the mid-1970s.[58] After 1979, the distribution of income also worsened considerably.

The downfall of the economy was a consequence of Marcos's outright plunder. Marcos's greatest legacy was, in the end, the extensive pillage of the nation's economy. Marcos and his wife, Imelda, granted family and cronies control over private enterprises (particularly those of political enemies); cornered government contracts and licenses; established monopolies over various sectors of the economy, including sugar, coconut, tobacco, construction, and shipping; received kickbacks from construction projects; laundered money and invested in real estate abroad through offshore holding corporations and dummy companies; and, finally, used the national treasury as their own private bank. The amount estimated to have been stolen by Marcos and his cronies was "five to ten billion dollars, or even beyond that."[59] This was plunder on an unrivaled scale, except for the neighboring Suharto regime in Indonesia.[60] With the treasury bankrupt, the Philippine debt ballooned at the end of the Marcos regime to $27 billion, ranking it as one of the ten most indebted countries in the developing world. In Marcos's last years, the economy had collapsed, its growth rates at one point declining by 14 percent, while inflation averaged 50 percent, and the unemployment rate rose to 24 percent.[61] Particularly disturbing was the finding that, in 1981–83, corporate equity investments were the highest capital outlay, ahead even of infrastructure.[62] This was done to make equity contributions to major government banks so that they would rescue debilitated crony firms. The use of government funds for family and cronies was exorbitant and had a devastating effect on the rates of poverty and the distribution of income, as resources were disproportionately channeled to the circle of favorites rather than the needy.

DEMOCRATIC RESTORATION

The 1983 assassination of the opposition leader Benigno Aquino precipitated the downfall of the Marcos regime. The groundswell for political change culminated in the four stunning days of the EDSA "People Power" revolution in February 1986.[63] But the euphoria of the bloodless revolution and the restoration of democracy quickly faded as Corazon Aquino, the wife of the slain opposition leader, faced the seemingly more difficult challenge of deepening the democratic revolution into the popular sector.

Caught between grassroots pressures for social reform and threatening maneuvers by the military, Aquino—herself a conservative oligarch—was forced to straddle a fine line between reform and reaction. Her first cabinet, a mixture of right-wing figures and left-leaning reformists, projected that tension. Under constant attack from a fragmented military—having faced four coup attempts in her first three years in office—Aquino sought not to antagonize the armed forces. She ended up retreating from a popular reform agenda, dropping some of her closest, left-leaning allies from the cabinet, and taking a more intransigent position against the communists.

The dilemma that Aquino faced was that she had a unique opportunity to make the EDSA revolution mean more than simply a return to electoral democracy, but she was constrained by her own class background, the various reactionary forces arrayed against her, and the absence of any institutional structure that could spearhead, mobilize, and enforce reforms. Although there were some immediate pro-poor initiatives, such as the Policy Agenda for People-Powered Development, the reality is that Aquino was neither ideologically inclined toward social reforms (owning herself one of the largest sugar plantations in central Luzon) nor did she have the institutional backing necessary for major structural changes. Above all, Aquino concentrated on preserving democracy against myriad antagonists. Had she swung too much in favor of social reform, she would have incited even more military resistance and would have lost the support of conservative landlords.

A longtime observer of the Philippines puts it thus: "During the period when President Aquino had virtually limitless power under the freedom constitution, she had dramatic opportunity to address frontally the social contradictions and economic tensions of her nation. But President Aquino lacked omnipotence . . . a chance to redistribute wealth and address issues of social justice was lost."[64] Aquino, in fact, had "limitless power" only on paper. She lacked a cohesive state apparatus and a loyal and disciplined military, let alone an organized party to provide institutional backing. But the fact is that, despite the institutional disadvantages within which Aquino was forced to operate, she exerted minimal efforts to use or create organizational power that might deepen reform. In the first post-Marcos congressional elections in 1987, Aquino neither joined a party nor led a party.[65] The party linked to Aquino, Laban ng Demokratikong Pilipino, was made up of many former Marcos supporters and oligarchs. Although intent on pursuing Aquino's agenda, it "lacked any defining ideology or agenda" and "was generally left to its own devices on the reform question; at several junctures, it failed to honor Aquino's wishes."[66] Furthermore, Aquino refused to use her decree-making powers to push through reform and allowed the agrarian reform bill to be drafted within a Congress dominated by oligarchs—in effect, feeding the sheep to the wolves.

The greatest example of the demise of social reform under Aquino was the fate of land reform. Aquino's hesitation to enforce major asset redistribution eventually doomed the Comprehensive Agrarian Reform Program. The program that passed in Congress was greatly diluted from what cabinet reformists such as the economist Solita Monsod had devised. From a projected 27.4 million acres to be redistributed, only 6.9 million was actually allowed. From 3 million projected beneficiaries, only 2 million were slated to receive land. Furthermore, sugar and coconut plantations were no longer required to have any upper retention limits. The actual state enforcement of the land-reform bill, key to success of any program of asset redistribution, was extremely weak. The *Manila Chronicle* noted tartly: "[T]he recently signed Agrarian Reform Law has confirmed resoundingly an old political truism: no class legislates itself out of existence."[67]

The failure of land reform under Aquino has been emblematic of the trend of social reform in the Philippines: much hope among the masses, followed by passage of a bill among the elites, and ending with its emasculation at every turn. The history of the Philippines has not been devoid of pro-poor initiatives, but it has been completely lacking in substantive implementation. Democratic oligarchs and patrimonial dictators alike have hinted at, and even pursued, reform. In the 1930s, Quezon astounded his fellow conservative elites with his social justice program dubbed "Quezonian communism" that was meant to assuage rural unrest.[68] In the 1950s, several influential U.S. missions to the Philippines called on the elites to implement land reform.[69] In 1963, President Macapagal reversed his earlier position and sought to pass the Agricultural Land Reform Code.[70] Even Marcos championed land reform as one of his major initiatives.[71] Some—but not all—of this may have been gamesmanship. But it is also clear that the elites realize that social reform is vital to the country's development. Yet they as individuals—not as programmatic parties—define the reform agenda, and without both institutional backing and institutional constraints, reform inevitably slips away.[72]

In the absence of institutionalized parties, as in Thailand, the burden for representing the poor has fallen heavily on civil society. Civil society in the Philippines is one of the most vibrant in Southeast Asia, but its fractious nature has limited its ability to advance substantive reforms.[73] There are numerous pro-poor civil society groups, but these have been deeply divided over tactics and end goals, thereby weakening the possibilities for institution building and blunting policy reform.[74] The more radical, exemplified by the national democratic front linked to the CPP, have sought armed seizure of the state and rejected moderate change. Other, more social democratic groups have made efforts to collaborate with the state to exploit the limited opportunities for reform.

The way that progressive groups addressed land reform in the post-Marcos era is indicative of the challenges civil society faces in advancing policy change. Popular groups built a united front on land reform, known as the Congress for a People's Agrarian Reform (CPAR). This was the broadest coalition created to address agrarian reform, but it was hampered by internal divisions. The front was split over how to deal with the loophole-ridden comprehensive agrarian reform law. Some social democratic nongovernmental organizations (NGOs) sought to test the law by exploring areas of collaboration and coordination with government, others sought to challenge the law, and more radical groups such as the national democratic left denounced the law and advocated land occupation and armed seizure of state power. In the end, member organizations in CPAR continued to "do their own thing" on the ground, leading to conflicting ends.[75]

Throughout the post-1986 democratic period, progressive groups in civil society have persisted in challenging traditional elite structures. But "in the absence of programmatic party competition, civil society fragmentation tends to reinforce elite democracy," argues Jennifer Franco, "and undermines the building up of a reform-oriented political pole capable of attracting popular support."[76] The "expose and oppose"[77] mode of civil society groups has been necessary and useful. But this kind of politics cannot penetrate deeply into policy and can be counterproductive at a certain point.[78]

Assessing the impact of rural development NGOs on land reform, James Putzel concludes that they were crucial in keeping agrarian reform on the political agenda through mass rallies, ties to the media, and lobbying with the executive and legislative branches but that "they have been less successful in altering the more deeply rooted structural causes of poverty."[79] Despite intensive efforts, the agrarian reform bill was shaped by congressional landed interests rather than by social forces in civil society. More generally, one study of civil society's role in advancing equitable development and democracy in the Philippines observes that "the impact of civil society on policy outcomes is decidedly mixed."[80]

I should be clear that NGOs in civil society play a vital role in sustaining a pro-poor agenda. But fragmentation within civil society, the prioritization of mass action over policy moderation and compromise, and reluctance in joining or allying with parties can weaken the gains made on the activist front. In contrast to a strategy driven primarily by civil society activism, one distinct position, known as the *bibingka* strategy, calls for a symbiotic alliance between social forces and reformist groups within the state.[81] This position, in essence a reworking of Peter Evans's idea of "embedded autonomy," moves away from excessive reliance on the state or social forces. But even this position, as its own advocate admits, is vulnerable to the ebbing of a reformist impulse within the bureaucracy.[82] By contrast, political parties, if institutionalized and programmatic, can sustain action in favor of a reform agenda, mobilize social groups in support of that agenda, and potentially have the means to directly influence the crafting and implementation of policy.

Akbayan is one of the few parties in the Philippines today that has the potential to spearhead a reform agenda. Founded by leftist groups who split from the CPP, Akbayan reflects the need "for a political vehicle that will carry a progressive reform agenda into the heart of the national electoral arena."[83] It understands the importance of strengthening the state, "particularly in terms of orientation and capability necessary to implement redistributive measures."[84] But the problem for Akbayan and a few other leftist parties, such as Bayan Muna, is that their opportunities for electoral growth are severely constrained by the peculiar rules of the party-list system in the Philippines that limit parties to a three-seat ceiling,[85] as well as by repressive attacks by conservative elites.[86]

Another party that offers some hope of reform and institutional depth is the long-standing Liberal Party (LP). Founded in 1946, it is institutionalized in the sense of continuity and adaptability, but the standard problems of the party system have long plagued it: personalism, clientelism, factionalism, and the absence of a programmatic agenda. However, consolidation in the post-Marcos period and a recent split precipitated by Gloria Macapagal-Arroyo's divide-and-rule tactics have helped the party develop into a smaller, more unified, and more programmatic institution.[87] The party lacks organizational complexity, but compared with other parties in the system, it has institutional value that transcends purely personalistic interests. The party is associated with a reformist agenda and often allies with progressive groups in civil society, but "there is no concerted effort to bind civil society groups to the party," nor does the party have a mass base that it can mobilize.[88] Quite significantly, the LP is close to Akbayan, sharing some of its goals, advisers, and candidates.[89]

The long-term trajectory of Philippine political development has been grim in terms of growth, equity, and institution building. The origins of this problem date back to the American colonial period in which landed elites entrenched themselves in elected offices and subsequently went on to gain a stranglehold over a weak state. On some level, the Philippines' claim to be the first democratic country in Asia has come to haunt its prospects for institution building and social reform. The legacy of the Marcos dictatorship, however, does not inspire confidence that there are better prospects under the aegis of authoritarianism. In both democratic and authoritarian regimes, equitable development has fared poorly precisely because the fatal weakness in the polity has been the fecklessness of political institutions.

Throughout Philippine history there have been a number of openings in which social reform or institution building could have gained momentum, yet none were sustained. The two most important moments came under Magsaysay and Corazon Aquino. Magsaysay may have been a more genuine reformer given his nonelite background, but Aquino did also show concern for the popular sector, at least initially, by appointing a number of prominent NGO leaders to the cabinet. Nonetheless, the same lesson holds for the general failure of reform under these two governments as for all previous governments: without institutions that can sustain and defend social reform, political will or sympathy for the poor from a political leader is simply not enough.

The prospects for equitable development in the Philippines ultimately lie with institution building, both within the state and within the party system. Although civil society must constitute one prong in the push for social reform, it cannot be the mainstay of reformists' hopes.[90] The Philippines today is not completely devoid of initiatives to strengthen institutions, as the examples of Akbayan and the Liberal Party have suggested. But compared with some of its neighbors in Southeast Asia, the Philippines has a much longer road to travel in the search for cohesive institutions. This, ultimately, must be the primary task of those who seek reform in a country that seems so stubbornly impervious to change.

Vietnam

With the backdrop of two major wars against Western powers, Vietnam's developmental trajectory has been impressive. In 1990, its GDP per capita was US$98. By 2009, it was US$1,032.[91] Growth rates in the 1990s were stellar, averaging 7.5 percent per year.[92] Although its GDP per capita still lags behind that of other capitalist Southeast Asian countries, its surge in the past two decades has begun to close the gap. This is especially evident in regard to its socioeconomic position vis-à-vis the Philippines.[93] Even more crucial in terms of this study is that the distribution of income has remained relatively healthy despite the turn toward market liberalization. This is due in large part to the earlier socialist policies of land reform, mass education, and primary health care. Like Japan, Korea, and Taiwan, early efforts toward equity have had a long-term impact on the developmental trajectory, which makes it more likely that the effects of growth will be more equitably shared.

The political explanation for this trajectory has to do with an institutionalized, socialist party that has been committed to social reform. The Vietnamese Communist Party (VCP) has been extremely effective at establishing roots in society, mobilizing its social base, changing leadership through systematic procedures, and maintaining a relatively disciplined organization. The VCP's coherence and rootedness in socialist ideology has kept the party on track with its policy agenda. The VCP's distinct characteristic, however, has been its ability to maintain a moderate course despite its strong socialist leanings. Compared with other similar communist regimes, the VCP has been willing and able to shift policy direction when it realized that its policy choice had not worked or when it had incited considerable opposition. This flexibility has enabled it to weather crises and maintain legitimacy among its social base.

ECONOMIC RECORD

Since Vietnam embarked on its *doi moi* (renovation) policy in 1986, its growth rates have been impressive. From 1993 to 2004, its average yearly GDP growth rate was 7.5 percent (see Table 7-4). Vietnam now spearheads the third generation of Asian Tigers. From 1993 to 2004, poverty declined by almost 39 percentage points. In 1993, the poverty rate was 58.1 percent; by 2002, it had gone down to 28.9 percent, and by 2004, it was 19.5 percent (see Table 7-5).[94] This extremely rapid decline in poverty in slightly more than a decade is a remarkable feat.

With the shift toward a market economy, Vietnam's traditionally egalitarian social structure came under greater scrutiny. Some argued that a wide array of data indicated worsening inequalities,[95] whereas some analysts at the World Bank wrote that "there is little sign of sharply rising income or consumption inequality."[96] If we look at the Gini coefficient, the only study that has calculated it on the basis of *income* reported a decline from .450 in 1993 to .378 in 2002, and then to .379 in 2006 (see Table 7-6 and Figure 7-2).[97] A recent report also concludes: "After more than a decade of reforming the economy from central planning into a market economy, the society of Vietnam today is quite equal in *relative* terms."[98] However, the

TABLE 7-4
Vietnam, GDP Growth Rates, 1985–2009 (percentage)

Year	Average growth rate
1985–89	4.5
1990–94	7.3
1995–99	7.5
2000–04	7.2
2005–09	7.3

SOURCE: World Bank WDI.

TABLE 7-5
Vietnam, Incidence of Poverty, 1993–2004 (percentage)

Year	Poverty rate
1993	58.1
1998	37.4
2002	28.9
2004	19.5

SOURCES: Luong 2003a: 1; VASS 2007; World Bank WDI.

same report notes that absolute inequality, defined as the gap between the top and bottom quintiles, has increased. Furthermore, the Gini coefficient calculated on the basis of *consumption* in this report shows a very slight increase in inequality, from .34 in 1993 to .35 in 1998 and .37 in 2004.[99]

If we look at the expenditures (consumption) of the quintiles, we see that the top quintile rose from 41.8 percent in 1993 to 44.7 percent of total expenditures in 2004, whereas that of the bottom quintile fell from 8.4 percent to 7.1 percent.[100] Hence, although the distribution of income in Vietnam remains quite low and its Gini coefficient has either been declining or remaining relatively constant in a period of market liberalization, it is also clear that the gap between the richest and the poorest has been widening. Given the decline or relative stability of the Gini coefficient, what this means is that the middle three quintiles are bunched more closely

TABLE 7-6
Vietnam, Distribution of Income, 1993–2006: Gini
Coefficient

Year	Gini coefficient
1993	.450
1998	.433
2002	.378
2006	.379

SOURCE: McCaig et al. 2009.

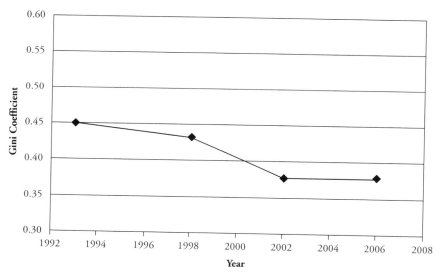

FIGURE 7-2 Vietnam, Trend in Income Inequality, 1993–2006
SOURCE: McCaig et al. 2009.

together—indicating a broad middle class—and the tails are widening. The gap between the highest and lowest quintiles is worrisome, but in the aggregate, the fact that the Gini coefficient still remains low, and that a study based on income shows it declining sharply while one based on consumption shows a very slight increase, suggests that the distribution of income is relatively even.

The relationship among growth, poverty, and inequality has been central to growth's positive effects on poverty reduction. Because Vietnam's level of inequality has been consistently low, growth rates have been able to reduce poverty more rapidly. The low level of inequality is, in turn, a direct result of the Viet Minh's policies of land reform and mass education. The recent land law promulgated in 1993 has continued the pattern of pro-poor land policy by making land allocation more efficient. Furthermore, growth has been explicitly pro-poor in the sense that the state has distributed the benefits of growth toward the poorer sectors of society, in terms of households and regions. Social transfers, including social insurance, social assistance, and education fee exemptions, were directed to the poorer households.[101] Interprovincial transfers have flowed from the richer to the poorer provinces.

Rural development has been a central pillar of Vietnam's equitable growth trajectory. Even in the 1990s, when Vietnam's liberalization policies began to take effect, it still maintained support for the rural sector. This contrasts with Thailand, where the rural sector has been given lower priority vis-à-vis industrialization during the economic takeoff of the 1980s. Compared with a select group of Asian countries, Vietnam's agricultural land productivity in the 1980s and 1990s was the fastest, and its impact on rural poverty was the strongest.[102] Liberalization policies, such as the dismantling of price controls, have benefited small-scale farmers and have contributed to the country becoming the world's second-largest exporter of rice.

To mitigate the destabilizing effects of economic liberalization, the state has also provided low-interest loans for small-scale entrepreneurs, partial or full tuition exemptions for the poor in primary and secondary schools, and health insurance cards for the poor. Public spending sharply increased in education from 10.9 percent in 1992 to 17.4 percent in 1998, and in health from 5.8 percent in 1992 to 8.5 percent in 1998. Furthermore, expenditures for education were reallocated toward primary and lower secondary levels, which tend to benefit the poor more.[103]

COLONIALISM AND THE BIRTH OF THE VIET MINH

The roots of the Vietnamese Communist Party (VCP) were forged in the anticolonialist struggle. While working in a photo shop in Paris, Ho Chi Minh was part of a delegation that called on the Allies at the Versailles peace conference to grant Vietnam autonomy. The Allied countries' dismissal of the Vietnamese delegation's requests, despite the granting of self-determination to numerous European nation-states, pushed Ho toward Marxism and away from his early attraction to Wilsonian democracy. Ho joined the Comintern and then founded the Vietnamese Revolutionary Youth League in 1925. As the league began to stress the importance of class struggle, it eventually transformed into the Indochinese Communist Party (ICP) in 1930 in Hong Kong.[104]

Having traveled to Moscow and closely studied Marxism-Leninism, Ho's model for the league and then the ICP was that of a strong Leninist organization with a clear and resolute ideology: "Only if the party is solid can the revolution succeed, just as only when the helmsman is firmly in control can the ship sail. If we want to have a solid party, it must have an ideology as its foundation, an ideology that everyone in the party must understand and follow. A party without an ideology is like a person without intelligence, a ship without a compass."[105] The party's ironclad discipline was also reinforced by the need to develop secret cells to evade the French *sûreté*. Compared with the Nationalist Party, another organization fomenting national revolution that met its demise, the ICP was more disciplined and cohesive and therefore able to survive repression from the French. Described by one analyst as "original, innovative, durable," the early party organization had territorial, functional, and external structures that enabled the party to develop cells across the country; to link up with social groups, including workers, farmers, students, women, and elderly villagers; and to liaise with international communist and labor movements.[106] Despite the intense repression the party suffered in this period at the hands of the French, its organizational structure began to take hold and form the core of its strategic imperative.

In the 1930s, the ICP upheld a proletarian agenda, but by the 1940s, it had moved away from class struggle as the core of its ideology. In the context of the Japanese invasion and the domestic preoccupations of the Soviet and Chinese communist parties, the ICP took a more pragmatic approach toward revolution, focusing on fighting imperialism through a united front that included the middle class and even landlords. In 1943, the Viet Minh emerged as a broad national front for the Communist Party, which would enable it to attract nationalists who did not necessarily share communist ideals.

A devastating famine in northern Vietnam in 1944 provided a window of opportunity for the Viet Minh to launch its revolutionary reforms and penetrate the countryside. As a famine ravaged northern Vietnam, colonial authorities and local notables showed little concern for the peasants' plight, instead hoarding paddy in granaries despite the miserable conditions in which the peasants found themselves. Peasants had long been seething at the colonial government's requisitioning of paddy at an unfair price.

General Vo Nguyen Giap led the Viet Minh army into northern villages and mobilized peasants to seize granaries and oust the local officials. As rice was distributed to starving peasants, the Viet Minh created village self-defense companies to protect villages that had sided with them. The Viet Minh's mobilization to provide peasants with food created the foundations for a loyal peasant base. This was the beginning of the Communist Party's roots in the peasantry. No other political force had made any effort to help the peasants of Tonkin, whose famine ended up claiming between five hundred thousand and 2 million lives.

Following its success in addressing the famine, the Viet Minh forged ahead in its push against the colonial authorities. The year 1945 was extremely tumultuous, as the Japanese formally took over from the French and were in turn ousted by the Viet Minh. The Viet Minh were not the only pretenders to replace the colonial powers. The Vietnamese Nationalist Party and several religious sects were also in contention. Yet the Viet Minh proved more skillful at recruiting members, mobilizing social groups, and articulating a vision of independence. A cohesive and disciplined organizational structure allowed it to decisively surpass its national rivals.

What was also critical at this stage of the revolution is that the Viet Minh forged the national front as a movement for nationalism rather than primarily for communism. In doing so, it was able to bring in middle peasants, landlords, the urban middle class, and intellectuals, who were united by the desire for independence. The Viet Minh was able to use its national salvation organizations to recruit many new members. Thus, "doctors, poets, soldiers, and bureaucrats attended the meetings of their respective national salvation associations to discuss what their members could do to create a new Vietnam."[107] The Viet Minh also targeted enlisted men and noncommissioned officers, locally powerful guilds like the weavers and fishermen, and machinists and skilled workers.[108] Peasant associations included rich peasants, middle peasants, poor peasants, and hirelings. Even labor unions did not follow a strictly communist agenda. Small owners of shops and factories were also recruited into labor unions.[109] Had the Viet Minh focused only on class struggle, the party would not have attracted the broad base of support that would be vital in fighting the returning French. Equally important at this time was the communists' targeting of youth organizations in the provincial capitals. The communists successfully co-opted the youth and sport program, developed by the French in Cochinchina, as a basis for social mobilization.[110]

Following the Japanese surrender in August 1945, the Viet Minh launched its August Revolution to claim sovereignty over the country. Building on the party's success in addressing the famine, the Viet Minh further consolidated the support of the peasantry by implementing many pro-poor policies. It confiscated and redistributed property of certain administrators and villagers who fled the arrival of the Viet Minh; it reduced land rents; it improved water storage and irrigation facilities; it instituted a single progressive tax to replace the much-despised French and Japanese body and land taxes; it began compulsory primary education; it enforced literacy campaigns across all social groups; it put forth labor laws to address the minimum wage and social insurance; it returned to the common pool communal land that landlords had appropriated; it allowed everyone who had lived in the village for five years the right to a piece of communal land; it reformed the bidding system for communal lands by creating a fairer process so that the rich could not stake their claim first; it prohibited evictions before the harvest or for small debts; and it improved women's rights by giving them a share of their land when their husbands were gone from the village.[111] These reforms were radical changes in the hierarchy of the villages and in the social lives of the peasants. At this point, however, they were not excessively alienating to the richer peasants or the landlord class because they did not expropriate property. Given the urgency of maintaining a cohesive national movement against the French, the Viet Minh made a conscious effort to advance progressive reforms that improved the conditions of the peasantry without excessively antagonizing the richer folk.

A critical aspect of the Viet Minh campaign was the ability to penetrate villages in Annam, Tonkin, and Cochinchina. The Viet Minh was much more successful in Annam and Tonkin, where the headquarters was based, than in Cochinchina, where it faced more competition from religious sects such as the Hoa Hao and Cao Dai, Catholics, and entrenched landlords closely allied with the French.[112] Initially in northern and central Vietnam, the Viet Minh formed intervillage administrations as a means of building support among the peasants. In effect, these were clandestine government structures parallel to those of the French. Eventually, the incipient administrations allowed them to erode the power of the local notables. The party's social reforms were extremely popular and provided the support base from which it could then take over the village administrations. As productivity increased because of peasants' greater food security and access to land and resources, the peasants became extremely supportive of the Viet Minh. The literacy campaigns that the Viet Minh developed, for example, were in marked contrast to the traditional elite, who had expressly sought to block peasants from improving their education. Once the Viet Minh had control of the village administrations, it would be able to mobilize peasants in the national liberation movement and establish a core social base for the Communist Party.

In Cochinchina, the Viet Minh had to struggle harder to establish control. Although the peasants in the south were more militant, the greater competition for loyalty was much more intense than in the central and northern regions. As peasants began to seize land from landowners, local communist groups decided to support the move. As in the north, the Viet Minh was able to advance a number of reforms that gained it the support of the peasantry. These included the formation of local courts, which gave the peasants a fairer hearing; the creation of peasants' and women's associations, which empowered both groups; and the establishment of literacy classes that were tailored to the needs of farmers, as classes were held during the slack period of agriculture.[113] The Viet Minh effectively used the social programs, such as the literacy classes, as a form of collective mobilization. The classrooms would serve as forums for discussing social issues and helping those with urgent social problems.[114]

The penetration of villages throughout Vietnam and the implementation of social programs that benefited the lives of the peasants strengthened the political position of the Viet Minh vis-à-vis the French and other rival political and religious forces. The Viet Minh was successful at this stage of the revolution because it was able to advance its agenda gradually in a way that gained the trust and loyalty of the peasantry. Although some of the richest landlords were driven out or fled, many landlords and rich peasants sided with the Viet Minh because of their support for the anticolonialist cause. The significance of the support of groups in the upper strata of the countryside is that it forged a broad coalition that allowed the Viet Minh to succeed in its goals of rural penetration and eventual defeat of the French.

It bears highlighting that what the Viet Minh brought in terms of social reforms to the countryside was a drastic change for the peasants, even
though the reforms themselves were not quite radical in a more communist
sense. Neglected by the landlords and repressed by the French, the peasants
saw a remarkable change of fortune with the leftist-nationalist movement's
push to improve peasants' living conditions. Samuel Popkin's interview with
one peasant in southern Vietnam captures this change from the point of
view of the peasant:

> [During the war] we had money but there were no clothes available to buy
> anywhere. We had one pair of pajamas. . . . When my wife went to the market I
> would stay in the house and then when she came back I would wear the pajamas
> to the field. . . . The pajamas wore out and all we had was a single rice sack. . . .
> When she wore the sack to market I stayed home. . . . Then I wore the sack to
> the fields. The only time we could go to the fields together was at night when no
> one could see us . . . we were so ashamed. . . . Then the Viet Minh came to our
> village. . . . They had some cloth and a few sacks and they brought some cotton
> seeds and taught us how to plant them.[115]

A formidable organizational structure underlay the success of the party
in advancing reforms in the villages and improving the living conditions
of the peasantry. It was especially during the first Indochina War that the
party sharpened its organizational apparatus to defeat the French and assert its authority throughout the countryside. Through cohesive leadership,
democratic-centralist decision making, disciplined and committed cadres,
well-honed communication mechanisms, and forceful and consistent ideology, the party was able to pursue its agenda and seize power. Without
organization, the party could not have fulfilled its promises of social change
to the peasantry.[116] "The party's true genius," writes Douglas Pike, "was its
ability to identify and then develop the great truths of organization. Some
were insights by Ho Chi Minh, some were borrowed from the Chinese,
some were the fruit of experience and experimentation. Combined, they
formed what amounted to a new discipline in sociology."[117]

LAND REFORM

The first major misstep of the party, however, came in the mid-1950s, when
doctrinal zeal gained the upper hand. Land reform began to take effect only
in 1953, once the war against the French was well under way and villages

were under the control of the party. These land reforms saw the party take a more radical turn in dispossessing many middle and rich peasants who had been at the heart of the nationalist movement. The land reform itself redistributed 2,001,553 acres among 10,514,000 peasants in 3,314 villages, which constituted 72.8 percent of the rural population.[118] In the annals of land reform, this was one of the more extensive campaigns. The reform destroyed the Tonkinese landlords, but it also wreaked havoc among middle and rich peasants. Many of the middle and rich peasants were wrongly classified as landlords by radical leaders and overzealous cadres who fanned out to the villages to implement the reforms. Although both middle and rich peasants owned some land, with the former being self-sufficient and the latter having enough land to hire extra labor, they worked their land themselves and had been committed members of the Viet Minh and the backbone of the resistance against the French.

The excesses of the land reform had to do with the cadres' belief that they were empowered and directed by the party leaders to restructure society and fulfill a stipulated quota of landlords to hunt down. But they also stemmed from a lack of training and paranoia that reactionary forces abounded in the villages and that these forces had to be ferreted out by any means. By directing the cadres to attack the middle and rich peasants, radical leaders in the party allowed some of its earliest members and some of its staunchest supporters to fall victim to violence and persecution. More than thirty thousand peasant households were misclassified, and many were denounced unfairly.[119] Not only were middle and rich peasants punished, but those who defended their neighbors were also subject to retaliation. Although the number of deaths resulting from the land reform is mired in controversy, recent estimates put the number at fifteen thousand.[120]

Part of the problem with the land-reform initiative was not simply excessive zeal of cadres and lack of adequate monitoring from party headquarters but, more fundamentally, a real tension in the goals of the revolution. The revolution was both a national and a social revolution, and once the national revolution was under way, the party moved toward its more socialist phase. The goal here was not just to alleviate the miserable conditions of the poor peasants but also to empower them so that they would become strong advocates of the party and active in local organizations. But in that move, party leaders came up against class divisions that they did not adequately assess and understand.

The party had earlier made a conscious effort to broaden out the social base to defeat the French, yet it appeared to have misjudged the tensions that would arise once this base was narrowed, assuming that only the true landlords, those who did not cultivate their land, would be dispossessed. The radical leaders and cadres who spearheaded the land reforms and mobilized the poor peasants to seize land believed that all peasants who owned land were to be punished and treated as landlords. The irony here was that most of these middle and rich peasants were the most ardent supporters of the national revolution, whereas many of the poor peasants had actually fought on the French side. Suddenly, the roles were reversed, with the poor peasants being given priority and the rich peasants being inexplicably punished despite their loyalty to the party.[121]

It took a while for the party to realize the extent of the damage being caused in the countryside, but once the last wave of land reforms had been executed, it began to conduct a postmortem. In August 1956, Ho Chi Minh admitted openly that the party had gone too far. In October 1956, General Giap, fresh from his victory at Dien Bien Phu, was placed in charge of national unity to address the rift between the poor peasants and the middle and rich peasants. Giap conceded that the party had failed to prevent "leftist deviations and unjust punishment."[122] The editorial in the party's newspaper then took full blame for the excesses of the campaign: "The errors which recently occurred were general errors of our Party. These errors harmed the whole people and the whole Party. They were not the particular errors of any particular comrades."[123] The party's willingness to accept collective responsibility for the "grave error" rather than scapegoat particular individuals is relatively unique in the annals of communist history. The general secretary of the party, Truong Chinh, was forced to resign from the politburo to take responsibility for the excesses of the land reform, and Le Duan, who had been in South Vietnam during the land-reform period and had therefore not been involved in the conflict, was appointed the new general secretary.

The party then made a major effort to bring back the middle and rich peasants. Former landowners were reclassified, and efforts were made to rehabilitate them. More than 50 percent of those who had been classified as landlords were reclassified and part of their property returned to them. The party had to make huge efforts to ease the tensions between the poor peasants, who in the reforms' aftermath were befuddled by the turn of events, and the rich peasants who held grudges against the poor peasants. One of the lessons the party learned was that, in the future, it had to conduct pro-poor reforms more carefully. This lesson was then applied to the collectivization programs, where the party initially moved gradually to increase the size of cooperatives.

COLLECTIVIZATION

The end of the first Indochina War gave the Viet Minh the opportunity to completely restructure the economy under its control, yet precisely because of the turmoil created by land reform and the concern not to alienate supporters any further, the "economic policies adopted immediately following the Geneva Conference were essentially moderate."[124] The government nationalized banks, utilities, and large enterprises, and it regulated wages, prices, and the allocation of goods. Yet, at least until 1958, it also made some initial concessions, by allowing manufacturing and trade to remain in private hands, and the middle class was told that its profits would be respected.[125]

Collectivization then took off in the late 1950s. The importance of collectivization for the state was that it improved agricultural productivity, provided surplus to finance industrialization, and granted poor peasants access to resources, such as draft animals, equipment, irrigation water, and increasing social welfare support. Collectivization occurred in three stages, first through the creation of seasonal labor exchange teams, then through the formation of small-scale cooperatives in which land and equipment were shared and a small rent given to former owners, and finally to the building of a socialist collective farm in which income was distributed on the basis of work points. In the early 1980s, more than 80 percent of all farm families in lowland areas in North Vietnam were incorporated in cooperatives.[126]

The cooperatives did not meet the expectations of the party. The main reason for this was the lack of incentive for output and productivity. The compensation system in the cooperatives functioned on the basis of "workdays." After parts of the produce were allocated to government agencies, the rest of the produce was distributed among the workers on the basis of workdays. The value of a workday per individual (e.g., its equivalent value in paddy) was based on dividing the remainder of the produce by the total number of workdays everyone in the organization had earned.[127] The problem with this was that the reward for work was far removed from the actual work conducted by the individual, and furthermore that individual had to believe that all others were working as hard as he, otherwise his share of workdays would be unfair. What was also problematic in Vietnam was the fact that peasants had never embraced collective farming, unlike land reform. Peasants were used to working as family units, and the total collectivity that the cooperatives required was anathema to villagers' work habits.[128]

Furthermore, the government also repressed the price of agricultural produce to create a surplus for industry, thereby pushing farmers to sell their goods on the black market and to focus on their household plots, whose goods they were allowed to sell on the open market. Income from these sanctioned private plots rose from 40 percent in the 1960s to 60–70 percent in the late 1970s.[129] The cooperatives did improve social equity by ensuring that peasants had food security, health-care programs, education, and social welfare (e.g., child care). Compared with other countries with similar per capita income, Vietnam's welfare conditions ranked much higher.[130] Yet real incomes actually declined precisely because there was no incentive for production.[131]

Debates about the pace and scale of collectivization were rife within the party from the very beginning. In the late 1950s, the party was embroiled in debates about whether to speed up or slow down collectivization. Local party officials were skeptical that collectivization was improving agricultural productivity and that peasants were supporting it.[132] Despite the fact that party leaders had decided by 1958 to speed up collectivization to expedite the creation of a centrally planned economy in which the rural sector would provide surplus for industrial takeoff, the issue was far from resolved among party officials. In 1962, government and party officials were still questioning the merits of cooperatives vis-à-vis family farming.[133] At a December 1963 meeting, several members of the party called for making the collective more similar to the Chinese model, to which the executive committee of the party responded that this was a position lacking a "spirit of independence."[134] On the other wing of the party, members criticized the politburo for having introduced agricultural cooperatives too early.[135]

Collectivization eventually collapsed because peasants simply saw no benefit to be gained from it. They did not find that they could produce enough for their own families, and they were outraged by corruption of cooperative leaders. In Benedict Kerkvliet's analysis, peasants expressed their discontent through "everyday politics." Without openly challenging the policy, peasants surreptitiously refused to comply or they more actively went against the directives of the cooperatives. They worked sluggishly in the collective fields and concentrated their energies on their household plots; they encroached on collective fields and took paddy from those fields; and they grew paddy and raised draft animals in their own plots rather than in the cooperatives. In most of these actions, local leaders gradually acquiesced, in part not to allow the whole system to collapse. By the early 1980s, national leaders were making numerous concessions, but by 1987–88, they accepted defeat and ended the cooperative system.[136]

Kerkvliet's argument that everyday politics was a fundamental cause of the demise of collectivization is compelling, but it represents only one part of the equation. The balance of this argument heaves greatly toward social forces. What such an argument does not address is why the party acquiesced to such resistance. The standard answer is that as the central base of support for the party, it would be dangerous for the party to alienate the peasantry, particularly because three-fourths of the population lived in the countryside.[137] Yet, as several authors have pointed out, the VCP's policies and behavior were relatively moderate compared with those of other communist states, including Stalinist Russia, Maoist China, and Pol Pot's Cambodia.[138] Kerkvliet himself writes:

> Authorities in Vietnam rarely used brute force to herd people into cooperatives, punish those who broke rules, or confiscate their possessions. When they encountered major problems, party leaders stressed management reforms, reorganization, and improved leadership and did not engage in the vicious campaigns against alleged subversives that occurred in other communist countries. . . . Unlike in Cambodia under the Khmer Rouge regime in the 1970s, families were not broken up or fused into communal living arrangements. Nor were villagers in Vietnam required to cook and eat together, as they had been in China during the late 1950s. Collective cooperatives in Vietnam even allowed families to produce a little on their own.[139]

This comparative perspective suggests that the answer to the VCP's acquiescence to peasant resistance to collectivization cannot rely solely on the party's need for peasant support. That is one part of the answer, but it is incomplete given that other communist parties have based their authority on rural support, and yet have had no compunction in employing violence against their own social base. Where we should look for an answer, then, is in the particular ideological makeup of the party—that is, that the VCP has historically been a pragmatic party committed to socialism but not excessively dogmatic about its agenda. This is a party that has been willing to make compromises to advance its twin goals of national sovereignty and a socialist state. Like Malaysia's UMNO, this party has had to weave between different directions, reversing course when it went too far left, but it has ultimately remained relatively moderate vis-à-vis other similar communist regimes. More important, it has kept its ear to the ground, never completely shunning popular opinion.

By contrast, not only were the policies of the Khmer Rouge, the Soviet Communist Party under Stalin, and the Chinese Communist Party under Mao extreme; these were parties whose institutionalization had eroded at the time of the excesses, or in the case of the Khmer Rouge, were largely devoid of an institutional structure. These parties were centered heavily on personality cults. Although the Soviet Communist Party initially was more institutionalized and returned to a more pragmatic position under Nikita Khrushchev, during the collectivization drive under Stalin, the party was marked by brutality. Furthermore, all of these parties at some point in their histories initiated mass campaigns of hysteria, whether in the likes of China's Cultural Revolution or in terms of the Khmer Rouge's paranoia toward middle-class and foreign enemies. In fact, the Vietnamese party leaders indicated their distaste for Mao's Cultural Revolution and did not persecute intellectuals, nor was class warfare against landlords or capitalists as extensive as it was in China.[140] The only period in which the VCP engaged in excessive violence was during the land reforms. Yet the party later acknowledged making a "grave error" and sought to redress this. Furthermore, the extent of violence was of a lower magnitude compared to purges executed under Stalin, Pol Pot, and Mao.

THE PRAGMATISM OF DOI MOI

Like the gradual about-face on collectivization, the state also came under pressure in regards to its centrally planned economy. The broad problem with a centrally planned economy is a lack of incentive for production and severe price distortions. By the late 1970s, the economy was caught in a chronic disequilibrium between supply and demand as industry failed to meet the demand for more resources. At the same time, shortages increased and resources were being channeled to the outside economy because of the difference between state and market prices.[141]

In response to the economy's stagnation, the state initiated some reforms in 1979 to grant enterprises more autonomy. After a number of stops and gos in policy reform, the government took an important step by implementing price liberalization in 1985, thereby ending the ration system and monetization of wages for state employees. A looming economic crisis in 1986 driven by rising inflation, declining productivity from state-owned enterprises, and the sharp reduction in aid from the Soviet Union pushed the state to implement more sweeping reforms, known as *doi moi*, or renovation. Some of the most important changes under *doi moi* included a law permitting foreign investment, the floating of the exchange rate, and an end to official prices. Liberal market reforms thus brought the Vietnamese economy to a 180-degree shift from its vision of a centrally planned economy. By the late 1980s, Vietnam's economy had begun to take off.

The political basis for wide-scale reforms was the sixth party congress in December 1986. At this congress, important changes were made in the main ruling bodies of the party. A generational shift accompanied these changes, as many of the founding members of the party had retired and the number of central, party, state, and military officials had declined. In their place were lower-level and provincial officials. Three of the top leaders retired, including General Secretary and President Truong Chinh. The simultaneous retirement of several leaders is significant, because in most communist parties this often occurs through purging or death in office.[142] This change allowed Nguyen Van Linh, a pragmatic reformer from the south, to take over as general secretary and to deepen party reforms.

The congress was unique in the amount of internal criticism that the party allowed, particularly in terms of the country's economic trajectory. Like UMNO in 1969, faced with an economic crisis, the VCP decided to reform its own institutions. The party debates pointed to the need for institutional rejuvenation and a cleaning out of reactionary and corrupt members. Approximately one-third of the Central Committee members were replaced.[143] The party committed to attack corruption and reform the party and bureaucracy by calling on the media, writers, and artists to criticize corrupt bureaucrats and party members. By 1991, 127,000 party members had been disciplined and 78,000 expelled.[144] As well, the National Assembly was vested with more public authority. Linh was committed to regenerating the state and party while still maintaining control over the country. At the seventh party congress in 1991, the party moved away from the aim of building a socialist state to that of stabilizing socioeconomic and political conditions.[145] The party continued to engage with ideas of economic and political liberalization as well as recognizing the value of technocrats and intellectuals. In the 1990s, deputies showed more autonomy in the Assembly, often challenging decisions coming out of the executive.[146] In 1992, the constitution strengthened the rule of law and created more of a separation between state and party. Two years earlier, the constitution had already dropped reference to establishing a "dictatorship of the proletariat."

Although Vietnam functions as a one-party state, like UMNO the VCP does not act without the interests of society in mind. Kerkvliet has called this a "dialogic" or "responsive-repressive" system, Brantley Womack has conceptualized the VCP as "mass-regarding," and Chris Dixon has called the regime "authoritarian-corporatist."[147] Rather than stamp out dissent, the state seeks to absorb it.[148] This is a state that—though intent on maintaining its grip on power—is willing to negotiate with social groups. Indeed, it is noteworthy that although democratic revolutions brought down communist regimes throughout the Soviet Empire, they did not affect Vietnam. In part, this is because of the party's willingness to listen to concerns coming from the popular sector. It dismantled the collectivization system when it was clear that the peasants would not accept it. It liberalized the economy and allowed the private sector to thrive again. Despite the fact that strikes are illegal, it has condoned strikes and public demonstrations—with some deputies voicing their support for aggrieved workers.[149] And in the past two decades it has hesitantly allowed some civil liberties and engaged a number of the middle-class intelligentsia. These are all signs of a party that, though not democratic in an electoral or liberal sense, is representative in the sense that it does address some of the interests of its citizens.

From its very beginnings, the VCP, in its earlier incarnations as the Indochinese Communist Party and the Labor Party, and through its broader front of the Viet Minh organization, has been a highly institutionalized party. The key element of the party's success throughout has been organization. Through Leninist tactics in which the party has maintained a cohesive top-down agenda, through the building of cells throughout the countryside, and by maintaining a collective leadership rather than falling into the trap of personalistic charisma, the VCP has been able to remain institutionalized. Its cohesiveness is also evident in the fact that it did not experience purges or succession struggles as severe as did the Soviet Union and

China.[150] In fact, the collective leadership "neutralized attempts by leading political personalities to monopolize power."[151] Its tight organizational structure enabled the party to push through a battery of social reforms that in turn solidified a social base, thereby further institutionalizing the party. The initial success of the party in the critical early years in the 1950s in penetrating villages in the north and then winning over the peasants was in large part due to the institutionalized structure of the party. Political organization was necessary to penetrate villages and then to mobilize them to restructure village institutions and hierarchies. Institutionalization was also central to the party's ability to withstand and overcome two imperialist powers as well as other religious and civil rivals.

Buttressing the party's organizational structure are numerous party-affiliated mass organizations that are used to incorporate and mobilize social groups. The most important is the Vietnam Fatherland Front, an umbrella organization that coordinates twenty-five mass organizations and is responsible for approving candidates for the National Assembly. Other important organizations include the Vietnam General Confederation of Trade Unions, the Ho Chi Minh Communist Youth League, and the Vietnam Women's Union. The peasant organization, Nong Hoi, now the Vietnam Peasants' Association, is also a critical organization, having been instrumental in helping the party push through land reforms and in "persuad[ing], encourag[ing], and coerc[ing] villagers to join agricultural collectives."[152] In 1996, the Peasants' Association had ten thousand chapters with 7 million members, and some of its recent efforts have included the provision of no-interest loans to improve peasants' social welfare.[153] The party has also worked more closely with the Women's Union in the past decades to address rising gender inequality due to market liberalization.[154]

These mass organizations are essential to the party because they provide an immediate force for mobilization, and they enable the party to control key social groups. The party, in fact, places members from the Central Committee in leadership positions to steer the organizations. But these organizations are not just used for the purpose of mobilization and control. They also serve a semidemocratic function by providing social groups with a channel for expressing their interests, albeit in a tightly controlled manner. These organizations act as the party's ears in society. The party holds meetings periodically with these organizations to receive feedback. At the second congress of the Vietnam Peasants' Association, General Secretary Do Muoi commented that the association "must serve as a backbone force in the mass movement, attentively listen to and promptly give feedback to the party on critical peasant views, as well as feelings and aspirations."[155] Such comments have fostered an environment in which members of associations are able to make demands on the party and express their views relatively openly. These meetings between mass associations and the party are thus of value both to the social groups and to the party. They contribute to the strengthening of the social base, the deepening of the party's roots in society, and an understanding of the needs and mood of society.

The second element of the VCP's success has been its pragmatic behavior. Although the party has long upheld a socialist vision, it has never been so dogmatic as to preclude alliances and changes in strategy. The party did take a sharp radical turn and commit some serious errors by allowing some of its most loyal supporters to be persecuted during the land reform campaigns. Despite this, however, the party has generally adhered to a relatively inclusive socialist ideology. When the party's goal of a centrally planned economy came up against discontent and dismal economic conditions, it retreated and changed strategy. In collectivization, the party chose not to brutalize the peasants who resisted but to make some compromises, which eventually led to the complete dismantlement of the program. More generally, the planned economy was given the boot once it became clear that such a system would not jump-start the economy. One study noted that "in comparison, for example, with North Korea, Vietnamese central planning was, in some senses of the word, hardly serious. At crucial points (the early 1960s, the late 1970s) the Vietnamese leaders turned away from the violent logic inherent in the neo-Stalinist program, refusing (or unable) to shed the blood needed to curb the development of the free market."[156] By comparison with the communist parties in the Soviet Union, China, North Korea, and Cambodia, the VCP has been quite moderate in its behavior. Its early strategy of allying with middle and rich peasants is in fact closer to that of the democratic Communist Party-Marxist (CPM) of West Bengal, India, than to the more rigid authoritarian communist parties.

Conclusion

By extending the theoretical argument of this study to two other countries in Southeast Asia, we have seen that institutional power and capacity have been a central force in driving Vietnam's politics, whereas it has been sorely absent in that of the Philippines. In both cases, historical origins explain a great deal of the institutional fabric of states and parties and the long-term trajectory of development. Colonialism in the Philippines strengthened provincial oligarchs without hardening a bureaucratic core. These oligarchs then used elections to dominate politics, with parties serving as convenient vehicles for personal agendas. In Vietnam, the struggle against the French required that the VCP function as a disciplined party. Once the party was able to penetrate villages during a catastrophic famine, it began to establish itself as an organized force for reform. The extensive reforms that the VCP implemented gained it a loyal social base that would further institutionalize the party.

Despite major crises in both countries, institutional structures have remained largely constant. The Philippines has faced several crises, including the Huk Rebellion and the economic and political crisis of the later years of the Marcos regime. In both crises, there was an opportunity for change. Structural constraints could have pushed elites to tackle the crises through policy reforms and institutional changes. On some level, Magsaysay did move in that direction, but his reforms lacked an institutional foundation and therefore a basis for continuity beyond his own political will. In the aftermath of People Power, Aquino initiated some reforms but ultimately failed to go through with them, as she sought to defend electoral democracy while protecting her own class interests. Vietnam also went through major crises, shaped by wars and economic stagnation. What enabled Vietnam to get through its crises was the organizational consistency of the VCP and its ideological flexibility. Committed to socialism, the VCP was savvy enough to know when to shift gears. Although some data indicate that inequality has inched up under *doi moi*, given the high growth rates Vietnam's developmental trajectory is still remarkably equitable.

A rare comparative study of Vietnam and the Philippines concluded the following: "In the Philippines, workers, peasants, and low income people have far greater freedom than their Vietnamese counterparts to organize and protest against particular officials, government policies, and even the government itself. Yet Filipinos have much more difficulty being taken seriously by government officials. Philippine authorities rarely listen." By contrast, in Vietnam, state and party structures "monitor what people are doing and saying. This can intimidate and stifle open dissent. *But the structures are also ways for authorities to learn about problems and seek solutions.*"[157] The fact that the Philippine democratic government rarely listens, whereas Vietnam's authoritarian regime does, raises doubts about the positive effect of democracy for social reform. But more crucially, it reinforces the point that the presence or absence of institutionalized mechanisms of representation is critical for addressing the interests of the lower classes. For authorities to listen, seek change, and sustain an agenda of reform, there must be an organizational structure that penetrates into society and channels its concerns into government. Vietnam has one of the most effective institutional structures to do this, and the Philippines one of the weakest.

EIGHT

Conclusion

This study has charted the politics of equitable development in four countries in Southeast Asia. What we have seen is that institutionalized parties, cohesive interventionist states, and pragmatic policies and ideologies have been crucial in achieving equitable development. The absence of one or several of these variables has made it less likely for a country to move in the direction of equitable development. The central idea advanced here is that powerful and capable institutions are fundamental for pursuing equitable development.

A comparative historical framework has reinforced the importance of historical factors and historical timing in shaping developmental outcomes. In Malaysia and Vietnam, opposition to a colonial regime or to a colonial project stimulated the formation of strong parties. In Thailand, the absence of colonialism limited the impulse for a nationalist party, whereas in the Philippines, the advent of democratic elections throughout the archipelago before the cementing of a bureaucratic core weakened the potential for institutional development. In the long run, these historical processes had a significant effect on institution building and on the prospects for social reform.

The two positive cases in this study, Malaysia and Vietnam, have both had relatively similar institutional features that have enabled them to achieve equitable development. In both countries, institutionalized parties have advanced reforms following major crises that significantly restructured social relations. Both the United Malays National Organization (UMNO) and the Vietnamese Communist Party (VCP) have been cohesive, disciplined, adaptable, programmatic, and rooted in society. Ethnic roots have kept UMNO linked to its social base and focused on ethnic redistribution. Ties to the peasantry have been the foundation of the VCP and have kept its ideology aligned with its social constituency.

Steeped in the late-colonial period's struggle for Malay rights, UMNO has always stood as the advocate of the Malays. Its genesis stemmed from the effort to block the British postwar plan to grant Chinese citizenship rights. Since the campaign against the Malayan Union, UMNO has staunchly advanced and defended Malay interests. Its success in pushing through social reforms for the Malays has come through its institutional depth. Although in the pre-1969 period the party made strenuous efforts to support the Malays, it did not go far enough to break with the structural patterns that were limiting Malay economic advancement. The party in the 1960s had become too personalized under Abdul Rahman. The state continued to follow a laissez-faire approach and, despite heavy public spending in the rural sector, did not intervene forcefully enough to improve the capacities of the Malays and increase their opportunities in the modern sector.

After the 1969 riots, UMNO restructured the party, making it more disciplined and cohesive; revamped its governing multiethnic coalition, making itself more hegemonic and co-opting most parties in the system; led the state in a significantly more interventionist direction; and crafted a policy agenda that was redistributive but also growth inducing. In rural development, UMNO made major inroads because it had a vast network at the grassroots level and constantly monitored policy implementation through feedback between the center and offices in the periphery. In terms of education, the state intervened aggressively to build an urban professional class by redistributing resources and by building numerous institutions that would improve the skills and capacities of the Malays. In the health sector, the state focused on improving access in the countryside, especially by focusing on primary care and low-cost interventions.

In Malaysia, UMNO has been able to penetrate the countryside and pursue its development policies through ubiquitous party branches built throughout the periphery. Representatives elected at the national and state level work constantly to advance the party agenda at the local level and routinely make themselves available to their constituents. Parliamentarians and state assembly members must always engage in dialogue with the branch unit to have a sense of the political currents in the villages and towns. The ability of UMNO to execute its goals and to adjust policy when necessary stems in large part from the party's responsiveness and rootedness at the local level. Even the Chinese, though disadvantaged in the political system, have parties to call on for support. In small towns in Kelantan, for example, despite the dominance of an Islamic-Malay party (PAS), the Chinese party—the Malaysian Chinese Association—still maintains branch offices, which serve as a place where constituents can articulate their needs and grievances.[1] In the mid-1970s, an analysis of Malaysian members of Parliament's (MP) work and meetings stressed the extensive tasks expected of and fulfilled by the party official: "[T]he MP is often seen as an arbitrator who is trusted to settle issues in a disinterested way. . . . [H]e is also involved in the whole range of problems that confront constituents in their dealings with the government; he is asked to champion their causes or plead their case."[2] Although this study has focused heavily on showing how UMNO has sought to represent its Malay constituency, a broader pattern evident in Malaysia is the effective representation (with one exception) of all ethnic groups through programmatic parties.[3] Equitable development can thus be attained in Malaysia because the parties are institutionalized and representative in the broadest sense.

The VCP's origins as a revolutionary organization challenging one of the more brutal colonial regimes in Southeast Asia provided it with the structural girders from which to develop into an institutionalized party. Like most communist parties, the VCP upheld a Leninist organizational structure that ensured discipline, cohesiveness, and territorial penetration. Once an opportunity arose to advance its agenda, the VCP forcefully initiated its pro-poor policies. In the 1944 famine and in the early 1950s, the VCP implemented a battery of pro-poor policies that generated loyalty and a deep social base among the peasantry. Through programs involving agricultural support, mass education, and primary health care, the VCP showed decisively that its raison d'être was based on a real representative function. Combining both organizational cohesiveness and deep roots in society, the VCP has become one of the more institutionalized parties in the developing world. This institutionalization has provided it with the consistency and power to continue sustaining its programmatic agenda.

Along with their institutionalized structures, UMNO and the VCP also share another critical property: moderation. In spite of its origins as the advocate of Malay interests, UMNO has rarely veered toward ethnic extremism. This moderation can be traced to the early years of the party's founding. The aristocratic and bureaucratic origins of the party's leaders; the exhortations of the British for a postcolonial, multicommunal democratic arrangement; and competition from more radical Malay parties anchored UMNO within a more pragmatic position. In the aftermath of the 1969 riots, UMNO acted more decisively in favor of Malay interests, but it did not succumb to the temptation of retaliatory acts against the Chinese. Rather, under Abdul Razak, the party first expelled the radical leaders who had advocated punitive action but then brought them back in and pursued their agenda for sweeping change. But through a pragmatic leadership, the party implemented an agenda for structural reform in a rationalized and restrained manner that was in line with the party's moderate instincts.

Despite its more hegemonic position in the post-1969 Barisan Nasional, UMNO still felt it necessary to stick to a multicommunal coalition. Its pragmatism in its policy direction, particularly in maintaining an agenda of growth with equity within the New Economic Policy, and of pursuing redistribution without seizure of assets, as well as later decisions, such as allowing Chinese private universities to gain a foothold, or closing an eye to so-called Ali Baba business partnerships that allowed Chinese to run government-favored Malay firms, suggest that the party has stuck to a centrist course. This effort to steer toward the center runs against the tendency among the more activist grass roots for extremist action,[4] as well as the pattern of other ethnically riven countries, such as Fiji, Guyana, or Sri Lanka, where the ethnic majority in control of the state has often lashed out against the economically stronger ethnic group. Furthermore, Malaysia has a much better record in terms of ethnic relations between Malays and Chinese than does its neighbor, Indonesia, where violence against the Chinese has been recurrent.

Like UMNO, the VCP has generally been quite moderate in its political behavior. This moderation stemmed from its efforts to create a broad nationalist front that would be able to overwhelm the repressive colonial regime. Initially, the party was willing to ally with landlords and rich peasants in pursuit of a common nationalist goal. But in its determination to deepen the social revolution, the VCP overdid its land-reform drive and persecuted thousands of middle and rich peasants who had been the backbone of the party's nationalist movement. Once the dust had settled, however, the VCP admitted that it had gone too far and made major efforts to rebalance its social base and rehabilitate the middle and rich peasants who had been attacked and stripped of their assets. This decision to acknowledge a party error, rather than blame individuals, is relatively unusual for a communist institution. The VCP also decided to move toward a more liberalized market in the face of a stagnating economy. Such decisions reinforce the view that the party leadership is relatively pragmatic and flexible, despite being rooted in a socialist ideology. To contextualize the VCP's pragmatism, it is useful to compare the party with other communist regimes, such as the Chinese Communist Party, the Cambodian Khmer Rouge, and the Soviet Communist Party. Unlike these other communist parties, the VCP has been more willing to shift course when it has gone too far to the left, whether in terms of land reform or in terms of collectivization. What we see, then, is that the VCP has been quite moderate in relation to its universe of ideologically comparable cases.

Lest it be misunderstood, we should be clear that the VCP is an authoritarian party and that coercion and repression are an integral part of its repertoire. Similarly, although to a lesser extent, UMNO operates with coercive force, using the state's weaponry to repress opponents during periods in which its power is threatened. Both parties function within illiberal regimes, with Vietnam being significantly more authoritarian. Yet the point is that, despite the authoritarian elements of these parties, they are not immune to societal interests and are both concerned with maintaining legitimacy through development. These parties' desire to maintain power through illiberal means has not prevented them from addressing the concerns of the grass roots, changing course in the face of solid resistance, and negotiating with societal groups who hold opposing views. The flexible behavior and moderate policies of UMNO and the VCP may thus best be understood within a "repressive-responsive" framework, which Harold Crouch used to describe the Malaysian polity, and which Benedict Kerkvliet applied to Vietnam's political system.

Both parties—UMNO and the VCP—would seem to be very different beasts, one ethnic, the other communist, and as comparative reference points, they may seem odd. But we should recall that the central theme of this study concerns the relationship between institutional structures and developmental outcomes. If we focus on institutions as the analytical pivot with which to compare these cases, this comparison becomes clear. From the point of view of institutional power and capacity, pragmatic policy making, and concern with equity, these are quite similar cases. Furthermore, it is especially by placing these cases within their own "ideological fields" that it becomes clear how similar they actually are. Unlike other ethnically divided nations and communist regimes, UMNO and the VCP have both been relatively pragmatic in addressing their pressing social problems.

The two negative cases in this study, Thailand and the Philippines, share similar features. Although Thailand has a relatively more cohesive and skilled bureaucracy than the Philippines and has achieved much higher growth rates, neither country has been able to make inroads on the equity front. This, I have argued, is largely because there have been no political parties with the requisite organizational capacity and ideology to advance social reforms. Early historical developments have had a long-term impact on the predicament of political parties. The formation of a strong bureaucratic military state in Thailand and the concomitant absence of a colonial power lessened the impetus for the creation of nationalist movements that have often been the precursors for institutionalized parties. In the Philippines, the establishment of electoral democracy at the turn of the century in the context of a weak bureaucratic center led to the strengthening of provincial oligarchs with no real organizational structure undergirding their power. In the postwar and contemporary period, there have been a number of instances in both countries when governments sought to advance reforms, but in each instance, they were either crushed by the military or oligarchs or organizationally incapable of following through.

Unlike in Malaysia or Vietnam, most political parties in Thailand and the Philippines do not fulfill the functions of political representation. Politicians join or build parties largely to further their personal interests. The bond that holds parties together is not ideological or programmatic; it is largely personal, centered on factions and based on friends, relatives, and followers. There is little sense among elites that parties are meant to advance a broader collective agenda and represent public interests. Organizationally, parties are often shallow and make minimal efforts to develop the institution or to cultivate a membership base.

In the absence of parties functioning as representative agents, in the Philippines and Thailand, citizens are left with their village patrons or nongovernmental organizations (NGOs) as sources of support. Neither of these provides institutional structures that can ensure that policy will be implemented and sustained. Village leaders are often susceptible to material incentives from elites that can lead to outcomes that are not in the interests of the poorer peasants. Often, NGOs play a crucial role in supporting the poor, but their ability to influence the crafting and implementation of policy is limited. As we have seen in the case of the Pak Mun Dam in Thailand, NGOs were indispensable in terms of raising awareness of the villagers' conditions, but they lacked concrete power to make sweeping changes. A major NGO coalition spearheaded efforts to advance land reform in the Philippines during the early Corazon Aquino years, but this coalition was too fragmented and unable to outmaneuver the oligarchs' emasculating tactics. Without allying with parties, NGOs do not have enough power to influence the direction of development policy.

Recent developments in Thailand and the Philippines do not bode well for institution building and social reform. The September 2006 coup that ousted Thaksin's Thai Rak Thai (TRT) government has been a setback for democracy and for political parties. In some sense, Thailand seems to have made a full circle from the turbulent 1970s, when grievances from the rural sector and the government's incapacity precipitated a military coup. In the current political crisis, heightened inequality and discontent have opened up a sharp rift between Thaksin's TRT and the rural sector on one side and the Bangkok middle class, the monarchy, and the military on the other side. There are many dimensions to this current crisis, but one of the most salient concerns the demands of the rural sector for more equitable distribution of resources and more effective representation.[5] The TRT Party may have been too closely tied to Thaksin to be considered an institutionalized party, yet the demise of TRT and the maneuvers to oust other parties that have sought to advance pro-poor populist policies ultimately deny the poor any institutional mechanism for pursuing their interests. Mobilization on the streets thus becomes the only means to gain a fair hearing. But with opposing groups so polarized, street politics is likely to lead to violence, as the events of April and May 2010 in Bangkok vividly demonstrated. Such an outcome was not to the benefit of either the rural poor or the urban middle class.

In the Philippines, the nine years (2001–10) under President Gloria Macapagal-Arroyo resulted in the decay of institutions and relentless attacks on leftists, progressive reformists in Congress, and NGOs. With the exception of a few leftist parties, such as Akbayan, and the reformist wing of the Liberal Party, there are no ongoing efforts to build more institutionalized organizations that might champion reform. Clientelistic figures who eschew the need for organizational structures dominate the polity. When reformists arise, they are invariably maverick candidates who can gain the backing of the middle class but who do not have a grassroots base from which to build a strong, long-lasting institution. The middle class itself is quick to support candidates who call for reform, but it appears less interested in building long-term institutions that might sustain reform programs.

The election in May 2010 of Benigno Aquino III, popularly known as "Noynoy," brings the more programmatic Liberal Party to the seat of the presidency. But whether this means that the party will usher in social change or seek to build more effective institutions is not clear. After all, Noynoy was catapulted into Malacañang Palace not on the basis of his achievements as congressman or senator but on a national wave of emotions spurred by the passing of his mother, Corazon Aquino, some nine months preceding the election.

Institutions, Power, and Reform

In this study, we have emphasized the significance of institutional structures for affecting trajectories of development. Institutionalized parties, cohesive interventionist states, and moderate ideology and policy have been at the core of the analytical framework. The significance of institutions for reform stems from inductive observation of the way politics plays out in Southeast Asia as much as from a deductive view that social reform cannot make headway without being undergirded by strong institutions. This view is fundamental to leftist hopes for social change, but as this study has shown, it does not belong solely to the left.

This study has also downplayed the importance of democracy, class struggle, and ethnic demographics as candidates for advancing equitable development. The core idea that these arguments share at their very root is that social mobilization and competition, especially in an open environment, will benefit the poor. The argument emphasizing democracy has gained particular salience today, given the legitimacy of democratic regimes across the globe. In an ideal world, pro-poor reforms would be achieved through a democratic system, such that there would be no contradiction between our desire for freedom and our desire for equality. One central point of this study, however, has been to emphasize precisely that social reforms may be pursued in a framework that is less than normatively ideal as long as the institutions themselves are powerful and capable.

This does not mean that we should not seek social reform under democratic auspices or that we should necessarily champion "benign" institutionalized-authoritarian regimes as a panacea for underdevelopment. It does mean, however, that if we are to seek the advancement of equitable development within a regime type that is now regarded as universally legitimate (i.e., democracy), we should not lose sight of what really matters for reform: the presence of cohesive institutions that represent collective interests and have the organizational means to channel, shape, and execute policy reform. In the absence of institutionalized parties and capable states, reform will wither even if civil society is mobilized and democratic competition is encouraged, precisely because personalistic and clientelistic structures remain so deeply entrenched in the developing world. Thus, what needs to be built and strengthened within democratic regimes, so that the regimes actually represent the poor, are institutions that articulate, advance, and sustain public interests. The imperative for equitable development can rest only with strong institutions.

Controlling for Social Structure
Fiji, Guyana, and Sri Lanka

The argument that Malaysia's social structure explains its developmental outcome cannot be sustained if we place Malaysia in comparison with other countries that have similar social structures: where one ethnic group, self-identified as "sons of the soil," controls the state and is economically weaker, whereas the other ethnic group is economically stronger. Fiji, Guyana, and Sri Lanka are all comparable to Malaysia in terms of social structure, but all have developmental outcomes that have ranged from civil war to cyclical coups. None of these countries has achieved growth with equity and political stability.

Fiji is perhaps the most similar country to Malaysia in terms of social structure. Officially colonized by the British in 1874, the same year as the takeover of Malaya, the Fijian polity is well balanced between the Fijians and the Indians. From 1945 to 1988, Indians outnumbered the Fijians by about 48 percent to 46 percent. Since the late 1980s, the numbers have reversed slightly in favor of the Fijians. Most Fijians work in the rural sector, own most of the land, and are the dominant group in the state. Indians are largely based in the sugar industry, in intermediate businesses, and in the professional and management sector. They are more likely to be salary earners and are also the highest taxpayers. The third significant group, Europeans, claim the large businesses, such as banks, hotels, and factories.

The two main parties are ethnically based, although they incorporate small sections of the opposing ethnic groups. The Alliance Party, established in 1966, is headed by the Fijian Association and comprises at the margins the Indian Alliance (Indian Muslims) and the General Electors' Association (Europeans and Chinese). The Alliance Party is largely concerned with maintaining the paramount position of the Fijians. The Fijian Association, created in 1956, is not a mass-based party like UMNO.[1] Its main goal is to ensure that the traditional hierarchical authority of the eastern chiefs is maintained, that land ownership of the Fijians remains unchallenged, and that Fijians maintain their political supremacy.[2] Similar to Malaysia, however, the British plans for constitutional reform and fears of losing ethnic dominance were what awakened the Fijian Association into the political vehicle that eventually coalesced as the Alliance. The main oppositional Indian party, the National Federation Party (NFP), began as a labor union representing Indian cane growers and has been, from its inception, mass based. It has sought to establish a multicommunal front, particularly by appealing to western Fijians long marginalized by the eastern chiefs of the islands. The NFP, like the Malaysian Indian Congress, is notorious for internecine factionalism among its leadership.[3]

The Alliance Party, like Malaysia's own Alliance and later National Front, has dominated elections since independence. Only on two occasions did it lose the majority vote, but on each occasion, events transpired that blocked the NFP from gaining the prime ministership. In 1977, intense factionalism wracked the NFP and derailed it from forming a parliamentary majority. In 1987, the NFP won elections for the second time—this time, however, in alliance with the newly formed Labor Party. Although the NFP astutely gave the prime ministership to a moderate Fijian, Bavadra, the Fijian traditional establishment, was unwilling to countenance such a change. The armed forces, which is 95 percent Fijian, launched a coup that subsequently restored power to the Alliance.[4]

Unlike Malaysia, the Fijian state has not exerted much effort in redistributing income or in promoting growth. In terms of affirmative action, it has been much more concerned with increasing its ethnic ranks within the military and the bureaucracy.[5] This is due to the nature of the elite of the Fijian Association. The Fijian Association, and the Alliance Party that it heads, is largely an organization driven by the interests of the eastern chiefly oligarchy, and as much as its base is Fijian, it is led by an elite that is most concerned with maintaining its historically based ascriptive power and its overwhelming land ownership. Strengthening the military and the bureaucracy secures this purpose, and growth and redistribution are only secondary goals. Furthermore, it is in the interest of the eastern oligarchs to keep the Fijians in an economically subordinate position vis-à-vis the Indian population so as to maintain their own traditional authority. As long as patronage is provided in state institutions and as long as the military upholds the power of the oligarchs, there is little purpose in initiating a Malaysia-style New Economic Policy.

In just more than two decades, Fiji has experienced five coups, the most recent in April 2009. These coups have been instigated largely by fears of the Indian ethnic population taking control of the state and threatening ethnic Fijian interests. In the first decade of the twenty-first century alone, there have been three coups, which have led to the country being described as having a "coup culture." Since the 2000 coup, the armed forces have become more dominant and, under General Frank Bainimarama, have increasingly militarized civilian institutions. The consequence of these coups has been perpetual instability and an economy in tatters.[6] The contrast with Malaysia, in terms of both development and stability, could not be starker.

Guyana provides an extreme case in which tension between an indigenous ethnic group in control of the state (Africans) and an ethnic group dominant in the capital sector (Indians) has led to implosion rather than accommodation. In 1980, Indians made up 51 percent of the population; Africans, 30 percent; mixed races, 11 percent; Amerindians, 5 percent; and Portuguese and Europeans, 1 percent.[7] A 1967 survey showed that Indians were predominantly based in agriculture, particularly rice and sugar, and in business, whereas Africans were more dominant in the civil service and in blue-collar jobs. Although Indians are economically more powerful because of their strength in business, they are also more heavily concentrated in the rural sector. Poverty levels are high in both ethnic groups, but among Africans, poverty and unemployment levels are significantly higher. In the 1967 survey, the majority of those with the lowest household incomes were Africans.[8]

The two major ethnic parties, the People's Progressive Party (PPP), representing the Indians, and the People's National Congress (PNC), representing the Africans, are socialist and well-organized institutions. The parties have fluctuated in power, with the PPP dominant in the 1950s and 1960s, and the PNC in the 1970s and 1980s. The PPP upheld free-market policies during its tenure but also increased expenditures for rural development to aid its Indian constituency. Angered by this ethnic bias, African urban workers destabilized the economy through strikes and boycotts in the mid-1960s, eventually creating a virtual civil war.

In 1968, the African PNC gained power. In 1970, its charismatic leader, Forbes Burnham, established a "cooperative republic" and, by the mid-1970s, had nationalized all foreign firms, thus providing PNC members with ample patronage. Burnham tilted the economy toward socialism largely as a means to weaken the Indian business sector. Furthermore, he reversed the previous government's subsidies for the rural sector. In response, the Indian community repeated the same strategy as African labor in the 1960s: destabilizing the economy by reducing agricultural output. By 1989, rice and sugar production had plummeted to less than 50 percent of output compared to 1979.[9] Per capita real income fell by 33 percent between 1975 and 1986. By 1990, Guyana was one of the poorest countries in Latin America, a place where, in effect, "economic suffering [had become] a leveler in material well-being for many Indians and Africans."[10]

The case of Guyana contrasts sharply with Malaysia in its economic outcome but also in the style of leadership. Although Guyana's parties are ethnically based and, as socialist organizations, highly institutionalized, they have also been deeply polarizing. Unlike Malaysia, pragmatic multicommunal politics did not succeed, although an effort was made when the Indian PPP initially brought Burnham into its fold in the 1950s. The failure to reach any accommodative bargain among the elites has allowed ethnic politics to spiral into extreme antagonism. As Premdas puts it, "The rival parties, linked to discrete ethnic clusters, confronted each other in a manner similar to military warfare."[11] Thus, the control of the state by one ethnic group seeking to ameliorate the economic position of its constituency does not predict a successful outcome of equitable development. Large numbers on both sides, ideally functioning as a stabilizing factor, have also not prevented Guyanese politics from veering toward polarization and fragmentation.

Sri Lanka is a country in which ethnic conflict and struggles over resources have led to open civil war. Although Sri Lanka has created a welfare state and its per capita income is relatively high within South Asia, economic development has stagnated largely because of civil war. The two main ethnic groups in Sri Lanka are the Sinhalese (73.8 percent) and the Sri Lankan Tamils (12.7 percent). The Sri Lankan Moors make up 7.6 percent and the Indian Tamils 5.5 percent of the population. The Sinhalese are largely Buddhists, whereas the Tamils are primarily Hindu.

The origins of the conflict between the Sinhalese and the Tamils can be traced to British colonialism. Through their policy of *divide et impera*, the British heavily favored the Tamils over the Sinhalese. Missionary schools were crucial in spreading education in Jaffna, where the Tamils are centered. Under the British administration, the Tamils were given a disproportionate number of professional and clerical jobs. In 1921, 28 percent of all lawyers and 44 percent of all doctors were Tamil, despite the fact that they made up only 12 percent of the population.[12]

After independence, the Sinhalese elites began to mobilize to redress their economic disadvantage. The Swabasha Movement sought to make Sinhalese the official language of Sri Lanka. Eventually, this movement became a "Sinhala-Only" policy in 1956 and was reinforced in the 1972 constitution. In the 1970s, the Sinhalese moved to restructure the educational system by making it easier for Sinhalese students to qualify for universities. Until the early 1970s, the Tamils still dominated in fields such as engineering (48 percent) and medicine (49 percent). A district quota implemented in 1972 cemented the restructuring: by 1974, Tamils made up only 19 percent of the science stream, down from 35 percent in 1970.[13] Changes in language and education policy had an impact on the structure of employment within the civil service, as the percentage of Sinhalese rapidly increased and that of the Tamils declined.

A critical problem in the Sri Lankan political system is the first-past-the-post (FPTP) system, which has created incentives for ethnic outbidding.[14] The FPTP system translates small vote differences into large seat differences, thereby making it more likely for Sinhalese politicians to appeal to ethnic extremism. The two dominant Sinhalese parties, the United National Party and the Sri Lanka Freedom Party, have both advanced Sinhalese policies and marginalized the Tamils. Any effort by one party to create some compromise with the Tamils has been attacked by the other party, forcing policy to move back to the more exclusionary position.

In 1983, civil war broke out between the Tamils and the Sinhalese. In 2004, the World Bank classified Sri Lanka as "one of the world's most politically unstable countries." The civil war ended in 2009 with a brutal crushing of the Tamil Tigers, trapped in a sliver of Jaffna. The end of the civil war reinforced the power of President Rajapaksa, who has maintained the authoritarian powers held during the war and dismissed constitutional and judicial restraints. With the crushing of the Tamil Tigers, the government has little incentive to accommodate the needs of the Tamil minority. The prospects for the Tamil minority thus look especially bleak.[15]

Compared to Malaysia, Fiji, Guyana, and Sri Lanka have thus all been wracked by systemic violence and instability. Despite similarities in ethnic and class structures, Malaysia is the only country in this group that has advanced equitable development in the context of political stability. This difference is due to the nature of institutions.

Notes

Chapter 1

1. Ness 1967: 240–41.
2. Saneh 1973: 89.
3. Huntington 1968: 24.
4. Kuznets 1955.
5. Fields 2001.
6. According to the development economist Gary Fields (2001: 70), "The highest payoff [for explaining the determinants of inequality] . . . would appear to be in-depth *country studies over time* and *comparisons* of the patterns found and reasons for them" (emphasis added).
7. World Bank, World Development Indicators (WDI; in current U.S. dollars).
8. Malaysia 2010: 145.
9. Ibid., 151.
10. Meerman 2008: 79.
11. Ibid., 109.
12. World Bank, WDI.
13. World Bank, WDI (in current U.S. dollars).
14. Medhi and Pranee 1991; Somchai 2001; World Bank 2001: 26; National Economic and Social Development Board 2003; Medhi 2008: 137; Warr 2009.
15. Pasuk, Sangsit, and Nualnoi 1996: 13.
16. Medhi and Pranee 1991: 1.
17. The term "organizational weapon" is from Selznick 1952.
18. Mainwaring 1999: 335.
19. By this, I mean bureaucratic capacities and structures in the form of technical and analytic skills and routinized and systematic procedures. "Iron cage" is

Max Weber's term, although he used it to connote the grim aspects of bureaucratization. See the last pages of any version of *The Protestant Ethic and the Spirit of Capitalism* (Weber 2002: 123–25). See also the creative use of the concepts of "iron cage" and "iron fist" in Slater 2003.

20. For example, some may see as negative the fact that the Gini coefficient still hovers in the middle range, but if we look at the origins of the problem and the long-term trend, it is hard to deny progress. The Gini coefficient can range from 0 (perfect equality) to 1 (perfect inequality). Most countries rank between .2 and .6, and Malaysia's 2009 Gini coefficient was in the mid-.4 range.

21. In terms of comparing parties or political institutions, there is also a void in the literature. But fleeting comparative observations on the strength of Malaysian parties and the weakness of Thai parties can be found in Huntington 1968; Von der Mehden 1974: 109–14; Kramol 1982: 39; Chai-Anan 1990: 291.

22. One of the more problematic aspects of modernization theory was its tendency to assume that "all good things go together." Huntington's (1968) work was compelling precisely because it pierced this liberal myth. Yet the idea that "all good things go together" is alive and well, for example, in the work of Sen 1999.

23. Central Intelligence Agency 2003. Data for Malaysia is from July 2002 and for Thailand from 2000. It is difficult to know the exact percentage of Chinese in Thailand, given the fact that the census does not break down data on the basis of ethnicity. Most estimates range between 12 percent and 15 percent.

24. I have been to Thailand every year since 2000 to do research. The major periods were 2000–01, 2003, and 2006. I conducted fieldwork in Malaysia in 2001, 2002, and 2006.

25. On deinstitutionalization within UMNO, see Slater 2003.

26. However, to the extent that a state pursues a battery of pro-poor policies, we should expect aggregate measures to reflect policy output.

27. It is important to highlight here the problems with World Bank data on the Gini coefficient. These problems can be grouped into three types: discrepancy within World Bank institutions, lack of uniformity within the World Development Indicators (WDI) data set, and anomalous data points. The World Bank's figures for the Gini coefficient in the WDI differ starkly from the data given by the local World Bank offices because the latter rely on the Gini coefficient as calculated by local economists. Compare the different data in the WDI to World Bank (2001: 26–27) published in Bangkok or to any issue of *World Bank Thailand Economic Monitor*. In terms of the WDI data set, the World Bank switches from income to consumption in its indicators. In the WDI, data are calculated for Malaysia on the basis of income but for Thailand on the basis of consumption. The effect of this in terms of comparing Gini coefficients would be to overestimate Malaysia's Gini coefficient and to underestimate Thailand's because income data

generally tend to have a higher estimate than consumption. Finally, the WDI data also exhibit unusual patterns that differ considerably from local sources. Malaysia's Gini coefficient, according to the WDI, was .49 in 1997 but decreased astoundingly to .38 in 2004. By comparison, the Malaysian government's figures were .443 in 1999, .462 in 2004, and .441 in 2009. In contrast, Thailand's Gini coefficient in the WDI appears to hardly move compared to what local economists discern. For all of these reasons, I have chosen not to rely on the WDI data set on the Gini coefficient. Note, furthermore, comments by the preeminent Malaysian economist Jomo K. S. (2006: 11, 27) comparing World Bank data and that of local sources. On Thailand: "There is no evidence supporting the World Bank's claim of a dramatic decline in income inequality in Thailand." On Malaysia: "Curiously, the World Bank's 1993 'Miracle Volume' suggests that Malaysia was the only exception to the regional trend of declining income inequality. In fact, it appears that government efforts to reduce inter-ethnic inequality during the 1970s and 1980s apparently reduced overall inequality as well."

28. For the reasons noted in the previous footnote, I am more confident in the validity of local data than in the data of the World Bank WDI.

Chapter 2

1. Recent works making the case for democracy as equity enhancing include Boix 2003; Sandbrook et al. 2007; Haggard and Kaufman 2008; McGuire 2010. Note that, although Haggard and Kaufman argue for a generally positive role for democracy, they also emphasize that other crucial factors, such as economic interests and coalitional alignments, combine with democracy to create pro-poor outcomes. See also their appendix summarizing quantitative studies relating inequality to regime type. Similarly, Sandbrook et al. emphasize other variables beyond democracy, particularly the types of institutions within democracies.

2. Marshall 1950; Frankel 1978; Lipset 1981; Przeworski 1985.

3. McGuire (2010: 9–10) provides a nuanced discussion of this. See also Lake and Baum 2001; Boix 2003: chap. 5; Wong 2004.

4. Sen 1999.

5. Even if the cases that match this theoretical position are not from Europe, they often have characteristics that mirror those of European social democracies.

6. Stephens 1979; Korpi 1983; Przeworski 1985; Esping-Andersen 1985, 1990; Hicks 1999; Huber and Stephens 2001.

7. Emblematic is Milne's (1967: 3) comment: "More than anything else, the racial composition of Malaysia is the key to understanding the whole picture. It dictates the pattern of the economy, has helped to shape the Constitution, and has influenced the democratic process and the party system." Or, as Mahathir puts it

in his own inimitably tautological way: "The politics of this country tend to be racial whether you like it or not, so whenever you talk about anything that has some identification with race, the chances are that politics will be dragged in" (quoted in Mauzy 1983: 136). See also Ratnam 1965; Means 1970; Von Vorys 1975; Vasil 1980; Jesudason 1989. But see Khoo 1995: xvii–xxii.

8. A similar line of argument is made in Funston 1980.

9. See also Esman 1987.

10. Among all Malaysia scholars whom I am aware of, this point is most forcefully made in analytical terms in Funston 1980.

11. See, e.g., Migdal, Kohli, and Shue 1994.

12. This thesis is most closely associated with Duverger (1959), particularly in relation to the French Socialist Party; see also Selznick 1952; Michels 1962; Epstein 1967: esp. chap. 6; Panebianco 1988.

13. Quoted in Huntington 1968: 461.

14. Kohli 1987; see also the extension of the argument in Harriss 2005.

15. Sandbrook et al. 2007.

16. Weyland 1996.

17. Levitsky and Way 2010.

18. I should be clear that by institutionalization, I am not referring in a very general sense to something that has staying power, as in "the norm of shame is institutionalized in Japanese culture." In that sentence, institutionalization is synonymous with something being entrenched or persistent. Institutionalization in the way it is used in the literature on political parties has to do in part with patterned continuity, but it is also much more specific and complex than that.

19. Huntington 1968.

20. On the specific concept of institutionalization, rather than general concern with institutions, the following works are especially significant: Welfling 1973; Panebianco 1988: esp. chaps. 1, 4; McGuire 1997; Levitsky 1998; Randall and Svasand 2002. Huntington's ideas can be traced to Selznick 1983 [1957]. Studies that operationalize the concept include Dix 1992; Mainwaring 1999; Kuenzi and Lambright 2001; Tan 2002; Tan 2010; Beatty-Riedl 2008; Hicken and Kuhonta 2011.

21. Mainwaring and Scully 1995.

22. Randall and Svasand (2002) note that autonomy may or may not be useful for institutionalization, depending on the form of interdependence. Where the party is the more dominant force in a relationship, then interdependence may be beneficial, but where the party is a more subservient force, then interdependence may be to the detriment of the organization.

23. The relationship between autonomy and rootedness can be compared to Evans's (1995) idea of embedded autonomy, particularly in his discussion of redistributive reforms in Kerala. Redistributive policies were successful in Kerala

because of a combination of mobilized farmers and workers and an effective civil service.

24. The nature of that rootedness must orient the party in some way to a pro-poor orientation, which can come from class or ethnicity.

25. Barnes 1966: 522–23, quoted in Sartori 1990: 170. Thanks to Antonis Ellinas for pointing out this quotation to me.

26. Selznick 1952.

27. Here I differ from Huntington's position, where he relates coherence solely with autonomy.

28. Kitschelt (1989) argues that parties' ideologies are closely tied to their efforts to maintain their followers' support.

29. Crouch 1996.

30. A split return means that in a constituency with more than one MP, and with voters allowed more than one vote, the voter chooses at least two different parties.

31. Hicken 2009: 97.

32. Siripan 2006: 139. Analysts, however, have questioned whether membership constitutes any credible activity. On TRT, see, e.g., Nelson 2002: 290–91; on the Democrat Party, see Chai-Anan (n.d.).

33. Siripan 2006: 73.

34. Kramol 1982: 33.

35. Askew 2008.

36. See also Weyland's (1996) discussion of organizational fragmentation.

37. Chambers 2005.

38. This occurred under Abdul Rahman and under Mahathir. The Mahathir effort is analyzed nicely in Slater (2003) and that of Abdul Rahman in Funston 1980.

39. This was especially evident in a public row throughout 2006 between Abdullah Badawi, Mahathir's successor, and Mahathir himself. With Mahathir no longer leading the party, UMNO leaders rallied around Badawi (author interview with UMNO MP Shahrir Samad, Kuala Lumpur, July 2006). Mahathir found himself shut out from the UMNO-dominated media and ironically had to resort to opposition media to air his criticisms.

40. See Dornbusch and Edwards 1991; Roberts 1995; Weyland 2001.

41. Thaksin Shinawatra's populist policies, however, differ sharply from the classic Latin American variant. This is discussed in Kuhonta (n.d.).

42. See Landé 1977.

43. Huntington 1968; Mainwaring 1999: 330.

44. See, e.g., the essays in Kitschelt and Wilkinson 2007.

45. Crouch (1996) makes a strong case for UMNO as a party driven by patronage.

46. Randall and Svasand 2002: 21.

47. A contrasting argument advanced by Zheng (1997), based on the case of China, is that a close relationship between state and party can be extremely detrimental to developmental goals, particularly state building. This is because the organizational basis and interests of a revolutionary party conflict with the need to rationalize state institutions.

48. Ammar et al. 1993; Pasuk and Baker 2002.

49. Jomo 2001: 480–82.

50. Johnson 1982; Amsden 1989; Wade 1990; Evans 1995; Woo-Cumings 1999; Kohli 2004.

51. See, among others, Huntington and Moore 1970; Pempel 1990; Smith 2005; Greene 2007; Friedman and Wong 2008.

52. In democratic Latin America, this issue has been analyzed less in terms of the concept of regime dominance and more in terms of party control over two institutions—presidency and Congress—which enables more effective policy implementation (see Corrales 2002).

53. Greene 2007: 297.

54. Ibid., 40–41.

55. For example, dominant regimes in the Middle East, such as in Egypt, Syria, or Iraq, have not matched the successful redistributive policies of the Asian regimes.

56. Rueschemeyer and Evans 1985: 56; see also Rondinelli 1979: 404: "[A] strong, integrated, and responsive party system extending down to the village level has been a *necessary adjunct to government agencies* in mobilizing popular support, eliciting participation, generating leadership, and ensuring administrative compliance with rural development policies" (emphasis added).

57. Shamsul 1986.

58. Herring 1991; Heller 1999.

59. Mencher 1980, quoted in Evans 1995: 237.

60. Wade 1990.

61. Grindle 1980: 8–9.

62. Horowitz 1989a: 279.

63. Note, for example, that almost all health ministers have been non-Malays.

64. Kohli 1987.

65. Comparative evidence reinforces the view that ideological moderation pays off in terms of both policy success and party dominance. See, e.g., Berman's (1998) argument regarding the Swedish Social Democratic Party's ideological flexibility compared to the German Social Democratic Party's adherence to ideological dogma.

66. Verba 1971: 302, 306. Note that institutionalization is used here in a broad sense—as both organizational structures and the development of accepted norms.

67. Grindle and Thomas 1989: 232.

68. Hirschman 1963: 261.

69. Johnson 1999: 53.

70. Horowitz 1989a: 256.

71. Gourevitch 1986: 9.

72. Grindle and Thomas 1989: 231.

73. Doner, Ritchie, and Slater (2005) argue that the condition of systemic vulnerability—an aggregate of three crises: domestic, external, and resource—will create an institutional response that will strengthen developmental capacities. This is a compelling argument, but it is problematic because it assumes, in effect, that a massive crisis will *necessarily* stimulate the building of developmental institutions. More likely, effective institutions were already present in some form before the advent of a massive crisis.

74. Crone (1993) advances a related argument that "strategic elites" must be present for a state to respond to a social crisis. But it is not clear why strategic elites will have great foresight.

75. This is what UMNO was pressured to do both by some party leaders and by social forces in the immediate aftermath of May 1969. Precisely because of its relatively cohesive structure, UMNO dismissed these calls. Note especially Esman's (1987) typology of ethnic groups that have used repression and those that have not.

76. A crisis is not one of the independent variables but is a background factor that can potentially spur political and institutional change. However, as I have emphasized, its effect in spurring change is not automatic; it depends on the kind of institutions already present in the polity.

77. An excellent discussion of configuration and relational contexts is Katznelson 1997.

78. "Development models are not simple packages of policies," write Haggard and Cheng. "They are configurations of political, institutional, and historical events" (quoted in Hutchcroft 1998: 15).

Part Two

1. Malaysia 1986, 1996.

2. World Bank, World Development Indicators (WDI; current U.S. dollars).

3. Malaysia 2010.

4. Ibid.

5. In this book, I do not address redistribution of corporate equity or the more general issue of Malay capital formation. Although this is an important—and highly contested—element of the NEP, the focus of this study remains squarely on questions of poverty and inequality.

6. World Bank 1993a.

7. Malaysia 1986.

8. Malaysia 1996: 5. Note that the rate of growth during the NEP was higher than during the prior period, when the government did not make as much of an effort to redistribute. Therefore, the view that redistribution hurts the rate of growth does not hold in this case.

9. Malaysia 2001.

10. Ragayah 2008: 114.

11. This rise in inequality in the early 1990s was due to a shift toward capital-intensive production; heightened demand for skilled workers; the influx of un-skilled foreign laborers, which in turn lowered the job opportunities for unskilled local labor; and the decline of the agricultural sector, which lowered the income of poorer farmers (Ishak and Ragayah 1995).

12. Malaysia 2010: 147.

13. Ibid., 145.

14. Jomo 2003: 27–28.

15. For earlier criticisms of government data, see "Review of Third Malaysia Plan—Academics Query the Figures," *Straits Times,* 21 May 1979.

16. Abdul Rahman Embong 2002: 2–3.

17. Malaysia 2010: 146. Bumiputera constituted 60 percent of architects, 53 percent of doctors, and 52 percent of engineers (ibid.).

Chapter 3

1. Quoted in Kratoska 1983: 207.

2. Emerson 1937: 185.

3. Lim 1984: 65.

4. Furnivall 1956: chap. 8.

5. Quoted in Gullick and Gale 1986: 25.

6. The definitive study of the development of the Federated Malay States (FMS) is Emerson 1937: chap. 4.

7. The nomenclature of the British officials depended on the region. In the FMS, the advisers were known as Residents; in the UMS, they were Advisers; and in Johor there was a General Adviser.

8. J. P. Rodger, British Resident of Selangor, stated in the *Annual Report on Selangor for 1896* that they should "make every effort to encourage and develop the capabilities of those who, had not the States been brought under British pro-tection, would now be in sole and absolute control of every district" (quoted in Khasnor 1984: 14).

9. Ibid., 116–17.

10. Non-Malays were employed in government, such as in the Clerical and Railway Services, but were largely absent in most sectors of the bureaucracy.

11. See, e.g., the comment by Hugh Clifford, a British colonial official (quoted in Kratoska 1983: 270).

12. Lim 1984: 37–38. Also see Jomo 1986: esp. chap. 3.

13. Emerson 1937: 184.

14. Lau 1991: 70, 276.

15. Concerning self-government, Noordin (2005: 17) noted that the Colonial Office "had to colonize in order to decolonize," because the Malayan states had never been legally annexed. Lau (1991: 277), however, argues that the language of self-government was a facade that the Colonial Office employed to make its post-war designs on Malaya more palatable.

16. The British turned to the Chinese first, rather than the Malays, for help in organizing resistance to the Japanese. The Chinese created the Overseas Chinese Mobilization Council to organize civil defense, propaganda, and a fighting unit linked to the British army. See Lau 1989: 224–25; Cheah 1988: 19.

17. See Purcell 1946; Rudner 1970.

18. Purcell 1946: 31–38; Noordin 2005: 20–25.

19. del Tufo 1949: 40.

20. Purcell 1967: app. 3.

21. Stockwell 1979: 69.

22. Ishak 1960: 61.

23. Ibid., 65.

24. Stockwell 1977: 511.

25. The fact that Malays came from the lower echelons of the bureaucracy made it easier for them to join UMNO's movement rather than support the colonial state. Compared with bureaucrats in other developing countries, such as India, these bureaucrats were not at the apex of the administration and were therefore not torn between the dictates of the colonial state and the vision of national independence.

26. Stockwell 1979: 160. *Mukim* is the administratively defined village. *Kampong* also denotes a village, but its delineation is not based on official administrative boundaries.

27. The quotation is from Rees-Williams (1947: 174) and from L. D. Gammans's press statement (quoted in Stockwell 1979: 89n12).

28. A concern of the British was that Malay protests might spin off into more radical agitation, as in Indonesia. "Malay opinion is roused as never before. By itself, this is not a bad thing," Governor-General MacDonald observed. "But [it] will be extremely unfortunate if this awakened political consciousness and interest gets railroaded into extremist and anti-British tendencies. If we can restore Ma-

lay confidence in Britain . . . [t]hen Malay nationalist movement is likely to . . . cooperate with us in political affairs instead of being swept into Indonesia anti-European currents" (Lau 1989: 231–32).

29. Citizenship rights were eventually liberalized in 1952 and then in the constitution in 1957. After the 1952 ordinance, Ratnam (1965: 93, and more generally 66–101) concluded, "Almost all persons born in the country were in one way or another eligible to become citizens."

30. Means 1970: 100.

31. Stockwell 1977: 501. Ishak (1960: 77) notes that only in 1951 did membership surpass one hundred thousand.

32. Roff 1967; Ongkili 1974: 267; Stockwell 1977: esp. 509–13; Harper 1999: 92.

33. Means 1970: 101.

34. Stockwell 1979: 170.

35. Harper 1999: 75–76.

36. Stockwell 1977: 510.

37. Stockwell 1979: 160.

38. Stockwell 1977: 498.

39. Harper 1999: 90.

40. The Malayan Security Service was keen to help UMNO establish itself against radical Chinese and Malay alternatives: "A big Government[-]supported agricultural and educational campaign by UMNO, fully publicized, would be the most effective method of countering the activities of the Communist Party" (Stockwell 1979: 115).

41. For this paragraph, see ibid., 108–28.

42. Ibid., 126. The creation of the women's section helped the party deepen its roots in society, such that by 1955, half of Malay voters were women. By contrast, only one in two Chinese women, and only one in four Indian women, voted. The women's section was especially useful during electoral campaigns in actively mobilizing voters. A letter to the secretary-general of UMNO noted: "Kaum Ibu in every division and branch have been requested to undertake the task of giving information, by going to the houses of UMNO members and supporters and explaining the Alliance symbol, so that they will know how to vote" (Manderson 1977: 221n27, 222).

43. In practice, these early programs did not go very far given the party's lack of resources, but the extensive planning revealed the importance the party gave to social and economic issues. For example, one circular sent by the secretary-general to district secretaries in July 1949 called on branches to use their offices for classes on bookkeeping, handicrafts, and health, and to create a fund for scholarships for primary students. For details, see especially Stockwell 1977: 500–09; Funston 1980: 83–87.

44. The first four leaders of UMNO were aristocrats and civil servants. Onn Jaafar was a district officer and later *mentri besar* (chief minister) from Johor; Abdul Rahman, a prince, was a deputy public prosecutor; Abdul Razak was an assistant district officer and later assistant state secretary; Hussein Onn, son of Onn Jaafar, was an assistant administrative officer in Johor and then a district officer in Selangor. Seven of eleven members of the original UMNO executive committee in 1946 were civil servants. Until 1969, nearly half of the executive committee members were from the bureaucracy (Puthucheary 1978: 34; Funston 1980: 106).

45. At the national level, 80 percent were educated in English; of that group, about half had tertiary education and most others had a secondary education. See Funston 1980: 102–06.

46. Milne and Mauzy 1978: 13.

47. A 1956 party document titled "The Basis of UMNO's Struggle" states: "The theory of nationalism pursued by UMNO is a broad concept. . . . [W]hile striving for the privileges, sovereignty and priority of Malays as the owners of this country, UMNO also acknowledges that members of other races who have already become citizens . . . also shall receive specified rights as citizens of Malaya" (quoted in Funston 1980: 139). On the importance of ideological moderation and pragmatism, see Ratnam and Milne 1965: 417; Milne and Mauzy 1978: 129, 131, 174, 204, 221; Funston 1980: 137–40; Mauzy 1983: 23, 136–41; Zakaria Haji Ahmad 1989: 235, 240; Case 1995, 1996.

48. Mauzy 1983: 23.

49. Funston 1980: 127. It is worth pointing out that Razak joined the Labor Party and the Fabian Society as a student in England (Shaw 1976: 73).

50. More generally, ethnic groups that are economically disadvantaged but numerically advantaged have often repressed their ethnic rivals (Esman 1987: 416n2).

51. The UMNO Youth has functioned as a feedback mechanism for the party because of its more radical orientation, at times acting like militant enforcers of the party agenda. During the NEP period, it was UMNO Youth that monitored progress of policy, meeting with bureaucrats and counting the ethnic makeup in government organizations. Yet, true to the party's moderating principle, UMNO warned the auxiliary unit: "You should not take direct action against anything considered to be an abuse of national policy, especially if you do not have sufficient evidence" (Milne 1976: 254).

52. Funston 1980: 183.

53. Ibid., 137, 139.

54. No one is perhaps more emblematic of this shift than the mercurial Mahathir Mohamad, who gained prominence as an ultra in the aftermath of 1969, was expelled from the party but then returned and rapidly rose up the ranks as a moderate, and then cracked down on radical elements in society.

55. Interview with UMNO Executive Secretary Osaini, Kuala Lumpur, June 2006; see also Ratnam 1965: 164; Ness 1967: viii.

56. Ratnam 1965: 22.

57. Ongkili 1974: 259; Mauzy 1983: 20.

58. Mauzy 1983: 12.

59. The Chinese elites, who would then form the MCA, came from business and professional backgrounds, traditional guilds and associations, and anticommunist KMT groups. See Heng 1988.

60. Rudner (1975: 25) writes: "Central to Alliance economic philosophy was an overriding faith in private enterprise as a logical concomitant of political democracy."

61. Horowitz 1985: 410–27.

62. The original "flank" parties on the Chinese side were the Labor Party and the People's Progressive Party.

63. As Horowitz (1985: 409) writes: "UMNO and the MCA leaders felt drawn together by the forces that surrounded them. Moreover, those forces consisted, in considerable measure, of segments of their communities which the UMNO and MCA leaders respected least: Chinese schoolteachers and Malay *ulama* (theologians), both regarded as intolerably parochial and chauvinistic."

64. Ishak 1960: 70.

65. Repudiated in his radical agenda, Aziz was later expelled from the cabinet. Notably, he was rivals with Razak, the head of the Ministry of Rural Development, to succeed Abdul Rahman as leader of the party, and this may also have influenced his fate in UMNO. Both Razak and Aziz were deeply concerned with improving the conditions of the rural Malays, but their methods differed sharply. See Ness 1967: 225–26; Means 1970: 248–49.

66. The 1969 Alliance manifesto stated: "We believe in free enterprise. The foreign investors are here by invitation. We seek their expertise, some of their capital, and our share in profits."

67. The war against communist insurgency, waged between 1948 and 1960.

68. Horowitz 1985: 402–03.

69. Onn had sought to make UMNO a multicommunal party in the early 1950s, but members of the party rejected his proposal.

70. Onn had unintentionally insulted one of the key leaders of the MCA.

71. Horowitz 1985: 402.

72. Jomo 1986: 247; see also Heng 1988.

73. In the 1955 elections, the Chinese share of the vote was much lower than its actual share of the population, as many Chinese had not yet been granted citizenship. In 1955, Malays made up 84.2 percent of the electorate. Many of the MCA seats were won in districts with Malay majorities, where Malays "cross-voted" for the MCA.

74. Means 1970: 211.

75. Rudner 1975.

76. Malaya 1961: 18.

77. Rudner 1975: 61–63.

78. This was the "First Malaysia Plan" after Malaya became the Federation of Malaysia in 1963.

79. Malaysia 1965: 6.

80. On the question of Chinese middlemen exploiting Malay farmers, see Ungku Aziz 1969.

81. Malaysia 1965: 79–81.

82. See, e.g., "Malaysia's Jobless Problem Worsened Last Year," *Straits Times,* 17 Apr. 1969; "Economic Drive," *Straits Times,* 10 July 1969; "Paying for Safety," *Straits Times,* 8 Oct. 1969; "Jobless on Increase in Malaysia," *Straits Times,* 4 Dec. 1969; "Government to Lead 'More Jobs' Drive," *Straits Times,* 24 June 1970; "Employment Problem in Malaysia," *Straits Times,* 26 Oct. 1970.

83. Malaysia 1969: 51.

84. Rudner 1975: 57.

85. Quoted in ibid., 58.

86. See, e.g., "Money for Development," *Straits Times,* 23 Feb. 1968.

87. Snodgrass 1980.

88. Shaw 1976: 129.

89. Zainal 2001: 82–83.

90. Ness 1967: 146–49.

91. The Ministry of Rural Development had a budget for "quick results money" that was granted to many district committees to enable the implementation of high-priority projects. Furthermore, state committees communicated quickly with district committees regarding the amount of funds to be disbursed (Ness 1967: 149).

92. Ibid., 148.

93. Ibid., 167–68.

94. Razak ended his first directive to the district rural development committees with a boldface "Results Are What We Want" (Ness 1967: 166).

95. Ibid., 169–70.

96. Ibid., 157.

97. Esman 1972: 101–02, 218. One incompetent district officer incurred the wrath of Razak for failing to collect information for the Red Book. He was dismissed from his duties on the rural development committee and blocked from promotion in the party (Ness 1967: 164).

98. Milne 1967: 157–58. The ministry's stated goal was to visit all seventy district offices twice a year.

99. "The Basis for Economic Development by Tun," *Straits Times*, 25 Oct. 1966.

100. Also, UMNO ensured that its message of development was heard loud and clear. In the 1960s, the Ministry of Information sent officials throughout the states screening films that espoused national unity and showed developmental programs that could benefit peasants.

101. Ness 1967: 156. The Red Book program was one of the most innovative structures of Malaysia's development machinery, but its very agenda limited the scope for major reform in the rural sector. The program disbursed significant funds but did not effect deep structural change in terms of economic relations or skills and capacities of the rural Malays.

102. One rural civil servant noted that the institutional framework was "only a sort of structural change superimposed on an old system of administration leaving the officials, their method of practices and their mentality very much as they have been before the Red Book" (quoted in Esman 1972: 224).

103. Rudner 1975: 74.

104. During the colonial period, Christian missionary groups were also discouraged from building schools in the heavily Muslim areas, in order to protect Islam.

105. The Malay-language schools would also have to offer compulsory English-language courses, whereas the Chinese-language schools would have to teach Malay-language courses and English-language courses.

106. The secondary level in Malaysia consists of three years of lower and three years of upper secondary school.

107. Quoted in Takei, Bock, and Saunders 1973.

108. "Getting to Grips with Poverty," *Straits Times*, 8 Sept. 1969.

109. Rudner 1975: 74–75.

Chapter 4

1. Abdul Razak 1971: 6.

2. Data from the first three Malaysia plans (Malaysia 1965, 1971a, 1973, 1976).

3. Sultanism is a concept developed by Max Weber (see Chehabi and Linz 1989).

4. Notwithstanding Abdul Rahman's centralization of party policy and decision making, UMNO local branches still pushed their own programs and maintained vibrant political activities, particularly in welfare projects. The UMNO yearly reports indicate that the main activities at the divisional level were increasing membership, building local party offices, organizing for elections, and providing information to the branches regarding government policy (Funston 1980: 176).

5. Ibid., 175. Abdul Rahman is known as Tunku Abdul Rahman. *Tunku* is an honorific that means "prince."

6. The relative success of the government in elections is based on its ability to muster two-thirds of the seats, which is necessary to amend the constitution.

7. National Operations Council 1969.

8. Slimming (1969: 47–49) argues that a conservative estimate of deaths is more than eight hundred. For a detailed account, see Von Vorys 1975. See also Abdul Rahman 1969; Gagliano 1970; Goh 1971; Vasil 1972. Surveying the literature on 13 May 1969, Funston (1975: 2) writes that it "is widely regarded as the most significant event in the country's turbulent post-independence history."

9. The Rukunegara states: "Our Nation, Malaysia, being dedicated to achieving a greater unity of all her peoples; to maintaining a democratic way of life; to creating a just society in which the wealth of the nation shall be equitably shared; to ensuring a liberal approach to her rich and diverse cultural traditions; to building a progressive society which shall be oriented to modern science and technology. We, her peoples, pledge our united efforts to attain these ends guided by these principles—Belief in God, Loyalty to King and Country, Upholding the Constitution, Rule of Law, Good Behavior and Morality."

10. Mauzy 1983: 47.

11. Milne 1976: 238.

12. Rogers 1972: 170.

13. This follows from Funston 1980: chap. 9.

14. Means 1991.

15. Funston 1980: 235.

16. Ibid., 237.

17. *New Straits Times*, 3 Sept. 1974, quoted in Ong 1976: 410.

18. Musolf and Springer 1979.

19. Ibid.

20. Some of the reforms eventually withered. Party meetings became less regular, monthly reports from party divisions were often not filed, and the Supreme Council meetings returned to the president's house rather than the party headquarters. But overall, Funston (1980: 242) concludes that "UMNO did not . . . slip back to the pre-1969 stage."

21. Von Vorys 1975: 393.

22. Ibid., 393.

23. For details, see Mauzy 1983.

24. In 1978, PAS broke away.

25. Mauzy (1983: 141) noted that opposition parties were "made more moderate by the responsibilities of sharing power, and were exposed to the tradition of accommodative attitudes and practices of the government."

26. *Straits Times*, 27 June 1974, quoted in Milne and Mauzy 1978: 190.

27. Hicken and Kuhonta 2011: 572–97.

28. Ghazali 1993: 6.

29. For this reason, Lustick's (1979) "control" thesis may be a better way of conceptualizing the BN, although the BN still retained numerous consociational features.

30. Funston (1980: 253) writes that the apportionment of cabinet seats to non-Malays "was not mere tokenism; cabinet portfolios and other seats were allocated with strict attention to providing an equitable share for each party. . . . It was thus shown that communal politics in Malaysia is not the zero sum game that many observers believed it to be."

31. Note, however, Funston's (1975: 13–14) discussion of the label "ultras."

32. Students called for defending Malay rights, confiscating Chinese property, and stripping Chinese of their citizenship rights, as well as maintaining authoritarian rule.

33. Musa Hitam, who later became deputy prime minister, noted that the difference between him and Mahathir in 1969 was that he was emphasizing accountability while Mahathir was obsessed with Malay ideology (author interview, Kuala Lumpur, July 2006).

34. Mahathir, who became prime minister in 1981, was expelled from UMNO in 1969 after he denounced Abdul Rahman in a publicly circulated letter, blaming him for the predicament of the Malays and for being excessively accommodative of the Chinese. He subsequently wrote *The Malay Dilemma* (1970), which was colored with chauvinist rhetoric against the Chinese (though replete as well with ample criticism of Malay backwardness). The government banned the book. When Mahathir was brought back into the party in the early 1970s, he clamped down on student demonstrations pushing for reforms. Thus, UMNO had disciplined and then reintegrated a leading light of the party who had moderated his position.

35. *Straits Times*, 1 Aug. 1969, quoted in Milne and Mauzy 1978: 82.

36. Quoted in Mauzy 1983: 156–57.

37. Horowitz 1989a: 259.

38. Some aspects of the NEP "had pre-1969 antecedents and were not wholly new," such as employment preferences for Malays on the docks in the 1950s and government agencies providing loans, scholarships, and training for Malays. Yet "the post-1969 innovations constituted a quantum leap in conception and resources" (Horowitz 1989a: 282n11).

39. The actual shaping of the NEP as a document espousing growth with equity was the result of internal debates between the Economic Planning Unit (EPU) and the Department of National Unity (DNU). In the aftermath of the

riots, the EPU remained wedded to a growth-oriented framework, whereas the DNU pushed for a more interventionist strategy in terms of poverty reduction, income redistribution, employment generation, and Malay corporate growth. The NEP reflects the merging of these two schools of thought, but with a significantly heavier emphasis on the DNU's interventionist position. On this debate, see Faaland, Parkinson, and Saniman 1990: 28–37.

40. Khoo 2005: 13.

41. Funston 1980: 221.

42. In all plans following the Second Malaysia Plan, national unity is the first goal articulated by the government. For example, Razak states in the foreword of the *Second Malaysia Plan* (1971): "The objectives, priorities, and strategies of the Plan have all been shaped by the overriding need to promote national unity." Fifteen years later, the government again stated in the fifth plan: "It has to be reiterated that national unity is the overriding objective and fundamental goal of the country" (Malaysia 1986: 5).

43. Malaysia 1971a: 43.

44. Author interview with Alihan Hamid and Ali Hamza, Distribution Section of the Economic Planning Unit, Putra Jaya, August 2002.

45. *Straits Times*, 2 Feb. 1971.

46. Malaysia 1971a.

47. In the traditional rural sector, the ratio of Malays to non-Malays was 3:1; in the traditional urban sector, it was 1:3; in the modern rural sector and in the modern urban sector, it was 2:5; in the government sector, it was 5:3. Ibid., 38.

48. Malaysia 1973: 80.

49. Ibid., 9.

50. Malaysia 1971a: 4–5.

51. Although FELDA has contributed to the rise in incomes in the rural sector, Shireen (1998) notes that declines in poverty came primarily from mobility into other occupations.

52. Two of the major *political* crises in Malaysia occurred during periods of severe unemployment. The 1969 ethnic riots erupted in the context of an unemployment rate of 8 percent. The 1987 struggle for the leadership of UMNO and the subsequent Operation Lalang in which more than one hundred people were arrested under the draconian Internal Security Act occurred with unemployment at 8.1 percent. See Malaysia, Ministry of Finance 1989.

53. Malaysia 1971b: 99. See also "Employment Problem in Malaysia," *Straits Times*, 26 Oct. 1970.

54. Malaysia 1971b: 99.

55. Razak also warned unemployed youths to take whatever jobs were available, as data in 1969 indicated that available slots were not even being actively

sought: "[A]lthough there are a number of jobs available as a result of this exercise [non-Malaysians were required to register for work permits to find out the number of jobs available], the number of Malaysians coming forward to fill these jobs has been disappointing. *I would like to stress once again that our youth must be prepared to take whatever jobs [are] available and must be prepared to roll their sleeves to play their part in the development of our country*" (emphasis in original). See Malaysia 1970: 9.

56. The government also created the National Trade Certification Board to formulate standards of training and the National Training Advisory Council to channel information from industries to a central coordinating body in which all training agencies are represented. See Malaysia 1971a: 27.

57. See, e.g., "Malaysia Acts on Jobs," *Straits Times*, 31 May 1971.

58. I thank Tan Siok Choo for pointing out to me the importance of the EPF (author interview, Kuala Lumpur, July 2002).

59. See Malaysia 1971b: 79; 1972: 32–33.

60. Meerman 1979: 18–19.

61. Ibid.

62. The tax effort is measured as a ratio of revenue to national income (Asher 1980).

63. Tanzi and Shome 1992: 57.

64. Ibid., 56

65. On the NDP, see Malaysia 1991b.

66. Ragayah 2008: 122.

67. Ibid., 130.

68. Malaysia 2010.

69. Malaysia 1991b: 31.

70. Milne (1976: 244) stresses the importance of organization for the business aspect of the NEP, but the point is true more generally.

71. On the broad outlines of the planning machinery, see Milne and Mauzy 1978: 253–57; Zainal 2001.

72. See the details in chapter 3 of this book; author interview with Rafisi Mohammed Muktar, director of the Social Division of the Implementation Coordination Unit, Putra Jaya, August 2002.

73. Author interview with Dr. Haflah, Malaysian Institute of Economic Research, Kuala Lumpur, July 2002.

74. Author interview with Rafisi Mohammed Muktar, Implementation Coordination Unit, Putra Jaya, August 2002.

75. Musolf and Springer 1979.

76. Ibid., 305.

77. Puthucheary 1978: 34.

78. Crouch 1996: 133.

79. Shamsul 1986: chap. 5.

80. This point is also made in Rogers 1975a.

81. Author interview with Abdul Hamid, UMNO public relations officer, Kuala Lumpur, June 2006.

82. The range of an MP's (government and opposition) workload and expectations from constituents is nicely described in Ong 1976.

83. In Bukit Tukuh in Kelanatan, the state assemblyman's house is adjacent to the UMNO division office and the local mosque, which suggests that the assemblyman plays a multifaceted role in the community. Fieldwork observation, Rantau Panjang, Kelantan, June 2006.

84. Author interview with Mat Zain, Rantau Panjang UMNO division leader and Bukit Tukuh state assemblyman, Rantau Panjang, Kelantan, June 2006.

85. At the house of Bukit Tukuh State Assemblyman Mat Zain, a woman complained at length to the assemblyman's wife about a schoolteacher's performance. Fieldwork observation in Rantau Panjang, Kelantan, June 2006.

86. Information on the branch level is based on interviews in Rantau Panjang, Kelantan, and Kuala Lumpur, in June and July 2006.

87. Rogers (1975a, 1975b) provides a description of the role of branches at the local level.

88. Ong 1976: 408.

89. Shamsul 1986; Rogers 1989, 1993: 116, 130.

90. A UMNO MP in Terengganu, Ahmad Shabery Cheek (author interview, Kuala Lumpur, July 2006), stresses that the branch level has a powerful pull on the national party. Shabery meets with the branches in his constituency three days during the week to gauge their needs. Higher-level officials, such as MPs or state assemblymen, must be extremely attentive to the demands of the branch leaders, as the latter deliver votes during elections.

91. Author interview with UMNO Executive Secretary Osaini, Kuala Lumpur, June 2006.

92. Author interview with MP Ahmad Shabery Cheek, Kuala Lumpur, July 2006. This is true also of opposition parties, as chronicled in Ong 1976.

93. Ratnam 1965: 163n51; Means 1970: 196–97.

94. Ratnam and Milne 1965: 403.

95. Rogers 1989: 782.

96. The first group of villagers paid their loans back and received title to their land in 1977, twenty-one years after they entered the settlement.

97. On the early trials and errors of FELDA, see "$2.5 Million Production Now, $260 Million Projected in 10 Years," *Straits Times*, 27 Oct. 1966.

98. Lee and Shamsul 2006: 52.

99. One aspect of its success, in contrast with the Rural Industry and Development Authority, that Ness (1967: 176–86) highlighted was its close organizational tie with its parent body, the Ministry of Rural Development.

100. Lee and Shamsul 2006: 52.

101. The Satu Wilayah Satu Industri (SAWARI) project, started in 2003, is divided into three industries: textile and embroidery, food, and handicrafts.

102. Jomo and Ishak 1986.

103. Halim 1992: 107–32.

104. Ibid., 115.

105. Ibid.

106. Wafa 1972, quoted in Jomo and Ishak 1986; see also Scott (1985: 136, 220–22) on UMNO's patronage in the villages.

107. Thillainathan 1976: 73–88.

108. Author interview with UMNO Executive Secretary Osaini, Kuala Lumpur, June 2006.

109. "Higher Living Allowances for Felda Settlers," *Star Online*, 9 June 2007.

110. Fong et al., 1982; Fong 1985: 149–70.

111. Jomo and Ishak 1986: 61.

112. Snodgrass 1980: 176–82.

113. Snodgrass (1980: 181–82) concluded in 1980: "[T]here is little doubt that the FELDA program is a bright spot in the rural scene. . . . [G]iven the surge of rural population and the distance Malaysia has to go before a large industrial work force is needed, the use of available land to create a halfway house for underemployed rural labor seems undeniably to have been a good thing." See also the positive assessment of Ness 1967.

114. Lee and Shamsul 2006: 23.

115. Ibid., 39.

116. Kinsey and Binswanger 1993.

117. Before 1970, the major concern of the government, other than language, was universal access. In the early 1990s, the government focused on improving quality.

118. Author interview with Zahri bin Aziz, principal assistant director of the Education Planning and Research Division, Ministry of Education, Kuala Lumpur, August 2002.

119. World Bank, World Development Indicators.

120. Primary school fees ended in 1961.

121. Contrary to earlier findings, Psacharopoulos and Tilak (1991) argue that secondary education has a more significant effect on income distribution than primary education. Because most countries have achieved almost similarly high

levels of enrollment at the primary level, the secondary level may be more critical in reducing income disparities.

122. Hoerr 1970.

123. Ramesh 2000: 124.

124. Author interview with Arshad Ayob, first principal of MARA Institute of Technology, Kuala Lumpur, July 2006.

125. Author interview with Arshad Ayob, Kuala Lumpur, July 2006.

126. Students previously received diplomas for professional courses and certificates for vocational training. Now they receive degrees.

127. This was an advanced diploma but technically was not a degree. Information from author interview with Arshad Ayob, Kuala Lumpur, July 2006.

128. Author interview with Arshad Ayob, Kuala Lumpur, July 2006.

129. See Asian Development Bank 1999; on Malaysia, see Hanafiah 1996: 766.

130. Malaysia, Ministry of Health 2000: 23.

131. Meerman 1979.

132. Asian Development Bank 1999.

133. Hanafiah 1996: 762.

134. World Bank 1992.

135. Norrizan 1999.

136. Hanafiah 1996; Malaysia, Ministry of Health 2006.

137. Author interview with Noraini Mohamed Ali, principal assistant director of the Social Division, Economic Planning Unit, Putra Jaya, August 2002; and author interview with Rohaizat bin Yon and Siti Zaharah Seman, Planning and Development Division, Ministry of Health, Kuala Lumpur, August 2002.

138. Rohaizat of the Ministry of Health emphasized that noninstitutional care is the key to Malaysia's success in health access and that it has served as a model for Hong Kong (author interview, Kuala Lumpur, August 2002).

139. Chee and Barraclough 2007b.

140. Hanafiah 1996.

141. Planning and Development Division, Ministry of Health.

142. Ahlburg and Flint 2001: 1–17.

143. Snodgrass 1980: 273.

144. Chee and Barraclough 2007b: 9.

145. This section on the privatization of health care relies on Barraclough 1996, 2000; Chee and Barraclough 2007a.

146. Malaysia 1991a: 88.

147. Vision 2020 is spelled out in Malaysia 1991a.

148. For example, private hospitals increased from 10 in 1980 to 128 in 2003 (Chee and Barraclough 2007a: 23, 31).

149. Grindle and Thomas 1989: 230.

150. Case 1995: 73–74.

151. See, e.g., class-based arguments, in Jomo and Ishak 1986: 99; Aliran 1989: 173–75; Chandra 1989.

152. The literature here is vast. For a balanced treatment, see Searle 1999. A sharp critique of money politics in the NEP is Gomez and Jomo 1997. Other critical studies on the capitalist class under the NEP include Jomo 1986; Mehmet 1986; Jesudason 1989. The abuse of the NEP by politicians at the rural level is described in Shamsul 1986.

153. Abdul Rahman Embong 2002: 191.

Part Three

1. Thailand 1997: 1.

2. World Bank, World Development Indicators (WDI; current US$).

3. However, comparing the rates in 2004 with previous rates is problematic because the poverty line was changed for the 2004 data (see World Bank 2005b).

4. Medhi and Pranee 1991. See also Pasuk, Sangsit, and Nualnoi 1996.

5. Debate surrounds the accuracy of the poverty threshold. Claiming that the poverty threshold line was too low and did not address changes since 1976, Medhi and Pranee adjusted the poverty line in 1988. The results show a huge gap between the adjusted and unadjusted poverty lines. Without adjustment, the incidence of poverty is calculated at 22.8 percent; with adjustment, poverty rises to 48.8 percent. See Medhi and Pranee 1991: table 2.15, 74, 250–51, and see 42–45.

6. A steep decline in farm prices and the value of agricultural production affected the poverty incidence in the mid-1980s, whereas in 1997–98, poverty increased as a result of the loss of jobs of factory workers in Bangkok, who returned to the countryside to sustain their livelihood.

7. World Bank 1993b: 6.

8. Somchai 2001.

Chapter 5

1. Wilson 1962: 280.

2. The debate over conceptualizing *sakdina* is not purely academic. It reflects deeply opposed positions on the role of the monarchy and the Sangha. See Reynolds 1987.

3. Akhin 1969: 22.

4. Wales 1965 [1934].

5. The argument that *sakdina* is equivalent to feudalism is made most famously in Jit Pumisak's trenchant critique of the premodern Thai polity, *Chomna sakdina*

thai (2000 [1957]). For an English translation, see Reynolds 1987: chap. 2. Reynolds notes that most Western and Thai scholars agree that *sakdina* does not match European feudalism (159, 167). Yet Reynolds defends Jit's position forcefully. An important analytical point that Reynolds makes is that conceptualizing *sakdina* as congruent with feudalism allows for comparability, and this in turn negates conservative claims of timelessness: "[R]esemblance between premodern Thai social formation and the European one [i.e., feudalism] is to assert the comparability of Thai society. Such comparability further suggests that each Thai social formation, including and especially the present one, is historical, contingent, and temporally bounded. If such institutions as the monarchy and Buddhist monkhood are historical and contingent then they will gradually decline in power and prestige" (168–69). This, in essence, captures what is at stake in the debate over *sakdina*. See also Reynolds and Lysa 1983.

6. See Chai-Anan 1976; Chatthip and Suthy 1981: 23–24.

7. Wales 1965 [1934].

8. Wales 1965 [1934]: 46–50, esp. 49–50.

9. There were actually three categories, including the *phrai suai*. These were commoners who lived in remote provinces and sent tax in kind (*suai*) to substitute for labor service.

10. In the 1800s, the amount of time required for corvée gradually declined from six months to three months to one month.

11. Akhin 1969: 57.

12. Pasuk and Baker 1995: 24.

13. Mead 2004: 42.

14. The Bunnags were of Arab descent and established themselves as key ministers during the Ayutthaya period. See Wyatt 1968.

15. Tej 1977: 12.

16. For an informative (and amusing) firsthand account of the battle and its broader consequences, see Smyth 1994: chap. 12.

17. A sense of how the Siamese perceived their losses to the French is evident in the maps provided by Thailand's great propagandist, Vichit 1941: 56–62.

18. Mead 2004: 41 (emphasis added).

19. For some middle-class views of Chulalongkorn as abolitionist, see Stengs 2009: 45–52.

20. The *nai* accumulated wealth by extracting a higher commutation tax from the *phrai* and withholding much of it for themselves. In a cash economy, they also took the surplus from the *phrai*'s labor in rice fields, and they levied fees on *phrai* working in the urban sector and estate lands. See Mead 2004: 41, 43.

21. Tej 1977: 175.

22. Skinner 1957: 97.

23. According to Skinner (1957: 125), half of the state's revenues came from the Chinese in the form of head taxes, fixed returns from tax farms held by the Chinese, from gambling, and from opium and spirits consumption.

24. Tej 1977, 14–17.

25. This discussion of the *thesaphiban* system summarizes Tej 1977: 61–75, 99–125, 163–84.

26. Battye 1974: 30–31.

27. Ibid., 216.

28. Ibid., 489.

29. Ibid., 398. Battye argues that the impetus for universal conscription was not internal pacification but external defense. Yet the evidence he provides suggests that it was a combination of external and internal concerns that mattered. See Battye 1974: 402, 413, 429, 439–41.

30. Battye 1974: 530–31.

31. Yet for all of Chulalongkorn's goals of creating a modern, rationalized nation-state, the Siamese state still remained very much a creature of patrimonialism. The king understood well that if bureaucratic rationalization were taken to its full completion, his authority would be threatened. Thus, he maintained patrimonial practices, insisting that bureaucrats come to see him in person rather than following bureaucratic norms of communication, that civil servants always attend the palace's ceremonial functions, and that judges make decisions based on the interests of the monarchy (Mead 2004: 101–04, 112–17).

32. The legacy of state building under Chulalongkorn is central to Riggs's (1966) thesis: "Clearly the foundations laid by Chulalongkorn had been lasting. Not only had they created a basic governmental structure which could stand the strain of revolutionary pressures generated by the abolition of the absolute monarchy itself, but they provided, in addition, a floor on which further growth and development would be possible" (131).

33. In a world-historical perspective, Chulalongkorn's structural reforms are often depicted as modernizing. Centralizing power, rationalizing the civil administration and military, ending slavery, establishing foundations for social equity, and stymieing imperial aggression—these are all rightly viewed as aspects of modernization. Emblematic of this position is historian David Wyatt (1969: 376): "A feature of great significance for Thailand's survival, however, was the fact that the transformation of her society and government was accomplished largely through action from above, by leaders who were more than leaders; visionaries who were sensitive to the needs of the age and who forced change upon their nation." However, Benedict Anderson's (1978) trenchant critique of Thai nationalism and the Thai monarchy has forced us to reconsider these truisms. In Anderson's view, we must conceptualize Chulalongkorn's reforms less as modernizing in a

nationalist sense than as efforts at dynastic preservation. When juxtaposed with other nationalist leaders in Southeast Asia or Japan, the conservative elements of Chulalongkorn's agenda stand in stark relief. The significance of Anderson's powerful critique is to point out that the reforms of the fifth reign essentially deepened the conservative elements of the Thai state rather than modernizing it in the direction of the national interest. Most obviously, these reforms strengthened the monarchy's authority and legitimacy. Even Tej Bunnag (1977: 16), despite his sympathetic view toward the monarchy, acknowledged this point: "The King was the herald of reform, not only because it was his duty to look after national interests, but because it was also the means of restoring power to the monarchy." These reforms sustained a monarchical strain in the Thai state that even the most constitutionally oriented reformists could not figure out how to undo. And this was to make modernizing reforms—understood in a more national sense—when they did arrive in 1932, ultimately incapable of ushering substantive institutional or social change into Thailand. For critiques of conventional Thai historiography, see Anderson 1978; Reynolds 1987; Thongchai 1994; Koizumi 2002. The work of Mead (2004), although less hard hitting than the previous works, also leans in a more critical direction.

34. Under Rama VII, royalists had increased their political power compared to Rama VI. The Supreme State Council and the Council of Ministers were dominated by princes. One event that had long rankled the army was the public flogging in 1909 of several army officers following a dispute with pages of Crown Prince Vajiravudh. The army considered the flogging "unjustifiable." See Mead (2004: 123; see also 117–25) for a description of the rising bureaucratic middle class.

35. Pasuk and Baker 1995: 248.

36. Pridi's father was a civil servant, but he was also related to the governor of Ayutthaya.

37. Pridi, quoted in Thak 1978: 52.

38. The Russian Revolution framed Pridi's time in Paris: "He arrived in Paris in 1920 when the Russian revolution was still struggling for consolidation. He left in 1927 when the first Soviet four-year plan had been launched." See Baker and Pasuk 2000: xii. When he was a high school student in Ayutthaya, Pridi (1974: 27–28) had already expressed interest in the Chinese and Russian revolutions.

39. Pridi himself noted many years later, "Each of us had different ideas about the need to develop society and about the principles and methods of social development. After we had the power of the state, these differences led to conflict among us." See Pridi 2000: 135.

40. The coup members were known as "Promoters" of change in the system, which identified them as the vanguard of the reform movement.

41. For a blow-by-blow account of how the coup unfolded from the perspective of its main strategist, see Song Suradet, in Thak 1978. The best detailed studies of the revolution are Thawatt 1962, 1972.

42. Prajhadipok's advisers rebuffed his efforts to create a constitution. See Batson 1984: 146–53.

43. On the People's Party Manifesto of 24 June 1932, see Pridi 2000. The *London Times*, 4 Aug. 1932, noted: "Following quickly on the arrest of the Princes, there came a proclamation of such a kind as might have been posted on a barricade in Paris during one of its nineteenth-century revolutions."

44. "It would seem that these leaders are not too confident that they have the entire country behind them, and therefore for the present they cannot take risks," reported the *London Times*, 4 Aug. 1932.

45. Yano 1978: 134.

46. See Pridi 2000: 73–79.

47. In the first stage, the Assembly would be made up of seventy members who were to be appointed by the military. This stage would last for six months. In the second stage, the Assembly would be composed of two categories of members of equal numbers. The first were those who were to be elected by the people from provinces with a population of more than one hundred thousand. These members would be elected through indirect voting and had to pass an examination on politics. The second group was composed of members from the original Assembly. The third stage of democratization would commence when more than half of the population had attained primary education, or within ten years of the implementation of the constitution. See Riggs 1966: 153–57.

48. Thawatt 1962: 148.

49. Thawatt (1962: 148) argues that Pridi's ideas derived more from Sun rather than from Marxism-Leninism.

50. Quoted in Stowe 1991: 30.

51. Compare the translations of the *Economic Plan* in Landon 1939 and in Pridi 2000.

52. Pridi 2000: 112–13.

53. The *Economic Plan* is characterized by Pridi's use of forceful and vivid language.

54. See Pridi 2000: 93, 94, 100, 103, 113.

55. Pridi (2000: 113) wrote that: "People will have equal rights in not going hungry, but not equality in the sense that if one person has a hundred baht it must be seized and shared equally among a hundred people at one baht apiece."

56. Fistié 1969: 60.

57. Ibid., 70, 73.

58. Pridi 2000: 30.

59. Fistié 1969: 77.

60. Ibid.

61. Baker and Pasuk 2000: xiii. They note that the only economist cited in the plan is German Friedrich List, an advocate of state-led industrialization.

62. Pridi 2000.

63. Pridi 2000: 107.

64. Decha n.d.

65. See "Minutes of a Meeting of a Committee to Consider a National Economic Policy at Paruskawan Palace, 12 March 1933," in Thak 1978. Most interesting in this meeting is the forceful questioning, but ultimate support, of the king's designated adviser on economic matters, Prince Sakorn, dubbed "the red prince."

66. Quoted in Thawatt 1972: 162.

67. Attacked by reactionary forces for being a communist, he was in turn lambasted by the communists for selling out. On 29 September 1932, the Communist Party of Siam distributed pamphlets in English, Thai, and Chinese that denounced Pridi and his government for being "false revolutionaries." Stowe (1991: 47) suggests that Ho Chi Minh was the writer of the pamphlets, as Ho had passed through Bangkok a few days after the pamphlets had been circulated. Ho had participated in meetings of Asian revolutionaries in Paris which Pridi had also attended.

68. See, for example, the *Bangkok Times*, 21 Oct. 1932.

69. Khana Chat had no ideological basis and was driven by hatred of members of the People's Party. Most of its members were civilian and military officials who had fallen from grace since the 1932 revolution. A key member was Vichit Vatakarn, a diplomat in Paris in the 1920s who had sympathized with the rebellious students but was offended when he was not rewarded with a plum position in the aftermath of the coup.

70. Murashima, Nakharin, and Wanthana 1991: 17–19.

71. Copeland 1993: 214.

72. *Bangkok Times Weekly Mail*, 22 Aug. 1932, quoted in Copeland 1993: 7. The archives of the *Bangkok Times* report recruitment activities of the People's Association from September 1932 until January 1933.

73. *Bangkok Times*, 30 Sept. 1932.

74. *Bangkok Times*, 26 Sept. 1932.

75. Brown 2004: 38–42.

76. Date of the 1932 revolution.

77. Kasian 2001: 35.

78. Ibid.

79. Stowe 1991: 30.

80. Quoted in Thawatt 1962: 85.

81. *Bangkok Times*, 21 Oct. 1932.

82. "Democracy in Siam," *Bangkok Times*, 6 Feb. 1933.

83. As Riggs (1966: 157) notes, in contrast to the People's Party, the KMT developed a grassroots base and military cadres.

84. Pridi admitted as much, particularly in regards to his choice of the conservative Manopakorn as prime minister. See Pridi 2000: 167–69, 241.

85. Riggs 1966: 161–62.

86. Coast 1953: 5.

87. Ibid., 6. Similarly, Fistié (1969: 111) comments: "If Pridi's program lacked realism it was not solely in the financial goals. . . . Pridi, in effect, seems to have had a lot of illusions about the possibility of mobilizing his compatriots and engage them in a collective effort in the framework of a planned socialist system."

88. Copeland (1993) claims that 1932 should be seen as a nationalist revolution, which in many ways was equivalent to the mass-based nationalist movements that rose up against colonial states in Asia. The revolution went against the patrimonial system of the monarchy and sought to completely transform the polity through a new constitution, representative Assembly, elections, the rationalization of state authority, the expansion of the public school system, and the revision of the tax code. Through the ideals that the Promoters sought to inculcate into the polity and because of their affinity to other mass-based nationalist movements, Copeland argues that the revolution was "an event which can be said to mark the figurative 'liberation' of the Thai nation" (vii). Those who battled against the monarchy were "those elements in society which formed the vanguard of nationalist movements in neighboring colonial states: Western-trained professionals employed in the civil and military bureaucracies; members of the urban intelligentsia; and representatives of ethnic groups residing under the authority of alien rulers" (10). Copeland's thesis is compelling, but the fact remains that the People's Party failed to mobilize the nation against the monarchy and was not committed to a republican government. These constitute significant differences from other anticolonial nationalist movements. See also Hewison 1989: 61–62; Reynolds 1992: 318; Nakharin 1992.

89. Riggs 1966: 112.

90. Pasuk and Baker 1995: 266.

91. Ibid., 266.

92. Darling 1965: 55.

93. Ibid., 59.

94. Wilson 1959: 82.

95. Sarit did create a political party known as Seri Manangasila, and his successor in 1963, Thanom Kittikachorn, established the United Thai People's Party. The function of these parties was mainly to provide patronage for loyal military and civil bureaucrats by giving them seats in an emasculated Parliament. However, the

military did not use these parties for the purpose of social mobilization. Unlike a praetorian state such as Indonesia under Suharto, the military did not take full advantage of the myriad functions a party could play. See Chai-Anan 1982.

96. Thak 1979: 167.

97. Muscat 1994: 88.

98. World Bank 1959.

99. The NEDB relied heavily on academic expertise, including forty-five specialists in economic development. Sarit had a favorable view of academics as long as they were not involved in politics: "In former times, academics received little status; economics was taken as common sense and those who never studied economics could talk about the subject . . . which led them to believe that they did not have to rely upon academic expertise. I have no such belief." Quoted in Thak 1979: 279.

100. Muscat (1994: 66) identifies three groups of technocrats who adhered to laissez-faire ideals. The first group comprised so-called elders in the mid-1950s, including Puey. The second group included graduates of Western universities who were rising up the career ladder at the Bank of Thailand and the Ministry of Finance. The third group was made up of young students of economics and public administration who were returning to Thailand after earning their graduate degrees in the United States and England.

101. Quoted in Muscat 1994: 68. Note that Puey's comments are as much against capitalist profiteers as they are against corrupt state elites.

102. Thailand 1961: 9.

103. See Thailand 1967: 39.

104. The Second Plan (Thailand 1967: 2) noted: "[S]evere regional inequality constitutes an economic weakness which outside infiltrators have been exploiting for subversive purposes."

105. Surachart 1988.

106. Thak 1979: 303.

107. Excerpts of speech by Sarit Thanarat, in Smith 1974: 40–45.

108. Oey 1978: 36.

109. Medhi 1981.

110. Oey 1978: 66, 71.

111. Ibid., 75.

112. During this period, the rice premium was one of the most contentious policies that facilitated the transfer of resources from the rural to the urban sector. Instituted in the early postwar period, the rice premium functioned as a tax on rice for export whose purpose was to stabilize prices, increase fiscal revenue for government, and most important, reduce expenditures for urban residents, particularly civil servants who had been hard hit by postwar inflation (Ammar and

Suthad 1989: 64; Ammar 1975). Between 1955 and 1966, the premium averaged about 12 percent of total government revenue (Ammar 1975: 17–18). The effect of the rice premium on farmers was to depress their incomes, and to discourage innovation and land intensification, by lowering the domestic price of rice (Ingram 1971: 255). At its height, between 1955 and 1974, the premium depressed the domestic price of rice compared to that in the international market by 35 percent (Dixon 1999: 141). From the 1950s until the late 1970s, it served as one of the central tools of government for generating a surplus from the income of paddy farmers to favor urban interests. The premium was terminated in 1986, at which point its significance for fiscal revenue had declined.

113. Baker and Pasuk 2000: xiv.

114. Fistié 1969: 114.

Chapter 6

1. Girling 1981b: 160.

2. *Far Eastern Economic Review Yearbook* (1972: 325), quoted in Neher 1975: 1100.

3. Race 1974: 194.

4. In the 1960s, enrollment in secondary schools increased by 43 percent, and in vocational schools by 81 percent (Darling 1974: 6–9). Anderson (1977: 17) captured the rising aspirations of families experiencing the economic boom of the 1960s thus: "It was possible to *imagine* within the confines of a single household a successful dry-cleaner father and an embryonic cabinet secretary son" (emphasis in original).

5. A detailed account of the 1973 events is Race 1974.

6. Stifel 1970; Arumugam, Low, and Rajaretnam 1973: 41–43; Puey 2000: 94–95.

7. *Bangkok Bank Monthly Review* (1973), quoted in Race 1974: 192.

8. Kramol 1982: 20.

9. Ibid., 33.

10. This was the most significant parliamentary showing for the left since 1946. Together, the three parties on the left won 14.4 percent of votes and thirty-seven seats.

11. The Seri Manangasila, which later became the United Thai People's Party.

12. Morell and Chai-Anan 1981: 261.

13. Electoral support for the left since 1946 has come largely from the northeastern peasantry, where income per capita is lower than in other regions. See especially Race 1975; Somporn 1976. On the relative continuity of leftist parties, see Wilson 1959: 95–98, but note 100; Keyes 1967: 42–47; Ockey 2005: 736.

14. See Morell and Chai-Anan (1981: 158–59) for figures on student demonstrations outside Bangkok.

15. Turton 1978: 129–31.

16. Calculated on the basis of Nikom 1978: 283; Morell and Chai-Anan 1981: 188.

17. Medhi and Pranee 1991: 120.

18. Suehiro 1981: 318.

19. Quoted in Arumugam, Low, and Rajaretnam 1973: 42.

20. Morell and Chai-Anan 1981: 214–15.

21. Ibid., 218.

22. Cohen 1983: 254.

23. The Bangkok Bank was a strong advocate of land reform and social reform in general. See 1970s issues of its *Monthly Review* (e.g., October 1971).

24. Morell and Chai-Anan 1981: 120.

25. Ibid., 127.

26. Ibid.

27. Girling 1981b: 203.

28. Village headmen and *tambon* leaders (*kamnan*) are elected to office, but once elected, they are in office in perpetuity. The reform bill called for elections every five years.

29. Morell and Chai-Anan 1981: 130.

30. Ammar et al. 1990: 274.

31. Ibid.

32. Even within Bangkok, reform initiatives went unfulfilled. Despite sharp increases in the minimum wage, some factories, particularly in the textile industry, refused to abide by the new wages. Yet when a worker could not work because of illness, his or her wage would be reduced at the rate of the minimum wage (Bt20) even if the worker were being paid only Bt12. See Morell and Chai-Anan 1981: 194–95.

33. Ibid., 230.

34. Although the Tambon Fund was more successful than other policies, it was also plagued by problems. For example, it did not employ as much local manpower as intended, with local construction companies getting many of the contracts. Furthermore, there were numerous reports of misuse of funds (Turton 1978: 118–19).

35. Despite not requiring coercion to succeed, another much-heralded reform, the price support program through the Farmers' Aid Fund, ended up benefiting local elites, such as rice millers, rather than small-scale farmers (Ammar and Suthad 1989: 41, 59).

36. For example, Cohen (1983: 255) found that northern peasants were reluctant to press their landlords for a fair share of the rent, as stipulated in the Land

Rent Control Act, in part because of the fear of eviction. Landlords also proved adept at manipulating a loophole in the act that enabled them to maintain their control over tenants.

37. Katherine Bowie and Brian Phelan, "Who Is Killing the Farmers?" *Bangkok Post Sunday Magazine*, 17 Aug. 1975.

38. Udomsak Yudhanaraweesak, "Thai Society Is Changing," *Bangkok Post Sunday Magazine*, 17 Aug. 1975.

39. Bowie and Phelan, "Who Is Killing the Farmers?"

40. The bill set 50 *rai* (20 acres) as the ceiling, despite the fact that the average farm size in 1975 was 14.7 *rai* (6 acres) (Ramsay 1982: 183).

41. Lin and Esposito 1976: 440–42; Suehiro 1981: 340; Ramsay 1982: 184–86. Although the central plains were given attention, the northern and north-central provinces were neglected (Ramsay 1982: 188).

42. Suehiro 1981: 338, 340. The Land Reform Act also included distribution of *public* land, but even there the results were dismal. As Suehiro (340) concluded: "Judged from results . . . there was very little difference between the land reform on state land and that on private land." See also Ramsay 1982: 186–87.

43. The newspaper *Ban Muang* observed that "even the CIA would not object to Kukrit as prime minister." Quoted in Prizzia 1985: 92.

44. Lin and Esposito 1976: 437.

45. Suehiro 1981: 342.

46. Author interview with Banthorn On-dam, NGO leader, Bangkok, January 2001; Bowie and Phelan, "Who Is Killing the Farmers?"; Suehiro 1981: 342.

47. The Democrat Party and the three leftist parties had joined together to force a no-confidence vote against Kukrit and form a new government.

48. The bill that would have created local elections to improve grassroots democracy and weaken the all-powerful Ministry of Interior collapsed precisely because of the short staying power of the Kukrit government.

49. This division was reflected in the policy platform of the party: in 1975 it advocated "mild socialism," but in 1976 it veered sharply to the right. See Somporn 1976: 24, 32–33.

50. The conservative group led by Samak Sundaravej also had close links with the Chat Thai, in effect undermining the Democrat Party in which it was nominally based. See Morell and Chai-Anan 1981.

51. Chai-Anan (n.d.), quoted in Kramol 1982: 26–27.

52. Krit was the army's commander in chief during the October 1973 uprising. He was instrumental in undermining Thanom and Praphat by double-crossing them and refusing to crack down on the students. This was the result of intense factionalism within the military.

53. On the massacre at Thammasat—a uniquely devastating moment in modern Thai history—and the events leading up to it, see Anderson 1977; Girling 1977; Puey 1977; Mallet 1978; Girling 1981b; Morell and Chai-Anan 1981; more generally, see Bowie 1997.

54. Leftist parties had some links with civil society groups. For example, the Farmers Federation of Thailand actively campaigned for the Socialist Party in the north (see Bowie and Phelan, "Who Is Killing the Farmers?"). But the left did not have enough seats to join the governing coalition and was then eviscerated by right-wing violence. Paramilitary groups conspired to destroy leftist parties, including assassinating the secretary-general of the Socialist Party, who was a professor at Thammasat University with a doctorate from Cornell University. In the 1976 elections, the leftist parties were decimated, falling from 14 percent of the vote to 2.2 percent. Their seat share collapsed from thirty-seven to six.

55. Student activism was crucial in terms of pressuring for policy reform, challenging social hierarchies, and putting the armed forces on the defensive, but activists also did not know when to moderate their demands, when to compromise, and how to forge alliances with some parties that might have met them halfway. Puey Ungphakorn (2000: 74)—rector of Thammasat during the height of the crisis in 1976 and an ally of the student movement—wrote the following assessment of the movement after leaving the country: "Most of the students are well-intentioned; they want freedom and democracy; they wish to help the underdogs; they have set about correcting social injustice." But flush with their success in 1973, "university students then became overconfident, arrogant and created too many enemies among officials, landowners, and businessmen. . . . They protested on so many issues that people became indifferent if not hostile." Girling (1977: 398–99) is similarly critical, but see also Zimmerman (1974), written at a more hopeful moment, and Prizzia 1985: chap. 4.

56. Quoted in Girling 1981b: 184n134.

57. Such an alliance might also have created a bulwark against the right-wing violence unleashed on the left and ultimately on democratic institutions. In defense, at the very least, of democratic institutions—if not of the left—both Kukrit's SAP and Seni's Democrats might have benefited from an alliance, for their parties also lost when reactionary elements executed their coup.

58. Morell and Chai-Anan 1981: 132.

59. On the structural adjustment period, see Doner and Anek 1994; Muscat 1994: chap. 6.

60. Doner 2009: 31.

61. Ibid., 31–32.

62. Pasuk and Baker 1995: 156–69.

63. Pasuk and Baker 1995: 153. In the mid-1980s, Thailand had one of the lowest labor costs in Southeast Asia (Dixon 1996: 41).

64. Pasuk and Baker 2008.

65. Medhi 1995: 36; World Bank, World Development Indicators; Doner 2009: 39; see Ammar, Suthad, and Direk (1993: 93) for Asia comparisons.

66. Pranee (1995: 228) suggests that a minimum-wage law has made the price of capital relatively cheap vis-à-vis labor, thereby lowering employment in industry.

67. Pasuk 1999. See similarly Chai-Anan (1995: esp. 236 and 244), who suggests that liberalization has been an elite phenomenon that has hurt the peasantry.

68. Muscat 1994: 65–71.

69. Ammar, Suthad, and Direk 1993; Pasuk and Baker 1995.

70. Hicken and Kuhonta 2011: 572–97.

71. The author calculated the effective number of parliamentary parties; parliamentary factions are from Chambers 2005.

72. Chambers 2005: 501.

73. Pasuk and Baker 1998: 246.

74. Chai-Anan 1990: 293.

75. Anek 1992: tables 2.2 and 2.3.

76. In 1974, more than half of the members of the executive committees of these three parties were businessmen. Although always business oriented, Chat Thai and SAP had eased out all factions centered on career politicians by the 1980s (Anek 1992: tables 2.2 and 2.3; 1988: 453).

77. Noranit (1987: 156) concludes that the party's organizational development has not been very effective because it lacks a social base that is committed to the institution. Rather than expanding through branches, the party needs central leadership that strengthens its functions so as to increase mass support. Similarly, Anusorn (1998: 423) finds that party branches were not effective in terms of social mobilization and party engagement—"the Democrat Party's attempt, so far, to be a party for the masses, has not been very satisfactory."

78. Noranit 1987; Sungsidh 1996.

79. Noranit 1987: 160.

80. Sungsidh 1996; Askew 2008: 44. Note also the controversy over Chuan's role in the May 1992 popular uprising (McCargo 1997a).

81. Sungsidh 1996: 111.

82. The Ministry of Industry has historically been under its grip.

83. Sungsidh 1996: 37.

84. Sungsidh 1996.

85. It supported the 1976 and 1992 coups, although it was also ousted in 1991 by the military.

86. This is a play on *kin muang*—literally "eat the province," or corruption.

87. He was known as the "walking ATM" because of his "generosity." His 1995–96 tenure was dubbed the "7-eleven government" (Pasuk and Baker 1998: 258, 260).

88. This is part of the title of McCargo's (1997a) insightful study on the party and its leader.

89. The actual policy agenda of the party was rather fuzzy, but its party pledge was distinct: "acting only in accordance with morality, refraining from vote-buying, not aspiring to political office, and not lying." Members who did not follow these principles would be expelled from the party (McCargo 1997a: 150–51).

90. Its founder, Chamlong, noted that the party was created to rectify the "lack of righteousness" in Thai politics (King 1996: 43). Prospective party candidates were carefully screened in terms of their moral standing.

91. This was particularly so for candidate selection, where there was ample feedback between local branches and central candidate selection committees.

92. McCargo 1997b: 125.

93. The school was begun by a former member of the SAP, who wanted to build a mass base for that party in the 1970s and who consciously modeled his agenda on Western European mass parties. At its height, the school had more than 8,500 graduates who could be mobilized for party goals. It published a newsletter with articles on parties and democracy, and it made efforts to target northeastern villagers (McCargo 1997a: 173–76; King 1996: 62).

94. King 1996: 56.

95. McCargo 1997a: 178–79.

96. Although factionalism in Palang Dharma was based not just on spoils and personal rivalries but also on substantive issues regarding party identity.

97. McCargo 1997b: 128.

98. Ibid.

99. King 1996: 66.

100. Author interview with Thamarak Karnpisit, deputy secretary-general of NESDB, Bangkok, January 2001.

101. See Thailand 1982: 278; Thailand 1987: 338, 345, 356, and 359.

102. Author interview with Thamarak Karnpisit, Bangkok, January 2001.

103. Economist Ammar Siamwalla argues that the NESDB is peripheral in policy making (author interview, Bangkok, December 2001). Under Sarit, Thanom, and Prem (all generals), the NESDB was highly influential (Muscat 1994). But since the Chatichai government and the creeping assertiveness of business-oriented parties, its significance has declined. This contrasts with the Malaysian planning body, the Economic Planning Unit (EPU), which dominates policy making on every level: from policy formulation to budget allocation and

implementation. One key difference from the NESDB is that the EPU has the power to allocate funding within its five-year plans and can therefore control the direction of policy and the relative emphases of the various ministries (the EPU sets the floor and ceiling of the budget but the Ministry of Finance does the sectoral allocations). This contrast reflects the greater institutional coherence of the Malaysian state than that of Thailand.

104. Worawut 2006: 158.

105. Author interviews with Nikhom Chandravitoon (Bangkok, 2000–01), a bureaucrat and senator who played a critical role in drafting the bill. Also important was Kraisak Choonhavan, Chatichai's son, who, unlike his father, is a leftist intellectual.

106. Reinecke 1993.

107. Ibid., 98 (emphasis in original).

108. Per capita income declined by 14.5 percent, and unemployment rose to 5.3 percent nationally; but in the northeast unemployment rose to 8.8 percent, and among those between the ages of fifteen and twenty-nine, figures were even higher: 18 percent for men and 15 percent for women (Pasuk and Baker 2000: 92, 94–95).

109. Baker 2005: 120.

110. Pasuk and Baker 2004: 68–69; McCargo and Ukrist 2005: 98.

111. Dornbusch and Edwards 1991; Roberts 1995; Weyland 2001; Anek 2007.

112. Baker 2005: 121. In subsequent elections, the Democrat Party aped TRT's platform, bettering it in some respects by calling for a universal health-care policy without the thirty-baht copayment. Yet it refused to call its programs populist (McCargo and Ukrist 2005: 92–93).

113. Chambers 2005.

114. In 2004, TRT had 14 million members and ten branches (Siripan 2006: 139). However, critics have noted that membership often overlapped among parties, whereas branches were hollow (Nelson 2002; McCargo and Ukrist 2005: 16).

115. McCargo and Ukrist 2005: 85; see also Ockey 2003; Pasuk and Baker 2004.

116. A farmer in the central plains stressed the importance of cash that leads to debt: "Buying rice seed; paying for the ploughing machine; inputting fertilizer, water and chemicals; hiring a harvesting machine; paying for transportation to silo . . . it's all about paying out cash" ("A Matter of Survival for Rice Farmers," *Bangkok Post*, 17 Feb. 2002). Another explained: "Farmers . . . might have a bad harvest one year, and have to borrow money in order to get by. Then they will try to get out of debt by increasing their acreage, which means they have to borrow even more. This is a cycle that is very difficult to get out of." See Sangkhom 1996.

117. This is compared to 12 percent to 14 percent from the BAAC (Ammar et al. 1990: 284).

118. See Suehiro (1981: 324) for the trend in land forfeiture in the 1970s.

119. The problem of land titles has been less of an issue in the central delta region because titles were issued early on.

120. Muscat 1994: 144.

121. World Bank 2000: 23.

122. Author interview with Decha Siripat, Technology for Rural Ecology and the Environment (TREE), Suphan Buri, May 2001; *Nation* (Bangkok), 15 Sept. 1999.

123. The market share of informal lenders has declined since the 1970s, but its absolute amount is still high (Ammar et al. 1990).

124. Ibid., 277.

125. Author interviews with farmers in Suphan Buri, June 2001. See also "Farmers' Adaptation to Alternative Agriculture: Case Studies of Farmers in the Four Regions of Thailand," *Thai Development Newsletter* 30 (1996): 27–36; and "Farmer Profiles," *Thai Development Newsletter* 30 (1996): 40–46.

126. But the cost of alternative agriculture is potentially lower yields. See *Bangkok Post*, 17 Feb. 2002.

127. Author interview with Decha Siripat, TREE, Suphan Buri, May 2001.

128. See "King Clarifies Sufficiency Idea," *Bangkok Post*, 5 Dec. 1998; UNDP 2003; NESDB Plans.

129. This section on the DMP draws partly from Kuhonta and Mutebi (n.d.).

130. Debt suspension meant a deferral on interest and principal, whereas debt relief entailed a 3 percent reduction in interest rate while still servicing the debt. Both programs had a three-year limit.

131. See the TRT's website (http://www.thairakthai.or.th/about/policy /policy_6.htm (in Thai) and http://www.thairakthai.or.th/article/bansat_nonpay .htm (in Thai, both accessed July 2003); see also "Thai Rak Thai Party Explains Its Policy on Debt Moratorium," *Nation* (Bangkok), 4 Sept. 2000; "Thai Rak Thai Unveils Rural Plan," *Nation* (Bangkok), 15 Jan. 2001.

132. For example, "Debt Moratorium Recipe for Disaster," *Bangkok Post*, 30 Aug. 2000.

133. The secretary of the Federation of Isaan Agricultural Cooperatives made his point very clear: "Farmers in nineteen northeastern provinces will stop repaying their loans from now because they have elected Thai Rak Thai due to its campaign platform calling for a three-year moratorium on farm debts." See "Farmers' Group to Stop Repayments Immediately," *Nation* (Bangkok), 23 Jan. 2001.

134. Secretariat of the Thai Cabinet 2004.

135. Suchanan 2004: 23–30.

136. Thammasat University 2004.

137. Surveys and focus groups were divided into those in the suspension program, those in the relief program, and those who exited the program.

138. Thammasat University 2004: 74–80, 95, 97–98.

139. Of those who joined the training program within the DMP, 51.3 percent and 53.7 percent believe that savings and assets, respectively, increased. In general, those who joined the training program did better than those who did not (Thammasat University 2004: 70–71, 80–82, 93, 96–97, 99–100).

140. Farmers in the debt suspension program and those in the debt relief program had Bt2.2 billion and Bt2.6 billion more in savings, respectively. See Secretariat of the Thai Cabinet 2004: 40. A subsequent document had even higher figures (Secretariat of the Thai Cabinet 2005: 14).

141. The exception is the BAAC (2004: 40), which reports that debt declined from Bt94,329 to Bt77,768. The decline was most notable for the group in the debt suspension program, and less for those in the debt relief program. Although the Thammasat University (2004: 75) report shows debt increasing, it converges with the BAAC in noting that the debt suspension program has better results than the debt relief program. It is not clear where this discrepancy comes from, but one possibility is that the BAAC (2004) does not include those who exited the program. Thammasat University (2004) includes this group, whose results are generally weak.

142. Between 2001 and the end of 2003, debt increased from Bt46,665 to Bt55,424 . The report notes that the finding that debt increased (53 percent reported increases) is inconsistent with other results (Thammasat University 2004: 75, 97, 144). But this is significant, as it suggests that increased capital may simply have added to debt.

143. For example, farmers may have a positive cash flow, but this is still woefully insufficient to pay off debt. Or they may have an improved asset-to-debt ratio, but their savings reflect less their capacity than the rules set by the BAAC (Thammasat University 2004: 78, 84). Furthermore, it is clear that another of Thaksin's pro-poor programs, the One-Million-Baht Village Fund, was used to pay off debt. After joining the DMP, the percentage using the fund to pay off debt increased by 8 percentage points. Furthermore, the percentage of those in debt who used income from agricultural products to pay off debt declined by 13 percentage points, which indicates that they were relying more on easy credit (DMP) than on productivity to pay off their debt. Somewhat more positive, the percentage of those relying on friends (informal lenders) to pay off debt declined from 9.4 percentage points (Thammasat University 2004: 78–79, 151).

144. In 2001, a National Statistical Office survey (*Bangkok Post*, 14 Feb. 2002) showed that agricultural workers' household debt declined by 23.7 percent. But Somchai and Jiraporn's (2003) data present a starkly different picture. Between 1994 and 2002 when the rate of debt increased overall, the rate of increase of the debt-to-income ratio of the ultra poor was highest between 2000 and 2002 (when the DMP and other pro-poor policies were implemented)—a jump of 3.7 points

from 11.5 to 15.2. The percentage of consumption debt between 2000 and 2002 also registered a huge rise for the ultra poor from 37.7 percent to 50.2 percent—an increase of 12.5 percent.

145. "Farmers Demand Better Debt Solution," *Nation* (Bangkok), 2 Apr. 2002. One of the complaints of farmers is that the three-year period is insufficient to start from scratch.

146. In the December 2007 elections, Chat Thai and Matchimathipatai advocated a debt moratorium plan as part of their platform. Once in power, the People's Power Party implemented such a plan, and the Democrat Party also supported this when leading government. See "Govt Woos Farmers, Reds with Debt Shelter Plan," *Bangkok Post*, 31 Mar. 2010; "Surapong Offers Farmers Debt Relief," *Nation* (Bangkok), 23 Feb. 2008.

147. Hirsch and Lohmann 1989.

148. Ibid., 446.

149. Thailand Development Research Institute 2000: 11.

150. Chayan 2000: 2.

151. Author interview with Khun Bundeum, Pak Mun Dam, March 2001.

152. Author interview with Khun La, Pak Mun Dam, March 2001. In my trips to the villages around the Mun River, villagers pointed out how their communities had become politically and geographically riven. Some groups of villagers who sided with EGAT stayed close to the river, whereas others who opposed the dam were displaced further away from the river.

153. Chayan 2000: 7.

154. Author interviews with villagers at the Pak Mun Dam, March 2001. One resettlement site with EGAT-constructed houses was virtually empty because villagers had chosen not to move into the new houses.

155. Author interview with Khun La, Pak Mun Dam, March 2001; Chayan 2000: 19.

156. Praphat 1998.

157. Missingham 2003.

158. Ibid., 167.

159. Ibid.

160. This is the complex of offices of the prime minister.

161. Author interview in Bangkok with two villagers, Khun Kamta and Khun Saengchai, from the district of Khong Jiam in the province of Ubon Ratchatani, July 2000.

162. *Nation* (Bangkok), 23 Apr. 1997.

163. Ubon Ratchatani University 2002.

164. *Bangkok Post*, 21 Dec. 2002.

165. Nipapun and Naowarut 1996: 171.

166. I use data from before 2001 to discuss geographical distribution and access, because after 2001, reforms under the Thaksin Shinawatra government significantly affected the health-care system. The following section discusses these reforms.

167. UNDP 2003: 83–85.

168. The Health Achievement Index was first employed in *Thailand Human Development Report 2003*. The health index is made of up of six indicators: (1) life expectancy at birth, (2) incidence of first-degree malnutrition in children younger than five, (3) incidence of AIDS, (4) incidence of mental illness, (5) population with unhealthy behavior, and (6) population per physician.

169. Thailand, Ministry of Public Health 2002: 253.

170. Author interview with Pongpisut Jongudomsuk, director of the Bureau of Policy and Planning, National Health Security Office, Bangkok, June 2003.

171. Supasit et al. 2000: 303–11.

172. Thailand, Ministry of Public Health 2002: 351.

173. Ibid., 350; "New Bill to 'Give Equal Benefits,'" *Bangkok Post*, 25 Aug. 1997.

174. Author interviews with Amara Pongsapich, Institute of Social Research, Chulalongkorn University, Bangkok, December 2001, and Pongpisut Jongudomsuk, National Health Security Office, Bangkok, June 2003.

175. Author interview with Pongpisut, National Health Security Office, Bangkok, June 2003.

176. Worawan 2003: 5–6; Pongpisut 2002.

177. National Health Security Office (NHSO) 2009a.

178. "Health," *Bangkok Post Economic Review 2004*; NHSO 2009a.

179. Pongpisut 2002.

180. NHSO 2009b.

181. Author interview with Pongpisut, National Health Security Office, Bangkok, June 2003.

182. See "Vinai Slams Scheme as Too Divisive," *Bangkok Post*, 22 Aug. 2002.

183. Author interview with Pongpisut, National Health Security Office, Bangkok, May 2006. The weighting of funding toward a population per capita basis is particularly important because district hospitals receive 90 percent of their revenue from the thirty-baht program, whereas regional hospitals are not as dependent on the thirty-baht program for their revenue.

184. Interview with Pongthep, head of the Rural Doctors Society, Bangkok, July 2006.

185. "State Doctors Slam Delays in Payments," *Bangkok Post*, 28 Aug. 2002.

186. "Budget Allocation Woes," *Bangkok Post Economic Review 2004*.

187. Interview with Suthath Duangdeeden, physician at Lerdsin Hospital, Bangkok, June 2003.

188. Interview with Suthat, Bangkok, June 2003.

189. The program was formerly housed in a gleaming high-rise on the outskirts of Bangkok and is now clustered with other major government agencies. It is institutionalized in every sense.

190. The debt moratorium program also continued in post-TRT governments.

Chapter 7

1. In 2005, Vietnam's population was 84.2 million, and the Philippines' was 83.1 million (*Economist* 2007).

2. Its GDP per capita at this time grew faster than that of all countries in Southeast Asia.

3. World Bank 1993b: 24.

4. In his monumental study, Myrdal (1968) categorizes the Philippines as a "soft state."

5. Hutchcroft 1991.

6. Landé 1977: 86, 88.

7. Hutchcroft 1998: 14.

8. Balisacan and Piza 2003: 2.

9. World Bank, World Development Indicators (WDI; current U.S. dollars)

10. Growth rates for GDP are calculated from the WDI; Canlas, Cham, and Zhuang 2009.

11. According to Balisacan's (1999, 2001) own estimations, the official poverty count is an overestimation.

12. Balisacan 1999.

13. Hutchcroft 2000: 277.

14. Agoncillo 1969: 45.

15. Quoted in Abinales and Amoroso 2005: 88.

16. Agoncillo 1969: 60.

17. Abinales and Amoroso 2005: 67.

18. Ibid., 87, 93.

19. Agoncillo 1969: 61.

20. Wurfel 1988: 5.

21. Abinales and Amoroso 2005: 77.

22. They offered usurious loans to the peasants through a system known as the *pacto de retrovendendi*. Land placed as collateral would be significantly undervalued, and credit made against the rice or sugar crop would be calculated on the basis of an abundant harvest and low price (Corpuz 1989: 423–24). A report in the early 1800s noted that, through these pacts, "the mestizos are acquiring all the lands in Filipinas; if the Royal Audiencia does not act to abolish this irregularity,

in a little time this clever nation [mestizos] will own the entire islands" (quoted in Corpuz 1989: 424).

23. These included fraudulent land surveys, wills and testaments executed by friars, and purchase of extensive communal or royal land tracts known as *realengas*. One of the critical problems was that peasants did not have legal title to their land and were granted only usufructuary rights. Furthermore, lands were not registered in a cadastre, which made it easier to deny villagers their claims (Corpuz 1997: 61–68; 1989: 426–30).

24. Constantino 1975: 123–25; Abinales and Amoroso 2005: 80–82.

25. Corpuz 1989: 423.

26. Corpuz 1997: chaps. 7–8.

27. Constantino 1975: 348.

28. Hutchcroft 2000.

29. Agoncillo 1969: 161, 174–75; Abinales and Amoroso 2005: 147.

30. Except for the difference between the Federalists and Nacionalistas, with the latter in favor of independence. But see Paredes's (1988) critique.

31. Constantino 1975: 320.

32. Ibid., 320.

33. Clientelism was also reinforced through the collaborative relationships between the caciques themselves and the colonial authorities, as well as the tendency of the Americans to build up a single national leader. See Paredes 1988.

34. He wrote in 1900: "While they [the *ilustrados*] deal in high sounding phrases concerning liberty and free government they have very little conception of what that means. They cannot resist the temptation to venality, and every office is likely to be used for the personal aggrandizement of the holder thereof in disregard of public interest" (Cullinane 1971: 15).

35. Ibid., 38.

36. Efforts were undertaken to check corruption at the municipal level by imposing more controls from the provincial governor and the executive bureau, but these were ineffective (Cullinane 1971).

37. Ibid., 18.

38. See, for example, Mark Twain's critique of the American war of pacification in Zwick 1992.

39. Hutchcroft 2000: 289.

40. Hayden 1942: 95–101.

41. This theme is a central point in Anderson (1996, 1998) and frames Sidel's (1999) analysis of local bossism. More generally, see Shefter 1977.

42. Grossoltz (1964: 86) observed that the family is "the strongest unit of society, demanding the deepest loyalties of the individual and coloring all social activity with its own set of demands."

43. McCoy 1994: 10.

44. Abueva 1969: 537.

45. Wurfel 1988: 79.

46. Hayden 1942: 128–30.

47. Wurfel 1988: 80.

48. However, Abinales and Amoroso (2005: 170) argue that in the early postwar years there was a difference between the Nacionalistas and Liberals, with the former committed to nationalism and centralization of power as a means of national progress.

49. Wurfel 1988: 96.

50. The classic study of this period is Kerkvliet 1977.

51. In his first month as secretary of defense, Magsaysay investigated and then charged twenty army officers. Nine constabulary officers were also court-martialed. See Abueva 1971: 163n13, 170.

52. Quoted in ibid., 163n10.

53. Quirino 1958: 63.

54. Ibid.

55. Kerkvliet 1977: 239–40.

56. Wurfel 1988; Kerkvliet 1996.

57. *Philippine Daily Express* 1973: 6 (quoted in Reidinger 1995: 8).

58. Steinberg 1990: 128.

59. Presidential Commission on Good Government, quoted in Aquino 1987: 1.

60. Transparency International estimates that Suharto's wealth was between US$15 billion and $35 billion.

61. Villegas 1986: 145; Boyce 1993: 31.

62. Villegas 1986: 162.

63. Epifanio de los Santos Avenue (EDSA) is a major thoroughfare in metropolitan Manila.

64. Steinberg 1990: 150–51.

65. Reidinger 1995: 115.

66. Ibid., 116.

67. Quoted in Steinberg 1990: 169.

68. Constantino 1975: 374–79.

69. Putzel 1986: chap. 4.

70. Ibid., 188–89.

71. See Putzel 1992: chap. 4.

72. For example, Macapagal's 1963 land-reform bill, meant to respond to U.S. pressure, did go through Congress but was emasculated and swamped by two hundred amendments (Putzel 1986: 188).

73. One 1995 estimate counts 70,200 NGOs in the Philippines (Clarke 1998: 70).

74. I refer only to divisions within the more left-progressive camp rather than within civil society as a whole.

75. Villanueva 1997; Putzel 1998: 96; Franco 2004: 113.

76. Franco 2004: 118.

77. Ibid., 113.

78. For example, Karina Constantino-David, an NGO activist in the Estrada cabinet, found herself often at odds with NGOs who in her view "seemed more comfortable dealing with promises than being told the facts" (quoted in Franco 2004: 121).

79. Putzel 1998: 100, also 95.

80. Silliman and Noble 1998: 302.

81. Borras 1999, 2007.

82. Borras 2007: 208.

83. Carmel Abao, first secretary-general of Akbayan, quoted in Franco 2004: 116.

84. Quoted in ibid., 116.

85. See Wurfel 1997.

86. For example, in 2006, President Macapagal-Arroyo sought to arrest Satur Ocampo of Bayan Muna and five other leftist congressmen. See "Veteran Revolutionary Trapped in the Halls of Power," *International Herald Tribune*, 18 Apr. 2006.

87. Notes from Liberal Party meeting, Manila, June 2006, and author's conversations in Manila and Montreal with LP official Chito Gascon and former LP congressman Neric Acosta. However, the party's programmatic orientation is more a result of individual members' specific policy interests rather than an overarching policy agenda (Bevis 2006).

88. Bevis 2006: 275.

89. For example, in the 1992 election, Akbayan was part of the Koalisyong Pambansa (National Coalition), headed by LP leader and presidential candidate Jovito Salonga. More recently, in the 2010 election, Akbayan congresswoman Risa Hontiveros ran on the LP senatorial slate. Joel Rocamora, member of Akbayan, has also advised the LP. For a comparison of Akbayan and LP, see Bevis 2006.

90. Kerkvliet (1996) argues that efforts to challenge elite power—"struggles to give substance to Philippine democracy"—cannot be dismissed. I agree; the question is how to channel and concretize those struggles into policy gains.

91. World Bank WDI (current U.S. dollars).

92. World Bank WDI; Luong 2003a: 1.

93. See a longitudinal comparison of Vietnam's and the Philippines' human development index in Kervkliet 2009: 97.

94. Vietnamese Academy of Social Sciences (VASS) 2007; Luong 2003a: 12.
95. See especially the essays in Taylor 2004.
96. Ravallion and van de Walle 2003: 4.
97. McCaig, Benjamin, and Brandt 2009.
98. VASS 2007: 16.
99. Ibid., 25.
100. Ibid., 26–27.
101. VASS 2007.
102. World Bank 2005a: 11, 17.
103. Luong 2003b: 95.
104. The ICP was called the Workers' Party (Dang Lao Dong Viet Nam) in 1951 and was renamed the Vietnamese Communist Party (VCP) only in 1976.
105. Quoted in Ho Tai 1992: 225.
106. Pike 1978: 16–17.
107. Popkin 1979: 221. On the relationship between intellectuals and the Viet Minh in the wake of the August Revolution, see Ninh 2002: chap. 2.
108. Popkin 1979: 224.
109. Woodside 1976: 249.
110. Popkin 1979: 218.
111. Woodside 1976: 229; Popkin 1979: 225–29.
112. Popkin 1979: 224–42.
113. Ibid., 236–42.
114. Ibid., 239.
115. Ibid., 238.
116. This is a key point in Migdal 1974: chap. 10.
117. Pike 1978: 91.
118. Moise 1976: 71; Thaveeporn 1995: 266.
119. Moise 1976: 83.
120. Moise's (1976) earlier estimate was five thousand. But recent work by Vo (1990), Moise (2001), and Vu (2010) all agree that the number was three times higher.
121. See Moise 1976: 78–81.
122. Thaveeporn 1995: 267.
123. *Nhan Dan*, quoted in Moise 1976: 84.
124. Duiker 1983: 102.
125. Ibid., 102.
126. Ibid., 104.
127. Kerkvliet 2005b: 18.
128. Ibid., 11–12.

129. Beresford 2001: 211.

130. Beresford 1995: 104–19.

131. Kerkvliet 2005b: 174, 207–08.

132. Ibid., 62.

133. Ibid.

134. Woodside 1976: 251.

135. Steinberg 1987: 369.

136. Kerkvliet 2005b.

137. Ibid., 242.

138. Woodside (1976: 251) notes that agricultural cooperatives were "relatively conservative" compared to in China. See also Duiker 1983; Thaveeporn 1995.

139. Kerkvliet 2005b: 13.

140. Steinberg 1987: 368; Chan, Kerkvliet, and Unger 1999: 9.

141. Beresford 1995: 212–13.

142. Le Duan, general secretary from 1960 to 1985, died in office in July 1985, making room for change. Without his death, these changes might not have occurred. Personal communication from Tuong Vu.

143. The VCP is made up of the Central Committee (CC) and the political bureau (politburo). The national party congress elects the CC every five years, and the CC then elects the members of the politburo. The politburo is the highest decision-making body in the party.

144. Thaveeporn 1995: 276.

145. Ibid., 282.

146. Luong 2003a: 23.

147. Kerkvliet 2001, 2005b, 2009; Womack 1987; Dixon 2004. See, similarly, Beresford 1989; Fforde 1989. Regarding a "dialogic system," Luong (2003a) writes: "As long as we understand *dialogue* in a broad sense of the word . . . and do not assume dialogue partners to have equal power," then state-society relations in Vietnam "may be described as dialogic. It can be argued that this extended back to 1956 when the state had to admit excesses in the land reform campaign." Note that although Kerkvliet (2001) distinguishes between a "corporatist" and "dialogic" system, I group them together because they are both structures within which social interests are taken into consideration, even though one may be more top-down than the other.

148. Fforde and Goldstone 1995.

149. Kerkvliet 2009: 88.

150. Thaveeporn 1995: 263. There were purges of high-ranking officials from 1967 to 1972. These were led by Le Duan and Le Duc Tho against Vo Nguyen Giap. Nonetheless, the purges were not of the same magnitude as in the Soviet Union or China.

151. Ibid., 288.
152. Kerkvliet 2001: 246.
153. Jeong 1997: 157.
154. Ibid., 159.
155. Quoted in ibid., 165.
156. Fforde and de Vylder 1996: 239.
157. Kerkvliet 2005a: 16 (emphasis added).

Chapter 8

1. Fieldwork observation, Rantau Panjang, Kelantan, June 2006.
2. Ong 1976: 419.
3. That exception is the Malaysian Indian Congress (MIC). Although it represents the Indian population, the party is widely considered ineffective. In part, this has to do with demographics, with the Indian minority at a significant disadvantage. But it also reflects the MIC elites' tendency to stick to a comfortable status quo.
4. At times, UMNO rhetoric at party assemblies may sound extreme, but this does not actually have much impact on policy output. The party seems to know how to galvanize the grass roots, especially the UMNO Youth, while still sticking to its pragmatic tendencies.
5. See my "Thailand Unraveling," *Gazette* (Montreal), 19 May 2010.

Appendix

1. During a 1963 Legislative Council debate, Ravuamu Vunivalu, an urban-based commoner, had this to say: "[T]here is a feeling abroad among the ordinary laborer, tiller of the soil, the carpenter, and the factory worker that there is no connection between them and the honorable members of this House. They feel that once members get elected to the Legislative Council, they forget the people who put them there, and their feelings are absolutely justified" (quoted in Lal 1986: 31).
2. Lawson (1991: 178) writes, "The early strategies devised by the Association's leaders required compliance, not involvement, from their followers, who were not encouraged to participate in decision-making. Although these strategies were modified, the notion persisted that the ascriptive status of the eastern chiefs entitled them to the foremost leadership roles."
3. See Lal 1986: 93–95.
4. On the 1977 and 1987 crises, see Lawson 1991; Howard 1991.
5. Milne 1981: 141.
6. Kurer 2001; Lal 2002.

7. Although the migrant ethnic group (Indians) are the majority, Guyana is still comparable to Malaysia and Fiji because the Indian community is economically more powerful, while the state is in the hands of the indigenous group (Africans).

8. Milne 1981: 87; Premdas 1995: 167.

9. Premdas 1995: 173.

10. Ibid., 181.

11. Ibid., 183.

12. Sowell 2004: 82.

13. De Silva 1997.

14. Horowitz 1985: esp. part 3; 1989b.

15. De Votta 2009; Chellaney 2009.

References

Thai and Malay names are listed beginning with the first name.

Abdul Rahman, Tunku. 1969. *May 13th—Before and After*. Kuala Lumpur: Utusan Melayu Press.

Abdul Rahman Embong. 2002. *State-Led Modernization and the New Middle Class in Malaysia*. New York: Palgrave Macmillan.

Abdul Razak. 1971. Speech on the Second Malaysia Plan in Dewan Ra'ayat (Parliament), 12 July. *Foreign Affairs Malaysia* (Ministry of Foreign Affairs) 4, no. 3.

Abinales, Patricio, and Donna J. Amoroso. 2005. *State and Society in the Philippines*. Lanham, MD: Rowman and Littlefield.

Abueva, Jose V. 1969. "Political Stability, Development and Welfare." In *Foundations and Dynamics of Filipino Government and Politics*, edited by Jose V. Abueva and Raul P. De Guzman. Manila: Bookmark.

———. 1971. *Ramon Magsaysay: A Political Biography*. Manila: Solidaridad.

Agoncillo, Teodoro A. 1969. *A Short History of the Philippines*. New York: Mentor Books.

Ahlburg, Dennis, and Darla Flint. 2001. "Public Health Conditions and Policies in the Asia-Pacific Region." *Asian-Pacific Economic Literature* 15, no. 2: 1–17.

Akhin Rabibhadana. 1969. *The Organization of Thai Society in the Early Bangkok Period, 1782–1873*. Ithaca, NY: Southeast Asia Program, Cornell University.

Aliran. 1989. *Nation on Trial*. Penang: Aliran.

Ammar Siamwalla. 1975. "A History of Rice Price Policies in Thailand: The Beginning of Thai Rice Exports Up to the Second World War." Unpublished manuscript, Thammasat University.

Ammar Siamwalla and Suthad Setboonsarng. 1989. *Trade, Exchange Rate, and Agricultural Pricing Policies in Thailand.* Washington, D.C.: World Bank.

Ammar Siamwalla, Suthad Setboonsarng, and Direk Patamasiriwat. 1993. "Agriculture." In *The Thai Economy in Transition*, edited by Peter G. Warr. Cambridge: Cambridge University Press.

Ammar Siamwalla, Chirmsak Pinthong, Nipon Poapongsakorn, Ploenpit Satsanguan, Prayong Nettayarak, Wanrak Mingmaneenakin, and Yuavares Tubpun. 1990. "The Thai Rural Credit System: Public Subsidies, Private Information, and Segmented Markets." *World Bank Economic Review* 4, no. 3: 271–95.

Amsden, Alice. 1989. *Asia's Next Giant: South Korea and Late Industrialization.* Oxford: Oxford University Press.

Anderson, Benedict R. 1977. "Withdrawal Symptoms: Social and Cultural Aspects of the October 6 Coup." *Bulletin of Concerned Asian Scholars* 9, no. 1: 13–40.

———. 1978. "Studies of the Thai State: The State of Thai Studies." In *The Study of Thailand*, edited by Eliezer B. Ayal. Athens: Ohio University Center for International Studies, Southeast Asia Program.

———. 1996. "Elections and Participation in Three Southeast Asian Countries." In *The Politics of Elections in Southeast Asia*, edited by Robert H. Taylor. Cambridge: Cambridge University Press.

———. 1998. *The Spectre of Comparisons: Nationalism, Southeast Asia, and the World.* London: Verso.

Anek Laothamatas. 1988. "Business and Politics in Thailand: New Patterns of Influence." *Asian Survey* 28, no. 4: 451–70.

——— 1992. *Business Associations and the New Political Economy of Thailand: From Bureaucratic Polity to Liberal Corporatism.* Boulder, CO: Westview Press; Singapore: Institute of Southeast Asian Studies.

———. 2007. *Thaksina prachaniyom* [Thaksin-Style Populism]. Bangkok: Matichon.

Anusorn Limanee. 1998. "Thailand." In *Political Party Systems and Democratic Development in East and Southeast Asia*, edited by Wolfgang Sachsenröder and Ulrike E. Frings. Aldershot, U.K.: Ashgate.

Aquino, Belinda A. 1987. *The Politics of Plunder: The Philippines under Marcos.* Quezon City: Great Books Trading.

Arumugam, Raja Segaran, Patrick Low, and M. Rajaretnam. 1973. "Thailand in the Seventies: Challenges of Stability and Security." *Trends in Thailand*, edited by M. Rajaretnam and Lim So Jean. Singapore: Institute of Southeast Asian Studies.

Asher, Mukul. 1980. *Revenue Systems of ASEAN Countries.* Singapore: Singapore University Press.

Asian Development Bank. 1999. *Policy for the Health Sector.* Manila: Asian Development Bank.

Askew, Marc. 2008. *Performing Political Identity: The Democrat Party in Southern Thailand.* Bangkok: Silkworm Books.

Baker, Chris. 2005. "Pluto-Populism: Thaksin and Popular Politics." In *Thailand beyond the Crisis*, edited by Peter Warr. London: Routledge.

Baker, Chris, and Pasuk Phongpaichit. 2000. "Introduction." In *Pridi by Pridi*, by Pridi Bhanomyong. Chiang Mai, Thailand: Silkworm Books.

Balisacan, Arsenio M. 1993. "Agricultural Growth, Landlessness, Off-Farm Employment and Rural Poverty in the Philippines." *Economic Development and Cultural Change* 41: 533–62.

———. 1994. "Urban Poverty in the Philippines." *Asian Development Review* 12, no. 1: 117–52.

———. 1999. "What Do We Really Know—or Don't Know—about Economic Inequality and Poverty in the Philippines?" In *Causes of Poverty: Myths, Facts, and Policies*, edited by Arsenio M. Balisacan and Shigeaki Fujisaki. Quezon City: University of the Philippines Press.

———. 2001. "Rural Development in the 21st Century: Monitoring and Assessing Performance in Rural Poverty Reduction." In *The Philippine Economy: Alternatives for the 21st Century*, edited by Dante B. Canlas and Shigeaki Fujisaki. Quezon City: University of the Philippines Press.

Balisacan, Arsenio M., and Sharon Faye A. Piza. 2003. "Nature and Causes of Income Inequality in the Philippines." Presented at Conference on Comparative Analyses of East Asian Income Inequalities, Bangkok, 27–28 January.

Bank for Agriculture and Agricultural Cooperatives (BAAC). 2004. *Pak chamra nii lae lot para nii* [Debt Suspension and Debt Reduction]. Bangkok: Bank for Agriculture and Agricultural Cooperatives.

Barnes, Samuel H. 1966. "Ideology and the Organization of Conflict: On the Relationship between Political Thought and Behavior." *Journal of Politics* 28, no. 3: 513–30.

Barraclough, Simon. 1996. "Health Care Policy Issues in Malaysia's Drive for Socioeconomic Development by the Year 2020." *Asian Studies Review* 20, no. 1: 5–19.

———. 2000. "The Politics of Privatization in the Malaysian Health Care System." *Contemporary Southeast Asia* 22, no. 2: 340–60.

Batson, Benjamin. 1984. *The End of the Absolute Monarchy in Siam.* Singapore: Oxford University Press.

Battye, Noel Alfred. 1974. "The Military, Government, and Society in Siam, 1868–1910: Politics and Military Reform during the Reign of King Chulalongkorn." Ph.D. diss., Cornell University.

Beatty-Riedl, Rachel. 2008. "Institutions in New Democracies: Variations in African Party Systems." Ph.D. diss., Princeton University.

Beresford, Melanie. 1989. *National Unification and Economic Development in Vietnam*. London: MacMillan.

———. 1995. "Political Economy of Primary Health Care in Vietnam." In *Health and Development in Southeast Asia*, edited by Paul Cohen and John Purcal. Canberra: Australian Development Studies Network.

———. 2001. "Vietnam: The Transition from Central Planning." In *The Political Economy of South-East Asia*, edited by Garry Rodan, Kevin Hewison, and Richard Robison. 2nd ed. Melbourne: Oxford University Press.

Berman, Sheri. 1998. *The Social Democratic Moment: Ideas and Politics in the Making of Interwar Europe*. Cambridge, MA: Harvard University Press.

Bevis, Gwendolyn. 2006. "Building Programmatic Parties in a Patronage-Dominated System: Akbayan and the Liberal Party in the Post-1986 Philippines." Ph.D. diss., University of Wisconsin–Madison.

Boix, Charles. 2003. *Democracy and Redistribution*. Cambridge: Cambridge University Press.

Borras, Saturnino M., Jr. 1999. *The Bibingka Strategy in Land Reform Implementation: Autonomous Peasant Movements and State Reformists in the Philippines*. Quezon City: Institute for Popular Democracy.

———. 2007. *Pro-Poor Land Reform: A Critique*. Ottawa: University of Ottawa Press.

Bowie, Katherine A. 1997. *Rituals of National Loyalty: An Anthropology of the Village Scout Movement in Thailand*. New York: Columbia University Press.

Boyce, James. 1993. *The Political Economy of Growth and Impoverishment in the Marcos Era*. Quezon City: Ateneo de Manila University Press.

Brown, Andrew. 2004. *Labor, Politics and the State in Industrializing Thailand*. London: Routledge.

Canlas, Dante, Maria Rowena M. Cham, and Juzhong Zhuang. 2009. "Development Performance and Policy." In *Diagnosing the Philippine Economy: Toward Inclusive Growth*, edited by Dante Canlas, Muhammad Ehsan Khan, and Juzhong Zhuang. Manila: Asian Development Bank.

Case, William. 1995. "Malaysia: Aspects and Audiences of Legitimacy." In *Political Legitimacy in Southeast Asia: The Quest for Moral Authority*, edited by Muthiah Alagappa. Stanford, CA: Stanford University Press.

———. 1996. *Elites and Regimes in Malaysia: Revisiting a Consociational Democracy*. Clayton, Australia: Monash Asia Institute, Monash University.

Central Intelligence Agency. 2003. *CIA World Factbook*. Washington, D.C.: U.S. Government Printing Office. http://www.cia.gov/cia/publications/factbook/index.html.

Chai-Anan Samudavanija. N.d. *Kan pathana khong pak karn muang thai: suksa chapoa korani khong phak prachathipat, 1975–1976* [Development of Thai Political Parties: A Case Study of the Democrat Party's Expansion].

———. 1976. *Sakdina kap phatthanakan khong sanghkomthai* [Sakdina and the Development of Thai Society]. Bangkok: Namaksonkanphim.

———. 1982. *The Thai Young Turks.* Singapore: Institute of Southeast Asian Studies.

———. 1990. "Thailand: A Semi-Stable Democracy." In *Democracy in Developing Countries: Comparing Experiences with Democracy*, edited by Larry Diamond, Juan Linz, and Seymour Martin Lipset. Boulder, CO: Lynn Rienner Publishers.

———. 1995. "Economic Development and Democracy." In *Thailand's Industrialization and Its Consequences*, edited by Medhi Krongkaew. New York: St. Martin's Press.

Chambers, Paul. 2005. "Evolving toward What? Parties, Factions, and Coalition Behavior in Thailand Today." *Journal of East Asian Studies* 5: 495–520.

Chan, Anita, Benedict J. Tria Kerkvliet, and Jonathan Unger, eds. 1999. *Transforming Asian Socialism: China and Vietnam Compared.* Sydney: Allen and Unwin.

Chandra Muzaffar. 1989. *The NEP, Development and Alternative Consciousness.* Penang: Aliran.

Chatthip Nartsupha and Suthy Prasartset. 1981. *The Political Economy of Siam, 1851–1910.* Bangkok: Social Science Association of Thailand.

Chayan Vaddhanaphuti. 2000. "Pak Mun Case Study: Social Aspects." Report submitted to the World Commission on Dams, January.

Cheah Boon Kheng. 1988. *Red Star over Malaya.* Singapore: Singapore University Press.

Chee Heng Leng and Simon Barraclough. 2007a. "The Growth of Corporate Health Care in Malaysia." In *Health Care in Malaysia: The Dynamics of Provision, Financing and Access*, edited by Chee Heng Leng and Simon Barraclough. London: Routledge.

———. 2007b. "Introduction: The Transformation of Health Care in Malaysia." In *Health Care in Malaysia: The Dynamics of Provision, Financing and Access*, edited by Chee Heng Leng and Simon Barraclough. London: Routledge.

Chehabi, H. E., and Juan J. Linz, eds. 1989. *Sultanistic Regimes.* Baltimore: Johns Hopkins University Press.

Chellaney, Brahma. 2009. "Sri Lanka's Elusive Peace Dividend." *Far Eastern Economic Review* 172, no. 8: 32–36.

Clarke, Gerard. 1998. *The Politics of NGOs in South-East Asia.* London: Routledge.

Coast, John. 1953. *Some Aspects of Siamese Politics.* New York: Institute of Pacific Relations.

Cohen, Paul T. 1983. "Problems of Tenancy and Landlessness in Northern Thailand." *Developing Economies* 21, no. 3: 244–66.

Constantino, Renato. 1975. *A History of the Philippines: From the Spanish Colonization to the Second World War*. New York: Monthly Review Press.

Copeland, Matthew Phillip. 1993. "Contested Nationalism and the 1932 Overthrow of the Absolute Monarchy in Siam." Ph.D. diss., Australian National University.

Corpuz, O. D. 1989. *The Roots of the Filipino Nation*, vol. 1. Quezon City: Aklahi Foundation.

———. 1997. *An Economic History of the Philippines*. Quezon City: University of the Philippines Press.

Corrales, Javier. 2002. *Presidents without Parties: The Politics of Economic Reform in Argentina and Venezuela in the 1990s*. University Park: Pennsylvania State University Press.

Crone, Donald. 1993. "State, Elites, and Social Welfare in Southeast Asia." *World Development* 21, no. 1: 55–66.

Crouch, Harold. 1996. *Government and Society in Malaysia*. Ithaca, NY: Cornell University Press.

Cullinane, Michael. 1971. "Implementing the 'New Order': The Structure and Supervision of Local Government during the Taft Era." In *Compadre Colonialism: Studies on the Philippines under American Rule*, edited by Norman Owen. Ann Arbor: University of Michigan Press.

Darling, Frank C. 1965. *Thailand and the United States*. Washington, D.C.: Public Affairs Press.

———. 1974. "Student Protest and Political Change in Thailand." *Pacific Affairs* 47, no. 1: 5–19.

Decha Sungkawan. N.d. "The Enhancement of Social Provisions in the Contemporary Thai Social Welfare: From Public Assistance Programs in the 1940s to the Social Insurance Scheme in the 1990s." Unpublished manuscript, Thammasat University.

del Tufo, M. V. 1949. *Malaya, Comprising the Federation of Malaya and the Colony of Singapore: A Report on the 1947 Census of Population*. London: Crown Agents for the Government of Malaya and Singapore.

De Silva, K. 1997. "Affirmative Action Policies: The Sri Lankan Experience." *Ethnic Studies Report* 15, no. 2.

De Votta, Neil. 2009. "The Liberation Tigers of Tamil Eelam and the Lost Quest for Separatism in Sri Lanka." *Asian Survey* 49, no. 6: 1021–51.

Dix, R. 1992. "Democratization and Institutionalization of Latin American Political Parties." *Comparative Political Studies* 24, no. 4: 448–511.

Dixon, Chris. 1996. "Thailand's Rapid Economic Growth: Causes, Sustainability and Lessons." In *Uneven Development in Thailand*, edited by Mike Parnwell. Aldershot, U.K.: Avebury.

———. 1999. *The Thai Economy: Uneven Development and Internationalization.* London: Routledge.

———. 2004. "State, Party, and Political Change in Vietnam." In *Rethinking Vietnam*, edited by Duncan McCargo. London: Routledge Curzon.

Doner, Richard. 2009. *The Politics of Uneven Development: Thailand's Economic Growth in Comparative Perspective.* Cambridge: Cambridge University Press.

Doner, Richard, and Anek Laothamathas. 1994. "Political Economy of Structural Adjustment in Thailand." In *Voting for Reform*, edited by Stephan Haggard and Steven Webb. New York: Oxford University Press.

Doner, Richard, Bryan K. Ritchie, and Dan Slater. 2005. "Systemic Vulnerability and the Origins of Developmental States: Northeast and Southeast Asia in Comparative Perspective." *International Organization* 59, no. 2: 327–61.

Dornbusch, Rüdiger, and Sebastian Edwards, eds. 1991. *The Macroeconomics of Populism in Latin America.* Chicago: University of Chicago Press.

Duiker, William. 1983. *Vietnam: Nation in Revolution.* Boulder, CO: Westview Press.

Duverger, Maurice. 1959. *Political Parties.* London: Methuen.

Economist. 2007. *World Pocket in Figures.* London: Economist Intelligence Unit.

Emerson, Rupert. 1937. *Malaya: A Study in Direct and Indirect Rule.* New York: MacMillan.

Epstein, Leon. 1967. *Political Parties in Western Democracies.* New York: Praeger.

Esman, Milton J. 1972. *Administration and Development in Malaysia: Institution Building and Reform in a Plural Society.* Ithaca, NY: Cornell University Press.

———. 1987. "Ethnic Politics and Economic Power." *Comparative Politics* 19, no. 4: 395–418.

Esping-Andersen, Gøsta. 1985. *Politics against Markets: The Social Democratic Road to Power.* Princeton, NJ: Princeton University Press.

———. 1990. *The Three Worlds of Welfare Capitalism.* Princeton, NJ: Princeton University Press.

Evans, Peter. 1995. *Embedded Autonomy: States and Industrial Transformation.* Princeton, NJ: Princeton University Press.

Faaland, Just, J. R. Parkinson, and Rais Saniman. 1990. *Growth and Ethnic Inequality: Malaysia's New Economic Policy.* Kuala Lumpur: Dewan Bahasa dan Pustaka.

Fforde, Adam. 1989. *The Agrarian Question in North Vietnam, 1974–78: A Study of Cooperator Resistance to State Policy.* Armonk, NY: M. E. Sharpe.

Fforde, Adam, and Stefan de Vylder. 1996. *From Plan to Market: The Economic Transition in Vietnam*. Boulder, CO: Westview Press.

Fforde, Adam, and Anthony Goldstone. 1995. *Vietnam to 2005: Advancing on All Fronts*. London: Economist Intelligence Unit.

Fields, Gary. 2001. *Distribution and Development*. New York: Russell Sage Foundation.

Fistié, Pierre. 1969. *Sous-développement et utopie au Siam: Le programme de réformes présenté en 1933 par Pridi Phanomyong*. Paris: Mouton.

Fong, Chan Onn. 1985. "Integrated Population-Development Program Performance: The Malaysian Felda Experience." *Journal of Developing Areas* 19, no. 2: 149–70.

Fong, Chan Onn, R. R. Hashim, Gee Heng Hock, I. Jajri, and Yuet Chun Low. 1982. *The FELDA Model of Integrating Population and Development: Its Impact and Efficacy*. Kuala Lumpur: Faculty of Economics and Administration, University of Malaya.

Franco, Jennifer. 2004. "The Philippines: Fractious Civil Society and Competing Visions of Democracy." In *Civil Society and Political Change in Asia: Expanding and Contracting Democratic Space*, edited by Muthiah Alagappa. Stanford, CA: Stanford University Press.

Frankel, Francine. 1978. *India's Political Economy, 1947–1977: The Gradual Revolution*. Princeton, NJ: Princeton University Press.

Friedman, Edward, and Joseph Wong, eds. 2008. *Political Transitions in Dominant Party Systems: Learning to Lose*. New York: Routledge.

Funston, John. 1975. "Writings on May 13th." *Akademika* 6: 1–16.

———. 1980. *Malay Politics in Malaysia: A Study of UMNO and PAS*. Kuala Lumpur: Heinemann Educational Books.

Furnivall, J. S. 1956. *Colonial Policy and Practice: A Comparative Study of Burma and Netherlands India*. New York: New York University Press.

Gagliano, Felix. 1970. *Communal Violence in Malaysia 1969: The Political Aftermath*. Athens: Ohio University Southeast Asia Program.

Ghazali Shafie. 1993. "National Unity: Key to the Ultimate Malaysian Society." Institute of Strategic and International Studies paper. Kuala Lumpur: Institute of Strategic and International Studies.

Girling, John L. S. 1977. "Thailand: The Coup and Its Implications." *Pacific Affairs* 50, no. 3: 387–405.

———. 1981a. *The Bureaucratic Polity in Modernizing Societies: Similarities, Differences, and Prospects in the ASEAN Region*. Singapore: Institute of Southeast Asian Studies.

———. 1981b. *Thailand: Society and Politics*. Ithaca, NY: Cornell University Press.

Goh, Cheng Teik. 1971. *The May 13th Incident and Democracy in Malaysia*. Kuala Lumpur: Oxford University Press.

Gomez, Edmund Terrence, and Jomo K. S. 1997. *Malaysia's Political Economy: Politics, Patronage, and Profits*. Cambridge: Cambridge University Press.

Gourevitch, Peter. 1986. *Politics in Hard Times: Comparative Responses to International Economic Crises*. Ithaca, NY: Cornell University Press.

Greene, Kenneth. 2007. *Why Dominant Parties Lose: Mexico's Democratization in Comparative Perspective*. Cambridge: Cambridge University Press.

Grindle, Merilee. 1980. "Policy Content and Context in Implementation." In *Politics and Policy Implementation in the Third World*, edited by Merilee Grindle. Princeton, NJ: Princeton University Press.

Grindle, Merilee S., and John W. Thomas. 1989. "Policy Makers, Policy Choices, and Policy Outcomes: The Political Economy of Reform in Developing Countries." *Policy Sciences* 22, nos. 3–4: 213–48.

Grossoltz, Jean. 1964. *Politics in the Philippines*. Boston: Little, Brown.

Gullick, John, and Bruce Gale. 1986. *Malaysia: Its Political and Economic Development*. Petaling Jaya, Malaysia: Pelanduk.

Haggard, Stephan, and Robert R. Kaufman. 2008. *Development, Democracy, and Welfare States: Latin America, East Asia, and Eastern Europe*. Princeton, NJ: Princeton University Press.

Halim Salleh. 1992. "Peasants, Proletarianisation and the State: FELDA Settlers in Pahang." In *Fragmented Vision: Culture and Politics in Contemporary Malaysia*, edited by Joel S. Kahn and Francis Loh Kok Wah. Sydney: Allen and Unwin.

[Muhammad] Hanafiah bin Juni. 1996. "Public Health Care Provisions: Access and Equity." *Social Science and Medicine* 43, no. 5: 759–68.

Harper, T. N. 1999. *The End of Empire and the Making of Malaya*. Cambridge: Cambridge University Press.

Harriss, John. 2005. "Do Political Regimes Matter? Poverty Reduction and Regime Differences across India." In *Changing Paths: International Development and the New Politics of Inclusion*, edited by Peter P. Houtzager and Mick Moore. Ann Arbor: University of Michigan Press.

Hayden, Joseph Ralston. 1942. *The Philippines: A Study in National Development*. New York: MacMillan.

Heller, Patrick. 1999. *The Labor of Development: Workers and the Transformation of Capitalism in Kerala, India*. Ithaca, NY: Cornell University Press.

Heng, Pek Koon. 1988. *Chinese Politics in Malaysia: A History of the Malaysian Chinese Association*. Singapore: Oxford University Press.

Herring, Ronald. 1991. "From Structural Conflict to Agrarian Stalemate: Agrarian Reforms in South India." *Journal of Asian and African Studies* 26, nos. 3–4: 169–88.

Hewison, Kevin. 1989. *Bankers and Bureaucrats: Capital and the Role of the State in Thailand*. New Haven, CT: Yale University Southeast Asia Studies.

Hicken, Allen. 2009. *Building Party Systems in Developing Democracies*. Cambridge: Cambridge University Press.

Hicken, Allen, and Erik Martinez Kuhonta. 2011. "Shadows from the Past: Party System Institutionalization in Asia." *Comparative Political Studies* 44, no. 5: 572–97.

Hicks, Alexander. 1999. *Social Democracy and Welfare Capitalism: A Century of Income Security Politics*. Ithaca, NY: Cornell University Press.

Hirsch, Philip, and Larry Lohmann. 1989. "Contemporary Politics of Environment in Thailand." *Asian Survey* 29, no. 4: 439–51.

Hirschman, Albert. 1963. *Journeys toward Progress: Studies of Economic Policy-Making in Latin America*. New York: Twentieth Century Fund.

Hoerr, O. D. 1970. *Education, Income, and Equity in Malaysia*. Cambridge, MA: Development Advisory Service, Center for International Affairs, Harvard University.

Horowitz, Donald L. 1985. *Ethnic Groups in Conflict*. Berkeley: University of California Press.

———. 1989a. "Cause and Consequence in Public Theory: Ethnic Policy and System Transformation in Malaysia." *Policy Sciences* 22, nos. 3–4: 249–87.

———. 1989b. "Incentives and Behavior in the Ethnic Politics of Sri Lanka and Malaysia." *Third World Quarterly* 11, no. 4: 18–35.

Ho Tai, Hue-Tam. 1992. *Radicalism and the Origins of the Vietnamese Revolution*. Cambridge, MA: Harvard University Press.

Howard, Michael C. 1991. *Fiji: Race and Politics in an Island State*. Vancouver: University of British Columbia Press.

Huber, Evelyne, and John D. Stephens. 2001. *Development and Crisis of the Welfare State: Parties and Policies in Global Markets*. Chicago: University of Chicago Press.

Huntington, Samuel P. 1968. *Political Order in Changing Societies*. New Haven, CT: Yale University Press.

Huntington, Samuel P., and C. H. Moore. 1970. *Authoritarian Politics in Modern Society: The Dynamics of Established One-Party Systems*. New York: Basic Books.

Hutchcroft, Paul D. 1991. "Oligarchs and Cronies in the Philippine State: The Politics of Patrimonial Plunder." *World Politics* 43, no. 3: 414–50.

———. 1998. *Booty Capitalism: The Politics of Banking in the Philippines*. Ithaca, NY: Cornell University Press.

———. 2000. "Colonial Masters, National Politicos, and Provincial Lords: Central Authority and Local Autonomy in the American Philippines, 1910–1913." *Journal of Asian Studies* 59, no. 2: 207–306.

Ingram, James C. 1971. *Economic Change in Thailand 1850–1970.* Stanford, CA: Stanford University Press.

Ishak bin Tadin. 1960. "Dato Onn and Malay Nationalism, 1946–1951." *Journal of Southeast Asian Studies* 1, no. 1: 56–88.

Ishak Shari and Ragayah Mat Zin. 1995. "Economic Growth and Equity in Malaysia: Performance and Prospects." In *Southeast Asia on the Growth Path*, edited by Ahmad Mahdzan. Serdang: University Pertanian Malaysia Press.

Jeong, Yeonsik. 1997. "The Rise of State Corporatism in Vietnam." *Contemporary Southeast Asia* 19, no. 2: 152–71.

Jesudason, James V. 1989. *Ethnicity and the Economy: The State, Chinese Business, and Multinationals in Malaysia.* Singapore: Oxford University Press.

Jit Phumisak. 2000 [1957]. *Chomna sakdina thai* [The Real Face of Thai Feudalism]. Bangkok: Dork Ya.

Johnson, Chalmers. 1982. *MITI and the Japanese Miracle.* Stanford, CA: Stanford University Press.

———. 1999. "The Developmental State: Odyssey of a Concept." In *The Developmental State*, edited by Meredith Woo-Cumings. Ithaca, NY: Cornell University Press.

Jomo K. S. 1986. *A Question of Class: Capital, the State, and Uneven Development in Malaya.* Singapore: Oxford University Press.

———. 2001. "Rethinking the Role of Government Policy in Southeast Asia." In *Rethinking the East Asian Miracle*, edited by Joseph E. Stiglitz and Shahid Yusuf. New York: Oxford University Press.

———. 2003. "Growth with Equity in East Asia?" In *Southeast Asian Paper Tigers? Behind Miracle and Debacle*, edited by Jomo K. S. London: Routledge.

———. 2006. "Growth with Equity in East Asia?" U.N. Department of Social and Economic Affairs Working Paper No. 33 (September).

Jomo K. S., and Ishak Shari. 1986. *Development Policies and Income Inequality in Peninsular Malaysia.* Kuala Lumpur: Institute of Advanced Studies, University of Malaya.

Kasian Tejapira. 2001. *Commodifying Marxism: The Formation of Modern Thai Radical Culture, 1927–1958.* Kyoto, Japan: Kyoto University Press.

Katznelson, Ira. 1997. "Structure and Configuration in Comparative Politics." In *Comparative Politics: Rationality, Culture, and Structure*, edited by Mark Irving Lichbach and Alan S. Zuckerman. Cambridge: Cambridge University Press.

Kerkvliet, Benedict J. Tria. 1977. *The Huk Rebellion: A Study of Peasant Revolt in the Philippines.* Berkeley: University of California Press.

———. 1996. "Contested Meanings of Elections in the Philippines." In *The Politics of Elections in Southeast Asia*, edited by R. H. Taylor. Cambridge: Cambridge University Press.

————. 2001. "An Approach for Analyzing State-Society Relations in Vietnam." *Sojourn* 16, no. 2: 238–78.

————. 2005a. "Political Expectations and Democracy in the Philippines and Vietnam." *Philippine Political Science Journal* 26, no. 49: 1–26.

————. 2005b. *The Power of Everyday Politics: How Vietnamese Peasants Transformed National Policy.* Ithaca, NY: Cornell University Press.

————. 2009. "Governance, Development, and the Responsive-Repressive State in Vietnam." Paper presented at the conference of Foreningen af Udviklingsforskere (Association of Development Researchers in Denmark), Copenhagen, 12–13 May.

Keyes, Charles. 1967. *Isan: Regionalism in Northeastern Thailand.* Ithaca, NY: Southeast Asia Program, Cornell University.

Khasnor Johan. 1984. *The Emergence of the Modern Malay Administrative Elite.* Singapore: Oxford University Press.

Khoo, Boo Teik. 1995. *Paradoxes of Mahathirism.* Kuala Lumpur: Oxford University Press.

————. 2005. *Ethnic Structure, Inequality and Governance in the Public Sector: Malaysian Experiences.* Geneva: UN Research Institute for Social Development.

King, Daniel. 1996. "New Political Parties in Thailand: A Case Study of the Palang Dharma Party and the New Aspiration Party." Ph.D. diss., University of Wisconsin–Madison.

Kinsey, Bill H., and Hans P. Binswanger. 1993. "Characteristics and Performances of Settlement Programs: A Review." Policy Research Working Papers, Southern Africa Department, World Bank.

Kitschelt, Herbert. 1989. *The Logics of Party Formation: Ecological Politics in Belgium and West Germany.* Ithaca, NY: Cornell University Press.

Kitschelt, Herbert, and Steven Wilkinson, eds. 2007. *Patrons, Clients, and Policies: Patterns of Democratic Accountability and Political Competition.* Cambridge: Cambridge University Press.

Kohli, Atul. 1987. *The State and Poverty in India: The Politics of Reform.* Cambridge: Cambridge University Press.

————. 2004. *State-Directed Development: Political Power and Industrialization in the Global Periphery.* Cambridge: Cambridge University Press.

Koizumi, Junko. 2002. "King's Manpower Constructed: Writing the History of the Conscription of Labor in Siam." *South East Asia Research* 10, no. 1: 31–61.

Korpi, Walter. 1983. *The Democratic Class Struggle.* London: Routledge.

Kramol Tongdhamachart. 1982. *Toward a Political Party Theory in Thai Perspective.* Singapore: Maruzen Asia.

Kratoska, Paul, ed. 1983. *Honorable Intentions: Talks on the British Empire in South-East Asia Delivered at the Royal Colonial Institute, 1874–1928*. Singapore: Oxford University Press.

Kuenzi, Michelle, and Gina Lambright. 2001. "Party System Institutionalization in 30 African Countries." *Party Politics* 7, no. 4: 437–68.

Kuhonta, Erik Martinez. N.d. "Was Thaksin a Populist?" Unpublished manuscript, McGill University.

Kuhonta, Erik Martinez, and Alex Mutebi. N.d. "The Politics of Pro-Poor Populism in Thailand." Unpublished manuscript, McGill University.

Kurer, Oskar. 2001. "Land and Politics in Fiji: Of Failed Reforms and Coups." *Journal of Pacific History* 36, no. 3: 299–315.

Kuznets, Simon. 1955. "Economic Growth and Income Inequality." *American Economic Review* 45, no. 1: 1–28.

Lake, David, and Matthew Baum. 2001. "The Invisible Hand of Democracy: Political Control and the Provision of Public Services." *Comparative Political Studies* 34, no. 6: 587–621.

Lal, Brij V., ed. 1986. *Politics in Fiji*. Sydney: Allen and Unwin.

———. 2002. "In George Speight's Shadow: Fiji General Elections of 2001." *Journal of Pacific History* 37, no. 1: 87–101.

Landé, Carl. 1977. "Networks and Groups in Southeast Asia: Some Observations on the Group Theory of Politics." In *Friends, Followers, and Factions: A Reader in Clientelism*, edited by Steffen W. Schmidt, James C. Scott, Carl Landé, and Laura Guasti. Berkeley: University of California Press.

Landon, Kenneth P. 1939. *Siam in Transition: A Brief Survey of Cultural Trends in the Five Years since the Revolution of 1932*. Shanghai: Kelly and Walsh.

Lau, Albert. 1989. "Malayan Union Citizenship: Constitutional Change and Controversy in Malaya, 1942–48." *Journal of Southeast Asian Studies* 20, no. 2: 216–43.

———. 1991. *The Malayan Union Controversy*. Singapore: Oxford University Press.

Lawson, Stephanie. 1991. *The Failure of Democratic Politics in Fiji*. Oxford, U.K.: Clarendon Press.

Lee, Boon Thong, and (Tengku) Shamsul Bahrin. 2006. *FELDA's Fifty Years*. Kuala Lumpur: Federal Land Development Authority.

Levitsky, Steven. 1998. "Institutionalization and Peronism." *Party Politics* 4, no. 1: 77–92.

Levitsky, Steven, and Lucan Way. 2010 *Competitive Authoritarianism: Hybrid Regimes after the Cold War*. Cambridge: Cambridge University Press.

Lim, Teck Ghee. 1984. "British Colonial Administration and the 'Ethnic Division of Labor' in Malaya." *Kajian Malaysia* 2, no. 2: 28–66.

Lin, Sein, and Bruce Esposito. 1976. "Agrarian Reform in Thailand: Problems and Prospects." *Pacific Affairs* 49, no. 3: 425–42.

Lipset, Seymour Martin. 1981. *Political Man: The Social Bases of Politics.* Baltimore: Johns Hopkins University Press.

Luong, Hy V. 2003a. "Introduction." In *Postwar Vietnam: Dynamics of a Transforming Society,* edited by Hy V. Luong. Lanham, MD: Rowman and Littlefield.

———. 2003b. "Wealth, Power, and Inequality: Global Market, the State, and Local Sociocultural Dynamics." In *Postwar Vietnam: Dynamics of a Transforming Society,* edited by Hy V. Luong. Lanham, MD: Rowman and Littlefield.

Lustick, Ian. 1979. "Stability in Deeply Divided Societies: Consociationalism versus Control." *World Politics* 31, no. 3: 325–44.

Mahathir Mohamad. 1970. *The Malay Dilemma.* Singapore: Times Books International.

Mainwaring, Scott. 1999. *Rethinking Party Systems in the Third Wave of Democratization: The Case of Brazil.* Stanford, CA: Stanford University Press.

Mainwaring, Scott, and Timothy R. Scully, eds. 1995. *Building Democratic Institutions: Party Systems in Latin America.* Stanford, CA: Stanford University Press.

Malaya. 1961. *Second Five-Year Plan 1961–1965.* Kuala Lumpur: Government Press.

Malaysia. 1965. *First Malaysia Plan 1966–1970.* Kuala Lumpur: Government Press.

———. 1969. *The 1969 Budget.* Kuala Lumpur: Federal Department of Information.

———. 1970. *The 1970 Budget.* Kuala Lumpur: Federal Department of Information.

———. 1971a. *Second Malaysia Plan 1971–1975.* Kuala Lumpur: Government Press.

———. 1971b. *The 1971 Budget.* Kuala Lumpur: Federal Department of Information.

———. 1972. *The 1972 Budget.* Kuala Lumpur: Federal Department of Information.

———. 1973. *Mid-Term Review of the Second Malaysia Plan 1971–1975.* Kuala Lumpur: Government Press.

———. 1976. *Third Malaysia Plan 1976–1980.* Kuala Lumpur: Government Press.

———. 1981. *Fourth Malaysia Plan 1981–1985.* Kuala Lumpur: Government Press.

———. 1986. *Fifth Malaysia Plan 1986–1990.* Kuala Lumpur: Government Press.

———. 1991a. *Second Outline Perspective Plan 1991–2000.* Kuala Lumpur: Government Press.

———. 1991b. *Sixth Malaysia Plan 1991–1995.* Kuala Lumpur: Government Press.

―――. 1996. *Seventh Malaysia Plan 1996–2000*. Kuala Lumpur: Government Press.

―――. 2001. *Eighth Malaysia Plan 2001–2005*. Kuala Lumpur: Government Press.

―――. 2006. *Ninth Malaysia Plan 2006–2010*. Kuala Lumpur: Government Press.

―――. 2010. *Tenth Malaysia Plan 2011–2015*. Kuala Lumpur: Government Press.

Malaysia, Ministry of Education. 1968. *The Educational Statistics of Malaysia: 1938 to 1967*. Kuala Lumpur: Art Printing Works.

Malaysia, Ministry of Finance. 1984. *Economic Report 1984/85*. Kuala Lumpur: National Printing Department.

―――. 1989. *Economic Report 1989/90*. Kuala Lumpur: National Printing Department.

Malaysia, Ministry of Health. 2000. *Annual Report 1999*. Kuala Lumpur: Government Press.

―――. 2001. *Malaysia's Health 2000: Technical Report of the Director-General of Health, Malaysia*. Kuala Lumpur: Government Press.

―――. 2006. *My Health: Health Status of Malaysia 2005*. Putra Jaya, Malaysia: Planning and Development, Ministry of Health Malaysia.

Mallet, Marian. 1978. "Causes and Consequences of the October '76 Coup." In *Thailand: Roots of Conflict*, edited by Andrew Turton, Jonathan Fast, and Malcolm Caldwell. Nottingham, U.K.: Spokesman.

Manderson, Lenore. 1977. "The Shaping of the Kaum Ibu (Women's Section) of the United Malays National Organization." *Signs* 3, no. 1: 210–28.

Marshall, T. H. 1950. *Citizenship and Social Class*. Cambridge: Cambridge University Press.

Mauzy, Diane. 1983. *Barisan Nasional: Coalition Government in Malaysia*. Kuala Lumpur: Marican and Sons.

McCaig, Brian, Dwayne Benjamin, and Loren Brandt. 2009. "The Evolution of Income Inequality in Vietnam, 1993–2006." Working Paper, Australian National University.

McCargo, Duncan. 1997a. *Chamlong Srimuang and the New Thai Politics*. London: Hurst.

―――. 1997b. "Thailand's Political Parties: Real, Authentic, and Actual." In *Political Change in Thailand*, edited by Kevin Hewison. London: Routledge.

McCargo, Duncan, and Ukrist Pathmanand. 2005. *The Thaksinization of Thailand*. Copenhagen: Nordic Institute of Asian Studies Press.

McCoy, Alfred. 1994. "An Anarchy of Families." In *An Anarchy of Families: State and Family in the Philippines*, edited by Alfred McCoy. Manila: Ateneo de Manila University Press.

McGuire, James. 1997. *Peronism without Perón: Unions, Parties, and Democracy in Argentina*. Stanford, CA: Stanford University Press.

———. 2010. *Wealth, Health, and Democracy in East Asia and Latin America*. New York: Cambridge University Press.

Mead, Kullada Kesobonchoo. 2004. *The Rise and Decline of Thai Absolutism*. London: Routledge Curzon.

Means, Gordon P. 1970. *Malaysian Politics*. New York: New York University Press.

———. 1991. *Malaysian Politics: The Second Generation*. Singapore: Oxford University Press.

Medhi Krongkaew. 1981. "Current Interest and Research on Poverty and Income Distribution in Thailand." Paper presented at the Workshop on Issues in Development Studies in the ASEAN Countries, University of Malaya, Kuala Lumpur, 14–16 December.

———. 1995. "Contributions of Agriculture to Industrialization." In *Thailand's Industrialization and Its Consequences*, edited by Medhi Krongkaew. New York: St. Martin's Press.

———. 2008. "Comment on 'Income Inequality in Malaysia.'" *Asian Economic Policy Review* 3: 135–39.

Medhi Krongkaew and Pranee Tinakorn. 1991. "Priority Issues and Policy Measures to Alleviate Rural Poverty: The Case of Thailand." Report submitted to the Economic Development Resources Center, Asian Development Bank (Manila).

Medhi Krongkaew and Ragayah Haji Mat Zin. 2007. "Income Distribution and Sustainable Economic Development in East Asia: A Comparative Analysis." IDEAs Working Paper Series No.02/2007.

Meerman, Jacob. 1979. *Public Expenditure in Malaysia*. New York: Oxford University Press.

———. 2008. "The Malaysian Success Story, the Public Sector, and Inter-Ethnic Inequality." In *Globalization and National Autonomy: The Experience of Malaysia*, edited by Joan M. Nelson, Jacob Meerman, and Abdul Rahman Embong. Singapore: Institute of Southeast Asian Studies.

Mehmet, Ozay. 1986. *Development in Malaysia: Poverty, Wealth, and Trusteeship*. London: Croom Helm.

Mencher, Joan. 1980. "The Lessons and Non-Lessons of Kerala: Agricultural Labourers and Poverty." *Economic and Political Weekly* 15, nos. 41–43: 1781–83.

Michels, Robert. 1962. *Political Parties: A Sociological Study of the Oligarchical Tendencies of Modern Democracy*. New York: Free Press.

Migdal, Joel S. 1974. *Peasants, Politics, and Revolution: Pressures toward Political and Social Change in the Third World*. Princeton, NJ: Princeton University Press.

Migdal, Joel S., Atul Kohli, and Vivienne Shue, eds. 1994. *State Power and Social Forces: Domination and Transformation in the Third World.* Cambridge: Cambridge University Press.

Milne, R. S. 1967. *Government and Politics in Malaysia.* Boston: Houghton Mifflin.

———. 1976. "The Politics of Malaysia's New Economic Policy." *Pacific Affairs* 49, no. 2: 235–62.

———. 1981. *Politics in Ethnically Bipolar States: Guyana, Malaysia, Fiji.* Vancouver: University of British Columbia Press.

Milne, R. S., and Diane K. Mauzy. 1978. *Politics and Government in Malaysia.* Vancouver: University of British Columbia Press.

Missingham, Bruce. 2003. *The Assembly of the Poor in Thailand: From Local Struggles to National Protest Movement.* Bangkok: Silkworm Books.

Moise, Edwin. 1976. "Land Reform and Land Reform Errors in North Vietnam." *Pacific Affairs* 49, no. 1: 70–92.

———. 2001. "Land Reform in North Vietnam, 1953–1956." Paper presented at the Eighteenth Annual Conference on Southeast Asian Studies, Center for Southeast Asian Studies, University of California, Berkeley, February.

Morell, David, and Chai-Anan Samudavanija. 1981. *Political Conflict in Thailand: Reform, Reaction, and Revolution.* Cambridge, MA: Oelgeschlager, Gunn, and Hain.

Murashima, Eiji, Nakharin Mektrairat, and Somkiat Wanthana. 1991. *The Making of Modern Thai Political Parties.* Tokyo: Institute of Developing Economies.

Muscat, Robert. 1994. *The Fifth Tiger: A Study of Thai Development Policy.* Armonk, NY: M. E. Sharpe.

Musolf, Lloyd, and Fred Springer. 1977. "Legislatures and Divided Societies: The Malaysian Parliament and Multi-Ethnicity." *Legislative Studies Quarterly* 2, no. 2: 133–36.

———. 1979. "The Parliament of Malaysia and Economic Development: Policy Making and the MP." In *Legislatures in Development,* edited by Joel Smith and Lloyd Musolf. Durham, NC: Duke University Press.

Myrdal, Gunnar. 1968. *Asian Drama: An Inquiry into the Poverty of Nations.* New York: Pantheon.

Nakharin Mektrairat. 1992. *Kanpatiwat sayam 2475* [The 1932 Revolution in Siam]. Bangkok: Social Sciences and Humanities Foundation.

National Economic and Social Development Board. 2003. "Profile of Income Distribution and Development." *Development News Bulletin* 20, no. 11 (November): 4–5.

National Health Security Office Thailand, Bureau of Policy and Planning. 2009a. "Annual Report." Bangkok: Mimeo, in Thai.

————. 2009b. "Fund Management Annual Report." Bangkok: Mimeo, in Thai.

National Operations Council [Government of Malaysia]. 1969. *The May 13th Tragedy*. Kuala Lumpur: Government Printing.

National Statistical Coordination Board (NSCB) website (Philippines). 2011. "2009 Official Poverty Statistics." PowerPoint presentation, February 8. Available at http://www.nscb.gov.ph/poverty/2009/default.asp.

Neher, Clark. 1975. "Stability and Instability in Contemporary Thailand." *Asian Survey* 15, no. 12: 1087–1113.

Nelson, Joan M. 2008. "Malaysia's Healthcare Sector: Shifting Roles for Public and Private Provision." In *Globalization and National Autonomy: The Experience of Malaysia*, edited by Joan M. Nelson, Jacob Meerman, and Abdul Rahman Embong. Singapore: Institute of Southeast Asian Studies.

Nelson, Michael H. 2002. *Thailand's New Politics: King Prajadhipok's Institute Yearbook 2001*. Bangkok: King Prajadhipok's Institute.

Ness, Gayl D. 1967. *Bureaucracy and Rural Development in Malaysia*. Berkeley: University of California Press.

Nikom Chandravithum. 1978. "Labor Relations: Thailand's Experience." In *Readings in Thailand's Political Economy*, edited by Vichitvong Na Pombhejara. Bangkok: Bangkok Printing.

Ninh, Kim N. B. 2002. *A World Transformed: The Politics of Culture in Revolutionary Vietnam, 1945–1965*. Ann Arbor: University of Michigan Press.

Nipapun Kungskulniti and Naowarut Charoenca. 1996. "The Future of Public Health in Thailand." In *Issues and Challenges of Public Health in the 21st Century*, edited by Khairuddin Yusof, Wah-Yun Low, Siti Norazah Zulkifli, and Yut-Lin Wong. Kuala Lumpur: University of Malaya Press.

[Mohammad] Noordin Sopiee. 2005. *From Malayan Union to Singapore's Separation: Political Unification in the Malaysia Region, 1945–65*. 2nd ed. Kuala Lumpur: University of Malaya Press.

Noranit Setthabut. 1987. *Phak Prachathipat* [Democrat Party]. Bangkok: Thammasat University.

Norrizan Razali. 1999. "Human Resource Development in Malaysia: A Study of the Government's Role." *ASEAN Economic Bulletin* 16, no. 3: 307–29.

Norton, Robert. 1977. *Race and Politics in Fiji*. New York: St. Martin's Press.

Ockey, James. 2003. "Change and Continuity in the Thai Political Party System." *Asian Survey* 43, no. 4: 663–80.

————. 2005. "Variations on a Theme: Societal Cleavages and Party Orientations through Multiple Transitions in Thailand." *Party Politics* 11, no. 6: 728–47.

Oey Astra Meesook. 1978. "Income Distribution in Thailand." Research Report Series No. 10, Faculty of Economics, Thammasat University.

Ong, Michael. 1976. "The Member of Parliament and His Constituency: The Malaysian Case." *Legislative Studies Quarterly* 1, no. 3: 405–22.

Ongkili, James P. 1974. "The British and Malayan Nationalism, 1946–1957." *Journal of Southeast Asian Studies* 5, no. 2: 255–77.

Panebianco, Angelo. 1988. *Political Parties: Organization and Power.* Cambridge: Cambridge University Press.

Paredes, Ruby, ed. 1988. *Philippine Colonial Democracy.* New Haven, CT: Yale University Southeast Asia Studies.

Pasuk Phongpaichit. 1999. *Civilizing the State: State, Civil Society, and Politics in Thailand.* Wertheim Memorial Lecture, Amsterdam.

Pasuk Phongpaichit and Chris Baker. 1995. *Thailand: Economy and Politics.* Kuala Lumpur: Oxford University Press.

———. 1998. *Thailand's Boom and Bust.* Chiang Mai, Thailand: Silkworm Books.

———. 2000. *Thailand's Crisis.* Chiang Mai, Thailand: Silkworm Books.

———. 2002. *Thailand: Economy and Politics.* 2nd ed. Kuala Lumpur: Oxford University Press.

———. 2004. *Thaksin: The Business of Politics in Thailand.* Chiang Mai, Thailand: Silkworm Books.

———. 2008. "Thaksin's Populism." *Journal of Contemporary Asia* 28, no. 1: 62–83.

Pasuk Phongpaichit, Sangsit Phiriyarangsan, and Nualnoi Treerat. 1996. *Challenging Social Exclusion: Rights and Livelihood in Thailand.* Geneva: International Institute for Labor Studies.

Pempel, T. J., ed. 1990. *Uncommon Democracies: The One-Party Dominant Regime.* Ithaca, NY: Cornell University Press.

Pike, Douglas. 1978. *History of Vietnamese Communism, 1925–1976.* Stanford, CA: Hoover Institution Press.

Pongpisut Jongudomsuk. 2002. "Achieving Universal Coverage of Health Care in Thailand through 30 Baht Scheme." Paper presented at the Southeast Asian Medical Information Centre Conference, Chiang Mai, Thailand, 14–17 January.

Popkin, Samuel. 1979. *The Rational Peasant.* Berkeley: University of California Press.

Pranee Tinakorn. 1995. "Industrialization and Welfare: How Poverty and Income Distribution Are Affected." In *Thailand's Industrialization and Its Consequences,* edited by Medhi Krongkaew. New York: St. Martin's Press.

Praphat Pintoptaeng. 1998. *Kanmuang bon thong thanon: 99 wan prawatisat kan doen khabuan chumnum nai sanghkom thai* [Politics on the Street: 99 Days of the Assembly of the Poor]. Bangkok: Center for Research and Production of Textbooks, Krik University.

Premdas, Ralph. 1995. *Ethnic Conflict and Development: The Case of Guyana.* Brookfield, VT: Avebury.

Pridi Banomyong. 1974. *Ma vie mouvementée et mes 21 ans d'exil en Chine populaire.* Paris: UNESCON.

———. 2000. *Pridi by Pridi: Selected Writings on Life, Politics, and Economy.* Edited and translated by Chris Baker and Pasuk Phongpaichit. Chiang Mai, Thailand: Silkworm Books.

Prizzia, Ross. 1985. *Thailand in Transition: The Role of Oppositional Forces.* Honolulu: University of Hawai'i Press.

Przeworski, Adam. 1985. *Capitalism and Social Democracy.* Cambridge: Cambridge University Press.

Psacharopoulos, George, and Jandhyala Tilak. 1991. "Schooling and Equity." In *Essays on Equity, Poverty, and Growth*, edited by George Psacharopoulos. Oxford, U.K.: Pergamon Press.

Puey Ungphakorn. 1977. "Violence and the Military Coup in Thailand." *Bulletin of Concerned Asian Scholars* 9, no. 3: 4–12.

———. 2000. *A Siamese for All Seasons: Collected Articles by and about Puey Ungphakorn.* Bangkok: Komol Keemthong Foundation.

Purcell, Victor. 1946. *Malaya: Outline of a Colony.* London: T. Nelson and Sons.

———. 1967. *The Chinese in Malaya.* Kuala Lumpur: Oxford University Press.

Puthucheary, Mavis. 1978. *The Politics of Administration: The Malaysian Experience.* Singapore: Oxford University Press.

Putzel, James. 1986. "The Ladejinsky Model of Agrarian Reform: The Philippine Experience." M.A. thesis, McGill University.

———. 1992. *A Captive Land: The Politics of Agrarian Reform in the Philippines.* New York: Monthly Review Press.

———. 1998. "Non-Governmental Organizations and Rural Poverty." In *Organizing for Democracy: NGOs, Civil Society, and the Philippine State*, edited by G. Sidney Silliman and Lela Garner Noble. Honolulu: University of Hawai'i Press.

Quirino, Carlos. 1958. *Magsaysay of the Philippines.* Manila: Carmelo and Bauermann.

Race, Jeffrey. 1974. "Thailand 1973: 'We Certainly Have Been Ravaged by Something . . .'" *Asian Survey* 14, no. 2: 192–203.

———. 1975. "The January 1975 Thai Elections: Preliminary Data and Influences." *Asian Survey* 15, no. 4: 375–81.

Ragayah Mat Zin. 2008. "Income Inequality in Malaysia." *Asian Economic Policy Review* 3, no. 1: 114–32.

Ramesh, M. 2000. *Welfare Capitalism in Southeast Asia.* Basingstoke, U.K.: MacMillan.

Ramsay, James Ansil. 1982. "The Limits of Land Reform in Thailand." *Journal of Developing Areas* 16, no. 2: 173–96.

Randall, Vicky, and Lars Svasand. 2002. "Party Institutionalization in New Democracies." *Party Politics* 8, no. 1: 5–29.

Ratnam, K. J. 1965. *Communalism and the Political Process in Malaya*. Kuala Lumpur: University of Malaya Press.

Ratnam, K. J., and R. S. Milne. 1965. *The Malayan Parliamentary Election of 1964*. Kuala Lumpur: University of Malaya Press.

Ravallion, Martin, and Dominique van de Walle. 2003. "Land Allocation in Vietnam's Agrarian Transition." World Bank Working Paper 2951.

Rees-Williams, D. R. 1947. "Notes and Comment: The Constitutional Position in Malaya." *Pacific Affairs* 20, no. 2: 174–78.

Reidinger, Jeffrey M. 1995. *Agrarian Reform in the Philippines: Democratic Transitions and Redistributive Reform*. Stanford, CA: Stanford University Press.

Reinecke, Gerhard. 1993. "Social Security in Thailand: Political Decisions and Distributional Impact." *Crossroads* 8, no. 1: 78–116.

Reynolds, Craig. 1987. *Thai Radical Discourse: The Real Face of Thai Feudalism Today*. Ithaca, NY: Southeast Asia Program, Cornell University.

———. 1992. "The Plot of Thai History: Theory and Practice." In *Patterns and Illusions: Thai History and Thought*, edited by Gehan Wijeyewardene and E. C. Chapman. Canberra: Richard Davis Fund and Department of Anthropology, Australian National University.

Reynolds, Craig, and Hong Lysa. 1983. "Marxism in Thai Historical Studies." *Journal of Asian Studies* 43, no. 1: 77–104.

Riggs, Fred. 1966. *Thailand: The Modernization of a Bureaucratic Polity*. Honolulu: East-West Center Press.

Roberts, Kenneth. 1995. "Neoliberalism and the Transformation of Populism in Latin America: The Peruvian Case." *World Politics* 48, no. 1: 82–116.

Roff, William. 1967. *The Origins of Malay Nationalism*. New Haven, CT: Yale University Press.

Rogers, Marvin L. 1972. "Malaysia and Singapore: 1971 Developments." *Asian Survey* 12, no. 2: 168–76.

———. 1975a. "Patterns of Leadership in a Rural Malay Community." *Asian Survey* 15, no. 5: 407–21.

———. 1975b. "The Politicization of Malay Villagers: National Integration or Disintegration?" *Comparative Politics* 7, no. 2: 205–25.

———. 1989. "Patterns of Change in Rural Malaysia: Development and Dependence." *Asian Survey* 29, no. 8: 764–85.

———. 1993. *Local Politics in Rural Malaysia: Patterns of Change in Sungai Raya*. Kuala Lumpur: S. Abdul Majeed.

Rondinelli, Dennis A. 1978. "National Investment Planning and Equity Policy in Developing Countries: The Challenge of Decentralized Administration." *Policy Sciences* 10, no. 1: 45–74.

———. 1979. "Administration of Integrated Rural Development Policy: The Politics of Agrarian Reform in Developing Countries." *World Politics* 31, no. 3: 389–416.

Rudner, Martin. 1970. "The Political Structure of the Malayan Union." *Journal of the Malaysian Branch of the Royal Asiatic Society* 43, no. 1: 116–28.

———. 1975. *Nationalism, Planning, and Economic Modernization in Malaysia.* Beverly Hills, CA: Sage Publications.

Rueschemeyer, Dietrich, and Peter Evans. 1985. "The State and Economic Transformation: Towards an Analysis of the Conditions Underlying Effective Intervention." In *Bringing the State Back In*, edited by Peter Evans, Dietrich Rueschemeyer, and Theda Skocpol. Cambridge: Cambridge University Press.

Sandbrook, Richard, Marc Edeleman, Patrick Heller, and Judith Teichman. 2007. *Social Democracy in the Global Periphery: Origins, Challenges, Prospects.* Cambridge: Cambridge University Press.

Saneh Chamarik. 1973. "Questions of Stability and Security in Thailand." In *Trends in Thailand*, edited by M. Rajaretnam and Lim So Jean. Singapore: Institute of Southeast Asian Studies.

Sangkhom Sanjorn [pseud.]. 1996. *Wikrao kaset tii rap lung phak klang* [The Agricultural Crisis in the Central Plains]. In *Thammachat, sapayakon, khon din din* [Nature, Resources, Villagers]. Bangkok: Committee to Support and Spread Development Work.

Sartori, Giovanni. 1990. "The Sociology of Parties: A Critical Review." In *The West European Party System*, edited by Peter Mair. Oxford: Oxford University Press.

Scott, James. 1985. *Weapons of the Weak: Everyday Forms of Peasant Resistance.* New Haven, CT: Yale University Press.

Searle, Peter. 1999. *The Riddle of Malaysian Capitalism: Rent-Seekers or Real Capitalists?* St. Leonards, Australia: Allen and Unwin.

Secretariat of the Thai Cabinet. 2004. *Summary Implementation Results of the Cabinet of Thaksin Shinawatra's Administration Third Year (26 February 2003– 26 February 2004).* Bangkok: Office of the Prime Minister.

———. 2005. *Four Years of Repairing Thailand.* Bangkok, Thailand: Secretariat of the Cabinet, Office of the Prime Minister.

Selznick, Philip. 1952. *The Organizational Weapon: A Study of Bolshevik Strategy and Tactics.* New York: McGraw-Hill.

———. 1983 [1957]. *Leadership in Administration: A Sociological Interpretation.* Berkeley: University of California Press.

Sen, Amartya. 1999. *Development as Freedom.* New York: Anchor Books.

Shamsul A. B. 1986. *From British to Bumiputera Rule: Local Politics and Rural Development in Peninsular Malaysia*. Singapore: Institute of Southeast Asian Studies.

Shaw, William. 1976. *Tun Razak: His Life and Times*. Kuala Lumpur: Longman.

Shefter, Martin. 1977. "Party and Patronage: Germany, England, and Italy." *Politics and Society* 7: 403–51.

Shireen Mardziah Hashim. 1998. *Income Inequality and Poverty in Malaysia*. Lanham, MD: Rowman and Littlefield.

Sidel, John. 1999. *Capital, Coercion, and Crime: Bossism in the Philippines*. Stanford, CA: Stanford University Press.

Silliman, G. Sidney, and Lela Garner Noble. 1998. "Citizen Movements and Philippine Democracy." In *Organizing for Democracy: NGOs, Civil Society, and the Philippine State*, edited by G. Sidney Silliman and Lela Garner Noble. Honolulu: University of Hawai'i Press.

Siripan Nogsuan Sawasdee. 2006. *Thai Political Parties in the Age of Reform*. Bangkok: Institute of Public Policy Studies.

Skinner, G. William. 1957. *Chinese Society in Thailand: An Analytical History*. Ithaca, NY: Cornell University Press.

Slater, Dan. 2003. "Iron Cage in an Iron Fist: Authoritarian Institutions and the Personalization of Power in Malaysia." *Comparative Politics* 36, no. 1: 81–101.

Slimming, John. 1969. *Malaysia: Death of a Democracy*. London: John Murray.

Smith, Benjamin. 2005. "Life of the Party: The Origins of Regime Breakdown and Persistence under Single-Party Rule." *World Politics* 57, no. 3: 421–51.

Smith, Roger M., ed. 1974. *Southeast Asia: Documents of Political Development and Change*. Ithaca, NY: Cornell University Press.

Smyth, Warrington. 1994. *Five Years in Siam: From 1891–1896*. Bangkok: White Lotus.

Snodgrass, Donald. 1980. *Inequality and Economic Development in Malaysia*. Kuala Lumpur: Oxford University Press.

Somchai Jitsuchon. 1987. "Sources and Trends of Income Inequality: Thailand 1975/76 and 1981." Master's thesis, Faculty of Economics, Thammasat University.

———. 2001. "An Inquiry into the Proper Measurement of Poverty in Thailand." Paper presented at the Federation of the ASEAN Economic Associations Conference on Poverty and Income Distribution in ASEAN: Status and Policy Measures, Bangkok, 20–21 December.

Somchai Jitsuchon and Jiraporn Plangpraphan. 2003. "Poverty, Economic Security and the Role of the Thai Government." *TDRI Quarterly Review* 18, no. 4: 20–27.

Somporn Sangchai. 1976. *Some Observations on the Election and Coalition Formation in Thailand, 1976*. Singapore: Institute of Southeast Asian Studies.

Sowell, Thomas. 2004. *Affirmative Action around the World*. New Haven, CT: Yale University Press.

Steinberg, David Joel, ed. 1987. *In Search of Southeast Asia*. 2nd ed. Honolulu: University of Hawai'i Press.

———. 1990. *The Philippines: A Singular and a Plural Place*. Boulder, CO: Westview Press.

Stengs, Irene. 2009. *Worshipping the Great Moderniser: King Chulalongkorn, Patron Saint of the Middle Class*. Singapore: National University of Singapore Press.

Stephens, John D. 1979. *The Transition from Capitalism to Socialism*. London: MacMillan.

Stifel, L. 1970. "Problems and Prospects of Siam." *Solidarity* 5, no. 4.

Stockwell, A. J. 1977. "The Formation and First Years of the United Malays National Organization (UMNO) 1946–1948." *Modern Asian Studies* 11: 481–513.

———. 1979. *British Policy and Malay Politics during the Malayan Union Experiment, 1942–1948*. Kuala Lumpur: Malaysian Branch of the Royal Asiatic Society.

Stowe, Judith. 1991. *Siam Becomes Thailand*. London: Hurst and Co.

Suchanan Tambunlertchai. 2004. "Government's Helping Hand: A Study of Thailand's Agricultural Debt Moratorium." B.A. honors thesis, Department of Economics, Harvard University.

Suehiro, Akira. 1981. "Land Reform in Thailand. The Concept and Background of the Agricultural Land Reform Act of 1975." *Developing Economies* 19, no. 4: 314–47.

Sungsidh Piriyarangsan. 1996. *Phak Prachatiphat: Jaak anurakniyom sulath seriniyom mai* [The Democrat Party: From Conservatism to Neoliberalism]. In *Jodsamneuk lae udomkarn khong kabuankan prachathipathai ruan samai* [Political Ideology and the Current Democratic Movement], edited by Sungsidh Piriyarangsan and Pasuk Phongpaichit. Bangkok: Department of Economics and Friedrich Ebert Foundation.

Supasit Pannarunothai, Samrit Srithamrongsawat, Manit Kongpan, and Patchanee Thumvanna. 2000. "Financing Reforms for the Thai Health Card Scheme." *Health Policy and Planning* 15, no. 3: 303–11.

Surachart Bamrungsak. 1988. *United States Foreign Policy and Thai Military Rule, 1947–1977*. Bangkok: Duang Kamol.

Takei Yoshimitsu, John C. Bock, and Bruce Saunders. 1973. *Educational Sponsorship by Ethnicity: A Preliminary Analysis of the West Malaysian Experience*. Athens: Southeast Asia Program, Ohio University.

Tan, Netina. 2010. "Access to Power: Hegemonic Party Rule in Taiwan and Singapore." Ph.D. diss., University of British Columbia.

Tan, Paige Johnson. 2002. "Streams of Least Resistance: The Institutionalization of Political Parties and Democracy in Indonesia." Ph.D. diss., University of Virginia.

Tanzi, Vito, and Parthasarathi Shome. 1992. "The Role of Taxation in the Development of East Asian Economies." In *The Political Economy of Tax Reform*, edited by Takashi Ito and Anne Krueger. Chicago: University of Chicago Press.

Taylor, Philip, ed. 2004. *Social Inequality in Vietnam and the Challenges to Reform*. Singapore: Institute of Southeast Asian Studies.

Tej Bunnag. 1977. *The Provincial Administration of Siam, 1892–1915: The Ministry of the Interior under Prince Damrong Rajanubhab*. Kuala Lumpur: Oxford University Press.

Thailand. 1961. *First National Economic Development Plan 1961–1966*. Bangkok: Office of the Prime Minister.

———. 1967. *Second National Economic Development Plan 1967–1971*. Bangkok: Office of the Prime Minister.

———. 1972. *Third National Economic Development Plan 1972–1976*. Bangkok: Office of the Prime Minister.

———. 1977. *Fourth National Economic and Social Development Plan 1977–1981*. Bangkok: Office of the Prime Minister.

———. 1982. *Fifth National Economic and Social Development Plan 1982–1986*. Bangkok: Office of the Prime Minister.

———. 1987. *Sixth National Economic and Social Development Plan 1987–1991*. Bangkok: Office of the Prime Minister.

———. 1992. *Seventh National Economic and Social Development Plan 1992–1997*. Bangkok: Office of the Prime Minister.

———. 1997. *Eighth National Economic and Social Development Plan 1997–2001*. Bangkok: Office of the Prime Minister.

Thailand, Ministry of Public Health. 2002. *Thailand Health Profile 1999–2000*. Bangkok: Ministry of Public Health.

Thailand Development Research Institute. 2000. "Pak Mun Dam Case Study: Synthesis Report." Report submitted to the World Commission on Dams, February.

Thak Chaloemtriana, ed. 1978. *Thai Politics: Extracts and Documents, 1932–1957*. Bangkok: Social Science Association of Thailand.

———. 1979. *Thailand: The Politics of Despotic Paternalism*. Bangkok: Social Science Association of Thailand.

Thammasat University. 2004. *Khrongkan prameun phonkan phak chamra nii lae lot phara nii hai kee kasetakon ray yoy* [Project Evaluation of the Debt

Moratorium and Debt Reduction Program for Small Farmers]. Bangkok: National Advisory Research Institute, Thammasat University.

Thaveeporn Vasavakul. 1995. "Vietnam: The Changing Models of Legitimation." In *Political Legitimacy in Southeast Asia*, edited by Muthiah Alagappa. Stanford, CA: Stanford University Press.

Thawatt Mokarapong. 1962. "The June Revolution of 1932 in Thailand." Ph.D. diss., Indiana University.

———. 1972. *A History of the Thai Revolution: A Study in Political Behavior.* Bangkok: Chaermnit.

Thillainathan, R. 1976. "The Public Enterprise as an Instrument for Restructuring Society: The Malaysian Case." In *Malaysian Economic Development and Policies*, edited by Stephen Chee and Khoo Siew Mun. Kuala Lumpur: Malaysian Economic Association.

Thongchai Winichakul. 1994. *Siam Mapped: A History of the Geobody of a Nation.* Honolulu: University of Hawai'i Press.

Turton, Andrew. 1978. "The Current Situation in the Thai Countryside." In *Thailand: Roots of Conflict*, edited by Andrew Turton, Jonathan Fast, and Malcolm Caldwell. Nottingham, U.K.: Spokesman.

Ubon Ratchatani University. 2002. *Project to Study Approaches to the Restoration of the Ecology, Livelihood, and Communities Receiving Impact from the Construction of the Pak Mun Dam* (in Thai). Ubon Ratchatani, Thailand: Ubon Ratchatani University.

UN Development Programme. 2001. *Human Development Report 2001.* New York: Oxford University Press.

———. 2003. *Thailand Human Development Report 2003.* Bangkok: UN Development Programme.

Ungku Aziz. 1969. "Three Papers on Rural Development." Faculty of Economics and Administration, University of Malaya.

Vasil, R. K. 1972. *The Malaysian General Election of 1969.* Kuala Lumpur: Oxford University Press.

———. 1980. *Ethnic Politics in Malaysia.* New Delhi: Radiant Publishers.

Verba, Sidney. 1971. "Sequences and Development." In *Crises and Sequences in Political Development*, with Leonard Binder, James S. Coleman, Joseph LaPalombara, Lucian W. Pye, Sidney Verba, and Myron Weiner. Princeton, NJ: Princeton University Press.

Vichit Vatakarn. 1941. *Thailand's Case.* Bangkok: N.p.

Vietnamese Academy of Social Sciences (VASS). 2007. *Vietnam Update Poverty Report 2006: Poverty and Poverty Reduction in Vietnam 1993–2004.* Hanoi, Vietnam: National Political Publisher.

Villanueva, Pi. 1997. "The Influence of the Congress for a People's Agrarian Reform (CPAR) on the Legislative Process." In *State–Civil Society Relations in Policy-Making*, edited by Marion Wui and Glenda Lopez. Diliman: Third World Studies Center, University of the Philippines.

Villegas, Bernardo. 1986. "The Economic Crisis." In *Crisis in the Philippines: The Marcos Era and Beyond*, edited by John Bresnan. Princeton, NJ: Princeton University Press.

Vo, Nhan Tri. 1990. *Vietnam's Economic Policy since 1975*. Singapore: Institute of Southeast Asian Studies.

Von der Mehden, Fred. 1974. *South-East Asia 1930–1970: The Legacy of Colonialism and Nationalism*. New York: W. W. Norton.

Von Vorys, Karl. 1975. *Democracy without Consensus: Communalism and Political Stability in Malaysia*. Princeton, NJ: Princeton University Press.

Vu, Tuong. 2010. *Paths to Development: South Korea, Vietnam, China, and Indonesia*. Cambridge: Cambridge University Press.

Wade, Robert. 1990. *Governing the Market: Economic Theory and the Role of Government in East Asian Industrialization*. Princeton, NJ: Princeton University Press.

Wales, H. G. Quaritch. 1965 [1934]. *Ancient Siamese Government and Administration*. New York: Paragon.

Warr, Peter. 2002. "Economic Recovery and Poverty Reduction in Thailand." *TDRI Quarterly Review* 17, no. 2: 18–27.

———. 2009. "The Economy under the Thaksin Government: Stalled Recovery." In *Divided over Thaksin: Thailand's Coup and Problematic Transition*, edited by John Funston. Singapore: Institute of Southeast Asian Studies.

Weber, Max. 2002. *The Protestant Ethic and the Spirit of Capitalism*. London: Routledge.

Welfling, Mary B. 1973. *Political Institutionalization: Comparative Analyses of African Party Systems*. Beverly Hills, CA: Sage Publications.

Weyland, Kurt. 1996. *Democracy without Equity: Failures of Reform in Brazil*. Pittsburgh, PA: University of Pittsburgh Press.

———. 2001. "Clarifying a Contested Concept: Populism in the Study of Latin American Politics." *Comparative Politics* 34, no. 1: 1–21.

Wilson, David A. 1959. "Thailand and Marxism." In *Marxism in Southeast Asia: A Study of Four Countries*, edited by Frank N. Trager. Stanford, CA: Stanford University Press.

———. 1962. *Politics in Thailand*. Ithaca, NY: Cornell University Press.

Womack, Brantly. 1987. "The Party and the People: Postrevolutionary Politics in China and Vietnam." *World Politics* 39, no. 4: 479–507.

Wong, Joseph. 2004. *Healthy Democracies: Welfare Politics in Taiwan and South Korea.* Ithaca, NY: Cornell University Press.

Woo-Cumings, Meredith, ed. 1999. *The Developmental State.* Ithaca, NY: Cornell University Press.

Woodside, Alexander B. 1976. *Community and Revolution in Modern Vietnam.* Boston: Houghton Mifflin.

Worawan Chandoevwit. 2003. "Thailand's Grassroots Policies." *TDRI Quarterly* 18, no. 4: 3–8.

Worawut Smuthkalin. 2006. "Political Regimes and Welfare State Development in East Asia: How State Leaders Matter to Social Expansion in Taiwan, Thailand, and China." Ph.D. diss., Stanford University.

World Bank. "World Development Indicators (WDI)." http://data.worldbank.org/data-catalog/world-development-indicators.

———. 1959. *A Public Development Program for Thailand: Report of a Mission Organized by the International Bank for Reconstruction and Development at the Request of the Government of Thailand.* Baltimore: Johns Hopkins University Press.

———. 1992. *Malaysia: Fiscal Reform for Stable Growth.* Washington, D.C.: World Bank.

———. 1993a. *The East Asian Miracle: Economic Growth and Public Policy.* New York: Oxford University Press, for the World Bank.

———. 1993b. *Sustaining Rapid Development in East Asia and the Pacific.* Washington, D.C.: World Bank.

———. 2000. *Beyond the Crisis: A Strategy for Renewing Rural Development in Thailand.* Bangkok: World Bank.

———. 2001. *Thailand Social Monitor: Poverty and Public Policy.* Bangkok: World Bank (November).

———. 2005a. "Agriculture, Rural Development, and Pro-Poor Growth." World Bank Agriculture and Rural Development Discussion Paper 21.

———. 2005b. *Thailand Economic Monitor.* Bangkok: World Bank (April).

Wurfel, David. 1988. *Filipino Politics: Development and Decay.* Ithaca, NY: Cornell University Press.

———. 1997. "The Party-List Elections: Sectoral or National? Success or Failure?" *Kasarinlan* 13, no. 2: 19–30.

Wyatt, David. 1968. "Family Politics in Nineteenth Century in Thailand." *Journal of Southeast Asian History* 9: 208–28.

———. 1969. *The Politics of Reform in Thailand.* New Haven, CT: Yale University Press.

Yano, Toru. 1978. "Political Structure of a 'Rice-Growing State.'" Translated by Peter and Stephanie Hawkes. In *Thailand: A Rice-Growing Society*, edited by Yoneo Ishii. Honolulu: University of Hawai'i Press.

Zainal Ariff Hussain. 2001. *Malaysian Experiences of Monitoring in Development Planning*. Bangkok: UN Economic and Social Commission for Asia and the Pacific.

Zakaria Haji Ahmad. 1989. "Evolution and Development of the Political System in Malaysia." In *Asian Political Institutionalization*, edited by Robert A. Scalapino, Seizaburo Sato, and Jusuf Wanandi. Berkeley, CA: Institute of East Asian Studies.

Zheng, Shiping. 1997. *Party vs. State in Post-1949 China: The Institutional Dilemma*. Cambridge: Cambridge University Press.

Zimmerman, Robert E. 1974. "Student 'Revolution' in Thailand: The End of the Thai Bureaucratic Party?" *Asian Survey* 14, no. 6: 509–29.

Zwick, Jim. 1992. "Mark Twain on American Imperialism." *Atlantic Monthly*, April, 49–65.

Index

Italic page numbers indicate material in tables or figures.

Made in the USA
San Bernardino, CA
27 September 2016